FOR BETTER
OR FOR
WORSE

FOR BETTER
OR FOR
WORSE

CANADA
and the
UNITED
STATES
to the
1990s

J. L. GRANATSTEIN
NORMAN HILLMER

Copp Clark Pitman Ltd. A Longman Company Toronto

ISBN   0-7730-5177-5 (cloth)
        0-7730-5166-X (paper)

Executive editor: Brian Henderson
Editors: Camilla Jenkins, Barbara Tessman, Deborah Viets
Design: Liz Nyman
Cover illustration: Kyle Gell
Typesetter: Carol Magee
Printing and binding: John Deyell Company

Canadian Cataloguing in Publication Data

Granatstein, J.L., 1939–
For better or for worse: Canada and the United States to the 1990s

Includes bibliographical references and index.
ISBN 0-7730-5177-5 (bound) ISBN 0-7730-5166-X (pbk.)

1. Canada – Foreign relations – United States.   2. United States – Foreign relations – Canada.   I. Hillmer, Norman, 1942–   .   II. Title.

FC249.G73 1991   327.71073   C91-095056-3   F1029.5.U6G73 1991

72213

Copp Clark Pitman Ltd.
2775 Matheson Blvd. East
Mississauga, Ontario
L4W 4P7

Associated companies:
  Longman Group Ltd., London
  Longman Inc., New York
  Longman Cheshire Pty., Melbourne
  Longman Paul Pty., Auckland

Printed and bound in Canada by John Deyell Company

In Memory of Charles P. Stacey
and for Helen Stacey

Contents

PREFACE

We have never found it easy to explain why there are relatively few journalists, commentators, and academics who specialize in Canadian–American relations. There have been, for example, only four attempts over the last eight decades to write a book like this—a broad survey of the evolution of a relationship surely vital to both partners—and it is almost impossible to find historians who make the subject their primary business. Perhaps, as Robert Fulford observed in *Saturday Night* magazine, the explanation on the Canadian side is that the pressures of proximity to a giant leave us "breathless and speechless." Just as likely is that Canadians think they already know everything about the U.S.: they encounter the American fact everywhere.

Fulford corrects this impression. Canadians ought to be the world's leading authorities on the United States, but they are not. They expend remarkably little energy in looking closely and seriously at the United States. Marshall McLuhan and his impenetrable, prose are freely criticized in these sophisticated days, but he at least appreciated the importance of trying to interpret the American phenomenon. He also saw, and frequently commented upon, the valuable perspective that a bit of distance gave a Canadian who wished to evaluate the United States.

One way towards understanding—mutual understanding—might just be to examine the remarkable history of Canadian–American co-existence. Why have Canadians stubbornly insisted upon the maintenance of their own separate identity, and why have Americans allowed them to do so? Is there really a "best friendship" rooted in an American respect for the plucky little ally–adversary to the north, or has Canadian collaboration simply allowed U.S. imperialism to take a refined form? Our own preference is for the view that the relationship is characterized by a continued tension between conflict and co-operation. We agree with Henry Kissinger that Canada has remarkably little freedom of manoeuvre in its dealings with the United States, but that it has used the freedom it has with skill and determination.

As we have suggested, the list of histories of Canadian–American affairs is not long. What there is on the subject is usually very specialized, and much information has to be found in books not directly focussing on Canadian–American relations. Nevertheless, we could not have written this book without the already existing literature, without the work of such distinguished American and Canadian historians as Robert Craig Brown, Gordon Stewart, and A.C. Gluek. We have avoided footnotes, but have tried to acknowledge our indebtedness to earlier work in the bibliography at the end of the book.

Some of our debts are closer to home. Our friend Robert Bothwell gave important support to the project, as did Elaine Granatstein and Anne Hillmer. For better or for worse, William Kaplan donated the title and other advice. Former diplomats Charles Ritchie and Basil Robinson shared their memories with us. William Christian drew our attention to the George Grant quotation that is used in the conclusion. Carman Bickerton advised on the Gulf of Maine dispute. Angelika Sauer did the same on the late 1930s, and Stephen J. Harris contributed to our understanding of Defence Scheme No. 1. William Constable prepared the maps, and Isabel Campbell helped with the research for the defence map. Gloria McKeigan and Sandra Johnston assisted in the preparation of the manuscript; Lisa Dillon and Vincent Rigby made suggestions as they proofread and worked on the index.

We relied on Ian M. Drummond and Roger Sarty for expertise on economic and defence matters respectively. Professor Drummond indulged us in long conversations and longer letters: he gave us the benefit of his research and gently corrected our errors and misconceptions. Dr. Sarty put his knowledge of the unknown and known corners of the Canadian military experience at our disposal. The research for and conceptualization of the First World War section are his. Neither Ian nor Roger, however, should be indicted as co-conspirators in the crime. They did not have an opportunity to see the final manuscript.

We have been exceptionally well served by our Copp Clark editors, Barbara Tessman, Deborah Viets, and particularly Camilla Jenkins. Ms. Jenkins got to the manuscript first, laying waste to a good deal of what she saw, clarifying our thinking and our prose. It is a pleasure to find a publisher where the editorial craft is still taken seriously.

We dedicate the enterprise to Helen and Charles Stacey. There is much of them in this book.

JLG
NH
Toronto and Ottawa
July 1991

Introduction

The twentieth century, Teddy Roosevelt confidently proclaimed, was destined to belong to "the men who speak English." The United States and Great Britain—the first on the rise, the second faltering just a little— were putting a pragmatic end to their historic quarrels, and good feelings were burgeoning all over Anglo-Saxondom. As 1914 approached, groups of prominent citizens in Britain, the U.S., and Canada organized themselves to arrange celebrations of the centenary of peace following the end of the War of 1812. The heroes of the long ago war were transformed from symbols of resistance and patriotism into the embodiments of transatlantic brotherhood. Commemorative monuments great and small were planned, as were a Niagara River bridge, water gates between Detroit and Windsor, and archways over the international highways at the British Columbia–Washington state border and at Rouses Point on the Quebec–New York frontier.

"... Never a Fortress!"

Another war in 1914 caused the cancellation of many of the centenary celebrations. But this new conflict was not one within the English-speaking family: the British Empire and the United States were on the same side—in sympathy if not, until 1917, in fact. A war made in Europe by Europeans, but unfortunately not for Europeans alone, reinforced the growing belief that Canada and the U.S. had evolved a different and better way of co-existence across the boundary line. There were tensions and suspicions still, but the distinctions between the Old World and the New seemed clearer than ever before. Europe had divided itself into alliances and ententes, and the race for armaments had inevitably brought war; meanwhile North Americans had been learning to live together and resolve their disagreements peaceably. The Americans might be imperialists from time to time, but their imperialism was ordinarily directed at other, lesser folk. The U.S. might be plagued by social, racial, and economic problems, but if Canadians were honest, they had to admit their country was no Utopia immune to the diseases of the modern industrial age. The prominent Montreal author Andrew Macphail wrote in 1914 that Canadians had thanked God they were not Americans for far too long: "We were not like those republicans and sinners . . . who lived to the southward, with whom it was dangerous for simpleminded people like ourselves to have any truck or trade." That belief merely masked the truth, Macphail argued, encouraging Canadians in their misplaced complacency and self-righteousness. In fact, as the Canadian jurist and historian W.R. Riddell asserted, the divisions of the past had been "merely skin deep, as compared with our essential and fundamental identity and unity."

Its geographical remoteness encouraged a sense that North America was a continent apart. The rest of the world was a long way away. A week was needed to reach Southampton or Le Havre by steamship from Montreal or New York; from Vancouver or San Francisco if was three long weeks to Tokyo, four to Australia. Relatively few North Americans travelled to such exotic climes. Most knew only what little they were told in their newspapers, which headlined conflict and crisis abroad, or in literature, which frequently taught distrust of the foreign and different. Prejudice was not likely to be tempered by experience or knowledge. Canadians and Americans were superior, pure, safe. To adapt the words of American historian Robert Wiebe, the mind's eye of a North American could sweep the world with almost unrestricted freedom. "So little obtruded upon the senses. The consciousness which centuries of abrasive contact had worked into men's psyches, the *Weltanschauungen* that bound 'us' and 'them,' nation inextricably interlocked with nation, into bundles of hates and hopes, simply did not apply. . . . East and west were the great buffer oceans, insulators against a jagged proximity."

Before the Great War, this attitude of moral superiority was regularly demonstrated during the annual conferences held at Mohonk Lake, New York. From 1904 to 1915, Canadian and American delegates met to discuss and recommend the application of law, conciliation, and arbitration, rather than force, to the settlement of disputes. This was the

Canadian–American way, "the answer of the new world to the war talk
of the old," the high-minded and earnest Canadian minister of labour,
Mackenzie King, told the gathering in 1910. "Let us not think," he
added, "that this is some little trumpery affair, for here we have an
opportunity to show the world that by this unfortified line running
between the two great countries, by this century of peace, we on this
continent have helped to work out the accomplishment of an epoch in
the course of Christianity itself." The Mohonk principles of arbitration
were explicitly endorsed by business groups, service and women's
clubs, and the Ontario legislature, and the shining example of the
"North American Idea"—a term invented by James A. Macdonald—was
the staple of the lecture circuit for years to come.

Macdonald was managing editor of the Toronto *Globe* until 1915. He
was a leading peace activist before the outbreak of war in 1914; after it
began he tried to combine support for the cause with a crusade for the
"New World idea of reason and international faith . . . pushed to the limit
of disarmament." In Macdonald's view, the two North American democracies were Europe's second chance, perhaps Europe's last chance. They
were the exemplars and trustees of freedom and justice; using those principles, which were the real North American Idea, they had evolved a system of civilized internationalism that was the hope of the world. As he
wrote in 1917, the year the United States formally entered the war that
emphasized North America's spectacular achievements and laid bare
Europe's "barbaric" failure:

> More than five thousand miles of North America's interna-
> tional boundary between the United States and Canada! More
> than five thousand miles where free nation meets free nation!
> where vital interest touches vital interest! . . . More than five
> thousand miles, with never a fortress! never a battle-ship!
> never a yawning gun! never a threatening sentinel on
> guard! . . . The United States and Canada, two democracies
> with their two flags, have kept the peace, the peace with hon-
> our, not for one brief spasm, or through one sudden outburst
> of good-will. For more than a hundred years, a hundred rest-
> less, turbulent years, while the boundary lines of every other
> continent have blazed in war and dripped with blood, the
> internationalism of North America has held; and to-day, in the
> smitten face of Europe's international tragedy, North America
> gives the unbroken pledge of a far greater peace for all the
> world through a millennium yet to come.

Unfortunately, Macdonald and others who carolled the North American Idea so loudly had forgotten much of their history.

THE DEFENDED BORDER

That history was not one of peace. The fate of nations, the boundary lines drawn on the map, had been decided more often than not by the arbitrament of war. From the earliest days of European settlement, there had been conflict, as the British and French jostled for supremacy and used their native allies to burn, pillage, and terrify. By taking Quebec in 1759, Britain had finally succeeded in driving France off the eastern half of the continent, but the revolution in the Thirteen Colonies to the south decisively altered the balance of power.

The American Revolution was one of the pivotal events in world history. Divided and torn by dissent as they were, the American colonies struggled against and defeated the power of Great Britain. Instead of a united British North America ruled from London, there was now a new nation, the United States of America, and several scattered and disaffected British colonies to its north.

The revolutionary armies had invaded the conquered province of Quebec in 1775, to be greeted most often by the indifference of the *habitants* and the stony silence of the Roman Catholic priests who had no reason to love the Protestant invaders; occasionally, however, there were eager offers of collaboration from those who sought to throw off the hated British yoke. But when the Americans' paper money proved all but worthless and when the seige of Quebec collapsed under the weight of smallpox and round shot, the French-speaking inhabitants and the relatively few British administrators, soldiers, and merchants breathed a collective sigh of satisfaction and relief. Their lives could go on much as before, something assured when the 1783 Peace of Paris, the settlement between Britain and the United States, confirmed the existence of British North America.

The existence of a non-American, indeed anti-American, way of life in North America was confirmed as well by the arrival of the Loyalists. The United Empire Loyalists were the losers in the Revolution, the inhabitants of the Thirteen Colonies who had remained loyal to King and Empire and who had fought bitterly and long against republicanism and independence. Driven from their homes in defeat, expelled from the established towns and rich farms of New York, Pennsylvania, Virginia, and the Carolinas, many Loyalists found themselves in the wilderness of Canada. To the inhabitants of the United States, the Revolution and its heroes had ushered in the New Jerusalem; to the Loyalists, scattered in Nova Scotia, New Brunswick, the Eastern Townships of Quebec, or in the trackless wastes of what would become Ontario, the Revolution, as Arthur Lower put it, was a "foul and treasonable occurrence."

The bitterness was profound, the gulf in understanding deep, the determination to make of Canada something different from the United States almost fanatic in the tenacity with which it was held. America was democratic and republican; Canada was ruled from the top down by London's appointed governors and was loyal to the Crown. America was confident, materialistic, and scornful of rank and order; Canada was unsure but idealistic in its relative poverty, and it revered the titles and knighthoods imported from the mother country. Above all, America appeared to be on the road to the future while Canada clung to the past, and the fear that they would be left behind rankled those who adhered faithfully to the lost cause. It would take time to heal these wounds, and time was in short supply.

The simple truth was that British and American interests were in conflict still, and Canada, raw and new as it was, was the convenient point for London and Washington to clash. The French, at war with Britain since 1793, made unfailing attempts to weaken their enemy by stirring up bad blood in North America. In the United States lingering concerns persisted over British efforts to raise the native tribes against the advance of American influence. As well, the British interfered regularly with American shipping. The U.S. claimed "freedom of the seas" despite the conflict in Europe, but Britain's navy was determined to shut down trade that might assist France, and the Royal Navy exercised the right to stop and search any vessel, and to remove from U.S. ships seamen suspected of being deserters from the British service. The Americans were divided about their chances in another war with England. Their military was weak and inefficient but, at the same time, they believed that it was merely a matter of marching across the border into Canada to give the unhappy colonists the opportunity to beg for admission to the United States. After all, in a phrase that would not come into vogue for a generation more, it was America's "manifest destiny" to be one nation.

The War of 1812 was not destined to be the cakewalk that Washington's politicians expected. The British North American colonists were largely unenthusiastic about the struggle, and there were many "late Loyalists"—Americans who had crossed into Canada well after the Revolution in search of land—whose loyalty was, to say the least, suspect. But the decisive factor in the conflict was that London had command of the sea and had well-trained regiments and a few able commanders in Canada.

The Americans, especially at the beginning of the war, did not. Though the fighting at times verged on the farcical, at others it was bloody indeed. The struggles along the Niagara frontier were probably the key to the outcome. At Queenston Heights on 14 October 1812, the British regulars and a few militiamen, led by the fatally wounded General Isaac Brock, drove off the attacking Americans, demonstrating irrefutably that Canada would be ably defended. That coalesced opinion among the dubious in British North America, those who had counted heads and assumed, wrongly as it turned out, that the Americans could not lose this war. Two years of fighting confirmed this. Most of the engagements were little more than skirmishes, though one at least—Lundy's Lane on 25 July 1814—was a hard fought if less than conclusive battle. The British side sustained more casualities, but the Americans withdrew to their side of the Niagara River, leaving Upper Canada secure. At sea, or on lakes Champlain, Ontario, and Erie, the two sides built bigger and bigger-gunned vessels in a race to achieve dominance. The United States Navy, under Commodore Perry, dominated Lake Erie; the Royal Navy probably had the upper hand on Lake Ontario. But the Atlantic seaboard was Britain's, and the Royal Navy's numerous men-of-war roamed almost at will, blockading the coast and landing the troops that burned Washington in retaliation, it was claimed, for the Americans' burning of York. The Peace of Ghent ended the war in March 1815. British North America had survived its fiercest test.

The war confirmed and strengthened the thirty-year-old stories of American lawlessness that the Loyalists had cherished. The U.S. army had fought most of the war on Canadian soil, and its troops had often behaved more like barbarians than disciplined soldiery. Looting and wanton destruction of life and property had reinforced British North America's deep detestation of the Yankees.

The Rebellions of 1837 would go some distance to keeping this antipathy alive. The rebellion in Upper Canada, led by the Scots newspaper publisher and politician William Lyon Mackenzie, was caused, so the "good citizens" maintained, by American ideas of democracy and republicanism. The "French" were to blame for the revolt in Lower Canada, though even here some saw the hand of American ideas at work. Worse still, after the rebels were crushed at Montogmery's Tavern just north of Toronto, Mackenzie fled to the U.S., and there were soon raids across the border, virtually unhindered by the United States government, as sympathizers sought to knock the ripe apple of British North America off the tree and into American hands. Was this not proof, if any were needed, of the Americans' insatiable desire to control all of the continent? Was their lack of success not the best evidence that British ideals were still cherished north of the line?

British ideals there were, but commerce and profits were important too. In 1847 Britain repealed the Corn Laws, moving decisively away from the mercantilism that favoured English interests and towards free trade. At about the same time, the United States slapped higher tariffs on goods entering the country. These two events led to considerable agitation, especially in Montreal where there were riots, the Parliament buildings were burned, and most of the city's leading merchants signed a call for annexation to the United States. British trade policies threatened ruination and there was fear among the Montreal merchant class that the policies of Lord Elgin, the governor, guaranteed French domination. Better to be part of the United States than to be bankrupt and under the control of the French, the businessmen shouted. For his part, Elgin wrote to London that "if England will not make the sacrifices which are absolutely necessary to put the Colonists here in as good a position commercially as the citizens of the States—in order to which free navigation and reciprocal trade with the States are indispensible . . . the end may be nearer than we wot of."

The annexationist storm of 1849 died out quickly, and it was succeeded by prosperity—brought by a reciprocity treaty with the United States. Signed in 1854 after many a false start, the treaty provided for free admission of natural products, a list that included grain, livestock, meat, and fish. The treaty was a boon for British North America: exports to the U.S. doubled between 1854 and 1855 (though there would be severe slippage from 1857 to 1859). And with prosperity, the annexationist ideas dwindled away, but never to nothingness.

By the beginning of the 1860s, great events were on the horizon. In the United States the struggle between the slave and free states was about to turn into rebellion, secession, and civil war; in British North America, the need for defence, expanded markets, and railways was beginning to push the separate and fractious colonies towards confederation.

North America's peaceful character, its penchant for arbitration over warfare, was largely a myth. There had been wars, rebellions, bloodshed, and strife aplenty as the relations between the two peoples sorted themselves out. But if nations need myths, and they do, surely it was better to believe in peaceful ones than in those that were redolent of conquest and violence. North American amity, something that slowly came into being in the decades after the U.S. Civil War and Confederation, was a great achievement. There were many false starts along the way, some crises that threatened war, and an enormous disparity in power between the two nations that became ever more obvious as the U.S. became a superpower—and Canada did not. How this co-existence was achieved is the subject of this book.

CHAPTER one

WHO WOULD NOT BE AN AMERICAN?

1 8 6 0 — 1 9 0 3

The governor-in-chief of the colonies of British North America was "fussed," his wife recorded in her diary on 20 October 1864. She was not quite sure why, but she thought it had something to do with the Civil War that raged in the United States, pitting South against North, Confederate against Yankee, over the great issues of slavery, states' rights, and the preservation of the American Union. Governor Lord Monck, about to leave Ottawa for an important conference in Quebec on the federation of the colonies, had just received word of a Confederate raid on the Vermont town of St. Albans, a few miles from the Canadian border. Three banks had been robbed, and $200 000 had been taken before the men escaped on stolen horses; they had done their best to set St. Albans alight as they galloped away. One person had been killed.

Monck knew that the affair had substantial implications for his colonies. The raiders had used Canada as a launching pad for their attack and they immediately returned there to seek sanctuary. An order went out from General John A. Dix, the commander of the Military District of the East, for northern troops to do whatever was necessary to capture the invaders, even if it meant violating Canadian neutrality. That would almost certainly mean war between President Abraham Lincoln's Union forces and Canada. And that in turn meant that Lincoln would be at war with Britain.

CIVIL WAR AND CONFEDERATION

Lincoln, wisely, drew back from the brink, refusing to approve Dix's edict. The Union now waited for justice to be done in Canada: fourteen of the St. Albans gang, after all, had been arrested, and they were bound to be tried and found guilty. But late in 1864 the charges were all dropped on technical grounds. The raiders were released.

The North was incensed. Its worst fears about Canada's (and Britain's) pro-Confederate biases had been confirmed. Dix issued his order once again. Canadians were told that they would need passports to cross the border. There was discussion about ending the 1817 Rush-Bagot Agreement, which limited naval armaments on the Great Lakes. Michigan Senator Zachariah Chandler gave notice of a motion to end an already unpopular reciprocal trade treaty between Canada and the United States that had been signed ten years before. Rapid British–Canadian–Union diplomacy smoothed over the cracks, but ill-feeling lingered in all three camps.

The St. Albans raid was more serious because it was part of a pattern of accident and misunderstanding. From the beginning of the Civil War in 1861, northerners could not comprehend Britain's sympathy for the Confederacy when their own cause was so righteous. Britain and Canada, on the other hand, had decades'-old suspicions of Washington and all its works—the Prince of Wales's peaceful visit to the U.S. in 1860 notwith-standing—and they were not at all convinced that the North's motives for going to war were completely pure. As if to reinforce such misgivings, the British Royal Mailship *Trent* was stopped by a U.S. naval vessel very early in the war, in November 1861, and two Confederate diplomats were removed by force. This was a flagrant contravention of neutrality rights, and one clearly supported by a public that resented Britain's toleration of southern belligerency. "I fear war is upon us," wrote a senior British official, as London rushed 11 000 soldiers to Canada. The release of the Confederates helped to calm the storm, but there was no apology from President Lincoln.

The case of the *Alabama*, one of a number of Confederate ships that were built in British ports, underlined and symbolized the tensions that continued to plague British–American relations during the Civil War. The North tried to convince the British to keep the *Alabama* from being launched, but it managed to escape—the Union said with London's connivance—and did great damage to northern shipping until sunk in mid-1864.

Nor did the difficulties in British–American relations or the threat to Canada subside with the end of the Civil War. For a while, the victorious northern army, one of the greatest armed forces in world history, seemed poised to get revenge for a half-decade of frustrations by attacking Canada. The force in the event quickly demobilized, but that happened just as the Fenian Brotherhood came into prominence. This band of Irish-Americans was determined to wrest independence for Ireland from Britain, and one way to hurt the British was to attack Canada. Taking strength from about 10 000 Civil War veterans, a substantial war chest, and the reluctance of U.S. politicians (their eye on the Irish vote) to intervene, the Fenians caused much agitation and considerable expenditure for defence along the Canada–U.S. border in 1866. Twice they struck, once in the area of the Niagara Peninsula, where they won a famous battle at Ridgeway, but withdrew fearing an encounter with more substantial forces; another move was directed at the Eastern Townships in present-day Quebec. A third time they threatened the Maine–New Brunswick border, but did not attack. The Fenian operations were ultimately all unsuccessful, but they made the British colonies, particularly in the Maritimes, think even harder about coming together rather than perishing separately.

The Civil War and its aftermath contributed mightily to the Confederation of the British colonies in 1867. To begin with, the British were confirmed in their belief that they could no longer adequately protect the colonies, and London pressed them to band together and provide their own defences. That took some convincing, but the argument, with the help of the Fenians, eventually took root. The end of the reciprocity treaty in 1866 further emphasized the vulnerability of the individual colonies, and highlighted the potential for economic co-operation in a united Canada.

Nevertheless Confederation did not ensure the country's future. The new Dominion of Canada comprised four provinces, not the ten it would eventually boast, and Quebec and Ontario had only a third of the territory they would later possess. The population of about three and a half million huddled in a thin line—what the American journalist and politician Horace Greeley called "an eelskin of settled country"—close up to the United States. The provinces were not linked by dependable transport, and Canadians looked southwards more easily than they did to one another. Movements that promoted annexation with the United States had sprung up in each of the provinces, and none was stronger than in an economically distressed Nova Scotia. Joseph Howe, who had fought Confederation valiantly but had come over to John A. Macdonald's side in 1868, warned the prime minister that "a clear, unfettered vote of the people" might take the province into the American Union.

Canada's Britishness was an asset, an immunization against American influences and a reminder to Americans that if they wanted Canada they would have to cope with more than Canadians. But the British connection also put Canada at a disadvantage: the U.S. was irked by the shadow of the British Empire on a continent where by all rights the odious connection to the Old World ought long ago to have been jettisoned. London itself, preoccupied by problems in Europe and realizing that the defence of Canada was an impossible proposition against the now considerable military and naval power of the United States, was anxious to settle the Civil War account and be done with North America. Canada was an inconvenience and, besides, a potential hazard to both of the great powers, particularly if a quarrel over the dominion should get out of hand.

NATURAL LINES MUST PREVAIL

Prominent American politicians and officials had no difficulty in imagining a United States whose reach ran deep into lands north of the forty-ninth parallel. The U.S. government acquired Alaska in 1867 partly in order to bring the British Pacific Northwest into Washington's orbit. Secretary of State W.H. Seward, who engineered the purchase, admitted to Congress that his intention was to put pressure on British Columbia, to squeeze it from the north as well as the south. Seward's successor, Hamilton Fish, who held the position under President Ulysses S. Grant, also coveted the vast possessions of the Hudson's Bay Company to the west and north of Ontario. Minnesotans had long eyed the same territory, with its wealth and long-standing economic ties to the United States. A group of U.S. senators (including the influential chair of the Senate Committee on Foreign Relations, Charles Sumner of Massachusetts) suggested that Britain hand Canada over lock, stock, and barrel. That would nicely compensate an aggrieved United States for Britain's Civil War transgressions. President Grant agreed, telling his Cabinet in November 1869 that he wanted to delay a bargain over the *Alabama* and other claims until the British were ready to pay by giving up Canada. Adopting a somewhat different strategy with the same end, Fish repeatedly told the British representative in Washington that

Canada and the rest of British North America wanted independence and that it must be granted. Then, Fish thought, everything would inexorably come America's way. The continent "is ours," bellowed Senator Zachariah Chandler. Canada was "a mere speck on the map," a "nuisance" which, if it was allowed to expand westwards, would become "a standing menace . . . that we ought not to tolerate and will not tolerate."

Grant and Fish were happy enough to claim Canada and the British Northwest, and they took great pleasure in the various annexation movements on both sides of the border, but the actions they were willing to or could take were limited. Less restrained was General Oscar Malmros, the fiery U.S. consul in the Red River settlement, who took up his post in the crucial summer of 1869. That was just as Hudson's Bay Company properties in the area were coming into Canadian hands through purchase, and just as Louis Riel was organizing to ensure that his French-speaking Métis people, a good half of the population of Red River, would be protected in the transition. By the end of the year, Riel had set up a provisional government in the region, while Malmros schemed unrelentingly to demonstrate that the Métis leader and the Red River would both be better off if they attached themselves to the United States. Authorities in Washington watched, listened, and did not discourage. They cannot have been insensitive to their consul's assertion that they could prevent the establishment of a rival "great confederation north of the United States" by acquiring the settlement, which was strategically located at the entrance to the West and already populated by numerous American immigrants.

It was in Riel's interest to keep Ottawa off guard by holding open the possibility of a liaison with the Americans. He went as far as to finance a newspaper called the *New Nation*, an arm of Yankee propaganda which urged annexation to the United States with blaring headlines:

> Consolidation!
> The Future
> of the
> American Continent
> One Flag! One Empire!
> Natural Lines Must Prevail

The *New Nation's* first edition contained an unsigned article by Oscar Malmros. "Annexation Our Manifest Destiny" argued that Canada and the British Northwest were separated by a "dismal waste of rocks and water"; they had nothing in common whatsoever. The United States and the Northwest, on the other hand, were one—economically, geographically, culturally, permanently. This was the rhetoric frequently employed by Malmros's champion in Washington, Senator Alexander Ramsay of Minnesota, who at the time was unsuccessfully urging Fish to give clandestine financial assistance to Riel's efforts.

In the final analysis, however, neither Riel nor most of the Red River settlers wanted marriage with the United States. Riel wanted "to treat if possible with Canada for a just union with that country or England." If that failed, he would look elsewhere, but only then. The people themselves had the already familiar northern mixture of emotions towards Americans: they were admirable in so many ways, but also crude, unruly, demanding, and materialistic, not at all like the sensible and sensitive folk of the Red River. Nor had Malmros's over-zealous tactics helped.

The government of John A. Macdonald had only to handle the situation carefully. It accomplished this by creating the Canadian province of Manitoba in April 1870, and by making certain guarantees regarding land and language to the Métis. Without doubt, the Métis leader had progressed further and more quickly in his negotiations with Ottawa because of the American annexationist threat. But Riel, a rebel and worse in the eyes of many Canadians, then had to flee to the United States when Macdonald sent a military expedition later in 1870 to consolidate his grip on the Red River. The prime minister mixed British regular troops with his Canadian militia in order to demonstrate to the government and people of the United States that Britain was behind him and behind Canada. England, he wanted it known, was resolved not to abandon her colonies and was far from indifferent to the future of the great West.

President Grant could only have won Manitoba by force, but was never prepared to go to that length. Certainly his secretary of state had no intention of doing so. Hamilton Fish talked a good deal, and he was willing from time to time to manipulate or threaten. For example, he was behind the Cabinet's order that the U.S. locks at Sault Ste. Marie be denied to Macdonald's Red River expedition. That decision was quickly reversed, however, when Canada warned the Americans that they might be jeopardizing their right to use the Welland Canal. The Canadian steamer *Chicora*, with a cargo of only food and general supplies, was refused passage of the canal at Sault Ste. Marie on its first try, but allowed through a matter of days later after the Cabinet had reconsidered. The Americans thought, as part of their discussions with

Ottawa, that at least they had extracted a promise of amnesty for Riel and his men. They were wrong. All they got for their trouble was more ill-feeling from Canadians outraged that their willingness to open their own canals to commercial shipping during the Civil War had not been fully and generously reciprocated when Canada needed help. The incident showed how easily the instinct to obstruct rose up in Fish and like-minded colleagues, and how quickly they were apt to withdraw in the face of a good argument or strong response.

At the same time that Manitoba came into being, British Columbia was making a decision about its future. The Pacific Northwest had strong ties to the United States, dating back to the Fraser Valley gold rush of 1858–59, and there had been an annexation movement in B.C. since 1866. Washington therefore had hopes, which were further encouraged by a petition of some of the area's residents requesting entry into the United States. Here too, however, the U.S. administration was generally cautious and discreet, and it lost the prize. British Columbia, which in fact was far more "British" than the Red River, agreed to join Canada in 1871. In return, the new province got a promise that its debts would be cleared and a railway from east to west built within ten years. Protests from the opposition in Parliament about the costs of this arrangement were met by reminders of some of the more extreme American boasts and threats about their intentions for the region.

Grant and Fish were realists. The expansionist movement was small, even though it was supported by powerful commercial interests. There was no will to use force against Canada: the Civil War had given Americans a lifetime of wounds and debts. Among the prominent annexationists, only Senator Chandler advocated a war to gain the country to the north. Canada, even a transcontinental Canada, did not pose a military or even political threat to the United States, and both Britain and Canada had gone out of their way to reassure Americans on that score. Most Americans probably agreed with the *Boston Daily Advertiser*, which wrote at the end of 1869, "There is no one in the country who desires to annex one of their provinces unless the mass of population desires it. Should they, in obedience to a natural law of centripetal force, gravitate to us, we will welcome them cordially . . . but until they are ready to come to us, we have not the slightest disposition to interfere in or to influence their affairs."

In a curious way, Canada profited from a general air of bewilderment in the United States that anyone would wish to resist the greatness it had to offer. After all, historian Charles Stacey once said, who would not be an American if she or he had the chance?

A Pertinent Question

Mrs. Britannia: "Is it possible, my dear, that you have ever
given your cousin Jonathan any encouragement?"

Miss Canada: "Encouragement! Certainly not, Mamma. I
have told him we can *never* be united."

Canadians had been fashioning a negative response to that question
for a long time. Goodness, stability, and strength of character, they
claimed, were much more important than greatness. American ideas
and institutions were distrusted, resisted, believed to be morally infe-
rior. Canadians had Queen Victoria and the British constitutional and

legal tradition; with them went a stable balance between freedom and authority. The Canadian constitution, the British North America Act of 1867, was an explicit rejection of its American counterpart, which was seen as having created a weak central government in Washington, an important cause of the Civil War.

The Americans had too much democracy and too few ways to check its excesses. The U.S. "spirit of universal democracy," Thomas D'Arcy McGee had said just before Confederation, was of particular note and danger to Canadians because it was inherently aggressive. Whatever Americans saw, they wanted to possess and make over in their image. There had always been in the United States, the great Irish-Canadian orator warned, a desire "for the acquisition of new territory, and the inexorable law of democratic existence seems to be its absorption. They coveted Florida and seized it; they coveted Louisiana, and purchased it; they coveted Texas, and stole it; and then they picked a quarrel with Mexico, which ended by their getting California. They sometimes pretend to despise these colonies as prizes beneath their ambition; but had we not had the strong arm of England over us, we should not now have had a separate existence." That would remain a common Canadian theme for many decades: a distrust of the United States, and a belief that salvation and survival lay not simply in British values but in the potential for an application of British power. Canada could not stand alone as an independent republic, John A. Macdonald said many times during his long political career. It needed England at its back.

THE HIGH COMMISSION ON JOINTS, WASHINGTON 1871

Yet the British wished to get out of the business of North America. They had been withdrawing military forces from all their forts and strong points in Canada except Halifax since the late 1860s. By 1871 the process was complete. That same year, Great Britain began a serious negotiation with the United States to deal squarely with the North American issues that divided the two countries. Canada was of course an interested party, a fact recognized by the appointment of Macdonald as one of the United Kingdom representatives to the talks. The Canadian prime minister discovered to his dismay, however, that the British had "only one thing on their minds—that is, to go home to England with a treaty in their pockets, settling everything, no matter what the cost to Canada."

Two attempts had already been made to solve the rift in Anglo-American relations caused by the Civil War, the most recent scuppered in the Senate by Senator Sumner. The aim this time was to resolve the difficulties between the two countries once and for all. The chosen method of negotiation was a Joint High Commission of five high-powered delegates from each of the two countries. Secretary of State Fish led the American group, a job carried out on the British side by Lord Ripon, a member of British Prime Minister W.E. Gladstone's Cabinet. The meetings, highly successful from a British and American perspective, were held in the U.S. capital—hence the resulting Treaty of Washington, 1871. "Our life here," the chief British delegate complained, "is rendered very intolerable by the endless feasts. We work all day and dine all night. And some wag in the newspapers says we are not a Joint High Commission, but a High Commission on Joints—the joke greatly delights the Washingtonians." Macdonald at first enjoyed the extravagant proceedings very much. He had been desperately ill just the previous summer, and he welcomed the good living and warm climate. But his pleasure evaporated as the days went by, the talks wore on, and he lost battle after battle.

A good part of the commission's success—and of Macdonald's unhappiness—can be accounted for by British eagerness for an accommodation. Thus they apologized for the "escape" from their ports of and the damage caused by the *Alabama* and "other vessels" built in Britain, and agreed to an arbitration of claims on terms that were bound to make them losers. An international tribunal later awarded the United States a staggering $15.5 million in compensation. The British also allowed a lesser point of contention, the ownership of the west coast San Juan Islands, which lay between British Columbia and the state of Washington, to be referred to a third party. The arrangement precluded a political compromise and ultimately disadvantaged Canada. In 1872, the arbiter, Emperor William I of Germany, gave all of the islands to the United States.

From Canada's standpoint, however, the real issue was the fisheries. The Americans had had a piece of the maritime provinces' inshore fisheries under the Reciprocity Treaty of 1854, but when they denounced the agreement in 1866 they lost the right to fish along the Canadian coast. They came anyway. Ottawa tried licences, first attaching small fees, and then demanding higher and higher rates, but the system was difficult to enforce. The Americans kept coming. Macdonald could refer airily to an 1818 convention between the United States and Great Britain that excluded the former from the inshore fisheries, but that was hardly sufficient to stem the tide. In the summer of 1870, the Canadian government had launched a small fleet of cruisers to rein in the rule breakers. American vessels violating Canadian waters were seized, and the outrage south of the border was palpable. It was bad enough to be disciplined by Britain, but to have it happen at the hands of a puny Canada was too much. President Grant sarcastically told Congress that the imperial government in London had apparently handed all or some of its jurisdiction over the fisheries to "the colonial authority known as the Dominion of Canada, and this semi-independent but irresponsible agent has exercised its delegated powers in an unfriendly way." In the genteel world of international diplomacy these were fighting words, and that is perhaps where the two countries were headed but for the Washington talks.

Macdonald was willing to give in on the fisheries in exchange for a return to the halcyon days of 1854–66, when reciprocity was thought to have delivered prosperity to British North America. Such a bargain never had a chance. The Congress was protectionist, and the American negotiators knew that they could get the fisheries from Britain for a lot less. The Treaty of Washington gave the Americans what they demanded: unrestricted entry for a period of at least ten years into the territorial fisheries of Quebec, Prince Edward Island, Nova Scotia, and New Brunswick, as well as free navigation in the St. Lawrence River. Canada was granted fishing rights in American waters north of the thirty-ninth parallel, and navigation rights in Lake Michigan and on three remote northern rivers; a cash payment to Canada as further compensation was to be decided by yet another international panel. The only reciprocity that the treaty allowed for was in fish products, which could now move back and forth across the border without tariffs. For the Canadian prime minister the arrangement constituted utter defeat. "Well, here go the fisheries," Macdonald told Hamilton Fish, only to have the U.S. secretary of state quickly retort, "You get a good equivalent for them." "No," came Macdonald's reply, "we give them away. . . . They are gone."

Macdonald fought hard, but decisions like this were still Britain's to make. His colleagues, all from the mother country, accused him of obstructionism, hucksterism, and treachery: what right had he to interfere in the reconciliation of two great powers? He had always known that his situation would be very difficult, and for that reason had agreed to participate reluctantly. If he kicked against the British traces, he would be thought narrow and selfish, an irresponsible figure who was giving Americans advantages to exploit; if he acquiesced too easily in a settlement that seemed unfair, he would surely be accused by his own electors of not doing enough for Canada. After he saw the way that the talks over the fisheries were clearly headed, Macdonald seriously considered going home without signing the treaty. He understood, rightly, that it was going to be very unpopular in Canada, and that he would be seen as culpable in an outrage against his own people. "Never, in the course of my public life," he wrote from Washington, "have I been in so disagreeable a position."

But sign the treaty Macdonald did. He justified it to the House of Commons a year later as Canada's only course, given its delicate predicament as a British country on an American continent. Not for the last time, a Canadian prime minister argued that a happy Anglo-American relationship was vital to Canadian security. Macdonald reported to the House what an American statesman had told him. "The rejection of this Treaty . . . meant war, not war to-day or to-morrow or at any given period but whenever England was . . . engaged elsewhere." Had the two countries not resolved their squabbles, the prime minister concluded, "England's difficulty would be the United States' opportunity." The Americans would grab the opening to declare war on Britain, and "Canada would be, as a matter of course, the battleground of the two nations. We should be the sufferers, our country would be devastated, our people slaughtered, our prosperity destroyed."

Macdonald found it easier to argue for the Treaty of Washington a year after the fact. London had agreed to compensate Canada for its losses at the hands of the Fenians, who had not simply made attacks on Canada in 1866, but had continued to lurk about in the months and years immediately after Confederation, menacing the border, frightening Canadians, and creating insecurity in the new dominion. On the Queen's birthday in 1870, the Fenians made a last foray across the Vermont–Quebec border. Their leaders could only muster a few hundred invaders and there was no chance of success, but they were helped by the unwillingness of U.S. federal and state authorities to confiscate caches of arms prior to the raid. Only after the fact did President Grant issue a denunciation. He acted more quickly in condemning the raids than his predecessor had four years before, but there was still the stink of something like official collusion. "I cannot wonder," the British foreign secretary exclaimed, "at the bitter feeling of indignation that animates the Canadians who if the United States Government had behaved decently would have been saved all the troubles, anxiety and expense that they have endured for several years." Macdonald had wanted Fenian compensation on the agenda of the Washington Treaty negotiations, and he of course wanted the United States to be the one to make restitution. He failed on both counts. It was the British who paid, in the form of loan guarantees, for the building of Canadian canals and railways. They did so to keep the dominion sweet and ensure safe passage for the treaty.

For all the humiliations real and imagined, the Treaty of Washington was a watershed in Canada–U.S. relations. C.P. Stacey, the historian who exploded the myth that there was an unguarded frontier between Canada and United States as early as the beginning of the nineteenth century, dates the era of good feeling in North America from the signing of the 1871 treaty: "After that treaty there was a genuinely undefended border, in great part because the causes of tension between the two neighbouring communities had been removed." There was still plenty of bad blood between the United States and Britain, and between the U.S. and Canada. Americans remembered the Revolution, and railed against British economic policy and investments in their country. Canadians remembered the War of 1812, and railed against the fisheries clauses of the Washington treaty and the injustice of having to take Fenian compensation, not from the United States where the raids had originated, but from London. Viewed from a broader international perspective, however, 1871 was undoubtedly the beginning of a stability valuable for all. It was the path to peaceful co-existence in North America.

"NORTHMEN OF THE NEW WORLD"

Canada was more secure in other ways too. Ottawa had extended its authority westwards: the nation now swept from the Atlantic Ocean to the Pacific. Railways would follow, so that it was soon possible to travel or ship goods on an entirely Canadian route from Halifax to Vancouver. The annexation movements in both Canada and the United States were losing their momentum, at least for now. Nor were there any more Fenians to contend with; an 1871 border scare turned out not to have been caused by them. In 1873, Prince Edward Island joined the Confederation. This was an important addition because the island had only recently flirted with a free trade arrangement with the United States, which would have allowed Americans an economic and perhaps strategic toehold in the Gulf of the St. Lawrence, uncomfortably close to Canada.

The Canadian nation was born of vision, good fortune, self-awareness—but would it be enough? Canada First was a small, consciously English-Canadian movement of the late 1860s and early 1870s with big ideas about engendering a powerful nationalist spirit to consolidate Confederation and ward off the American disease. Members of the group used the country's northern climate and geography, as many Canadian nationalists have since, to differentiate between Canada and the United States. "We are the Northmen of the New World," one of them wrote, while another proclaimed, "The old Norse mythology, with its Thor hammerings, appeals to us,—for we are a Northern people,—as the true out-crop of human nature, more manly, more real, than the weak marrow-bones superstition of an effeminate South." There was hardiness, purity, and discipline in Canada, the argument went, but only passion and excess in the United States. The poet Charles Mair, an original member of the group, wrote that Americans were "a living exemplification of the danger of wild assumptions and wild interpretations in politics and morals." How could it be otherwise, he wrote a little later in life, when an entire generation was "fed on tales of villains elevated into heroes, Peck's Bad Boy and the like sickly rubbish, is full of aversion from honest work, sees successful fraud on all hands rolling in ostentatious and pretentious wealth."

For all their bluster and condescension, however, Canada Firsters at bottom reflected the uncertainties of their new nation. They worried about a country too easily divided against itself, not conscious enough or proud enough of its unique position in the world. They were profoundly concerned, in the context of the Treaty of Washington, about a Britain too anxious to quit the continent. Where would Canada be without a connection to the powerful British Empire? Where would the Monroe Doctrine and Manifest Destiny lead if Canada were exposed and unprotected?

In the federal election of 1872 the unpopularity of the Treaty of Washington was one of the issues that cost Macdonald votes. He won the slimmest of victories. Then the Pacific Scandal struck: Macdonald's Conservatives had taken campaign money from the syndicate that received the contract to build the Canadian Pacific Railway. Some of that money, moreover, had come from American entrepreneurs who wanted to control the railway. The government fell in 1873, and a solid, honest Scot named Alexander Mackenzie suddenly found himself in the premier's chair. Macdonald's political career was almost certainly over.

Mackenzie, like Macdonald, sought a return to reciprocity with the United States. In February 1874, only weeks after taking power, the prime minister delegated George Brown, the owner of the Toronto *Globe* and a hugely important fellow Liberal, to seek out a trade agreement with the U.S. The aim was to get reciprocity in natural products—the U.S. wanted to include manufactures as well—and to give the Americans access to the inshore fisheries in return. The ensuing drama unfolded in Washington over several months. Although the British minister hovered nearby to make it clear that Mother Knew Best and that Canada was not yet a nation in the international sense, the negotiation was almost entirely a Canadian–American affair, one of the first of its kind. A draft treaty emerged but it is difficult to believe that the Grant administration, which still sported Hamilton Fish, was fully serious in intent. The White House and the State Department did not put their weight behind the treaty, and a high-tariff Senate simply let it languish.

The international arbitration to decide upon a cash settlement for the Canadian inshore fisheries, stipulated by the Washington treaty, was completed in 1877. The decision called upon the U.S. to pay Canada $5.5 million, but it was a decision that pleased neither side. Canada wanted more, much more, while the Americans were so put out that they took the first opportunity, in 1885, to walk away from their commitments under the terms of the Treaty of Washington. A fish war promptly started.

Another Canadian–American diplomatic battle was waged in these years over Sitting Bull, the Sioux chief who arranged for the massacre of U.S. army General George Armstrong Custer and his entire force at Little Big Horn in 1876. Sitting Bull and his followers migrated to Canada the next year, encountering as their only resistance a North West Mounted Police major and four troopers—quite a contrast to their usual reception by the U.S. cavalry. For the next five years the Canadian and American governments negotiated over Sitting Bull's fate. Perhaps so little has been said or written about this part of the Sitting Bull tale, historian John Jennings muses, because the Sioux chief "was a great disappointment to those who looked on him as the scourge of the West, the embodiment of all that was savage and degraded in the Indian character." During the Canadian years there were "no scalpings, and nobody murdered, in fact nothing to whet the popular appetite at all."

The Canadian government, while not sharing the U.S. view of Sitting Bull as a hostile and dangerous warrior, did not wish him to remain in their West. Nor did the Americans really want to have him back. In June 1877, the Canadian minister of the interior, David Mills, made a pilgrimage to Washington in order to see what could be done. Mills saw President Rutherford B. Hayes and dispensed some good Canadian advice about Ottawa's superior wisdom where the Indians were concerned. The British, who were in charge of Canadian diplomacy, were not happy with this unofficial visit, but Mills was able to extract a promise that an American commission would be struck to facilitate Sitting Bull's return to the U.S.

Sitting Bull would not come back on the terms offered, which required that he surrender all arms and horses and settle on a reserve. The U.S. government then sent troops to the Canadian–American border, preventing Sitting Bull and other natives from crossing over into the United States and in the process interfering with long-standing hunting practices. Eventually, as Jennings says, starvation accomplished what diplomacy could not. Sitting Bull was unable to find sufficient food north of the border, and he could get no permanent assistance or assured status from a Canadian government anxious to avoid establishing a precedent. On 19 July 1882, Sitting Bull finally accepted the capitulation of his nation and told his young son, "My boy, if you live, you can never be a man in this world because you never could have a gun or pony."

COMPETITION AND IMITATION: THE NATIONAL POLICY

The resilient John A. Macdonald had meanwhile miraculously regained the premiership, assisted by a world-wide depression that made the Liberals vulnerable and by his own Conservatives' promise to build a tariff system to protect and promote Canadianism. The cry for a "National Policy" of big tariffs, which was incorporated into the Conservative platform during the period when Macdonald was inching his way back to respectability, was an effective political counter to the Liberals. Their obsessively low tariffs, critics said, had allowed U.S. products in while Canadian ones were forced to jump high hurdles at the American border. The famous cartoonist, J.W. Bengough, depicted Uncle Sam battering Canadian industry with the club of his protective tariff, while the Liberals watched and hesitated to help out; in the background were factories, closed, broken, suspended, or working half-time.

During the campaign that returned him to power in 1878, Macdonald pointed to the working people "gone off to the United States. They are to be found employed in the Western States, in Pittsburgh, and, in fact, in every place where manufactures are going on. These Canadian artizans are adding to the strength, to the power, and to the wealth of a foreign nation instead of adding to ours." Higher tariffs, judiciously applied, would enhance prosperity and develop national character by building a varied economy in which many occupations would be possible, creating opportunity, teaching skills, and keeping Canadians in Canada. Macdonald put his new policy in place early in 1879, and since it seemed to usher in a period of plenty, his compatriots must have thought that he knew what he was doing. Few perhaps noticed that the 1879 law held out the possibility of lower rates on a number of natural products (the National Policy did not apply to manufactures alone) if the United States were to extend reciprocal treatment.

The National Policy appealed to Canadians for obvious enough reasons; as a future prime minister would put it, the promise was "jobs, jobs, jobs." Nevertheless, Robert Craig Brown, who has carried out a systematic study of the 1880s and 1890s in Canadian–American relations, argues that a strategy was emerging that went far beyond balance sheets and tariff schedules. "Fundamental to the thinking of the framers of the policy," he writes, "was the idea that the United States was much less a friendly neighbour than an aggressive competitor power waiting for a suitable opportunity to fulfill its destiny of the complete conquest of North America." If there was to be a Canada, therefore, the construction of a strong economy with an industrial base and secure markets was not desirable but imperative. Brown sees the tariff as having fairly rapidly become synonymous with "the nation," a way of safeguarding what was distinctive. He demonstrates how the thinking behind the national policy was extended and applied by the governments of the time to all the great problems of Canadian–American relations: the protection of the inshore fisheries, and the attempt to use them as a negotiating tool to demand commercial benefits for all Canadians; the battle to assert the right of sealers to ply their trade in the Bering Sea, where U.S. officials claimed authority, barred Canadian ships, and seized interlopers; and the controversy over the boundary of the Alaska panhandle, an area in which Ottawa believed it had national economic and strategic interests to promote. This was the politics—and the economics—of survival and competition. A politician like John A. Macdonald, a late nineteenth-century Canadian nationalist who looked with pride at Great Britain and its immense empire, was by definition an anti-American.

But support for the National Policy was also motivated by a wish to *imitate* the United States: if this is a contradiction, it is a very Canadian one. Citizens of the dominion could not help looking enviously southwards. As business historian Michael Bliss writes, "the desire to create a great industrial country like the United States was overwhelming. The

"Old Tomorrow": John A. Macdonald in 1883.
(National Archives of Canada/C 21596)

"Canadians believed protection for their manufacturers was the best way to avoid becoming or remaining a nation of hewers of wood and drawers of water, of farmers, fisherman, and fur traders." The National Policy had the advantage of attracting American capital and know-how, allowing U.S. firms to circumvent the tariff by establishing branch plants in Canada. This factor was apparently understood by some businesses and politicians from the beginning, but it became more and more prominent as a somewhat incongruous rationale for high tariffs. Soon the press, politicians, and business people were marvelling at the magical impact that the tariff had on investment. "Score another for the N.P." and "another monument to the glory and success of our National Policy," the magazine *Canadian Manufacturer* trumpeted as American subsidiaries were set up or contemplated.

By 1887, the secretary of the Canadian Manufacturers' Association could testify to a royal commission that there was at least one branch plant in almost every important Ontario town. The policy was also going down well in Quebec because it helped to staunch the flow of emigration to the textile mills of New England. Keeping people at home was crucial if the French Canadian identity was to be preserved and enhanced. Thus the Canadian economic nationalism of the period had an American face. Bliss comments that it "operated and was known to operate to induce Americans to enter Canada and participate directly in the Canadian economy. . . . The funny thing about our tariff walls was that we always wanted the enemy to jump over them. Some walls!" Americans who were Canada's competitors in the United States, he adds, became invaluable economic allies simply by virtue of crossing the border. The "dangers" of "foreign investment" would not be an issue in Canadian life for many decades to come.

CONTINENTALISM REVIVED

The pan-Canadian nationalism that had been urged by the Canada First movement and promoted by the rhetoric and achievements of the National Policy did not come easily. The 1880s and 1890s were a period of serious regional, racial, and cultural divisions. Wilfrid Laurier, speaking shortly after his elevation to the leadership of the Liberal party in 1887, mused about the strong possibility of the country's "premature dissolution."

The problem was partly economic and psychological. The prosperity of the early era of the National Policy, helped by the tariff and by investment in the great transcontinental railway, did not last to the satisfaction of many Canadians. Historians frequently fall into the trap of listening too much to contemporary bleating about the economy, concluding that the period from the mid-1880s until 1896 was one of stagnation and depression. It was not. Population, gross national product, and exports all grew. Nevertheless, many individual Canadians, particularly in the West, had economic difficulty. Many others thought that the country was in trouble, to some extent making it so. The American example, or Canadians' perception of it, was in this regard crucial. As historian P.B. Waite perceptively states, "Canada developed later than the United States; Canadians at the time expected too much too soon. They were forever looking to the south, and wanting to realize at once what the United States had done, or was doing. Given this perennial juxtaposition—they are still at it—it was understandable that some Canadians at the time should have been restless and dissatisfied."

The young and the restless flocked south, providing a concrete statistic for those Canadians who wanted to tell themselves just how bad things were. The country gained 1.5 million people in the 1880s, but at the same time a very large number emigrated. It did not take much imagination to guess where most had gone. The 1890 U.S. census showed that almost a million persons born in Canada now lived in the United States; one estimate was that a quarter of all men and women born in Canada were ending up as American citizens, an astonishing and troubling figure. A popular novel of the time told the tale of a young man who sought the larger horizons of the United States; finding fame and fortune there, he returned home to retrieve his Canadian sweetheart. This was the quintessential Canadian parable. Opportunities for success and a better way of life lay to the south, there could be no doubt. But goodness, still, resided in Canada. When sentiment for closer continental co-operation of one sort or another revived—for one last fling?—in the last two decades of the century, it was an affair of the purse and political advantage, seldom of the heart.

Annexationism flared up but mainly in the central parts of Canada, not in the Maritimes or British Columbia. A Manitoba agitation for union with the United States in 1884–85, one strand of a movement of agrarian discontent, generated rumours of rebellion and a rebirth of Fenianism in the province sufficient to rock Prime Minister Macdonald. He privately admitted that he feared an all-out revolt. In Ontario, a growing sympathy for annexation was reported by various sources, particularly in areas such as Essex County, where Canadians could peer across the border at a thriving U.S. The *Clarion* wrote in 1889 that it was true Windsor was filled with annexationists; "The people here . . . know that in many lines [of manufacture] the prices in Detroit are lower by just the amount of the tariff. They see a city of one quarter of a million on one bank of a river while on the other bank . . . the population is less than ten thousand." The year before, the Toronto *Globe* had asked readers for comments on the country's future. In a city renowned the British Empire over for the strength of its imperial loyalty, twenty-five of seventy-five respondents plumped for annexation and had the temerity to sign their names.

And for the first time, French Canada also had its annexationists. The hanging of Louis Riel in 1885 divided Canadians along racial lines and made some of Riel's followers wonder if they would not be better off on their own or as part of the United States. French annexationists could look to the "bestarred flag" of the United States for comfort and tolerance, even though their English colleagues might support union with the Americans for the diametrically opposed aim of ending French and Roman Catholic "privilege." Both, at least, could agree that political marriage would bring good economic times.

Yet one should not make too much of these enthusiasms. They were minority opinions that mirrored Canadian-made fears and insecurities, and it was hard to find very many encouraging words in the U.S. for an amalgamation with the northern neighbour.

Canada's annexationist-in-chief was Goldwin Smith, a transplanted English publicist, historian, and journalist with considerable wealth and a caustic pen. Smith had trouble seeing the point of Canada: it was an artificial construct which defied nature, geography, and destiny, all of which would sooner or later demand a coming together of Canada and the United States. An unrepentant Anglo-Saxon, Smith believed that a vast English-speaking continental union would swamp the French of Canada and speed the way to the repair of the great rupture of 1776 between the United States and Great Britain. Those were developments devoutly to be wished, because in bringing English-speaking countries closer to "moral federation," their cause, and the world's, would be advanced.

In the late 1880s, Smith championed the call for a complete economic union of Canada and the United States. Commercial Union, as the movement was known, argued for continental free trade but also for a common North American tax system and an agreed tariff against the rest of the world. Smith spoke and wrote widely and was not shy about putting his own money behind the cause, which he said was nothing but convincing the regions of Canada to admit what they must know instinctively, that their economic ties were with their counterparts in the U.S., not with each other. He liked to quote J.W. Longley, the Nova Scotia attorney general: "Inter-Provincial trade is unnatural, forced and profitless, while there is a natural and profitable trade at our very doors open and available to us." For Smith, the continent was an economic whole, the tariff line that separated it insanity.

Commercial Union clubs sprouted up not simply in Canada but in the United States, where the leading light was Erastus Wiman. Wiman was a rich Canadian businessman who lived in New York, possessed mining and railway interests and strong Canadian connections, and had plenty to gain from closer economic ties between the two countries. Wiman and Smith both claimed that Commercial Union was an economic arrangement, pure and simple, which in no way implied political union or the subversion of Canadian independence. Wiman was probably sincere. Smith carried no conviction on the point whatsoever.

The involvement of an out-and-out annexationist like Smith did not help Commercial Union, which had only the shortest of lives. Reciprocity was to be desired, sought, and encouraged, but the majority of Canadians had never been—could never be—in favour of the absorption of what they had been building into a larger United States. Nor did the concept of Commercial Union have substantial or coherent support in the United States. Representative Benjamin Butterworth of Ohio, who wanted a North American economic alliance against the Old World, was one of the very few backers of the idea in the U.S. Congress, and he would have accepted almost any policy or agreement to improve economic relations. The fact was, then as now, that Americans were not very interested in Canada. They had, or so they believed, little to gain from closer ties—as the New York *Sun* put it, nothing from "a social and intellectual point of view and next to nothing in a commercial way."

COMMERCIAL WARFARE

What interest Americans had in Canada, indeed, was almost always negative: Canada was an economic competitor and could never be a real friend as long as it clung to the British and indulged in deliberately anti-American schemes such as closing the fisheries and building the Canadian Pacific Railway. Their neighbour was, in the words of a potent lobbyist, "a riddle to the American mind," a nation residing on the same continent, headed in many of the same directions, yet persisting in being an unreliable commercial belligerent. This view was not the only one (one prominent U.S. official described Canadians in 1892 as "our Northern neighbors, bound to us by so many ties of race and community of interest"), but it was common enough.

We have noted that the United States escaped from the fisheries commitments of the Treaty of Washington in 1885, as soon as it was possible to do so under the treaty's terms. The Americans had been infuriated by the large cash payment that an international tribunal had required them to make for their use of the Canadian fisheries, especially when they discovered that they were paying for a diminished resource, the much-sought-after mackerel having migrated southwards to U.S. waters. From 1885, then, Canada lost free access to the United States fish market and in turn began again to prevent American fishers from harvesting a crop in the inshore fisheries. This new state of affairs was accompanied by the redeployment of Canadian protection cruisers to arrest U.S. vessels found in forbidden waters. In the Pacific Ocean, meanwhile, the situation was reversed: American ships were seizing Canadian sealing vessels in the Bering Sea, ostensibly for the purpose of conserving the seal herd, although Canadians thought it was to conserve the interests of the Alaska Commercial Company, a U.S.-owned concern. These developments on the two coasts, dangerous enough individually, combined to create an explosive diplomatic situation.

Another Joint High Commission was convened in 1887–88 to confront the accumulating problems of the relationship. The commission represented some progress for Canada over the 1871 incarnation—the British commissioners were not inclined to run roughshod over Canadian interests this time—but in other respects the outcome was less satisfactory. The American secretary of state, Thomas Bayard, had hinted at the possibility of reciprocity in return for access to the inshore fisheries, but this was never a real possibility given the devaluation of the resource and the protectionist state of mind in the Congress. The Americans refused, too, to discuss the sealing problem in this forum: a compromise had to be found five years later by international arbitration.

The dealings of the commission therefore came down to one issue, the everlasting fisheries, and Canada had little with which to bargain. The resulting treaty did contain a definitive American repudiation of their right to fish the Canadian inshore waters, but it also made bows to the U.S. position that were readily characterized in Canada as an unnecessary sell-out. In any event, the document was rejected by the U.S. Senate, and the two countries were thrown back on a temporary agreement under which Canadian authorities could sell licences allowing American fishers to do business inshore—purchase supplies, for example—but not fish there. This modus vivendi, meant to last only until Senate ratification of the treaty, was to govern Canadian–American conduct in the North Atlantic fisheries into the twentieth century. Whatever the imperfections, and the gripes that inevitably went with them, the arrangement was better than the alternative—open commercial battling that might lead to something worse. While deploring "a surrender of most valuable rights that belong to Canada," Wilfrid Laurier nevertheless supported the rapprochement with a defence similar to Macdonald's of the Treaty of Washington two decades before. Good Anglo-American relations were necessary for Canada, and they could not be taken for granted. "The greatest calamity which could befall the civilized world would be an armed collision between the two greatest branches of the Anglo-Saxon race. . . . [I]t would be almost as criminal and as guilty as a civil war." Canada might be victimized by the alternative, but it would be for all the right reasons. In truth, of course, it was not as bad as that. In the fisheries and the Bering Sea disputes, Canada did not suffer unduly because of its lack of power or diplomatic punch.

"VEILED TREASON": THE 1891 ELECTION

Reciprocity remained the Holy Grail of Canadian politics—mystical, alluring, tantalizingly out of grasp. Almost every politician of the late nineteenth century supported it, although just what "it" consisted of might differ substantially, sometimes even among members of the same party. John A. Macdonald's preference was for a reciprocal trade agreement covering natural products only, like the one in 1854; in that way, the essence of his National Policy could be preserved. In 1888, after another Macdonald election victory the year before (his fourth since 1867), the Liberals incorporated something quite different into their agenda—"unrestricted reciprocity," or free trade. Their chief economic spokesman, Sir Richard Cartwright, told party leader Laurier that they must act in the name of political self-preservation: "Adopt this project or go to pieces."

Obviously, Commercial Union had appeal; just as obviously, it went too far. Laurier's party was trying to tap into the widespread Canadian desire to snuggle up to the American economic dream through the expedient of unrestricted reciprocity, while avoiding the accusation that it would countenance any reduction of Canadian autonomy. That the Liberals gained ground under their new banner cannot be doubted. In advocating the dismantling of the tariff, however, they could be accused of advocating the dismantling of the nation itself. That is exactly what happened in the election of 1891.

The campaign of 1891 really began the previous year, at a time when Americans seemed to be mounting a concentrated economic attack on Canada. First came the McKinley Tariff, named for its author,

Laurier (second from left) and his Liberals plot the takeover of Canada—Conservative party propaganda from the election of 1891. (National Archives of Canada/C6539)

a true believer in the tariff and a future president of the United States. That measure, with average duties of 49 percent, stacked the wall high against Canadian agricultural exports. Soon thereafter, Ottawa discovered that negotiations were afoot for a wide-ranging commercial agreement between nearby Newfoundland, a separate British colony, and the United States, giving the former's fish and fish products a marked advantage over their Canadian counterparts in the U.S. market, while handing American products a favoured position in the Newfoundland market. "Jingo Jim" Blaine, President Benjamin Harrison's secretary of state, had Hamilton Fish–like hopes for Canada. He was quoted publicly as having suggested that "Canada is like an apple on a tree just beyond our reach. We may strive to grasp it, but the bough recedes from our hold just in proportion to our effort to grasp it. Let alone, and in due time it will fall into our hands." Privately, however, Blaine was tougher, revealing some of the traditional hostilities towards Canada of Maine, his home state, where memories of border and fish battles ran deep. He advised the president: "The fact is we do not want any intercourse with Canada except through the medium of a tariff, and she will find she has a hard row to hoe and will ultimately, I believe, seek admission to the Union."

The McKinley Tariff was already hurting the Conservatives. A Newfoundland–United States agreement would hurt more. The Liberals, with their forceful plan for a new economic order, were a threat Macdonald took very seriously.

Macdonald sought to meet his delicate political situation by getting in on the action that was taking place in Washington. He requested, and with British help got, agreement in principle to hold formal trade talks of his own with the Americans. It is interesting, and undoubtedly indicative of the strong support that some sort of U.S. option had in the Canada of those days, that Macdonald chose this path rather than one of denunciation of the Americans. He would demonstrate to the Canadian electorate that their prime minister was as capable as the Liberals of getting them good things from the United States. The idea was to make known that the Americans had consented to a "negotiation," scooping the Liberals, and then to call an election and sweep to another victory.

Unfortunately for Macdonald, Blaine refused permission to let the Canadian people in on the glad news. Worse, the American secretary of state, a great friend of the Liberals, stated for the public record that there were "no negotiations whatever on foot for a reciprocity treaty with Canada, and you may be assured no such scheme for reciprocity with the Dominion confined to natural products will be entertained by this Government." The prime minister had put himself in a corner. The momentum towards an election was unstoppable, and the only possibility left open to him was a last-ditch stand against the creeping Americanism represented by closer economic ties between Canada and the U.S.—a stand for Canada, national policies, and the vaunted British connection. "We have burned our boats," Macdonald lamented, "and now we must fight for our lives."

All great politicians are lucky. Macdonald was no exception. An annexationist pamphlet written by a Toronto *Globe* reporter and Liberal sympathizer, Edward Farrer, was leaked to the prime minister, and it was exactly what he needed to dramatize his pro-Canadian case. The Liberals' design, he shouted from platforms across the country, was to ensnare Canada in the American net: unrestricted reciprocity was really a disguise for Commercial Union; Commercial Union would bring annexation. "I say that there is a deliberate conspiracy, by force, by fraud, or by both, to force Canada into the American union." Macdonald would have none of it: "A British subject I was born—a British subject I will die. With my utmost effort, with my last breath will I oppose the 'veiled treason' which attempts by sordid means and mercenary proffer to lure our people from our allegiance."

Macdonald won the debate and the election, taking a majority of seats in every province in English Canada except Prince Edward Island. He was clear in his own mind about the campaign's defining issue. "We worked the 'Loyalty' cry for all it was worth and it carried the country." Although he had ruthlessly manipulated the situation to his own benefit, there was nothing insincere about the prime minister's statement of his devotion to Britain and the empire. Like a great many other English Canadians, he thought of the old country as "home," and not simply because that was where one's relatives and one's roots were to be found. Britain was the repository of the ideals and values that made Canada different and worth preserving. In this sense there was no distinction to be made between loyalty to the empire and loyalty to Canada.

Continentalism had been defeated, narrowly but decisively, in the election of 1891. But the movement in its various forms was not dead, not quite yet. In 1892, the Continental Union League was formed, with headquarters in New York and Toronto, and with an impressive corps of U.S. backers, including the financiers Andrew Carnegie and John Jacob Astor, and major public-figures-to-be Elihu Root, John Hay, and Theodore Roosevelt. The irrepressible Goldwin Smith—and his money—was again at the forefront on the Canadian side. He saw real hope in the chatter about political union that swirled through the political constituencies and seemed to be making headway in the Liberal party. Prominent Liberals, however, saw something else. Sensing a threat to their country, they were already moving against annexationist sentiment. The party followed in 1893, abandoning its unrestricted reciprocity platform forever. The downturn in the American economy in that year administered the coup de grâce to the forces of political union. Who would be an American if it did not make them rich?

After five lacklustre Conservative years without Macdonald, who had died shortly after the unrestricted reciprocity election, the Liberals came to power in 1896 under the elegant, fluently bilingual Laurier. He quickly showed himself to be in the grand Macdonald mould: cautious, durable, carefully modulated, possessing a broad vision of the country which he was able to articulate. Laurier's team made the inevitable reciprocity pilgrimage to Washington in 1897, just as the Conservatives had done after the 1891 election and so often before. The Liberals met American good will and yet another high-tariff device, this time bearing the name of Representative Nelson Dingley. Reciprocity, however, was no longer their chief policy goal. They denied it, but once in office they were vigorous supporters of the Macdonald National Policy and imperial trade; in 1897, they extended unilateral preferences to British imports to Canada. As the minister of finance, W.S. Fielding, told the House of Commons, the Liberals would love a trade agreement with the Americans. But "if it shall not please them to do that, we shall in one way regret the fact, but shall nevertheless go on our way rejoicing, and find other markets to build up the prosperity of Canada independent of the American people."

"LET THE FIGHT COME": VENEZUELA AND ALASKA

In the 1890s, the United States was poised for a career as a world power. It was a prodigious economic success story, the international leader in manufacturing output, a vast transcontinental industrial nation of more than seventy-five million people; it was fairly bursting at the seams, hard times in the mid-nineties and the evaporation of the American frontier only accentuating a desire to seek and conquer new markets abroad; and it was becoming a military force to be reckoned with, building a first-class modern navy of steel battleships. With all this, caused to some extent by all this, went a growing confidence that Americans were going to do great things together, that their moment in history had come. "Americans," the U.S. foreign-policy historian Thomas Paterson has suggested, "had traditionally thought themselves exceptional. Almost everybody who counted knew this exceptionalism to be so; they felt it, even measured it, and they were quick to correct any affronts to their assumption of national greatness." The leaders of the immediate post–Civil War era, such as Grant and Seward, had considered the United States an international leader even then. The difference, Paterson says, was that their successors of the 1890s believed the country must now begin to act the part. By decade's end the U.S. had fought and won a war with Spain, subjugated Cuba, seized control of Puerto Rico and the Phillipines, annexed the Hawaiian Islands, and jumped into the international struggle for empire in China, while continuing to assert that it had special rights, privileges, and responsibilities in the western hemisphere.

The new phase of American expansionism was signalled by a dispute with Great Britain over the boundary between what was then British Guiana and Venezuela. For years U.S. governments had urged London to send the matter to arbitration and British governments had resisted. Because commercial interests were at stake, and because there seems to have been genuine outrage at the British position, the administration of President Grover Cleveland decided to take a much stronger stand in 1895. The asking stopped, the demanding began, and in language that was unmistakable in its tone. "Today the United States is practically sovereign on this continent," the secretary of state intoned, "and its fiat is law upon the subjects to which it confines its interposition." Infinite resources and geographical superiority made the United States "master of the situation and practically invulnerable as against any or all powers." The British were being warned that the 1823 Monroe Doctrine was alive and well and living in the hearts and minds of Americans; the United States was determined not to allow any state in North or South America to fall under the sway of "a European power." Great Britain had better agree to arbitration of the boundary, or face the unspecified consequences.

Washington's first challenge was turned aside. The bulky Cleveland became "mad clean through" when he read the perfunctory British communication on the subject. On 17 December 1895, in a special message to Congress, he issued what sounded like an ultimatum, beating on the drums of war for good measure. British Prime Minister Lord Salisbury was not impressed, believing that "the American conflagration . . . [would] fizzle away," but his Cabinet voted for arbitration. Said one minister, "We expect the French to hate us and are quite prepared to reciprocate the compliment if necessary; but the Americans, No!" The world's greatest power had backed away from confrontation with the United States.

The Venezuelan crisis had profound implications for Canada. The country to the north was a natural American target, a fact immediately remarked upon by Theodore Roosevelt, who was then an expansion-minded Republican politician on the rise. "Let the fight come if it must," he said. "I don't care whether our sea coast cities are bombarded or not; we would take Canada." The commander of the U.S. army, General N.A. Miles, was more cautious. He worried about the parlous condition of American home defence. He advised against pushing Britain too hard, but he did not doubt that the invasion and capture of Canada could be accomplished "if we wanted to." And he was of course correct. Though Canadians prepared for conflict as best they could and by their standards on a very large scale, they were no match for the Americans, and Britain could have done little to help. There were, however, plenty of moderate voices like Miles's on both sides, and an Anglo-American war over Venezuela was never very likely.

The British were determined to reduce the possibility further. To see American-style patriotism in full cry, and directed at them, had been a sobering experience for those who ran Britain's vast but vulnerable empire. They made a headlong rush towards placating the U.S., soon abandoning the hemisphere to an American sphere of influence and pledging never to go to war with the United States.

Canada did not want war between Great Britain and the United States, but peace had a price. The Alaskan boundary dispute was another encounter with the hard problems of being caught in the squeeze of great-power lovemaking. Canada realized perhaps that good Anglo-American relations were vital to its survival in the long term, but bitterly resented the sacrifice of its interests along the way. The Alaska controversy was settled through arbitration but the outcome was predetermined by American manoeuvring and pressure. That Canada's case was weak is beside the point. It never had a chance.

The United States had purchased Alaska from the Russians in 1867. The territory, very substantial in its northern mass, had a thin tail—the "panhandle"—which snaked south along the Pacific coast towards Vancouver Island as far as the lower tip of Prince of Wales Island. At issue was the size and shape of the panhandle, and whether the Anglo-Canadian claim to the inlets that penetrated deep into the coastline was justified. Ocean access to Canada's Yukon territory depended on the answer, and the great gold rush of 1896–97 gave the matter prominence.

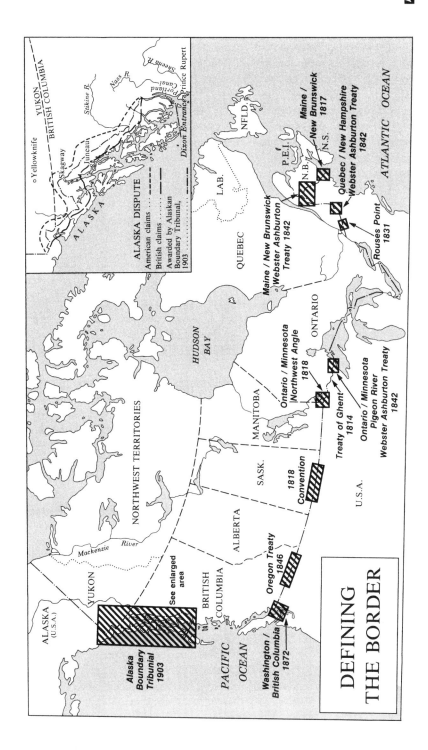

DEFINING THE BORDER

The United States had a strong case arising out of use and occupation. As one American expert proclaimed, "citizens of the United States have entered and occupied the strip, built cities and towns, and established industrial enterprise thereon" under the territorial claim and protection of their government. At the head of the most crucial of the deep inlets, Lynn Canal, were the towns of Dyea and Skagway, two long-established American possessions. From Lynn Canal across the Chilkoot and White passes lay the gold fields. Canada was willing to concede Dyea and Skagway, but demanded a nearby harbour and corridor of territory to connect it to the Yukon and the gold. A settlement was almost reached along these lines by a third Joint High Commission, which met in 1898–99, this time with Canadians sitting in five of the six "British" seats at the table. The deal, however, and the commission blew up when American public opinion took possession of the impending compromise. A provisional boundary was agreed upon in 1899, but that was all that seemed possible.

The prime minister of Canada was nevertheless confident. He had a case of his own, based on the original Anglo-Russian boundary treaty of 1825, which gave British subjects the right of free navigation, "without any hindrance whatever," of all the waters leading to the Pacific Ocean. Laurier's confidence, however, was badly misplaced. The British were beset with complications and challenges to their position in Europe, and, with the Boer War in South Africa preoccupying them as well from 1899, were anxious for good relations with the United States and reduced commitments in the western hemisphere. As the British ambassador in Washington wrote to his prime minister, "America seems to be our only friend just now and it would be unfortunate to quarrel with her." Thus the London government gave its permission in 1901 (necessary because of an Anglo-American understanding half a century earlier) for the U.S. to build a fortified canal across the isthmus of Panama connecting the Atlantic and Pacific oceans, despite Laurier's wish for that decision to be made contingent on a settlement of the Alaska problem. Britain's, and now Canada's, bargaining power suddenly diminished drastically.

Shortly after the Panama decision, the U.S. president, William McKinley, died at the hand of an assassin in Buffalo, New York. President-in-waiting Theodore Roosevelt was a tough and belligerent new actor in the drama, and he was determined to have a quick resolution of the Alaska dispute in his favour. Extremely intelligent, politically shrewd, Roosevelt strutted and paraded American power; even the tamer members of his own Cabinet winced at his bluster. One of the president's advisers did intimate that Roosevelt was prepared to give in to Canada on questions other than Alaska, and "not to press the American case upon these other points to its full value." But dealing on the boundary, which had become inseparable in the Rooseveltian mind with America's national honour, was impossible. Roosevelt was certain he had both power and truth on his side, a combination difficult to combat. He told the British that he was "going to be ugly" on Alaska, sending eight hundred troops to the region to underline the point.

Roosevelt was so sure of himself that he agreed to an arbitration panel with the power to decide the issue. The British were clearly behind him, anxious to get this irritant in the Anglo-American relationship out of the way once and for all. Laurier had to acknowledge that the forces against him were formidable. During a trip to London in 1902, the Canadian prime minister displayed "a conceding mood." He modified his demands and acquiesced in a tribunal of six members, three from each side. Since there would be no impartial third party represented on the panel, Laurier had made a major concession. He then shepherded his agreement with the British through a Cabinet that contained two reluctant senior members, W.S. Fielding and Clifford Sifton.

Laurier had the consolation that Roosevelt's representatives would be distinguished and impartial jurists. So he had been told by the British ambassador, who had done the deal with the United States; so he believed. Indeed, the Canadian leader had been led to expect a couple of U.S. Supreme Court justices. Instead the president named three political allies whose allegiance to the American claim was indelible: Elihu Root, Roosevelt's own secretary of war; Henry Cabot Lodge, the British-Empire-hating senator from Massachusetts, who had called Canada's case "baseless and manufactured"; and George Turner of the State of Washington, which was not an area disinterested in the fate of nearby Alaska. Laurier's biographer, O.D. Skelton, wrote that "all were lawyers of eminence, men of outstanding capacity, honourable men, but to term them 'impartial' was a wrench to the English language." Just as bad, Canada could not count on even a hint of support in London. The British ratified the whole arrangement without waiting for Canada's concurrence: "a very unceremonious and uncourteous proceeding," Laurier complained bitterly, "nothing short of a slap in the face."

The outcome, in light of these developments, was predictable, yet Roosevelt left nothing to chance. He instructed his representatives that there would be "no compromise," and through them he bombarded the British government with threats about what he would do if the panel did not carry out his will: "I am going to send a brigade of American regulars up to Skagway and take possession of the disputed territory and hold it by all the power and force of the United States." The British member of the tribunal, the lord chief justice of Great Britain, Lord Alverstone, voted with the U.S. members and left the Canadian panelists (hardly impartial themselves) sputtering betrayal. They refused to sign the award. A line was drawn between the respective claims, but it gave the Americans the lion's share of the land, the heads of all the inlets, and two of four contested islands in the Portland Canal at the lower end of the panhandle. The decision on the islands particularly galled Canadians and their representatives. That proved Lord Alverstone's perfidy. He set aside the very powerful Canadian claim to all four islands and chose to take the road of compromise, demonstrating from the Canadian viewpoint that the whole exercise had been a farce. It was being rubbed in that Canada did not count in the final analysis. Simple justice did not count. "I do not wonder that they are furious," wrote U.S. Secretary of State John Hay lightheartedly to his wife. "But . . . 'serves 'em right, if they can't take a joke.'" The Americans could afford a sense of humour. They had the superior claim and they had the battalions.

By the time of the Alaska decision, the great gold rush days in the Yukon were over. Little has been done to develop the land of the panhandle since. The fishing grounds of the Dixon Entrance directly south of Prince of Wales Island, however, have become a matter of contention as lawyers quarrel over where the 1903 boundary line cuts across the waters of the entrance—straight and tight underneath the island, as the Canadians would have it, or loose and jagged, giving the Americans many miles of lush hunting. More than one hundred years after the fish wars of the 1860s and 1880s, Canadian and American authorities patrol the disputed territory and, from time to time, seize one another's vessels.

"NO RECIPROCITY WANTED— EXCEPTING..."

1 9 0 3 — 1 9 1 8

The Ottawa *Evening Journal* captured the lonely feeling that many Canadians experienced in the immediate aftermath of the Alaska boundary award. "Cut loose from Britain, we would of course be robbed by the United States whenever opportunity occurred, and bullied if we protested. But we are that now. The only difference is that Englishmen inform us that it is justice and have the right to compel us to accept it as justice. And as Canada shouts 'stop thief' while Brother Jonathan is disappearing with the goods, the British press sings 'For He's a Jolly Good Fellow' and deplores that we don't join in." Great Britain, the mother country, had done precious little mothering of late.

The behaviour of the Americans was of course less surprising. They were different, morally and spiritually. Sir Wilfrid Laurier looked southwards at the "social condition of civil society" in the U.S.—lynchings, divorces, murders—and gave thanks that "we are living in a country where the young children of the land are taught Christian morals and Christian dogmas." The prime minister claimed that he liked and admired Americans, but he also knew that they were grasping, selfish, and self-seeking, "caring only for Canada in so far as it may serve their purpose to be friendly."

The Alaska settlement left its imprint on diplomacy. Laurier was not built for revolutionary action—there would be no sweep forward towards formal Canadian independence—but the wound lay close to the surface, needing only the slightest prod to provoke anger or recrimination or determination. The Liberal government would not actively seek any further accommodations with the United States. If others sought them, Laurier would insist, for national, political, and now deeply personal reasons, that Canadian rights and interests be fully respected. This new attitude contributed to a significant change in Canadian–American relations over the next decade. Against the background of rising Anglo-Saxon sentiment and celebrations of the tranquillity of the border between Canada and the U.S., the two countries dramatically settled all their outstanding diplomatic problems. The Alaska settlement may have been hard for the Canadians to take, but it laid the groundwork for rapprochement by sweeping away the last of the great boundary disputes.

SWEETENING AND SOFTENING

The best and brightest period in Canadian–American relations could not begin immediately—not so long as Britain's chief representatives in North America were the lamentable ambassador in Washington, Sir Mortimer Durand, and the self-indulgent governor general in Canada, Lord Minto. Minto's glimpse of Americans from the perspective of Britain's most important self-governing colony accentuated his long-held views about their insincerity and unreliability. It was all very well, he wrote to his brother, "for people in England to romance about the sentimental love of the Anglo-Saxon Races on either side of the Atlantic—but mercifully England has the ocean between her and her love. . . . What the Canadian sees and hears is constant Yankee bluff, and swagger, and that eventually he means to possess Canada for himself." Only "the cream" of the American people could "one . . . accept as ordinary beings." Minto's prejudices reinforced Laurier's and prevented him from seeing or seizing upon opportunities for better relations with the United States in the wake of Alaska.

Durand, who arrived in Washington at the end of 1903, prided himself on his open-mindedness towards the United States. But his mind, it appeared, was too open. A polo-player, tiger-shooter, and Civil War buff, he looked the perfect envoy to Teddy Roosevelt's America. The president liked what he saw in the beginning, but that did not withstand deeper examination. After eighteen months, he pronounced Durand slow and shy. Later, stupidity was added to the catalogue of adjectives. "He seems," wrote Roosevelt, "to have a brain of about eight-guinea-pig power. Why, under Heaven the English keep him here

I do not know . . . but it is useless to have a creature of mutton-suet consistency like the good Sir Mortimer." Durand discovered early on that Canadians believed his embassy was indifferent to their views and interests. He vowed to correct the impression, but did nothing. Canada was one of the ambassador's major clients, but he travelled there only once, for a few summer days in Quebec. Business was apparently far from his mind.

With the appointment of the next British governor general and the next ambassador to Washington, the Canadian–American relationship finally experienced a real chance for improvement. The fourth Earl Grey

The self-assured Theodore Roosevelt in 1907.
(National Archives of Canada/C 10056)

succeeded Minto as the King's representative in late 1904; James Bryce replaced Durand in Washington at the beginning of 1907. Both were passionate advocates of British–American friendship—the old country had to have that to survive the challenges of a dangerous new century—and they actively pursued improvements in the disturbingly volatile relationship between Canada and the U.S. as a vital element in the advancement of the greater Anglo-Saxon cause. Grey was an energetic busybody, unwilling simply to indulge in the good life of relaxation, ceremony, and sport that was the governor general's usual lot. His eye fell immediately on the long list of differences that plagued Canada–U.S. relations, from fish and seals to boundary waters and salvage operations, and he began to do what he could to initiate a systematic cleaning of the slate.

Grey had limitations, personal and constitutional. Bryce, however, was a respected author, scholar, lecturer, and journalist who was well known and well connected in the U.S. even before he took up his duties in Washington. He had, moreover, a wide scope for action. Chastened by the outcry over Alaska and annoyed by the frustrations of dealing with the unruly Canadians, London was unlikely to interfere, and did not, even when the ambassador began to deal directly with Canada without going through the time-honoured home government channels.

Canada generated three-quarters of the British Embassy's business, Bryce discovered, and patching up long-standing problems in the relationship seemed the most natural of occupations for an ambitious ambassador. Within a matter of weeks of arriving in Washington, Bryce was in Canada, the first of many visits. He got a rude reception. Laurier introduced him to one audience as part of a line of British representatives who had donated large tracts of Canadian land, some in Alaska, to the United States. But the ambassador persevered, winning trust with his openness and disarming manner, and following up with dynamic action to bring Canadians and Americans together. In 1911, a Laurier minister spoke for his colleagues when he wrote to Bryce: "You have been 'our ambassador.'"

Something else was needed for a Canadian–American rapprochement: an ally in the United States. That appeared in the person of Elihu Root, Roosevelt's secretary of state from 1905. One of the country's celebrated corporate lawyers, Root was a smooth administrator who could delegate, a shrewd, pragmatic negotiator, and a clever politician who kept Congress and the president sweet.

Root abhorred disorder, and disorder was everywhere in America's relations with the parts of the British Empire to the north. When confronted with the problem of the Newfoundland fishery, the secretary of state discovered that it could not be solved without reference to the Canadian fishery. That issue in turn was tangled up with myriad other gripes and grievances. It was all "a mess." Root found an expert New York lawyer, Chandler P. Anderson, to assist him with the details, and called in the British ambassador to suggest that Canada and the United States ought to examine their mutual concerns together. Laurier, putting aside his anti-American rhetoric, did not turn away from the opportunity. Root then came to Canada in 1907 and managed to overcome much of his reputation as one of the Alaska boundary dispute's "impartial judges" with a stirring speech acknowledging Canada's nationhood and emphasizing its positive links with the United States.

With Bryce arriving in Washington not long after Root got back from his voyage to Canada, the last ingredient for action was in place. Replacing Grey as the key figure on the "Canadian" side, Bryce pushed and prodded and insisted in both Washington and Ottawa. He was particularly effective in bringing along the always inefficient Canadian prime minister. Bryce began slowly, thinking (correctly as it turned out) that if the smaller puzzles could be dealt with satisfactorily, that would "sweeten and soften the feeling between the two countries" and provide the atmosphere for further agreement. By 1911, eight treaties and agreements had been signed which, the ambassador boasted, "so far as human precision can go . . . dealt with all the questions that are likely to arise between the United States and Canada." Three were noteworthy. The North Atlantic fisheries quarrel was referred to the International Court at The Hague in 1909: the decision came down a year later. A Boundary Waters Treaty was signed in 1909, creating the International Joint Commission (IJC) as a permanent body with a mandate to examine the inevitable problems arising from the use and sharing of the waters along the frontier. And in 1911, a major international accord was reached for the regulation of the fur seal trade in the North Pacific.

Each of the main sticking points in the relationship was thus removed, and to the substantial benefit of Canadians. The Hague court upheld the bulk of the Canada–Newfoundland claim to the North Atlantic fishery. Under the seal agreement, the U.S., Russia, and Japan provided compensation and a share of their annual catch to Canada, this at a time when the Canadian industry was all but moribund. And the IJC gave Canada equal representation—there were to be six commissioners, three from each country—in an arena in which agreement could be sought far from the glare of public debate. As A.C. Gluek, the leading expert on this period in Canadian–American relations has written, Bryce had laid siege to long-held Canadian beliefs. It was impossible to argue still that Britain always sacrificed Canadian interests to save itself; the British ambassador had acted consistently for Canada and sometimes even against Britain. Nor could it be said that Canadians invariably lost the diplomatic game to conniving Yankees. The reality was that Canada had done extremely well during the slate-cleaning era, bettering or breaking even with the United States in agreement after agreement.

THE INTERNATIONAL JOINT COMMISSION

The victories were not Bryce's alone, indispensable as he was. Laurier and his colleagues mattered as well, the best example of their influence being the Canadian–American agreement to create the International Joint Commission. The prime minister selected George Gibbons, a western Ontario lawyer, as his boundary waters negotiator; the strong-minded Gibbons would not be denied in his quest for a commission to confront problems on an independent and permanent basis. Root opposed both independence and permanency, preferring to take each issue as it arose and to retain as much authority as possible in Washington. Besides, he said, the Senate would not wish for or approve such a board anyway. Bryce reluctantly recommended that the Canadians capitulate; the obstacles were insurmountable. But Gibbons would have none of it and Laurier backed him to the hilt. They believed that there could be no fair play without an independent body deliberating from fixed principles and therefore no justice in the adjudication of disputes. The Canadians got their commission, along with a written promise that each side would have "equal and similar rights" in the use of all boundary waters.

Canadian diplomacy, such as it was, had begun to operate more freely and forcefully in relations with the United States after Alaska. There could be no doubt, however, that the machinery of government, such as *that* was, creaked and groaned under the strain. Grey likened it to a "swollen impossible cork, the extraction of which almost bursts a blood-vessel." "Considering what a brisk and go ahead country Canada has now become," Bryce complained to the governor general, "I am surprised at the long delays before I get [an] answer to my requests for expression of the views of your Ministers." Some of this was caution and procrastination—Laurier had replaced John A. Macdonald as Canada's "Old Tomorrow"—but some of it resulted from the cumbersome way in which colonial Ottawa had to and chose to do business.

The invention in 1909 of a Canadian Department of External Affairs, another development urged by Bryce and Grey, was a small organizational step towards efficiency and autonomy in diplomacy. The first undersecretary of state for external affairs, Joseph Pope, made himself immediately useful as an adjunct to Bryce's initiatives, playing a role of some significance, for example, in the settlement of the North Pacific sealing dispute. Pope had an ordered mind, a passion for filing cabinets rather than policy making. This was appropriate, since no one in Canada was yet arguing for a gallop into international affairs or disengagement from the foreign-policy apparatus of the imperial government in London. That, for one thing, might put Canadians right up against a too-powerful United States.

The International Joint Commission was an important innovation in Canadian–American relations, an agreement to institutionalize co-operation, consult regularly, and try to find ways of diminishing conflict, current and future. Beginning its labours in 1912, the IJC was a response to the serious environmental concerns of the age: pollution had already appeared in some parts of the Great Lakes and connecting tributaries, such as the Detroit River; irrigation schemes affecting the waters that crossed the Montana–Alberta border caused tension; the exploitation of the Niagara Falls and River for shipping and hydro-electricity was set against issues of conservation and tourism. Over its life, and it lives still, the IJC has done much useful work, and it has certainly been fuel for wordy celebrations of the Canadian–American arrangement.

In truth, however, Laurier and Gibbons were not as successful in the IJC negotiations as some Canadian historians suggest. The Americans saw to that. The commission was never a really powerful body, except in the narrow area of the use and apportionment of boundary waters, where a great deal of its activity was concentrated in the first thirty years of operation. More recently, problems of water and air quality have come to the fore. That work, limited to the recommendation of solutions, can be valuable: the IJC's research had much to do with the Great Lakes Water Quality Agreements of 1972 and 1978.

Most of the commission's functions, even so, are advisory and highly specialized, and its limits are notable. The commission's binding arbitration power, which is outlined in Article 10 of the Boundary Waters Treaty and may theoretically be applied to any Canadian–American disagreement, cannot be invoked without Senate approval in the U.S. and Cabinet sanction in Canada. With hurdles like that to sur-mount, the article has not been employed and is unlikely to be. The knowledgeable therefore give thanks for what the IJC does and express their frustration and disappointment that it does not do more. After considerable study of the commission's record and conversations with many of the diplomats and public servants who have tried to make it work, the American environmental authority John E. Carroll and the former governor of Maine and U.S. ambassador to Canada, Kenneth Curtis, have delivered a balanced assessment of the IJC:

> The Boundary Waters Treaty of 1909 and the treaty's vehicle for implementation, the International Joint Commission, have built a foundation that has underlain bilateral environmental relations between Canada and the United States for nearly three-quarters of a century. Touted world-wide as a unique model of what can be accomplished by two nations with sufficient will, the treaty and the commission have long been respected for their unusual spirit of collegiality; for their long record of sound scientific and technical findings, for the unique nature of their organization and approaches; and, perhaps most significantly, for their success in conflict avoidance. Recognition on all of these grounds is justified, though a caveat is in order: the commission's task under the treaty has been narrow and specialized; its work has been relegated to noncontroversial areas where there was already diplomatic recognition that agreement could be achieved; and most of its efforts, especially in recent years, have led to nonbinding recommendations that the two governments can (and often do) ignore. Hence the work of this in many respects admirable treaty and vehicle is confined and its impact limited. (*Canadian–American Relations: The Promise and the Challenge*, 27–28)

Canadian boosters of the IJC extol it as a vehicle through which their country can defend and advance its interests on the basis of a rough equality. The same is said about other Canadian–American institutions and arrangements that came after the IJC and were to some extent modelled on it—for example, the Permanent Joint Board on Defence, the St. Lawrence Seaway Authority, and the North American Air (later Aerospace) Defence Command. Bureaucracy has taken hold within these institutions, however, and many observers suspect that an over-structured process—indeed, any process at all—can restrict the freedom of action of both partners and actually increase the potential for conflict in the relationship. The possibility of true fairness or objectivity, moreover, diminishes in inverse proportion to the self-interest of the larger partner. In the IJC, Carroll writes, "collegiality is more difficult to maintain and nationalism to avoid" when the stakes are high.

GUNBOAT DIPLOMACY

The boundary waters that straddled the two countries, the Great Lakes in particular, posed other kinds of problems than political and environmental ones. By the turn of the century the United States was a major naval power. Surely the Americans could not be held to the confining terms of the Rush-Bagot Agreement, now almost one hundred years old.

Some background is in order. Because of the primitive nature of land transport, control of the Great Lakes had proved crucial during the War of 1812. Not only were there pitched naval battles on the lakes, albeit on a small scale, but by 1814 both the United States and Great Britain were engaged in a naval-building race. The construction and maintenance of ships and the upkeep of bases was extremely costly, however, and it made sense to limit firepower on the lakes as part of the postwar settlement, even though that would put the faraway British at a disadvantage in the event of an Anglo-American war. Under the Rush-Bagot Agreement of 1817, the U.S. and Great Britain agreed to hold themselves to only four small armed vessels each on the whole of the Great Lakes and Lake Champlain. Nevertheless, both parties pushed at times beyond the agreed limits along the nineteenth century's mythically unfortified Canadian–American frontier. In the 1840s, for example, the British and Americans had gunboats on the Great Lakes, and during the Civil War, the U.S. very seriously contemplated the abrogation of Rush-Bagot as part of an effort to build up defences against a possible Confederate or British attack.

The agreement was again challenged in the 1890s, when the U.S. began to construct a modern navy of steel warships. Pressure for a revised agreement came from the U.S. navy, concerned that small British warships could lurk in the superior Canadian canal system and move quickly onto the lakes during a crisis. The navy also wanted to be able to use the lakes' vast waters for training the militias of surrounding states. Pressure came too from the American Great Lakes shipbuilders, who lusted after their share of the business generated by the big new navy. Construction on the lakes even of warship hulls, which would later be armed, was forbidden under the Rush-Bagot Agreement.

Even so, the British government in London and the Canadian Conservative administration in Ottawa turned the other cheek when *Gresham*, a nine-hundred-ton revenue cutter with modern guns, was launched at Cleveland in 1895. It was not a warship, they reassured themselves, although they knew full well that it could become one. The Americans thereafter chewed away further at the edges of Rush-Bagot, and in the spring of 1898 offered a concrete proposal for a new accord at meetings of the Joint High Commission: no warships; two armed, unarmoured training vessels; and as many as six revenue or police cutters, limited in size and armament. Prime Minister Wilfrid Laurier and the British were prepared to accede to this arrangement, knowing that the U.S. might well do as it wished anyway. When the commission failed over Alaska, however, the opportunity for a changed and more realistic agreement was lost.

The Americans carried on regardless. They did not build or deploy warships, but revenue boats with lots of muscle and naval training vessels regularly appeared on the lakes, breaking both the spirit and letter of Rush-Bagot. From 1900 to 1907 Laurier and the British quietly acquiesced in this state of affairs, and explicitly allowed the entry of training warships into the Great Lakes through Canadian waters, even though the U.S. went a good deal over the agreed limit. When permission was sought and given in late 1907 for the *Nashville*, by far the largest U.S. navy trainer yet, to use the Great Lakes, a British official wrote excitedly that this would make "9 vessels in all!"

Yet what could Britain and Canada do? Both countries feared that the U.S. would abrogate the agreement, inflaming public opinion on both sides of the border and possibly triggering a naval arms race on the lakes for which neither the British nor the Canadians had the stomach. Laurier whispered to the British ambassador in Washington that he lived "in fear and trembling all the time" of the repercussions of going against the U.S. For that reason he turned a blind eye to "violations more or less notorious."

The British had already conceded that a war against the United States for Canada would be unwinnable. Gone, as of 1906, were Britain's squadrons at Halifax and Esquimalt. Gone was the pretence of defending Canada from attack. A British officer sent to assess the military situation along the border found a lone soldier at Fort Lennox, Montreal's bulwark against the south, who seemed to be there mainly to serve as an escort for picnickers from Plattsburgh, New York. The same officer concluded after surveying the Great Lakes that only the "famous lamp of Aladdin" could save Canada from a U.S. incursion into the area, which would put American forces in a position to halt the railways and sever east from west. The Canadian government and its military for their part had not completely given up on the country's defences. A number of measures were taken at the time—notably the garrisoning and modernization of Halifax—to stave off a major American offensive should it come. But should it come, realists knew that it would pose insurmountable problems.

The USS *Nashville* finally sailed in the spring of 1909. Shocked by its size and firepower, the Canadian press and opposition in Parliament made the ship's passage into a prominent issue. One correspondent pictured the *Nashville* "in frightening fullness, its four-inch guns capable of throwing a thirty-pound shell nearly five miles" and this "on the frontier which the Rush-Bagot Convention is supposed to keep clear of war-vessels, big guns and the apparatus of fighting."

Ever the responsive politician, Laurier decided to take a stand, if a quirky one. In deference to Rush-Bagot, the U.S. naval training ships customarily dismounted their guns while moving through Canadian waters. *Nashville* had done so, reinstalling its armament only after reaching Buffalo. Purely as a courtesy, and probably because of the inexperience of the new administration of William Howard Taft, the U.S. had asked Canada's permission (as it had not done on previous occasions) to remount *Nashville*'s guns in American waters. Ottawa did not answer, and the United States navy had reasonably enough proceeded on its way, undoubtedly taking silence as consent and remembering the many unopposed training missions of the recent past. Well into the summer, however, two months "after the horse was taken out," as a British official put it, Laurier decided to close the stable door. Permission would be refused for the Americans to do what they had already done!

Laurier had to channel this potentially explosive message through mother Britain. The British warned in traditional terms of the dangers of such a step—the Americans might denounce the Rush-Bagot in its entirety—and Laurier stepped down from his decidedly shaky high horse. The prime minister's concerns were nevertheless transmitted to Washington by the British ambassador. They had an impact. Taft agreed that the United States would attempt in the future to adhere more closely to the terms of Rush-Bagot. The president appreciated, he said, Ottawa's "wish that nothing should happen which would create any sentiment of disquiet or suspicion in the minds of any section of the people of Canada." Thus the United States moved back towards the original intentions of the 1817 document's drafters. By 1914, the Great Lakes were again all but disarmed, with only a few revenue and training ships, the latter less menacing than they had been only a few years before. The Rush-Bagot convention has been occasionally redefined over the years, and remains in effect to this day.

"CANADIANISM OR CONTINENTALISM": THE ELECTION OF 1911

President Taft was accommodating on Rush-Bagot and other Canadian–American issues, it seems, because he had a larger goal in view. He was desperately seeking reciprocity. For decades the high priests of U.S. protectionism had successfully fended off Canadian proposals to try the freer trade experiment of the mid-nineteenth century one more time. Now it was the government of the United States that took the lead, only to discover that big tariff nationalism had gained a strong following in Canada, especially in the central provinces, over the many years since the American retreat from reciprocity in 1866. In the midst of a great economic boom, suspicious of gift horses from the south, Canadians would think twice before embracing a revolution in their economic affairs.

Nevertheless, the reciprocity that Taft proffered in 1910–1911 struck Prime Minister Laurier as a very good idea at the time. The Liberal government, elected in 1896, was old, tired, bruised by scandal, and badly in need of an issue to galvanize the party faithful and make the electorate forget the messy details of a lengthy stay in power. Throughout 1910, farmers from the West made clear to Laurier their interest in larger markets and cheaper prices on manufactured imports, such as agricultural implements, coming from the United States. The business people of central Canada, with a heavy investment in the National Policy and an east–west pattern of trade flowing towards Britain, of course wanted no such thing. The Canada–U.S. trade agreement reached in 1911 was designed, in true Laurier on-the-one-hand, on-the-other-hand style, to give a large measure of comfort to the farmer while not alienating the manufacturer: it provided for reciprocal abolition of duties on natural products from the farm, and continuing protection for the vast majority of finished goods made in Canada. The combination seemed unbeatable, all the more so because it found a way around a trade war that had been brewing over recent changes in the tariff structure of the two countries. The Laurier Liberals were going to be in power forever.

Lower tariff sentiment had been building in the United States since the turn of the century. The reciprocity agreement was a response to pressure from the Democrats and from some of Taft's own Republicans in Congress, who were in turn answering a call from processors, manufacturers, and publishers interested in access to cheaper raw materials. Americans were realizing increasingly that Canada was important to their future. The northern country took 60 percent of its imports from the U.S. and its market was growing, while others, such as those in Europe, were not. Americans investors, particularly in mining and timber, were attracted by sheer propinquity, and by the similarity of language, outlook, and methods. Was Canada not simply an extension of the United States?

Yet danger loomed. Canada belonged to a rival empire which was apparently pushing towards a greater unity of purpose and policy. The British Empire appeared to be transforming itself into a more thoroughgoing economic system by such means as extending the trade preferences that Canada had given Great Britain in 1897.

In fact it was doing no such thing, but the threat seemed real enough to many Americans and certainly to President Taft. It was at this time and in these circumstances, historian Gordon Stewart argues, that the U.S. began to seriously think out and formulate its policy towards Canada for the first time: "The American goals were to continue to detach Canada from the empire, increase the U.S. share of the Canadian market, gain readier access to Canadian natural resources, and encourage, in general, Canadian integration into a unified North American economy." Stewart's research, and that of American historian Robert Hannigan, is noteworthy because never before has it been suggested that United States policy makers at that time entertained such a coherent view, or any real view of Canada at all. These historians place Taft's interest in reciprocity and political rapprochement with Canada in the context of the American search for an open door to economic opportunities and markets around the world, especially in Asia and South America.

An open door was one thing. In the Canadian case, Stewart says, U.S. officials apparently wanted to pry the door right off the hinges. Hannigan adds that a push for reciprocity in natural products and reductions in tariffs on manufactures constituted a move to "attain a guaranteed long-term source of natural products that would hold down prices in the American market. It would block closer British–Canadian relations and all that they entailed. It would set a precedent for still further and more sweeping reduction of duties in the future. Industries such as flour would be assisted to maintain their competitiveness on the world market, and an expanding volume of commerce along the north–south axis would be assured." President Taft wrote to Theodore Roosevelt that the measure "would make Canada into only an adjunct of the United States. . . . I see this argument made against Reciprocity in Canada, and I think it is a good one."

To the detriment of his cause in Canada, Taft was remarkably frank about his motives in public. He told the Congress that America's economic growth and position in the world was threatened by the country's increase in population and consumption on the one hand and the necessary limits of its natural resources on the other. Reciprocity offered the prospect of a certain supply of food and the necessities of life without injury to the producing and manufacturing classes; those classes, indeed, would be better off as the U.S. used the Canadian agreement to move towards control of the international wheat market and an expansion of outlets for American products. Taft (a regular visitor to his summer home in Murray Bay, Quebec) said that Canadians were an "active, aggressive, and intelligent people," but they were "coming to the parting of the ways." They must soon choose whether or not to be a member of a developing and necessarily exclusive British Empire economic club or to continue and deepen their commercial friendship with the United States. They could not do both.

In front of a New York audience of newspaper publishers, a group that had been in the forefront of the proponents of reciprocity, Taft predicted that it was now or never for reciprocity and close Canadian–American trade ties. The Canada–U.S. trade agreement would be a crucial and beneficial obstacle to the "forces which are at work in England and in Canada to separate her by a Chinese wall from the United States and to make her part of an imperial commercial band reaching from England around the world to England again by a system of imperial preferences." It was in the interests of all North Americans to keep Canada out of the clutches of the British. But Canadians were apt to feel that it was Taft's clutches they must avoid, however much a warm-hearted local hero he might be to the villagers of Murray Bay.

We are ahead of our story. President Taft and the Canadian minister of finance, W.S. Fielding, had agreed to trade talks in April 1910, and these were completed in Washington during the following January. The Americans were prepared to negotiate complete free trade; Canada would only consent to something more limited. The accord was to be implemented through concurrent legislation in the two countries, not in the form of a treaty, which would have brought the British into the process. Just as in 1854, the heart of the agreement lay in a reciprocal bargain to allow the free entry of such natural products as grains, fruits, vegetables, fish, and livestock. A few manufactures were added to the free list; a larger number (including farm implements) were to undergo the same tariff cuts on both sides of the border; and there were two further brief schedules that exchanged one set of reductions for another, in areas for which a complete understanding had not been possible. Cuts in the U.S. tariff on Canadian paper and wood pulp were also envisioned, but only once the provinces got rid of their own barriers to those exports. Fielding made the announcement in Parliament on 26 January 1911.

No one had expected an agreement so big or so soon. The Conservatives were stunned. Their honest, uninspiring leader, Robert Borden, had held on through humiliation and defeat and insubordination over ten hapless years in opposition. "I hereby give my consent to your getting out of politics—and quick," his wife had once counselled Borden, only partly in jest. As he replied to Fielding in the House of Commons, he groped for an alternative strategy. The agreement was unnecessary. Unlike a treaty, it was dangerously indefinite. It went against the grain of the Conservative party's policy of "reciprocity within the British Empire." But the best answer, at least for now, was to sit down quickly. That Borden did. At a caucus meeting the next morning, he recalled in his autobiography, there was the "deepest dejection in our party, and many of our members were confident that the Government's proposals would appeal to the country and give it another term of office." Reciprocity seemed likely to deliver the coup de grâce to Borden's leadership.

Borden and his MPs did not need to despair. Questions had already begun to be asked as the negotiations unfolded, and within days of Fielding's announcement, boards of trade and other significant interest groups had publicly registered their discontent. The parade continued on 20 February when eighteen Toronto business leaders and bankers, most of them with Liberal connections, signed a manifesto of opposition. Then, on the 28th, Clifford Sifton told a hushed House of Commons that he was joining the anti-reciprocity crowd. A wealthy western Canadian and a Laurier Cabinet stalwart until his resignation in 1905, Sifton had remained in Parliament and in the party. But the time had come, he said to the house, when he and the Liberals must part company.

As Sifton told the tale, the issue—and the menace—was the greatest to confront the country in his many years as a public figure. Reciprocity would ruin several Canadian industries and hurt farmers more than they knew. More importantly, the proposal directly contradicted decades of effort to bring the disparate Canadian regions together in transcontinental unity. The trade agreement would accentuate the north–south pull that was so easy, logical, and natural. Pressure would follow for more free trade, this time across a broad range of manufactures, pressure on a country less able to resist because it had acquiesced in the first accord. In short, Sifton feared reciprocity for precisely the reasons that Taft and his circle supported it: the agreement and the changes coming in its train would transform Canada into an economic dependant and North America into a single economic unit. "Sir," Sifton concluded, "we are putting our heads into a noose. . . . These resolutions, in my judgement, spell retrogression, commercial subordination, the destruction of our national ideals, and displacement from our proud position as the rising hope of the British Empire."

Borden took courage from both new allies and old allies such as the Conservative premier of Ontario, who had wired him only hours after the Fielding announcement urging that this move "from Imperialism to continentalism" be fought vigorously. Conservative MPs also told Borden the good news they were hearing from their constituencies. The agreement was vulnerable after all. The Conservative leader decided to obstruct and delay in every way possible; there was a country and a political career to save. The nation, he told Canadians, had worked hard to establish itself. Prosperity reigned. The British Empire had given Canada so much, and had more to offer. What sense did it make to sacrifice it all for the prospect of becoming the Americans' economic playground? Reciprocity was another attempt to conquer Canada, said one of Borden's colleagues, this time "by peaceful means and large gifts." Even as supporters flocked to his banner—an Anti-Reciprocity League was formed in Montreal, and the Canadian National League in Toronto—Borden had to outmanoeuvre his enemies within the party through yet another round of questioning about his leadership.

The momentum in Canadian politics, however, had shifted astonishingly. The Conservative leader had an issue that captured the imagination. By the end of March, Lord Grey judged that "the feeling in Montreal and Toronto against the Agreement could hardly be stronger if the United States troops had already invaded our territory." Borden acted with increasing skill and confidence. He was helped by the slow progress of the reciprocity legislation through the American Congress and by Taft's "now or never" speech, delivered to the newspaper publishers on 27 April. The Conservatives in the House of Commons, who now had the Liberals spending most of their time defending themselves, were able to push the day of decision back farther and farther until it began to conflict with Laurier's commitment to attend the coronation of King George V in London. The prime minister did not wish to leave Ottawa, but the Cabinet convinced him otherwise. The House was adjourned from mid-May to mid-June, giving Borden further time to build support in the course of a successful trip to the West.

Laurier's last gasp as prime minister of Canada, September
1911. (National Archives of Canada/C 3930)

When Laurier returned home, he was greeted by more obstruction-
ist tactics. Without the closure weapon (which was yet to be adopted by
Parliament) and with no end to the debate in sight, he dissolved the
House on 29 July and called a September election. Why he did so,
becoming the first prime minister in Canadian history to voluntarily
bring on a campaign after only three years in power, is not completely
clear. Yet his action is perhaps not so surprising. He had invested heavily in reciprocity, both politically and emotionally. It was going to be the
means to reunite Canadians and to reconcile them to his leadership after
the difficulties of the past months and years. The most prominent and
divisive of Laurier's problems had been the searing debate over the separate national navy he had created. English Canadians thought that

Laurier's navy would not do nearly enough to help defend the British Empire against a rising German menace; French Canadians thought it did far too much. The alternatives to a reciprocity election—continuing stalemate, withdrawal of the proposed legislation, or driving on to a bloody victory that might require weeks or months—were doubtless all unpalatable, especially for a leader who had been the undisputed champion of Canadian politics for fifteen years.

"What a salad!" exclaimed Laurier when he contemplated the forces arrayed against him in the 1911 campaign. There was Sifton and the disaffected Liberals; the "non-partisan" Canadian Manufacturers' Association; and, in Quebec, the alliance between the Conservatives and the Quebec nationalists, the latter led by Henri Bourassa. Bourassa was a former Laurier member of Parliament and adviser determined to bring his old boss down for having, to the nationalist way of thinking, consistently neglected to protect the interests of his French compatriots and his home province. The Conservatives and the nationalists in Quebec had little in common except their stand against Laurier and his navy. That was the predominant issue in Quebec, and that was enough to tie Laurier down in the province and make inroads on his traditional support.

Everywhere else voters and politicians alike seemed to talk of little else but reciprocity. Borden, concentrating on Ontario and spending little time in Quebec, played on sentiments of national pride and imperial loyalty, adapting the "parting of the ways" theme to his own purpose. Canada was at the crossroads all right: "We must decide whether the spirit of Canadianism or Continentalism shall prevail on the northern half of the continent. . . . With Canada's youthful vitality, her rapidly increasing population, her marvellous natural resources, her spirit of hopefulness and energy, she can place herself within a comparatively brief period in the highest position within this mighty Empire." The future lay in a strong Canada within a revitalized British Empire, not in a reciprocity agreement that was bound to lead to political union, whatever its economic consequences. Almost every Conservative speech and pamphlet quoted the words of one of the leading politicians in the United States, Champ Clark, the soon-to-be speaker of the House of Representatives: "I am for it [reciprocity] because I hope to see the day when the American flag will float over every square foot of the British North American possessions, clear to the North Pole." Other American politicians said the same thing, if less colourfully, and Taft's private letter to Roosevelt, saying that reciprocity would make Canada into a U.S. satellite, somehow found its way into the glare of public attention.

The Conservative press had a field day. Huge streamer headlines, red ink, and Union Jacks carried the message that it was either "Borden and King George, or Laurier and Taft." Was it for this sell-out, the Toronto *News* demanded to know, "that the illustrious heroes of our British history fought their age-long battles, and freely gave their lives? Was the soil of England empurpled by a hundred wars to vouchsafe to succeeding generations the right of the subject to the untrammelled ballot, only to have this priceless heritage torn from our grasp by the greedy magnates and the designing demagogues of the United States?" The emphasis on the British connection was a way of celebrating the distinctiveness of Canada. English history and values were a shield against the "many corrupt influences arising and fostered in the United States."

For the supporters of reciprocity, the Conservative rhetoric contained a contradiction. During an election rally, a Liberal politician was struck by the irony of "seeing a long procession of automobiles all imported from the United States pass in procession along the streets of Ottawa fairly swarthed in bunting upon which was printed the legend, 'No truck or trade with the Yankees.'" If mounting imports from the U.S. since 1900 had not caused annexation, Laurier's partisans said, how could mounting exports to the United States bring it? How could the Canadian banker with reserves in Wall Street, the company director drawn to grain terminals in Chicago, the manufacturer who thought nothing of Canada–U.S. mergers, ordain that their fellow citizens did not have the same right to economic freedom and closer commercial ties with a neighbour? Why could Saskatchewan homesteaders not sell their beef or wheat without selling their country and their souls with it?

Such logic made no impression. Laurier and his trade agreement were soundly defeated on 21 September 1911. Clearly the Liberals had been a party in decline for some time; clearly too the powerful Conservative party provincial machines in Manitoba, British Columbia, and especially Ontario were crucial, delivering a combined eighty-eight seats to the Liberals' fifteen. This has made some election watchers wonder just how important the Canada–U.S. accord was in most voters' calculations: it was only a matter of time for the tired old Liberals anyway. But reciprocity cannot be ignored in any assessment of the election outcome. It first brought the Liberals misplaced confidence, then revealed their weaknesses, and finally propelled them in frustration towards an election in which they would inevitably be on the defensive. It gave coherence and enthusiasm to the Conservative cause. It made Canadians think hard about their future. Contemporary observers noted, with commentator Andrew Macphail, the "spectacle of a whole people swept by a wave of emotion and sentiment. In all sincerity many good and loyal souls were seized by a genuine alarm that their nationality was in danger."

AMBIVALENCES

Laurier had offered a vision to Canadians in 1911, one "which would astonish the world by its novelty and grandeur, the spectacle of two peoples living side by side along a frontier nearly four thousand miles long, with not a cannon, with not a gun frowning across it on either side, with no armaments one against the other, but living in harmony, in mutual confidence and with no other rivalry than a generous emulation in commerce and the arts of peace." Such talk was all very much in fashion, and indeed Laurier's words might just as well have been written by the new prime minister himself. After the 1911 election Borden hastened to explain that there was "no spirit of unfriendliness or hostility to the United States." Before the end of the year, the minister of finance and the minister of trade and commerce had both addressed New York audiences. No two countries understood each other better, they affirmed, and Canada was still open for business, for trade, and for investment. The rhetoric of the election campaign seemed to have meant nothing.

Borden and his colleagues were not only reflecting the realities of living next door to a giant, but also that acceptance of and good will towards the United States was permeating the body politic. Examples of the things held in common could be found everywhere, and they amounted to far more than commerce or economics. Canadians and Americans shared a disdainful view of other countries that were unable to run their affairs efficiently and democratically, or to get along with one another as North Americans did. Cultural links were strong and increasing. One observer wrote that "laymen's missionary movements and professional baseball leagues know no boundary line; the edicts of *Ladies' Home Journal* on fashion or morality run north as well as south of forty-nine. Canadians and Americans attend the same plays, eat the same breakfast food, sling the same slang." The two countries exchanged immigrants on a huge scale, with all the implications that held for leavening the differences of history and allegiance. The American-born population in Canada rose to a total of 497 249 during the first decade of the century; by 1910, there were 1 204 637 Canadian-born in the United States. The movement of American farmers, very much encouraged by the government in Ottawa, to the prosperous Canadian Prairies was especially formidable, and U.S.-born people in Alberta constituted the biggest non-native group in the province.

Anti-Americanism still figured prominently in the national psyche. Despite the extent to which the two populations and cultures mingled,

"Canadianism or continentalism?" Robert Borden, shortly
after becoming prime minister.
(National Archives of Canada/C 18632)

Canadians generally speaking rejected the American way of life.
University Magazine noted that Canadians divorced less often than their
raffish cousins to the south. A member of the women's contingent of the
Anti-Reciprocity League worried that the agreement would mean "injury
to home life and the marriage tie, a lessening of national religion, morals
and patriotism." Film censorship boards established in the years 1911–13
acted quickly to ban or edit films with "unnecessary display of the
American flag"; it was a flag, the Saint John *Standard* insisted, "conceived
in treason and born in rebellion." In the view of many British loyalists,

Americans who came to Canada did not understand the country and mis-interpreted its needs. They were among the "new Canadians" who were thought less capable of understanding what was at stake in the reciproc-ity measure and more susceptible to the propaganda of political and eco-nomic union. "Old Canadians," their stout-hearted Britishness at the ready, knew better. "It is quite untrue," a resentful Albertan wrote Borden at the height of the 1911 campaign, "that the American immigrant becomes a good Canadian."

Americans had resentments of their own. The Canadian tariff was too high (although in fact much lower in the aggregate than the American). Too many people and too much capital migrated north. Ontario, Quebec, and British Columbia all but prevented the export of pulpwood by insist-ing on the domestic manufacture of the harvests from Crown lands. An American film trade paper, *Moving Picture World*, did not oppose censor-ship of the U.S. flag, but it could not refrain from passing comment on the way Canadians always seemed to want to have the best of both worlds: "Canadian Imperialists are complaining about having to witness too many deeds of Yankee valour in moving pictures. No reciprocity wanted—excepting Yankee dollars."

CONTINENTAL ECONOMICS

The U.S. did not officially criticize the defeat of freer trade in 1911 or attempt retaliation. There was undoubtedly private bewilderment and annoyance, but Washington's goals of weakening the empire and devel-oping an interlocking North American economic system were being advanced nonetheless—even without reciprocity.

There had been, indeed, a gradual movement for many years to-wards a continental economy, though generalizations to this effect are easily overdone. The United States was gaining ground on Britain as a market for Canadian exports: in 1900, $96 million worth of Canadian goods were sent to the British, and $52 million to the United States; in 1911, $132 million went to Great Britain, $104 million to the U.S. (and only $38 million to all other countries). In 1913, the U.S. removed the duty on newsprint paper, resulting in substantial increases in Canadian exports of that product. Overall, however, the British market was more important and would continue to be throughout the First World War and into the early 1920s. The United States did provide more of Canada's imports than

Britain, and had been doing so since the 1880s. By 1911, some $276 million or 60 percent of all of Canada's imports came from the United States.

The lion's share of total outside investor capital in this period came from Great Britain, but flows from the United States were increasing. Moreover, American investment was largely direct, in the sense that U.S. firms and individuals, unlike their British counterparts, were very apt to become participants in the Canadian economy, setting up and managing branch-plants, or establishing and controlling resource companies, particularly in the forest industry. Little is known about American branch-plant operations in Canada during this time; the one available record lists 451 American-owned enterprises in 1913, some obviously small and others not. These were good times in Canada, and an American company that set up business there could find an easier way into the domestic and British Empire economy. Imperial Oil, Canadian Westinghouse, and Ford of Canada were among the U.S.-controlled companies to gain a foothold before 1914.

The First World War produced remarkably little permanent impact on the continental economy-in-embryo. Trading patterns, although they changed during the war itself, were not substantially altered: in 1913, 39 percent of Canadian exports went to the U.S.; in 1919, only 37 percent travelled south. Imports of U.S. products into Canada did rise substantially during the war, but the percentage fell back in the 1920s.

One wartime innovation was Canadian federal government borrowing on the New York money market. The economist Ian Drummond succinctly explains the circumstances in which this took place. "Before 1914, Canada had blithely bought far more in the United States than she had sold there, paying the excess by converting the proceeds from exports to Britain and from borrowings on the British market. After 1914 this was no longer possible: Britain could not lend convertible currency to Canada, which now, in addition, found itself financing a large part of Britain's Canadian purchases." American money was therefore very useful in helping to cover the costs of U.S. exports to Canada for the duration. It should be noted, however, that New York borrowing was not revolutionary; Canadian provincial and municipal governments and corporations had long borrowed in the United States. And U.S. wartime borrowings by Ottawa were minor—some $300 million over the course of the war—compared to the amounts raised in Britain and in Canada itself.

Still, the government was anxious to have American dollars and was correspondingly distressed by the ban Washington slapped on foreign borrowing after the U.S. entered into the war in 1917. Sir Thomas

White, Borden's minister of finance, did his best to help secure an exemption to the new rule. In a letter to W.G. McAdoo, President Woodrow Wilson's son-in-law and the secretary of the treasury, the finance minister hit a note designed to appeal to U.S. self-interest and perhaps to threaten just a bit as well: "I might point out to you that the balance of trade between Canada and United States is greatly in your favour and this is a strong reason why we should be permitted to borrow. Unless we can obtain credit in [the] United States, it would appear to me that our purchases there must necessarily fall off."

Later, White (who also visited Washington to make his arguments) tried to stress the "hands across the border" approach. "We have in your time and mine always been good neighbours. Occasionally a verbal brickbat has been thrown across the fence but we have always sympathized with each other when brickbats have come from any foreign source. . . . Our people are very much alike and understand each other better I think than any other two peoples in the world today." This was clichéd language no doubt, but it is perhaps worth pointing out that White was one of the Liberals who had defected to the Conservatives over Laurier's reciprocity agreement in 1911, one of the key election strategists who had wrapped Borden's campaign in the cloak of Anglo-Canadian patriotism and denounced the hated Yankees without let. McAdoo allowed Ottawa to raise certain sums of money on the private capital market. White for his part was delighted that Ottawa did not have to borrow from the American government. "We shall have to pay a fairly stiff rate of interest," he told a colleague, but he did not want to borrow from Washington. "I would rather we should 'hoe our own road.'"

Wartime co-operation took other forms. Munitions production in Canada began to trail off in the fall of 1917 as London's orders decreased. To fill the gap and to keep the factories working, the Imperial Munitions Board, a British agency operated in Canada by Canadians, turned to the War Department in Washington. Striking a deal with the Ordnance Department ensured that Canadian surplus capacity could be used to provide munitions for the United States Army. The *Financial Post* called the deal a "most important development," a way of keeping orders up and employment high. Later the Canadian business newspaper exulted, "Canada's Prosperity to Depend on Close Co-operation in Aims and Objects with the United States."

But now another threat placed Canadian war production in jeopardy. After its entry into the war, which resulted in initial organizational chaos, the United States government had brought order to its effort with an array of boards and commissions possessing sweeping powers. Steel was controlled, for example, with supplies allocated where they were most needed. But Canada imported steel from the U.S. Without that, munitions production in Montreal, Toronto, and Winnipeg would grind to a halt. To resolve such problems, and they extended over the whole range of vital imports, Ottawa created the Canadian War Mission in Washington on 2 February 1918 to lobby American decision-makers and to ensure that Canadian plants got their fair share of scarce supplies. The mission, Canada's first organized representation in its neighbour's capital, thus carried out some important commerical functions. Other allies had similar missions in Washington.

Prime Minister Borden visited President Wilson on 27 February 1918. Borden had not been greatly impressed with Wilson, viewing him as a "Great rhetorician but a weak and shifty politician." But he had to deal with the man. His mission was to persuade the president to resist the bureaucratic move to have American resources devoted entirely to U.S. industrial needs and to place orders only in American factories. The prime minister got his way, and this architect of the defeat of reciprocity in 1911 reported on his return to Canada that the president had "expressed the view that the resources of the two countries should be pooled in the most effective co-operation and that the boundary line had little or no significance in considering or dealing with these vital questions."

THE FIRST WORLD WAR: THE ENEMY WITHIN

The First World War in fact demonstrated just how important the border remained. In August 1914, when Europe plunged into the great conflict that would reshape the world and cause the ruin of great powers and the rise of others, Canada went to war automatically. The United States did not. The British declaration of war bound Canadians and exposed their shipping and their ports to attack from the Central Powers of Germany and Austria–Hungary. But the legalities were unimportant. No one coerced Canada into war; no one had to do so. The simple truth was that Canadians wanted to defend Britain and British values. Besides, the war was expected to be brief and certain to lead to glory and victory.

American abstention from the war upset few Canadians initally. There seemed no need for America to join in the struggle. The Royal Navy and the French army would do the job on their own. But by 1915 when the war continued and by 1916, when Allied victory began to seem a fading prospect, the tone in Canada changed. Now, Canada objected to the fact that the United States was hanging back from partic-ipating in a crusade for democracy and against militarism and autoc-racy. Canadians resented that Americans were, in President Wilson's phrase, "too proud to fight." It was almost as if the American people were unwilling to believe that anything could be accomplished through fighting. In Ralph Connor's 1917 novel, *The Major*, a book designed to stimulate recruiting and stir up flagging Canadian idealism, the charac-ters were crude but revealing symbols. One had been raised by a Quaker mother, and clearly represented the United States. This fellow was initially a pacifist. However, after his chums died heroically in action, he rejected his earlier stance and seized the sword. This was bla-tant self-righteous propaganda drenched in patronizing sentimentality and chauvinist racism, but it nonetheless expressed something of the mood of wartime English Canada.

Once the U.S. entered the war in 1917, the complaint changed as American films appeared emphasizing the importance of Uncle Sam's contributions to the cause. Almost every Canadian newspaper printed editorials attacking American war films, overwhelming in quantity, poor in quality, boastful to a fault. And in the postwar years, Canadians would become very annoyed at American books and articles claiming that the United States had won the war. The response in Canada, expressed best by men like George A. Drew, a veteran and later a Conservative provin-cial and federal politician, was to compare casualties and campaigns and to argue that little Canada had done at least as much to win the war as the United States.

In Canada, as in other nations, the outbreak of war had brought panic about the "enemy within": secret agents gathering intelligence, saboteurs planting bombs, and fomenting insurrection. The Royal North West Mounted Police took note early on of the "many thousands of alien enemies in the Canadian West," and internments began soon thereafter. The U.S. declaration of neutrality heightened the alarm by arousing memories of the Fenian raids of the 1860s, the more so because Irish nationalists—in Ireland and in North America too—were still intent on winning independence from Britain by whatever means they had at their disposal. Enemy agents working through the embassies, consulates, and business interests of the Central Powers in the United States had ready access to the undefended border. They could find, or so it was thought, ample support among the large concentrations of German and Irish Americans in the northern states, and count on active co-operation in Canada, where over five percent of the population was of German or Austro-Hungarian extraction.

The government in Ottawa was inundated with reports of subversive plots. The most influential of these came from Sir Cecil Spring Rice, the British ambassador in Washington, who was profoundly disturbed by the flood of warnings he was receiving from British consular officials and other sources. Spring Rice's raw information, much of it unsubstantiated, was transmitted to Borden's government through the governor general, the Duke of Connaught. Connaught was a haughty career soldier, not blessed with critical powers, who had served with the British forces in Canada at the time of the Fenian raids, and he firmly believed that the country faced a menace to its very existence, just as it had at the time of Confederation.

Prime Minister Sir Robert Borden had little choice but to take the warnings seriously. A month after war broke out, he advised his acting defence minister that he feared serious threats to internal security were already present or immediately on the horizon:

> (1) Organized attacks by thugs, gunmen and other lawless individuals, instigated by German emissaries. Such persons are likely to undertake for hire the destruction of bridges and other vital positions of railways and canals, the blowing up of important public buildings, such as Post Offices, Custom Houses, Parliament Buildings, etc. There is some evidence that men have already been hired for this purpose in the large cities of the United States.
>
> (2) Organized attacks on a large scale by German and Austrian Reservists, as many thousands of these are at present in the United States out of work, destitute and desperate. We have reason to believe that these men are being instigated to attack Canada. . . .

Canada was by no means undefended. Over 10 000 permanent force troops and militiamen called out on active service ran the fortified ports of Halifax, Quebec City, and Victoria–Esquimalt, British Columbia, and protected major communications facilities thought vulnerable to sabotage, such as the Welland Canal. In October 1914, in a decision that was heavily publicized to quell public disquiet, the government announced that the raising and dispatch of troops overseas to the European theatre would be arranged in such a fashion that 30 000 men would always be available at training camps across the country for home defence. In November that number was raised to 50 000. During 1915–16 the total force in Canada climbed to over 65 000 troops. In addition, prominent individuals across the country created local home guard units to prepare for what one newspaper called the day of Armageddon.

The home defence force would have been bigger still had it not been for the restraining influence of Major-General Willoughby Gwatkin. This respected British officer had been seconded for two tours of duty with the Canadian militia since 1905, and in 1913 the Borden government appointed him chief of the general staff, the professional head of the land forces. Gwatkin worked relentlessly in the face of vested local political interests and popular alarm to trim the garrisons so that qualified personnel would not be held back from the European theatre where the war would be decided. He was fully aware of the large-scale preparations that would be required to mount a substantial cross-border raid, and was confident that such activity would be detected in ample time by the secret service that Colonel Sir Percy Sherwood, Canada's chief commissioner of police, had organized in the United States at the outbreak of war. Little is known of the service and its agents, which recalled a similar organization that had helped to counter the Fenians fifty years before.

Sir Percy's importance, however, is undeniable. With eyewitness evidence he was able to debunk many of the reports of enemy activity in U.S. border towns. The steady flow of detailed intelligence from Sherwood's agents, who were prowling bars, restaurants, and clubs favoured by expatriate Germans and Austrians, allowed Gwatkin to give blunt assurances to Connaught that there was no substantial cause for concern: "In the existing circumstances we have to protect ourselves not against open attack with which the soldier can deal, but against the lone incendiary or dynamitard whose hand the Civil policemen best can stay."

One should add, however, that Connaught's imaginings were not so far away from German ambitions. Betraying an understanding of North America reminiscent of pulp novels, the German foreign ministry seriously considered recruiting 650 000 German and Irish-American cowboys to gallop across the border and conquer Canada. In 1915 there was also a scheme afoot to blow up several of the Canadian Pacific Railway's key bridges. However, the efforts of Captain Franz von Papen, the German military attaché in the U.S., to bomb this network of bridges collapsed as it became clear that his gang of expatriates and sympathizers were as short on skills and commitment as they were long on bold talk. One of the conspirators, Werner Horn, not informed that the attack was off, detonated a few sticks of dynamite which damaged the American–Canadian bridge at Vanceboro, Maine. American authorities quickly arrested him, but treated him leniently because he seemed unbalanced. The Canadian government took the affair more seriously, initiating lengthy extradition proceedings that were not successfully concluded until 1919. Horn was committed to a ten-year term in Dorchester Penitentiary after a short trial in New Brunswick. He was returned home in 1921 at the insistence of the German government.

Although the Borden government believed the Americans had all but turned a blind eye to the violation of their neutrality in the Vanceboro incident, the U.S. government was closely monitoring German and Austrian activities. Later in 1915, American agents and British naval intelligence uncovered evidence of ambitious and in some cases successful plots to plant bombs on ships carrying supplies for the Allies from U.S. ports. Enemy sympathizers also sabotaged industry and infiltrated labour unions to slow down the manufacture of products for the Allies. As a warning to the Central Powers, the Wilson administration leaked evidence of these activities to the press. It also arrested and prosecuted foreign agents and expelled the Austrian ambassador and the German naval and military attachés at the end of 1915.

The fear of enemy subversion continued in Canada. As the historians of Canada's home defences in the First World War, Roger Sarty and John Armstrong, have pointed out, "Traces of a foreign accent, mildly unpatriotic sentiments, or the possession of a camera, binoculars or a mysterious package were enough to trigger suspicion. Accidental fires and explosions, sounds resembling gunshots, moving lights at night and unidentified aircraft were taken as sure evidence of insidious enemy activity. When the Centre Block of Parliament burned in February 1916, some were convinced the totalitarian powers had struck at the heart of Canadian freedom." In February 1917 opposition members asked the government about the danger of a desperate attack on Canada by German-Americans as the United States edged closer to war with the Central Powers. Prime Minister Borden admitted in Parliament that he shared their concern and that he had asked the defence department to further reinforce the garrisons, although the chief censor excised all references to the United States in the published debates. It was not until the spring and summer of 1917, after the United States had entered the war without a crisis on the border, that Gwatkin was able to send much of his home army overseas.

THE BRIEF ORIGINS OF DEFENCE CO-OPERATION

Border defence was only part—and the less difficult part—of Canada's security problem during the First World War. The country had a long, vulnerable coastline, and the Borden government learned that membership in the world's greatest maritime empire and friendly proximity to a major naval power by no means guaranteed adequate protection. The immediate danger on the outbreak of war came from four German cruisers that were loose in the eastern Pacific and western Atlantic. In addition, over fifty German merchant ships had interned themselves at U.S. ports, mostly in the north and especially at New York, using the cover of American neutrality to prevent being captured by Britain's navy. Several of the merchantmen were fast liners, well suited to take on armament and go to sea as raiders themselves, and all could serve as sources of coal and other supplies for German warships.

On the Atlantic, it soon became clear that German raiders were confining their operations to the Caribbean and the South American coast. British cruisers had arrived on the Canadian east coast and, using Halifax as a base, had established a patrol off New York that—despite American protests—guarded against the escape of the interned German merchant fleet. The ancient Royal Canadian Navy (RCN) training cruiser, HMCS *Niobe*, struggled into service with the New York patrol.

On the west coast, the appearance of two German cruisers at San Francisco caused a full-blown panic in British Columbia. The only defence immediately available was the Canadian navy's ill-equipped west coast training cruiser, HMCS *Rainbow*, which had dutifully put to sea during the last days of peace. The Canadian navy recruited its own secret agents, who rushed down the U.S. Pacific coast and into Mexico in an effort to get information about the German warships and to interfere with arrangements to refuel them. Meanwhile, the premier of British Columbia, Sir Richard McBride, had used his connections in Seattle, Washington, to purchase two submarines that were being completed there on a Chilean contract. The submarines found their way to British Columbia, managing to evade U.S. navy neutrality patrols, and Borden immediately had them commissioned into the RCN for coastal patrols. In the event, the German Pacific squadron attempted to break through to the Atlantic in December 1914 and was destroyed by the British Royal Navy at the Battle of the Falkland Islands, ending the main threat to the west coast.

By that time local naval defences on the east coast were becoming increasingly worrisome. The Royal Navy's blockading forces in the

North Sea would not have been able to prevent the breakout of powerful raiders from Germany, and the British admiral commanding in the western Atlantic informed the Canadian government that his thinly stretched cruiser squadron might well be caught off guard by such an action. The enemy was likely to operate in Canadian waters because North America was Britain's most important source of overseas supplies; most shipping from the United States and Canada went near Nova Scotia and south of Newfoundland, the short "Great Circle" route to the British Isles. More alarmingly, reports of suspicious activity aboard the interned German ships in U.S. ports suggested that these vessels were about to mount or support a raid on the Canadian coast. The RCN was especially concerned because the British navy exerted virtually total control over the Canadian east coast organization. And in contrast to the information about events on the border that was reaching Ottawa from its own agents and the British Embassy in Washington, very little intelligence about developments at sea was being transmitted to the Canadian capital.

Borden and the Duke of Connaught—often with the support of the British admiral in the western Atlantic—repeatedly asked the Admiralty either to loan Royal Navy coast defence ships or to assist in constructing them in Canadian shipyards. The Admiralty maintained that the margin of risk was acceptable, and that no British ships or shipbuilding experts could be spared. Warship production in Canada was impractical. Canada should continue to concentrate on providing land forces for the European theatre. That Canada faithfully did, but the sense of grievance grew, particularly after the government discovered, in January 1915, that British authorities had conspired with American companies to evade American neutrality laws by having components for ten submarines secretly imported to the Vickers shipyards in Montreal. There, under the guidance of expert U.S. workers who had illegally entered Canada, the vessels were assembled, finished, and dispatched to European waters. The British government had no sooner apologized for having failed to inform the Canadian government of this small detail than it transpired that hundreds of fast U.S. coastal motorboats were being built for the British in Canadian yards through a similar subterfuge.

In the spring of 1915, the Germans began their devastatingly successful submarine (U-boat) campaign against merchant shipping in the western approaches to the British Isles. Britain's surface ship squadrons proved incapable of countering the threat; they were utterly powerless against underwater attack from the U-boats. Reports came in that German spies from the United States were planning to establish refuelling depots on the isolated stretches of the Canadian and Newfoundland coast, so that the interned German merchant ships could escape and operate at will. Canada could only look to its hodgepodge of armed yachts and civil government steamers. Ottawa's nightmare was that one of many virtually unprotected liners carrying Canadian troops from east coast ports to Europe would be destroyed by a surprise German torpedo attack, just as the RMS *Lusitania* had been in the Irish Sea during May 1915.

The British refusal to allocate patrol warships to Canada and their seizure for the European theatre of many Canadian civil ships that might have been converted for coastal duty forced the Ottawa government to violate American neutrality again. In the summer of 1915, private Canadian sailors (acting secretly on behalf of the RCN) purchased four large yachts in the United States, and brought them to Halifax where they were armed and commissioned.

The alarms about the German navy's plans for the 1915 shipping season were all false. In July 1916, however, the new German freighter submarine *Deutschland* made a successful passage to Baltimore, where it offloaded a cargo of valuable German goods, and took on strategic U.S. materials. British protests and patrols failed to prevent its departure and safe return to Germany. When it made a second trip, in November, Sir Robert Borden was appalled at reports that the nickel it loaded—vital for German munitions production—had been mined at Sudbury, Ontario, before the war.

More disturbing still was the voyage of the combat submarine U-53 in October 1916. Without any prior intelligence warnings, it surfaced in Newport, Rhode Island. Crew members invited officers of the U.S. navy aboard to see its sophisticated equipment and powerful armament. It then cast off, and in a leisurely fashion destroyed five Allied merchant ships off Nantucket Island. The full implications of American neutrality were driven home for Canadians as never before. Over a dozen U.S. destroyers arrived on the scene, but they merely kept clear of the torpedo tracks and rescued downed crews and passengers. In response to reports that U-53 might be only one of a group of U-boats that could saturate the Halifax approaches, the British admiral in the region pulled his helpless cruisers into port and called for protection from small Canadian coastal craft.

The British pressed the Canadians to build as many anti-submarine ships of their own as possible, and quickly. But Canada could cobble together only the most rudimentary vessels. There were difficulties in building even these, because many of the steel components and engines had to be procured in the United States. The entry of the U.S. into the war in April 1917 only exacerbated the problem. Canadian orders now had to compete with the Americans' own mobilization requirements. The U.S. navy was unable to provide assistance either. They gave vague promises of occasional cruiser patrols into the southernmost reaches of Canadian waters. That was all.

All the while, supplies from the Canadian east coast were becoming increasingly vital to the Allied war effort, and therefore an even more important target for German raids. In the spring and summer of 1917, as a measure of last resort against the U-boats, the British began to sail transatlantic shipping in defended convoys, a tactic of desperation that ultimately proved to be decisive in denying victory to the submarines. Halifax and Sydney, Nova Scotia, because of their location on the Great Circle route, became major convoy ports.

Canada was learning, nevertheless, how little it mattered in the Anglo-U.S. maritime alliance. Without any consultation, in early 1918 the British diverted fast ships that carried valuable perishable cargoes from the St. Lawrence and Halifax to meet American needs. By this time, the Canadian navy had received warnings that long-range German submarines would almost certainly strike in Canadian waters during the spring and summer. The British, while delivering this bad news, promised that twelve warships, the bare minimum needed to give the tiny Canadian patrol vessels effective reinforcement, would be dispatched to Halifax. As spring neared, the Admiralty was forced by the situation in European waters to renege on this promise, advising instead that the Canadians approach the Americans for help.

The best the Americans would offer the Canadians was six wooden "submarine chasers." These were only marginally more capable than the best of Canada's small ships, but they were promptly dispatched to Nova Scotia and performed invaluable convoy escort services. U.S. navy seaplane units arrived at Halifax and Sydney too late in the season to play a significant part in the operations, but the navy's Boston Command agreed to defend the mouth of the Bay of Fundy and the southern tip of Nova Scotia. The Americans lacked the craft, however, to mount a permanent patrol in the region and they had to arrange to borrow vessels that were still being built in Canadian yards. In early August 1918, as these ships were being transferred to the U.S. navy, the German submarine U-156 suddenly appeared in the Fundy approaches and sank a large Canadian sailing ship. U-156 lingered in Canadian and northern U.S. waters until the end of the month; two other submarines made briefer strikes into the Canadian area in late August and mid-September en route to and from the American coast. The U.S. contributed an old gunboat, the USS *Yorktown*, to Canadian defences on 24 August, and it almost immediately began patrols out to the Grand Bank of Newfoundland. The RCN concentrated its own meagre forces to protect the ocean convoys and large ships on the coastal routes: only two steamers were sunk by the three submarines. Yet little could be done to guard the widely scattered fishing fleets, which suffered heavy losses.

The RCN's senior officers had high praise for the U.S. chasers that served under their command, but were bitter about the inadequate equipment and resources that hindered their own efforts. They freely predicted disaster if conditions did not improve and if, as expected, the U-boats returned in greater strength in 1919. Robert Borden was angry about the poor state of his naval service, and unhappy about having to rely on American assistance for the defence of Canadian national waters. At his direction, the navy again appealed to the British for destroyers, only to receive the familiar answers and a new commitment that the United States would provide assistance. Borden's directive to

SC 242, one of six U.S. submarine chasers that served with the Canadian navy in 1918. (Department of National Defence/CN 3280)

speed organization of an RCN air-patrol service for the 1919 season did bring results, largely because the Americans were willing to provide equipment and train personnel. The armistice on 11 November 1918 soon overtook these developments.

Friendly as co-operation had been between the Royal Canadian Navy and the U.S. navy in 1918, this first North American joint defence initiative was short lived, designed solely to meet a specific emergency. The Americans had appeared to give grudgingly; the Canadians accepted the help, but cautiously. The whole business was another illustration, as Alaska had been, of the difficulties in dealing with powerful friends when big international issues were at stake. Borden concluded, as Laurier had before him, that Canada was going to have to become more self-reliant.

C H *t\h* P *r* e *e* R

THE STING OF COMPETITION

1 9 1 9 — 1 9 3 5

In July 1923, Buster Brown and a colleague drove their McLaughlin Six automobile from Ottawa into Quebec, and then towards the United States. They encountered a Canadian customs official a few miles from the border—and a party of five Americans happily escaping their country's prohibition against alcohol—but found no post of any kind when they crossed the frontier at Highgate Springs, Vermont. Brown and his friend did all the things expected of assiduous tourists: chatted to the natives, snapped photographs, collected postcards, studied the history and geography of the region. Inevitably they stopped a few miles from Highgate Springs at St. Albans, the scene of the famous Confederate bank robbery and Fenian raids across the border in the 1860s. Inevitably, too, they drew superior Canadian conclusions about the "fat" and "lazy" Vermonters who crossed their path, friendly though they seemed to be to "Canady."

DEFENDING THE UNDEFENDABLE

Colonel James Sutherland "Buster" Brown, the Canadian army's director of military operations and intelligence, was not on holiday. He was carrying out, in the vernacular of the military, in-depth reconnaissance supporting his plan to foil an American invasion of Canada in the event of war between the U.S. and the British Empire. Defence Scheme No. 1 called for a first strike across the United States border at key points to a depth of a few hundred miles. Brown's ambition was to shock and sur-prise the enemy, gaining time while the forces of the empire rushed to Canada's side. His first-hand research confirmed his belief that the American people might be reluctant warriors. Many were of British extraction and would not enter wholeheartedly into a war with Great Britain or Canada unless a very strong cause existed. Indeed, a large constituency was displeased with "democracy as it exist[ed] in the United States of America," and had a sneaking regard for British laws and customs. Americans in addition had "a great love of the almighty dollar." Interference with trade and commerce might cause some parts of the U.S. "to be lukewarm or to take no action at all."

Once his papers were discovered by later generations, Buster Brown became all too predictably a figure of fun: a raving imperialist unable to put aside the anti-American prejudices of his Loyalist forebears; a ludi-crous Don Quixote trying to conquer the unconquerable; an ignorant anachronism, unwilling to adapt, out of step with his contemporaries and out of touch with the tranquil new realities of Canadian–American relations. Nevertheless, putting aside Brown's undeniable excesses, it is the responsibility of the planner to canvass all contingencies. A war between the United States and Great Britain was not out of the question in the 1920s, and Canada was bound to be involved. Other senior mem-bers of the Canadian armed forces, including the central figure of the period, Major General A.G.L. McNaughton, shared Brown's concerns about an unchecked U.S. military hegemony on the North American continent. More than most, the military knew that the history of Canada had been a gigantic struggle against nature and geography. The natural sea and land communications of North America ran in a north–south direction, which meant that a powerful United States held the continent in its hand. It needed only to squeeze.

Seen in this light, Colonel Brown's Defence Scheme No. 1 was neither stupidity nor lunacy but a rational precaution against the day, which might never come, when the "presently friendly" United States became hostile. Certainly the Americans did not rule out the possibility. Well into the 1930s, after Ottawa had scrapped Brown's document as unworkable and unnecessary, U.S. military planners were allowing for the contingency of an invasion of Canada more or less as Brown im-agined it. If there was an irony in the whole affair, it was that Brown's scheme had been predicated on the assumption that the British would not be far off—in spirit and, soon enough, in concrete action. The likelihood of a British bail out, however, was diminishing with each passing year. More and more Canada was alone on the North American continent.

Canadian military spies near Lake Placid, New York, in the early 1920s.
(Department of National Defence/PMR 87-512)

O BRAVE NEW WORLD

Professionals like Brown are paid to think thoughts of war. But North Americans had just fought to make the world safe and they might be forgiven for believing that their work was done. The British Empire and the United States had stood shoulder to shoulder in the First World War to preserve and extend their democratic way of life. Japan and Italy were among their allies. The German and Austrian empires had been decisively defeated and broken up. A brightly polished League of Nations was at the world's disposal, aiming to solve international problems by peaceful solutions if they could be found and collective security if they could not.

At war's end Canada and the United States, in James Eayrs's evocative phrase, "turned away from Europe, leaving behind their dead." After playing a decisive role at the peace conference, the U.S. decided not to become a member of the League because of public apathy, partisan politics, and powerful opposition to the League's forceful but inflexible exponent, President Woodrow Wilson. Canada did join the new organization but a steady stream of its delegates to the League fought hard against the notion of collective security, frequently making clear their compatriots' distaste that they should be asked to ensure the well-being of a corrupt Old World. It was, senior statesman Newton Rowell told the First Assembly of the League in 1920, "European policy, European statesmanship, European ambition, that drenched this world with blood and from which we are still suffering and will suffer for generations. Fifty thousand Canadians under the soil of France and Flanders is what Canada has paid for European statesmanship trying to settle European problems." Liberal Senator Raoul Dandurand lectured the same body some years on: "Not only have we had a hundred years of peace on our borders, but we think in terms of peace, while Europe, an armed camp, thinks in terms of war." Canadians were "fellow North Americans," the *Chicago Tribune* agreed. "Italians do not think of Germans or Frenchmen in anything like the same sense. They are suspicious where we have confidence."

Canada and the United States, however, differed in one important respect. Part of Canada and Canadians resided abroad—in the connection with Great Britain and the British Empire. Canada was a separate country, freely able to conduct virtually all of its internal affairs, but it remained tied to Britain in important ways. Canada had obtained, not without a fight, recent recognition of its fledgling international personality: separate representation at the 1919 Paris Peace Conference; signature of the Treaty of Versailles ending the war with Germany; and membership in the League of Nations. Nevertheless, Canada could not and did not wish to divorce itself from the Old World. The country's slowly emerging status, moreover, was easily misunderstood, at times scarcely acknowledged. It had no independent right to conduct diplomacy with other jurisdictions, and that was the classic test of true nationhood. Canada could not make treaties on its own. Its signature at Versailles came after that of the British prime minister, who had already placed his name on the treaty on behalf of the entire British Empire, Canada included. One of the arguments that American opponents of the League put forward most vigorously was that Canada and the other self-governing dominions had no business claiming individual membership in the international body. "Dominion," in fact, said it all. Canada and its imperial colleagues would simply vote as the British told them to, allowing them to gang up on other unfortunate nations.

THE LAST GASP OF A UNITED EMPIRE

In 1920, Sir Robert Borden worked out an agreement that provided for a Canadian minister in Washington to conduct the nation's business directly with the U.S. government. This was to be the country's first diplomatic representative in a foreign land, but there were carefully pre-scribed limits on what Great Britain and the United States would allow. The minister would be resident in the British Embassy in Washington, under the watchful eye of the imperial ambassador. The diplomatic unity of the empire—the theory that Great Britain alone spoke for all the dominion governments in matters of foreign policy—still held sway. In other words, Canada was understood to be part of an empire. It had no separate diplomatic existence. The Americans for their part refused to give the Canadian representative the same precedence in the diplomatic corps as the ministers of other foreign governments possessed. The Liberal opposition scoffed at the Conservatives' "kindergarten school diplomacy"; "pink teas and 10 o'clock dinners in Washington" did not make a nation. As it turned out, the position was not filled, partly because the search for a candidate with the right combination of wealth, prestige, and political good faith was not successful. The British and Americans, whose reaction had been grudging at best, were just as happy to see the untidy experiment delayed.

Borden had been content with an arrangement that provided for the closest possible relationship between the British ambassador and Canadian minister in Washington. He believed in building up Canada by building up the British Empire, and wanted co-operative policies worked out through consultation between the governments and prime ministers of Great Britain and the self-governing dominions of the empire. Full partnership was the objective: new national responsibilities with a new national status to match. The future belonged to an increasingly autonomous Canada firmly embedded in an empire (a more appropriate term, Commonwealth of Nations, was coming into fashion), which was stronger because its constituent parts had a significant role to play. Some glimmer of this ideal had been achieved in the Imperial War Cabinet of 1917–18 and at the Paris Peace Conference.

Borden's Conservative heir, Arthur Meighen, subscribed to the same beguiling vision, which was calculated to offer the best of both nationhood and empire. In practice, however, the idea of a co-operative empire was doomed to failure. The war, with its unifying impulses, was over. National reconstruction was the preoccupation. The dominions were far from one another and for the most part from Great Britain. Regular meetings of imperial leaders would be difficult, especially if busy prime ministers were to attend—and if not prime ministers, who? The British had an empire to run and no great interest in consultation with the hicks from the colonies. And, as Meighen would demonstrate in his brief eighteen months as prime minister, unified policies were difficult, even for the apparently committed, to find and pursue.

Like Borden, Meighen put great store in smooth relations between Great Britain and the United States. The Anglo-American relationship had always been important to Canada; after the First World War it was more so than ever because America had emerged with accentuated power, wealth, and prestige. The U.S. was a force to be reckoned with, and that made clashes inevitable with the reigning king of the hill, Great Britain. The two big powers of the postwar world had much in common, and they would again be allies in the Second World War, but throughout the 1920s and 1930s they were frequently at odds over vital economic and security issues. As the world moved from war to peace in 1919, one of Wilson's closest aides warned the president that there was a new antagonism in England towards the U.S. "The English are quite as cordial and hospitable to the individual American as ever, but they dislike us collectively. While the British Empire vastly exceeds the United States in area and population and while their aggregate wealth is perhaps greater than ours, yet our position is more favourable. It is because of this that the relations between the two countries are beginning to assume the same character as that between England and Germany before the war."

Arthur Meighen therefore went to the Imperial Conference of 1921 against a background of emerging and very serious Anglo-American competition. He was determined to promote good feelings between the U.S. and Great Britain, but also to make the point forcefully that Canada's voice had to be heard in matters affecting relations between the two great powers. As the Americans' closest neighbour, he claimed, Canadians had a unique expertise in gauging U.S. opinion. Moreover, they had a special right to be involved because, if things went badly wrong, Canada would be the battleground, the Belgium of a great British–American war.

The issue at hand in 1921 was the Anglo-Japanese alliance, which had been in force since 1902 as a mutual assistance treaty against unprovoked aggression. The pact was up for renewal, and was strenuously opposed by the United States. The U.S. did not wish to contemplate the combination of Britain and Japan, its greatest naval rivals, threatening American interests in the Far East and elsewhere. Meighen pushed the case against the alliance very hard, even to the extent of saying that he would opt out of any decision that did not please him. He was ultimately successful, in large measure because there were many senior people in London who agreed that a contented United States must be the central aim of British foreign policy. The Anglo-Japanese alliance was jettisoned as part of a complicated series of agreements reached at the Washington Conference of 1921–22, the most notable being a five power naval limitation treaty between the U.S., Britain, Japan, France, and Italy.

The alliance was gone, but at what price? Meighen had insisted on having his way, arguing that in imperial questions affecting North America the views of Canada must be paramount. The Australians and New Zealanders also had regional concerns, however, and the British government had a responsibility to defend an entire empire. Meighen has long been given credit for interpreting the United States to Britain, yet it went unnoticed that Meighen had dealt a body blow to the concept of unified policies reached in the interests of the whole empire and pursued even when there was not unanimity. He would prevail, or else.

Great Britain's decision to let the Japanese treaty fall by the wayside had serious implications for its position as an imperial power. Because they could not rely on the friendship of the Japanese, the British had to plan for possible aggression in the Far East as well as in every other part of their empire. They proved too weak to do so, and they received no tangible reward or support from the United States that would help their cause in return for abandoning the alliance. The appearance of a vast and impregnable worldwide network of possessions and interests was just that. The chair of the British chiefs of staff rightly pointed out in the 1930s that the empire, larger than ever before, was "disjointed, disconnected and highly vulnerable. It is even open to debate whether it is in reality strategically defensible."

An overextended Britain meant a weakened Canada. Neither Meighen nor the British saw that, without the Japanese alliance and the stability it guaranteed in the Pacific, Canada would be forced to rely all the more on the United States for its defence in some future crisis. If, furthermore, the British could not hold the peace, they would again call upon the senior dominion to be at their side in a big war. The call had been irresistible in 1914. Would it be the next time as well, and would it again divide Canadians against themselves? For Meighen these had not been pressing questions. His successor as prime minister was preoccupied by the problem.

A NEW LEADER AND A NEW POLICY

William Lyon Mackenzie King did not exactly sweep to power in the federal election of 1921. The war-weary troops of Arthur Meighen were reduced to a rump of fifty members, without representation in six of nine provinces including Quebec, which had most resented the Conservatives' imposition of compulsory military service four years before. King's Liberals, even so, won only 117 constituencies, not enough for a majority government. The problem was the Progressives, a party of farmer discontent that took almost all the Prairie seats and a good chunk in Ontario for a total of sixty-five. A handful of independents held the balance of power. The Progressives, committed to a low tariff on the way to none at all, bitterly remembered the defeat of reciprocity in 1911. King, then the labour minister, had been rejected in that election himself, and his stand on the tariff during the 1921 campaign showed that he was already a master of the devious caution that would be his hallmark as prime minister. He found a vague position between the Conservatives' firm stance for protection and the freer trade platform of the Progressives, and there he steadfastly stayed despite pressure to be more precise. Tariffs were needed, he said, but simply "tariffs for revenue," a term which he manipulated according to his audience. Meighen exploded: "Those words are the circular pomposity of a man who won't say what he means. He might as well say he favours a perambulatory tariff, or an atmospheric tariff, or a dynamic tariff."

The Conservative leader was unequivocal, as usual. He noted that the Americans were piling on the tariffs and assured voters, "I stand for a protective tariff, and I have always done so." At the height of the campaign, however, he was robbed of some of his reputation for plain dealing by a minor but telling incident. His wife bought a baby grand piano made in the United States, and the fact became well known. This seemed a direct contradiction of Conservative rhetoric about the protection of Canadian manufacturers and encouragement of domestic production. Meighen was not enough of a politician to do more than issue the feeblest of justifications. With enemies like that, King had little need of friends. A contemporary journalist wrote that Meighen was a master in debate, irony, satire, and in the thrust of the verbal rapier. But he always seemed to lose the fight.

Mackenzie King dominated national politics for the next three decades. He was the most successful of Canadian prime ministers, and the most maddening, constantly avoiding and obscuring as a deliberate act of policy. No one could attack what they could not pin down, he reasoned. When King died in 1950 after a brief retirement, the poet F.R. Scott reminisced,

> He skillfully avoided what was wrong
> Without saying what was right,
> And never let his on the one hand
> Know what his on the other hand was doing.

This technique was at the ready in King's management of foreign policy, the most divisive of Canadian questions. Secretary of state for external affairs almost as long as he was prime minister, he ran Canada's business with other nations virtually single-handed, letting only the odd politician or official in on the game. He defined the issues and decided the ground on which the few foreign policy debates he allowed would be fought.

The new prime minister lacked, as we now like to say, charisma. He was a small man, three years short of fifty in 1921, with a pale, broad, ordinary face, and a prissy demeanour and reedy voice that seemed to fit a preacher more than a politician. He was deeply religious, pathologically superstitious, and terribly lonely. He never married, had few friends, and desperately missed his mother, who had died in 1917. Much has been made of his devotion to his dogs, but they were almost his only steady, unswerving companions over a long public career. Ultra-sensitive to every slight, he sought attention and approval at the drop of a social occasion. "He is really excessively friendly," wrote a British diplomat after an Ottawa party. "My wife says that after a conversation with him she feels as if the cat had licked her all over and she ought to go and have a bath." King found an outlet for his repressions and insecurities in his diary, which he kept faithfully over more than fifty years, and in the world of the beyond, which consoled him that he was not alone. His diary could not talk back, and the ghosts of his mother and Sir Wilfrid Laurier (among other Liberal stalwarts) told him that he was always right. Another of King's ghosts was his grandfather, William Lyon Mackenzie, the leader of the 1837 rebellion in Upper Canada. Apparently the most establishment of men, King also fancied himself a rebel, an outsider, and he saw his career as a vindication of grandpapa's life and work.

This delicate man was also a tough, resourceful politician. King specialized in timing—in knowing when to act, and more importantly when not to act. Politics, he said, were like preventive medicine. "You keep the disease from developing. The important thing is not what action you take to make desirable events happen, but the action you take to keep bad ones from happening." Only too aware of his limitations, he added that "it's the result that counts, not the figure you cut while getting there." He told his aides to avoid at all costs the writing of striking phrases into his speeches. King did not want the public to remember anything he said.

King searched for a foreign policy that would not divide. He was by nature a compromiser and conciliator, but the structure of his political support and of the country itself helps to explain his approach. Quebec provided King and the Liberals with a solid core of seats in Parliament. He won all sixty-five in 1921. The French-speaking population of that province was sceptical of the empire connection. They wanted peace: no commitments abroad; no involvement in the affairs of other nations; no alliances that might bring conflict. Nor were Quebeckers alone in their desire to remain isolated from the world's problems. The majority of Progressive supporters probably agreed with their party's leader, who said that Canada had had entirely too many foreign affairs of late. Yet Canada was also a British country, and the empire connection made a great many Canadians, particularly the substantial number of British origin, feel special and powerful. It conferred economic and military advantages, and a sense that Canadians were different from and better than their neighbours.

The desire for the tranquillity and isolation of North America on the one hand and for taking on some of the joys and responsibilities of being British on the other could meet in a single person. It did in King himself. The one safe course that would ensure national unity was to promise that Canadians alone would determine their fate. King put emphasis on this, and on the development of a still young and fragile country in the shadow of the great giant to the south. Each day that he spent in the House of Commons was a reminder to be careful. King led a minority government in his first two Parliaments of the 1920s, and in the mid-1920s he was briefly knocked from power by Meighen's Conservatives. Even in the 1926 election, he did not win a big victory.

Soon after becoming prime minister in late 1921, King was off to Washington to show his diplomatic wares. They consisted primarily of a proposal to modernize the ancient Rush–Bagot Agreement of 1817, which limited naval armaments on the Great Lakes. The contemplated treaty would have had undoubted political and military benefits, and would have showed Europe and Asia how the peaceful folk of North America regulated their affairs. Nothing came of it, but King had struck out in the direction of a more independent external policy. He had let Washington know that a fresh breeze—or at least a different breeze—

was blowing in Canada. And he had informed the august authorities in London's Whitehall that he expected full powers to sign, without British participation, agreements that affected North America only.

The prime minister was back at Britain's door at the beginning of 1923 with a Canada–U.S. accord for the regulation of the continental Pacific halibut fishery. Canada had negotiated similar commercial agreements for decades, but they had always been countersigned by the British, usually by their ambassador in the United States. King demanded the right to sign the document alone. The British put up a vigorous counterattack, but King would have none of it, threatening immediate action to establish a "direct" diplomatic presence in Washington. He had been going slowly on this front, but would insist on a representative in the American capital if the British would not give Canada the freedom to complete its own treaties. The British capitulated. They had no desire to see a Canadian diplomat popping up in Washington, complicating their life and damaging their cherished imperial diplomatic unity. Although most Americans, and that included the inhabitants of the U.S. Senate, remained blissfully unaware that anything much had changed, King had carried out a tiny revolution on behalf of his vision of the British Commonwealth, one quite different from Borden's. Each part of the self-governing empire would autonomously carry out its diplomacy; they would consult and co-operate with each other only when necessary and feasible. For the first time a treaty had been entirely negotiated and signed by and for Canadians. Generations of schoolchildren ever since have memorized the name and date of the 1923 Halibut Treaty as part of the litany of Canadian nation building. Only in Canada, readers might think, and they would be right.

A MASSEY ON MASSACHUSETTS AVENUE

A Canadian representative in Washington was an idea whose time would soon come as well. By 1926, King had won the day in his campaign for a decentralized commonwealth, and he was ready to install Vincent Massey as Canada's first diplomat in a foreign country. Importantly, Massey was to take up residence in a separate legation, a departure from the Borden arrangement of six years before which envisioned the Canadian representative as part of the British ambassador's entourage. Massey was a former president of his family firm, the Massey-Harris farm implement company, and he had briefly held a minor Cabinet position in the King government without having been elected to Parliament. He failed to win a seat in the election of 1925 and could not gain a nomination in 1926. There he was: available, rich, prominent, articulate, cultured, and a bit of a pain in the neck to the prime minister. What better solution than to send him out of the country on a diplomatic errand? The public, if we are to judge from one reporter's conclusions, "regarded the creation of a Legation in Washington as puerile swank on the part of a Prime Minister with false boyish notions of our national importance, or as a means of providing a cosy berth for one of Mackenzie King's friends who did not fit into the political picture, but who had to be taken care of, as the heelers so charmingly phrase the fine art of providing for their own." This was an indication that there were still Canadians who regarded such an appointment as unnecessary. Some saw it as a slap in the face to the British and, worse, another step towards separation from the empire and engulfment by the United States. And for what? Tommy Church, a Conservative member of Parliament and former mayor of Toronto, said that all Massey's appointment did was "lower Canadian status to that of the other 26 Latin Republics represented in Washington."

Massey himself was not enamoured of the position. Oxford-educated, a rebel against his family's pro-American views, he was a thoroughgoing Anglophile capable—to steal a line from the poet Irving Layton—of making even the English feel unspeakably colonial. So far as public service was concerned, his highest ambition was to be Canadian high commissioner in London. Washington and the United States were distinctly second rate and second best.

Massey instantly got off on the wrong foot. He insisted that the Canadian government spend $500 000 to purchase a very grand building at 1746 Massachusetts Avenue to house the new legation. It was a lot of money, although it proved a very good investment over the years, and it reinforced many views about a man frequently dismissed as simply an over-rich playboy. But Massey committed himself to the job, and when he left Washington in the summer of 1930, the *Times* of London heaped on the praise. He had won "golden opinions" from all sides, the newspaper wrote. It was a common view. The journalist who had described adverse public opinion towards Massey in 1927 reported a sea change in attitude. "Even those roughneck voters who peer down their noses at his dilettante ways . . . admit he has done well in his job."

Massey's time in the American capital was an undeniable success for precisely the reason that he was so frequently criticized in Canada.

He was a dazzling public performer—a trained actor like his famous brother, Raymond—and he thrust himself and his country forward with aristocratic self-assurance. He delighted in arranging ceremonial occasions, such as the 1927 visit to Washington of the Canadian governor general, Lord Willingdon. Travelling widely and speaking often, Massey argued for Canada's position as a new North American nation with an ancient British allegiance, uniquely qualified to act as an interpreter and peacemaker in Anglo-American affairs. He remained a critic of the materialism and provincialism of American life and the "pep, punch, push" of U.S. business, but his views moderated considerably with experience. The British Empire man learned to look more fondly on the American colossus. Still, Washington was not a real job. That would only come when he was dispatched by King to his beloved London in 1935.

One of Massey's unappetizing tasks as Canadian minister arose out of the U.S. Eighteenth Amendment of the Constitution and the Volstead Act (both 1919), prohibiting the sale, manufacture, and transportation of alcohol. The booze poured southwards from Canada at hundreds of frontier locations, with the Windsor–Detroit route perhaps the most well worn: across the Detroit River by boat, over the winter ice in fast "Whiskey Six" cars, by cable under the water, and in innumerable hiding places as goods and people made their ingenious way across the border. Off the Atlantic seaboard, "rum row" was just outside the legal reach of U.S. authorities, and another favourite spot to offload Canadian whiskey, Caribbean rum, and French wine and brandy from St. Pierre and Miquelon in the Gulf of St. Lawrence. Massey's legation became used to hearing the complaints of outraged American law-enforcers and hard-done-by Canadian entrepreneurs, both of whom claimed to be within their rights, and both of whom frequently were not.

The most famous Canadian–American squabble over alcohol was that of the *I'm Alone*, a ninety-ton, Canadian-registered but American-owned rum-running schooner. In March 1929, the ship, bound from the Caribbean towards the Louisiana coast with a cargo of three thousand cases of alcohol, was intercepted, pursued two hundred miles into the Gulf of Mexico by the American Coast Guard, and sunk with the loss of one crew member. The Newfoundlander captain of the vessel, J.T. Randell, did not deny that he was bootlegging alcohol, but asserted that he had been first approached by the Coast Guard cutter *Wolcott* outside the agreed territorial jurisdiction of the United States, as laid down in a 1924 treaty and agreed to by Canada and the U.S. He had been brought down, moreover, by another Coast Guard vessel, the *Dexter*, which joined the chase after two days and could not by any stretch of the imagination be considered to have been part of a legitimate "hot pursuit." Randell was a swashbuckling character who captured the public imagination. Massey gushed that he was "in spirit an Elizabethan—he belonged to the days of Drake. He was a man of great rectitude in other matters, but disliked the principle of prohibition." One arbitrator for each country was named, and their report vindicated Randell. The sinking of the *I'm Alone* had been unjustified, and financial compensation was due to the Canadian government and the crew alike. Yet the law moves slowly and international law even more slowly. The report was issued in 1935, six years after the incident and two after the repeal of prohibition.

THE MOUNTING AMERICAN THREAT

After Massey presented his credentials to President Calvin Coolidge in 1927, the United States had answered with an appointment of its own. William Phillips became the American minister in Ottawa. As a senior figure in the State Department and a former undersecretary of state, he was a blockbuster choice, a stunning compliment, it was widely said, to the young country of Canada. It was particularly so because Phillips had stepped down in both rank and salary from the heights of ambassador in Belgium to become a mere minister in backwoods Ottawa. We are told that having heard of Washington's interest in Canada, Phillips "consented" to the "demotion." But the interest is unlikely to have originated in the White House; welcoming Massey to the United States, the stolid Calvin Coolidge had asked "whether Toronto was near the Lakes and if this was the first Canadian diplomatic mission."

Phillips was a member of a fine Boston family and was private school and Harvard educated. He had turned his back early on "the pallid career of family trustee," launching himself instead into career diplomacy in search of stimulation and adventure. Phillips "stoops to conquer," wrote the *New York Telegram* of his appointment to Canada.

The British saw Phillips as part of a mounting threat to their hold on Canada. The rivalry between Britain and the U.S. had not ceased with the death of the Anglo-Japanese alliance, and ill feelings between the two countries, primarily over the size of their navies, had reached such a state by 1927 that Winston Churchill was thinking the unthinkable. Himself half-American and a champion of Anglo-American relations, the chancellor of the exchequer told his Cabinet colleagues that war with the U.S. would be "foolish and disastrous," but that it might have to be. The British could not afford to put themselves in the power of the United States or in a position that would allow the Americans to give "orders about . . . [British] policy, say, in India, or Egypt, or Canada."

Canada was the biggest and most influential of the British dominions, the one most vital for the mother country to keep if the empire was to be maintained. Yet it was next door to the U.S., subject to all the temptations and influences of North America. Some of the English who came to Canada, distressed that they did not find a perfect reproduction of the homeland, concluded the worst. Canada would soon be lost to the empire. Other British visitors found Canada less Americanized than they had expected or feared. Wrote one in 1928, "Certain unessential external features of life, such as the make-up of their press, the perfection of their plumbing arrangements, the enormous consumption of iced water, down to such comparative trifles as the adoption of college yells and Greek Letter Societies, have been lifted bodily from the States, but in fundamentals they seem to me . . . to have left room in their lives for something other than the mere thirst for wealth." In fundamentals, that is, the current generation of Canadians was as "true as steel" to British values and interests. They considered themselves to belong to a superior political civilization.

The noise and flair of the great American experiment nevertheless made it difficult for the British to imagine that Canadians could think of anything else. A process of peaceful penetration was so obviously underway: American trade, American capital, American industry, American media. The alarm was raised by no less than the prime minister of Great Britain, who visited Canada for the Diamond Jubilee of Confederation in 1927. Stanley Baldwin wrote to King George V that the Phillips appointment must be countered by a British representative able to show "that we . . . take as great an interest in Canada as the Americans do." Too many industries were passing under American control, with the potential for U.S. financial interference in Canadian politics. The British must encourage more capital as a counterweight, helping Canadians "to repurchase, in time, the control of Canadian industries now in American hands." A year later Baldwin warned the man who would succeed him as prime minister that "American money power is trying to get a hold of the natural resources of the Empire. They are working like beavers." A high commissioner was sent to Ottawa in short order to fight these influences.

AMERICAN MONEY POWER

The influence of "American money power" was undoubtedly increasing in Britain's senior dominion. American investment in Canada had been just three-quarters of a billion dollars in 1914, distinctly second to that of the British. Within a decade, the United States' capital investment had surpassed Britain's. By the end of the 1920s, the American figure was almost $3.8 billion, the British total only $2.1 billion. Part of the American capital was used to develop Canadian natural resources: pulp and paper and nickel were sent in large quantities to the U.S. and helped to account for the boom in Canadian exports during the 1920s. Another part established American branch plants in Canada, allowing businesses to beat the domestic tariff and take advantage of trade preferences given to Canada by Great Britain and British Empire countries. Every leading car producer, for example, was a satellite of an American firm. Automobiles were among Canada's leading exports and a high percentage of them went to the empire. Conversations with American entrepreneurs demonstrated that they felt almost completely at home in Canada, regarding it as only a "slightly peculiar" northwards extension of their own domestic market. President Warren G. Harding, the first of his kind to visit Canada while in office, told a Vancouver audience in 1923 that U.S. investors accounted for "a huge sum of money and I have no doubt [it] is employed safely for us and helpfully for you."

Most Canadians liked what they saw. W.C. Clark, the dominant figure in the Department of Finance in the 1930s and 1940s, pointed out that the influx of capital from the United States "has transformed our whole economy—opened up many of our waste places, reshaped much of our industrial fabric, conditioned our standard of living, and affected to an important degree the whole tempo of our national life." And, after all, Canadians invested in the United States too, more per capita than Americans in Canada. The cash nexus, "the most extraordinary example in world history of the financial interrelationship of two countries," was the tie that bound Canada and the United States so closely together, and in ways that went far beyond the economic. This was good for both countries, despite the dangers and difficulties; the bonds of capital were likely to contribute "to a better mutual understanding and a closer fellowship between the two countries," Clark predicted.

Some Canadian business professionals and a few politicians expressed disquiet about the implications of U.S. investment, which did not substantially diminish with the Depression. But the majority view was one of confidence. The banks, railways, buses, airways, newspapers, and radio remained Canadian controlled, and the key sectors of the staple export trade, with the exception of pulp and paper and base metals, were almost entirely in Canadian hands. Any foreign company, the *Financial Post* editorialized in 1930, "establishing a permanent branch in Canada to give good service at a fair price is a Canadian institution. As a country with nearly two billions of dollars invested abroad, with a million native-born Canadians living outside our borders, with a national heritage larger than we can ourselves quickly and fully develop, we should be economically broadminded. Most Canadians are."

THE MOVEMENT OF PEOPLES

Yet Canada and the United States were rivals too. Mackenzie King's campaign for a more independent Canadian foreign policy can be partially explained by his government's desire to present a country that was just as free, peaceful, and secure as the United States to potential immigrants and investors. Immigration, indeed, became a major issue in the 1920s, although not because of a competition to import the best and brightest of Europe. Instead the worry was that Canadian citizens, well established and often well educated, were being driven or seduced southwards in large numbers. W.A. Irwin wrote in *Maclean's* magazine that Ottawa had spent thirteen million dollars from 1921 to 1926 to bring 667 349 immigrants into the country, but that 630 016 Canadians had emigrated to the U.S. during those same years. Irwin's assumption, and that of many leading commentators, was that "strangers" were invading the land and displacing "good" Canadians of upright character and long-standing residence in the dominion. Why bother, then, to spend time and money on a search for immigrants, expecially of the non-British, non-French variety which made up an increasing proportion of the Canadian population? It was time worse than wasted.

The reality was more complicated. There were certainly some Canadians dislodged for one reason or another by the recently arrived, just as there were immigrants who, once safely in Canada, made their way to the United States as soon as possible by fair means or foul. More tellingly, however, the United States economy had expanded rapidly after the First World War, while Canada's remained depressed until 1923. Needing labour, America drew on the young, urban population of Canada. The trend continued through the 1920s, even after the recovery of the global and national economies, and was no doubt aided by the size and dynamism of the United States and the admission of persons born in Canada to the U.S. as non-quota immigrants. The journalist J.W. Dafoe told the story of a young teacher, "who was extremely active in saving Canada and the British Empire from the traitorous conspiracies, American-inspired, which he saw all about him. One day we missed him; and upon inquiry it was found that, having been offered a better post in the United States, he had, practically without a moment's consideration, left Canada and the Empire to their fate. His case was that of tens of thousands of others." "We were taught," wrote that famous Canadian export, John Kenneth Galbraith, in his evocative memoirs of a boyhood in southwestern Ontario, "that Canadian patriotism should not withstand anything more than a $5-a-month differential. Anything more than that, and you went to Detroit."

Movement was not all one way. In 1929, Canada's biggest postwar immigration year, 30 000 of the 165 000 newcomers were from the United States. Overall, it is true, Americans were coming to live in Canada in fewer numbers than during earlier decades—the country's U.S.-born population actually diminished during the 1920s—but there were still 344 574 permanent American-born residents in Canada in 1931. Taking into account the American workers, tourists, and other travellers who were also to be found in Canada on a given day, one out of every ten people whom a Canadian was likely to meet would be from the United States. As one contemporary study put it, "The influence is ubiquitous; it renews itself daily; it embraces all classes."

The army of Canadians in the United States, again including workers and visitors, was immense. The dominion statistician estimated that "if we count all of Canadian stock, perhaps a third of us are south of the line." A Canadian paid a visit to the U.S. six or seven times as often as an American did to Canada, although Canadians were less likely to set down permanent roots in the United States than Americans were in Canada. Surprisingly, the Canadian-born element of the U.S. population only grew from 1 124 925 to 1 286 389 in the 1920s. The number might reflect the fact that some Canadians returned home as the North American economy crashed at the end of the decade; we know that almost 100 000 came back between 1930 and 1936. The Depression certainly brought emigration to the U.S. almost to a standstill, sadly restricting, as Dafoe said, "a Canadian industry—the equipping of young men in our universities for opportunities in the United States." In addition, it brought to an end "the old easy relationship along the frontier by which people could live in one country and work in another." The impact on the border towns and cities of Canada was catastrophic.

THE DEFENCE OF MASS CULTURE

Canadians were at a natural disadvantage in the arena of mass culture. In the face of the sheer size, proximity, and allure of the American marketplace, English- and French-Canadian nationalists alike worried about the invasion of materialistic and low-minded Americanism. By 1926, fifty million American magazines were bought annually in Canada, with *Ladies' Home Journal* (circulation 152 011) and *Saturday Evening Post* (128 574) leading the parade. The main Canadian national periodicals drew a much smaller readership than their southern competitors: *Maclean's* (82 013), *Canadian Home Journal* (68 054), and *Saturday Night* (30 858). In fact, eight magazines were imported from the United States for every one printed in Canada. Canadian publishers sought protection from what they labelled unfair competition, and asserted that they were as entitled to it as the manufacturers of lamps and lingerie. They also suggested that the materials flowing into Canada were full of smut; Canadians needed to be protected against immoral American influences. Indeed, the nation itself needed protection. As the editor of *Saturday Night* wrote, "Without the slightest notion of flag-waving or sloppy patriotism, it must be apparent that if we depend on these United States centers for our reading matter we might as well move our government to Washington, for under such conditions it will go there in the end. The press is a stronger cohesive agent than Parliament."

In 1928, publishers were able to gain a very substantial rebate on the tariff paid for certain paper imports. The circulation of Canadian magazines immediately rose significantly. Then, in 1931, came a much greater victory. Ottawa began to tax imported periodicals, resulting in a sharp decline in American magazine sales and big advances for Canadian products. "The imposition of tariffs against imported magazines," historian Mary Vipond states, "was an unprecedented act. Never before had a Canadian government taken upon itself to help a cultural industry by measures designed to discourage the import of foreign products." These tariffs, which inevitably encouraged U.S. publishing firms to establish branch plants in Canada, were ended by the Liberals after their return to power in 1935. Magazine imports from the United States quickly doubled.

To protect or not to protect? Both sides of the debate were moved, not surprisingly, by self-interest. Vipond has discovered that the principal allies of the magazine publishers were other members of the business community who supplied products to the industry or wished to curtail the invasion of advertising for goods that competed with their own. Yet the issue had other ingredients. Opponents of protection believed that

Canada's future lay with North America and the free, open, progressive values they associated with the United States. A tariff against ideas would be narrow and parochial, not to say unfair to all those accustomed to cheap literature from a wide variety of sources. Advocates of protection on the other hand emphasized Canadian distinctiveness, and had a strong distaste for and fear of the American way of life.

United States radio programming, for Canadian nationalists, was a greater menace than magazines. It had a more immediate, visceral impact; and it was omnipresent, because radio frequencies knew no frontiers. "The radio audience of North America is North American," noted Graham Spry of the Canadian Radio League, "but the performance is American; the audience listens not to North America, but to the United States." All of the populated areas of the country were in range of powerful U.S. transmitters, which broadcast such popular shows as "Amos 'n Andy," but fewer Canadians could pick up the always much punier stations operating in their own country. A west coast reader of *Maclean's* complained, "We can tune in regularly to stations in Seattle, Oakland, San Francisco, Cincinnati, St. Louis, Denver, etc., but consider it an achievement to get a station at Vancouver, Victoria, Calgary or Edmonton." Canadian National Railways, wanting entertainment for long-distance travellers, had developed a radio network—Moncton, Ottawa, Montreal, Toronto, and Vancouver—but it could provide only three hours of national programming a week by 1929. By then the great American network giants NBC and CBS were in full cry and attracting large Canadian urban stations like Toronto's CFRB into their stable.

Spry and his Radio League put the problem starkly. It was either the State or the United States. Given the choice, the government was for the State. The result was the 1932 Canadian Radio Broadcasting Act, which aimed for a publicly owned and controlled national network under the auspices of the Canadian Radio Broadcasting Commission. The work went slowly, and four years later a new act created the Canadian Broadcasting Corporation, a more effective instrument whose programming reached 76 percent of the population by 1937. Spry explained the wellsprings of his lobby movement in traditional Canadian terms. "The positive aspect of the national motive was the use of broadcasting for the development of Canadian national unity, and the negative aspect was the apprehension of American influences upon Canadian nationality, particularly as it concerned public opinion."

The movies were another American-dominated medium of mass communication coming into great prominence. There had been a spate of activity in Canada during and immediately after the First World War but the production of films soon declined and the home grown Allen Theatre chain was taken over in 1923 by Famous Players, as Hollywood asserted control over distribution and exhibition in the North American film industry. *Carry on Sergeant!*, a drama about the Canadian experience in the Great War, was the one major feature film made in the country during the late 1920s. It won critical acclaim, but died at the box office. In the 1930s Hollywood was encouraged by Ottawa to make "quickie" productions in Canada in order to slip them into British theatres, which were required to show a set quota of Commonwealth films. This practice was such a blatant abuse that Great Britain ended it in 1938. Without a real commercial industry to call their own, Canadians had to be content for most of the interwar years with hilarious distortions of their life and history in countless Hollywood films, and with the knowledge that "America's sweetheart," Mary Pickford, and three of the first four Oscar recipients for best actress, Pickford, Norma Shearer, and Marie Dressler, were born in Canada. American films and the values that went with them were not, of course, swallowed whole. One study of Canadian attitudes carried out in the mid-1930s noted the many protests against U.S. motion pictures, some on moral, some on cultural, and some on patriotic grounds. Far from popularizing and advertising the United States, films could arouse "a dislike of American life and a contempt for American civilization." That happened in the U.S. as well, the study suggested sardonically, but the difference was "that in Canada it can take the form of nationalist protest and give comfort to the sense of moral or even cultural superiority."

At the end of the interwar years, there were again small signs of life in the Canadian film industry, not least the formation of the National Film Board in 1939 under John Grierson. But a battle in which only scattered resources and a tiny population could be mustered would always be against the odds.

AUTOMOBILES: AN EXPERIMENT IN "CANADIAN CONTENT"

High tariffs were a fact of life on both sides of the border. Nowhere was the sting of Canadian–American competition felt more deeply by ordinary North Americans: tariffs directly and visibly affected jobs, prices, and business opportunities. Canadian consumers knew, for example, that they paid substantially more for automobiles than Americans did.

U.S. farmers resented imports of cheap Canadian food and demanded that they be penalized or excluded. The promise to nurture and shield domestic producers was a staple of every major North American election campaign of the period. During the Depression and even before, the tariff was also seen as a diplomatic weapon, a tool to be used in negotiation, or a means to force the recalcitrant to the bargaining table.

Yet Canadian–American trade boomed in the 1920s despite the tariff. By decade's end, the dominion received $847 million in imports from the U.S., 67.9 percent of the Canadian total. In 1930 Canada sent 46 percent of its exports—some $515 million—to the U.S. From the mid-1920s Great Britain was no longer Canada's leading market.

Mackenzie King cautiously balanced protectionist and lower-tariff sentiments in his caucus, in Parliament, and in the country. Washington had increased tariffs significantly in the early 1920s but King was not tempted to retaliate. Indeed, duties were lowered on certain products like sugar, textiles, and farm implements. For the most part, however, the Liberals kept things as they had been for many years. They talked freer trade but were generally protectionist, although a bit less so than their Conservative cousins.

The prime minister's balancing act was evident in the government's 1926 decision to slash the tariff on U.S. car imports from 35 to 20 percent on all products valued at not more than $1200—the vast majority of imports—and from 35 to 27.5 percent on luxury automobiles. The tariff on parts imports remained the same, but the minister of finance introduced a new wrinkle. In Canada cars were produced from materials and parts that could either be imported or made in Canada. Imported parts were subject to duty, but if at least 50 percent of the car's value—including the work done in the assembly plant—resulted from its being produced in Canada, the minister announced, a company could claim a 25 percent rebate on all duties it had paid on materials and parts. As the economic historian Tom Traves has commented, "these regulations marked the first time that made-in-Canada content requirements had been attached to the tariff schedule."

Automobiles had in fact become one of Canada's leading industries. There were more private cars in Canada than in any other country except the U.S. itself. King, ever the astute politician, steered a course between consumer pressures for lower automobile prices and economic nationalism, which demanded continuing protection. Traves points out that during the 1920s "nationalist sentiment rose sharply. Organizations such as the Canadian Manufacturers' Association supported and encouraged this tendency by massive advertising campaigns urging consumers to purchase Canadian-built products in order to build up the country's manufacturing base. The drawback provision of the new schedule finally provided a mechanism whereby nationalist sentiments could be translated into action." A British Columbia businessman commended the government for this reform, saying that it all came down to a question of whether "American manufacturers who have no interest in the country except profits for themselves" would be allowed to exploit Canada.

The Canadian car manufacturers directly affected by the changes could not have disagreed more, claiming that it was now less expensive to import a finished U.S. car than to assemble or manufacture an automobile in Canada. The government modified its plan slightly to appease industry executives who threatened—unconvincingly—that auto companies would close down altogether. But the essence remained, with mixed results for auto firms and Canadian consumers. Sales of Canadian-made cars doubled in the late 1920s, and so too did the use of Canadian parts, as auto-makers moved rapidly towards meeting the content incentives. Nevertheless, U.S. imports also increased dramatically, and a substantial part of the capacity of Canadian plants was going unused. Further representations from U.S. branch plants in Canada were inevitable. But they were unsuccessful until the Depression took hold and a new government came to power. The Conservatives agreed in 1931 to fight off American competition in the time-honoured way, with tariffs even higher than those of the mid-1920s.

SMOOT-HAWLEY AND THE SEAWAY

All through the 1920s successive U.S. Republican governments, backed by strong contingents of the same stripe in Congress, stood foursquare for high tariffs. That was the philosophy and policy of presidents Warren Harding and Calvin Coolidge, and it was Herbert Hoover's pledge to the people of the United States during the election campaign of 1928. Hoover's particular promise was to the farmers, who had suffered badly over many years despite the 1922 Fordney-McCumber tariff designed especially for them.

The American minister to Ottawa, William Phillips, tried to alert Hoover on the day before his inauguration as president that Canadians had very harsh feelings against higher tariffs and that retaliation would be the likely response. The president apparently knew something of the country, having presided over a major export thrust into Canada as secretary of commerce under Harding and Coolidge. Yet, he insisted, "there is no practical force in the contention that we cannot have a protective tariff and a growing foreign trade." Hoover diverted the U.S. minister to Congress, where he met members of the key House of Representatives Ways and Means Committee. Phillips warned the politicians in the strongest terms not to treat Canada lightly. But he noted puzzlement. Where and what was Canada? Phillips called for an atlas, and showed members the geography of their northern neighbour. Polite thanks were issued, but no minds were changed. The minister was sent on his way with the certain knowledge that exports were the last thing on the Congressional mind. The legislators wanted only to *prevent* imports, and they were perfectly frank and unashamed about it.

A specially convened session of the U.S. Congress took the matter in hand, and their efforts resulted in a ratcheting up of the tariff across the board until it stood at unprecedented heights. Despite protests from a pack of over a thousand leading economists, President Hoover did not have the imagination or courage to reject the bill, even though it went much further than he had asked or wanted. The Smoot-Hawley Tariff Act of 1930 was, according to one American historian, a virtual declaration of economic war. While this vastly exaggerates the importance of the act, it was nonetheless deeply unpopular with the world at large. Imports were cut drastically, but so too were exports as country after country slipped into depression, generally establishing their own barriers. From 1929 to 1933, U.S. exports to Canada plummeted from $868 million to $232 million; American shipments to other major trading partners fell in roughly similar proportions. The farmer, the original object of Smoot-Hawley, was even worse off than before.

While the edifying spectacle of the Smoot-Hawley process was underway, the Canadian government watched public opinion, which had initially been pro-Hoover, harden in favour of retaliation. Its own actions, however, were restrained. King did hint to the president that the development of a St. Lawrence seaway might be able to proceed if the U.S. did not take strong tariff measures against Canada. The project had been pushed hard by the Americans ever since 1919 and was devoutly desired by U.S. farmers. Hoover himself had been interested in the idea since his commerce department days, when he had headed the St. Lawrence Commission.

The creation of a major international water highway had been a dream in North America since the seventeenth century, but a dream it remained because the river's many natural obstacles were the least of the seaway promoters' problems. C.P. Stacey explains:

The progress of the great idea was marked by a variety of conflicts of interests such as few projects have had to contend with. The fact that the boundary settlement at the end of the American Revolution made the St. Lawrence an international river and the Great Lakes an international boundary rendered canalization a matter of foreign policy. But it was not just a question of reconciling two national points of view. On each side of the border, with the passage of time, regional and local and special interests might take sides for or against the plan. Many communities in the American Middle West were strongly for it; but inevitably New York and other Atlantic ports saw it as a menace. In both countries the railways disliked it, seeing it as a potential dangerous competitor. Local governments, state and provincial, had strong views that had to be taken into account. And the project had great possibilities for the generation of electric power as well as for the improvement of navigation, and the interests of power and navigation were not the same. And all these rivalries affected the political balance in both countries. *(Canada and the Age of Conflict*, vol. 2, 108).

The political balance in King's Canada, particularly in the province of Quebec, weighed against the seaway, and the prime minister was correspondingly wary. When Hoover appeared to show some interest in a clause in the Tariff Act exempting Canada from Smoot-Hawley in return for a bargain on the St. Lawrence project, King slammed the door in his face. Linkage, as we now call it, was out of the question: "A proposal of this kind would be interpreted as a threat or bargaining lever on the part of the United States to force Canada into a policy which it would not otherwise accept." Since it had been the prime minister who had raised the matter in the first place, Hoover was no doubt mystified. Perhaps King balked at anything other than a secret agreement. Perhaps he had simply been practising the tactics of delay and diversion, as he was inclined to do.

HIGH TARIFF DIPLOMACY

The American journalist Drew Pearson deplored the Hoover administration's use of "high tariff diplomacy" against Canada, but on the other side of the fence King was deciding to indulge in a mild version of his own. Even before seeing Smoot-Hawley in its absolutely final form, the Liberals prepared for an election with a budget that carried a moderate but unmistakable message. The prime minister had already told the Americans that he would nudge closer to Britain if the U.S. closed in on itself. The 1930 Dunning Budget, named for the minister of finance, unilaterally enlarged the list of preferences given to trade from the United Kingdom while hiking tariffs against imports from the U.S. The American Legation in Ottawa estimated the damage to the United States at $175 million, especially to iron and steel companies and fruit and vegetable farmers. In addition, Dunning let it be known that Canada was prepared if necessary to exchange misery with the Americans by introducing a "countervailing duty" on a small number of items, mostly agricultural. The government would raise duties to precisely the levels brought about by any outside increases.

The Liberals, it is clear in retrospect, had not done nearly enough to satisfy the public. King's middle way had worked in the past, but the fear and hostility of Canadians was keeping pace with the disastrous downturn in employment and wheat sales and the turning inwards of the United States. King had preached lower tariffs for so long that the protectionism of the Dunning Budget seemed too little, too late. Critics could say that the prime minister had gone through "nine years of wasted effort" before betraying the cause of freer trade. "It did not take Judas that long."

The Conservatives faced no such internal contradictions. They had always sworn to protect, protect, protect. Now that seemed the right policy, and along with it they had a leader who seemed right for the times. R.B. Bennett was the wealthy and well-fed champion of the status quo but he conveyed an impression of dynamism, movement, and change. "Listen," he boomed, "you agriculturist from the West, and all the other parts of Canada. You have been taught to applaud free trade. Tell me where did free trade ever fight for you? You say our tariffs are only for the manufacturers. I will make them fight for you as well. I will use them to blast a way into the markets that have been closed to you."

Bennett dispatched Mackenzie King from power in the election of 1930, winning a large majority and support in every part of the country. A commentator who knew and observed both prime ministers over many years recalled that King and Bennett were "able, obsessive, hardworking, religious men. Both were devoted to their mothers, and neither ever married. Both were lonely men, but Bennett at least was loved by his intimates." While King was "suave, cunning, indirect, pedestrian in manner and speech, Bennett was direct and forceful; he was an orator who used words as weapons. He was a dictator in his cabinet. His

R.B. Bennett, the faithful worshipper, 1932. (Winnipeg Free Press)

aggression was close to the surface and was revealed in speech and mannerisms, down to his unsmiling thrusting handshake at receptions, propelling his guests forward." As another acquaintance put it, "R.B. is partially educated, but wholly uncivilized."

Bennett immediately put his aggressiveness on display. In 1930 and again in 1931 he drove the tariff up in revolutionary style, and abrasively recommended that Great Britain do likewise, though it was essentially a free trading country.

In 1932, Bennett convened an imperial economic conference in Ottawa, which put into place the Ottawa Agreements. These were a generalized system of empire preferences and discrimination against foreign goods. The Americans were bound to be livid, even though the agreements amounted to nowhere near an imperial *Zollverein*. The United States, moreover, had started the world's gallop towards protectionism. The anti-Smoot-Hawley group of U.S. economists had predicted that other nations would follow suit, and they were right.

R.B. BENNETT AND AN EFFORT AT
RAPPROCHEMENT

Bennett always insisted that he was not anti-American. His passion was for Great Britain, however, and he ended his life as Viscount Bennett, a member of the British House of Lords. As prime minister, Bennett regarded himself as a neophyte in international affairs, and he looked to the British for guidance. There lay experience and even-handed wisdom. The United States, by contrast, Bennett judged irresponsible and untrustworthy. "My experience leads me to believe that, while the individual American leaves nothing to be desired, when you come to international politics he does not seem to have either the inclination or the desire that his country should pull its load." America's rejection of the League of Nations was completely in character and the "dead hand" of the country's first president, George Washington, an isolationist who had wanted to avoid the world's entanglements, still ruled in the United States. After the Japanese invasion of Manchuria in the fall of 1931, Bennett was drawn to the U.K.'s moderate effort to find a basis for conciliation under the auspices of the League, while his top counsellors were more inclined to the tougher rhetoric of the U.S. This made for some confusion—and high comedy—in the Canadian foreign policy of the time, yet in the final analysis, neither the United States nor the League had the will to face down the Japanese. The world was worse off for that.

Bennett was never uninterested in a rapprochement with the United States. Even at the height of ill feeling over Smoot-Hawley, he talked about a Canadian–American agreement on trade as one of the government's policy options—though admittedly one of the few. Bennett was an intelligent man, and he understood only too well the importance of the U.S. As he once said to Arthur Meighen, "Give me the control of the tariff policy of the United States for a period of ten years and I can do more for the welfare of Canada than I could do for it as Prime Minister." In 1931 he visited Hoover at the White House to discuss the St. Lawrence waterway and the tariff. Bennett did his best, it is true, not to be noticed, going so far as to refuse to have his picture taken with the unpopular president, but he followed up his Washington trip by naming his closest adviser, William D. Herridge, as minister to the United States.

Herridge was a war hero, lawyer, businessman, vocal nationalist, former confidant of Mackenzie King, and the inheritor of a great deal of money from his first wife, who had belonged to the prominent Booth family of Ottawa. He had turned up rather unexpectedly at Bennett's side in the 1930 election campaign, and they made a potent political partnership. It was Herridge who wrote the stirring "Canada First" speeches that helped rocket Bennett to power. And it was Herridge, not the senior people from the Department of External Affairs, who accompanied the prime minister to London and Washington in 1930–31. His appointment to the U.S. was commented upon unfavourably by many journalists, who called Herridge "the man who enlisted in the Conservative party as a Field Marshal," but influential Conservatives were happier to see him in the American capital than too near to them and Bennett in Ottawa. The British high commissioner commented

> Personally I find Major Herridge a man of culture and considerable charm, handicapped by a somewhat neurotic psychology. He is a prey to moods, during which he has been in the habit of denying his company to his best friends for several weeks on end, showing great ingenuity in preventing them from making contact with him by telephone or otherwise. Such tendencies would seem rather serious drawbacks in view of the heavy social demands of diplomatic life, but on the other hand, when Major Herridge entertains he does so with excellent taste; he knows how to make himself very pleasant to his guests; and is a ready conversationalist.

Shortly after presenting his credentials in Washington, the new minister sailed off to Europe with his new bride, who just happened to be the prime minister's sister. If there was ever any doubt about Herridge's influence, it ended there, even though his relationship with Bennett was frequently strained beneath the surface because the fiery diplomat tended to forget just which one of them was the prime minister.

Herridge's term in Washington was difficult at first. He was in the shadow of the previous minister, Vincent Massey, who had been effective and at ease in public speaking and grandiose entertainment, two areas in which Herridge felt insecure. But he was a powerful if often headstrong representative of Canadian interests: he forged links with the people who counted, and they knew that he had the most important of diplomatic credentials, access to the prime minister. Some of his most impressive contacts were with the "New Dealers" of the Roosevelt administration. He was instrumental near the end of Bennett's tenure in convincing his brother-in-law to embrace a Canadian version of the New Deal, Roosevelt's program of social and economic reform through a strong government presence. Herridge wanted to marry that with a free trade system in North America, beginning with natural products. He had come to believe that the North American continent was, in the final analysis, an economic unit, and he regretted that national interests apparently compelled an arbitrary division into two warring sides. Lower tariffs and economic planning were to be essential elements in Herridge's new Tory nationalism.

Herridge played a major role in the St. Lawrence Seaway diplomacy of the period. The seaway had been a plank in Bennett's election platform in 1930, as it had been in King's, and like his predecesssor the Conservative procrastinated at first. Hoover put on the pressure, apparently to the extent of arranging for a piece of academic bribery, an honorary Harvard degree for Bennett. The St. Lawrence Deep Waterway Treaty was signed in 1932, providing for the shared construction of a route "not less than twenty-seven feet in depth, for navigation from the interior of the Continent of North America through the Great Lakes and the St. Lawrence River to the sea, with the development of the water-power incidental thereto." The treaty became ensnared in politics, however, and in the competition between regions and between various interests that had long plagued the project. It failed to get the necessary votes for ratification by the U.S. Senate, and there would not be another agreement for a decade.

The seaway had been Hoover's pet project. His "whole attitude towards Canadian affairs hinges upon it," wrote the minister in Ottawa. But there were no other components in Hoover's "attitude." Richard Kottman, the American historian who has studied this period most closely, concludes that "the thirty-first President of the United States cared little about relations with Canada, was largely indifferent to Canadian interests, particularly the economic requirements of the dominion, and like most of his countrymen took Canadian friendship for granted." Kottman illustrates Hoover's lack of commitment to Canada by describing his appointment of two Republican Party war horses with few qualifications as his representatives to Ottawa.

Hanford MacNider, the minister from 1930 to 1932, was at least a likeable and energetic campaigner for American causes such as the seaway—and he could claim a Canadian grandfather. N.W. MacChesney, the next in line for the Canadian plum, had absolutely no connection with or knowledge of Canada. The State Department had to recommend that he rush to the bookstore for a dose of Canadian content. But even if he did his homework, this labour came to naught. Noting that the president who had nominated him was in his last weeks of power, the Senate refused to confirm MacChesney. MacNider's successor and many after him would be named by the new president, Franklin Delano Roosevelt.

Roosevelt had more interest in Canada. He quickly signalled it by inviting Bennett to Washington in April 1933. The president and the prime minister issued a statement agreeing "to begin a search for means to increase the exchange of commodities between our two countries." During Bennett's stay, however, the White House dog bit him, and that turned out to be prophetic. Roosevelt became preoccupied with domestic concerns and the administration did not build its very cumbersome machinery for reciprocal trade agreements until 1934. There were also delays on the Canadian side. It was late in August 1935 when actual negotiations for a Canadian–American commercial accord began, and Bennett was by then on the verge of calling a general election because his five-year term was soon to expire. Much preliminary work had already been done, but it was too late to put all the pieces of an agreement together, especially when there were fundamental differences on several of the Canadian demands for concessions.

An aristocratic twosome: R.B. Bennett and Franklin D. Roosevelt, Washington, 1933. (National Archives of Canda/PA 145058)

Bennett was to some extent the victim of his own economic nationalism. American officials had difficulty believing that he was sincere and reliable, and they were determined not to let it be said that Bennett's punitive tariff regime had brought them to their knees and forced an agreement. Bennett and Herridge's bold tactics, trying to protect their position with Canadians and publicly prod the U.S. into action, probably did not help either. Roosevelt could afford not to hurry. He knew that the Depression had left the Canadian government and its political hopes in shreds. The next crowd that came to power in Ottawa would almost certainly be more accommodating.

CHAPTER four

THE BEST OF NEIGHBOURS

1 9 3 5 — 1 9 3 9

On 18 August 1938, the prime minister of Canada and the president of the United States officially opened the Thousand Islands International Bridge, a magnificent iron sculpture spanning the St. Lawrence River from Ivy Lea, Ontario, to Collins Landing, New York. William Lyon Mackenzie King and Franklin Delano Roosevelt extracted all they could from the symbolism of the moment. Germany, Italy, and Japan were on the march, building armaments and enmities. How much better it was, King said, to know how to build bridges. Despite their many cultural and racial similarities to Europeans, the peoples of Canada and the United States had not chosen to solve their problems and quarrels by force or bluster. Coming through the turbulence and conflict of their early relationship, North Americans had discovered better methods to secure and maintain stability, and had devised techniques of conciliation like the International Joint Commission. In Roosevelt's homey language, Canadians and Americans needed only two simple words at their frontier, "Pass, friend." It was time for the world to take notice of this example before it was too late.

Earlier that day Roosevelt had been in nearby Kingston, Ontario, to accept an honorary Doctor of Laws degree from Queen's University. He warned a huge crowd that war was in the air: not war in North America, but war abroad from which North America would not be immune. Calling for solidarity to preserve their mutual freedoms, he gave a pledge that acknowledged Canada's British history while underlining its American geography: "The Dominion of Canada is part of the sisterhood of the British Empire. I give to you assurance that the people of the United States will not stand idly by if domination of Canadian soil is threatened by any other empire." Those words, as famous as any in the history of Canadian–American relations, had been written by the president himself as he travelled by train from Washington to Kingston.

Mackenzie King, on the platform with Roosevelt at the Queen's stadium, instantly recognized the importance of what he had heard. According to the jottings in his notebook, he told Roosevelt that he had "dropped a bomb." Canadian, American, and British newspapers alike agreed, calling the speech "one of the utterances that change the face of things." In the view of the British newspaper, the London *Daily Telegraph*, Roosevelt was stating his personal belief that "in matters of peace or war there can be no separation between the two great democracies of the American continent." The *New York Times* added that the president had promised "perpetual vigilance over the Dominion against foreign aggression." More pointed was the comment in the Toronto *Globe*: the Monroe Doctrine had come to Canada.

A response was called for if Canada were not simply to accept the role of a helpless neighbour. King explicitly gave that in Woodbridge, near Toronto, two days later. Canadians were grateful for Roosevelt's statement of support, he claimed, but they were bound to feel that it only added to their obligations "for maintaining Canadian soil as a homeland for free men in the western hemisphere." In particular, their responsibility was to expend enough effort to keep the country as safe from attack or possible invasion "as we can reasonably be expected to make it," and to prevent an enemy from pursuing its way across Canadian territory to the United States. Canada had already slowly begun to improve its defences, especially on the two coasts. Roosevelt, King knew, was saying that Canada had better do more.

The years between the two world wars were, if the speeches of public figures like Roosevelt and King are to be believed, an age of good neighbourhood, entirely removed from the long decades of mistrust and suspicion. There is much in this. Canadians and Americans were co-operating, exchanging goods and people and ideas as never before and to the general benefit of both. But neighbours can be selfish and irksome. They are apt to have expectations and make demands. Behind the lofty rhetoric of Roosevelt's Kingston speech, as Canadian politicians and officials well understood, lay a tough assertion of self-interest and an urgent request for action. Neighbourhood was no guarantee of equality or genuine friendship.

MACKENZIE KING, AGAIN

Mackenzie King had cruised back to power in the October 1935 federal election. One hundred and seventy-eight out of 245 seats were his. The Liberals were dominant everywhere except Alberta and British Columbia, and even there they had a presence. King was aware of the problems that too many members of parliament and a feeble opposition could cause—there were now many friends to satisfy and perhaps too few enemies to keep the party in fighting trim—but his current situation was infinitely preferable to the tight political corners of the 1920s. Promising an end to government by the fist of the "pugilist" Bennett and a return to the healing hand of the physician, King told an American official that he was "very much opposed to the dramatic way of doing public business that the former Prime Minister of Canada had followed. . . . I was desirous to have people realize that government was concerned with thought more than with display." King's critics replied that such rhetoric was simply a prescription for inaction. He would never do anything unpopular unless compelled to.

Despite his reputation, King was determined to take forceful measures. His aim from the first moment was economic recovery through freer trade. King had told voters in the 1935 campaign that the Depression "was nothing more or less than absence of trade; and I may state the reverse as being equally true, that trade—plenty of trade—means the end of depression." Within two years King and his Liberal party, advocates of lower tariffs since the days of John A. Macdonald, had concluded trade agreements with the United States, Great Britain, and Germany, and ended Bennett's embargo against imports from the Soviet Union.

King put particular and immediate emphasis on the improvement of Canadian–American ties. His only hard-edged election promise in 1935 had been a trade agreement with the United States, and on his first day in power, Canadian Thanksgiving, he took the highly unusual step of calling upon the American diplomatic representative in Ottawa. An embarrassed Norman Armour, who "felt it was for me to come to see him," returned the favour the next day. King made it clear in the course of these two wordy encounters that he wished Canada and the United States to present a united front to the world. It had always been his policy "to seize every occasion possible to show Canada's solidarity with the United States on matters affecting their mutual interest and well-being."

King explained to Armour that together Canada and the United States must do something to put an end to economic nationalism, which led not simply to isolation and ruination at home but also to bitterness and poisonous relations between the countries of the world. The answer lay in striking down tariffs, in the rapid movement of goods, and in breaking with the protectionist "beggar-thy-neighbour" policies of the earlier 1930s. If other nations could see two important countries iron out their trading difficulties, standing ready to face the international situation together, that would be a powerful example of and incentive for change. The New World could show the Old how to practise the creative art of peace rather than the destructive craft of war—and this at a time when Japan and Germany had left the League of Nations and Italy was attacking Ethiopia.

PEACE, POLITICS, AND PROSPERITY: THE 1935 TRADE AGREEMENT

King did not then know the state of the Canadian–American trade talks that had been suspended at the end of Bennett's tenure. Even so, he told the American minister that he wanted to visit President Roosevelt in Washington in order to strike a bargain immediately. The prime minister knew that the pressures of the 1936 presidential and congressional elections, against compromise or hasty action or action at all, would soon become very nearly irresistible. A great believer in symbols, King concocted the idea that an announcement on 11 November, Armistice Day, would add weight to his argument that North America had a peaceful lesson to teach a warring world.

They would have to move fast. King had promised the electorate a trade agreement in ninety days, but Armistice Day was little more than two weeks away. Canadian negotiators scurried to the American capital, and the prime minister himself arrived on the famous train, the Washingtonian, on 7 November. He first visited American Secretary of State Cordell Hull, who shared King's view that armies would cross international boundaries if trade could not. A sympathetic Roosevelt was next, and the two leaders, meeting for the first time as the heads of their respective governments, quickly got down to what they knew best: the realities and problems of domestic politics.

There were certain things that could not be done. Roosevelt, for example, was reluctant to touch the tariff on potato imports. As he told his aides, "I cannot approve any reduction in the tariff on them. . . . I know my potatoes!" Roosevelt meant that he knew his potato-producing regions, Maine in particular. Unfortunately, Roosevelt told King, Maine was the first state to vote in a presidential contest, and there was a saying in American politics, "as Maine goes, so goes the United States." The president did agree to take a risk on potatoes used strictly for seeding, but those grown to be eaten were beyond negotiation.

The two leaders found enough common ground to lead the way to an exchange of concessions. The officials had done the hard work at the mundane level of frozen blueberries, ice skates, and pipe organs, and the politicians now injected the political will. Roosevelt took up the idea of an Armistice Day announcement, asking his speech writer to add a paragraph on the trade agreement to his Arlington Cemetery speech scheduled for that day. The power of good example, he said on 11 November, "surpasses preachments; it excels good resolutions; it is far better than agreements unfulfilled." For his part, King enthused in his stilted prose: "What possible tribute to the date could be greater than that the cause . . . [of] international good-will, as against international hate, should receive an enduring monument."

There was one last obstacle. Even as Roosevelt was about to depart for Arlington, his treasury secretary, Henry Morgenthau, asked for a delay, questioning the proposed 50 percent reduction in the tariff on whisky. The treasury had quite different plans for Canadian liquor manufacturers, who had poured the demon alcohol illegally into the United States throughout the prohibition era. Just as scandalously from the bureaucratic point of view, in doing so they had contributed no tariffs or taxes. Canadian companies would have to pay $100 million in penalties, the treasury said, or risk the prospect of seeing their booze banished entirely from the United States. Either of these alternatives would naturally be very much to the taste of the American distillers, who did not yet have properly aged liquors ready for the market and were therefore not in a competitive position. Roosevelt was able to overcome Morgenthau's objection, and he proceeded to Arlington with the secretary's agreement that the accord could go ahead. The treasury complained vigorously on the matter well into the next year, so much so that the Canadian government began to threaten denunciation of the entire trade agreement. In May 1936, after a long-distance telephone conversation with King, the president finally ordered Morgenthau and his department to accept a payment from Canadian firms of $3 million for their sins past. King was gushingly grateful.

Roosevelt insisted that the trade agreement ceremony take place with appropriate pomp and circumstance at the White House. King and

Cordell Hull signed their names on 15 November 1935, with Roosevelt smiling nearby and his entire Cabinet present by presidential edict. The first commercial accord between the two countries in over seventy years was not a treaty, although King twice called it that in his short speech after the signing, and it therefore did not need the consent of the United States Senate. It had been negotiated under the 1934 Reciprocal Trade Agreements Act, which gave the president of the United States the power to proclaim international trade agreements without the approval of Congress so long as certain conditions were met: no existing U.S. tariff, for example, could be cut by more than 50 percent.

In the 1935 agreement Canada conferred, for the first time, most-favoured-nation (mfn) status on the United States. That is, in addition to the cuts specified in the Canadian tariff on 180 U.S. exports, mostly manufactures, the U.S. received all the reductions in import duties that Canada had negotiated with its best foreign trading partners. "Foreign" was an important word, however, because the preferential system put in place by British Commonwealth countries at Ottawa in 1932 was considered to be a family affair. The Americans did not get the benefit of those lower rates. Imperial preference remained intact, much to the annoyance of Roosevelt, Hull, and their colleagues, who were extremely suspicious of British trading practices and feared an imperial plot to divert Canada out of North American channels.

The U.S. government agreed that it would continue to accord mfn treatment to Canada. It guaranteed easy entry to a variety of wood products, and gave tariff reductions on certain species of fish, most types of lumber, and cheddar cheese, live poultry, and maple syrup. Cattle, cream, seed potatoes, and Douglas fir imports from Canada also benefited from either reduced tariffs or quotas.

The Americans privately believed that the trade agreement was a great triumph, and for this Mackenzie King must take part of the blame or credit. As the prime minister had told U.S. minister Norman Armour in Ottawa, there were two roads open to Canada. King claimed that he wished to travel the American road, strengthening Canadian–American attachments and achieving closer political and economic relations. These were seductive words for American officials and politicians, who were inclined to see North America as a unit but knew the strength of the old imperial connection. Here was a leader, as Roosevelt's advisers told him, more inclined to play "the game." King could help them to break Canada's last ties with Britain, which had too long interfered with the natural geo-economic order of things. The trade agreement seemed to the Americans an excellent commercial bargain, but it was something much more important. It would bring Canada finally and irrevocably into the U.S. economic and political sphere of influence.

King's motives were rather different. Whatever he might have told the U.S. minister, he was British and Canadian to his core. Like many Canadians, he believed that Americans were too extreme, too zealous, and that their country was not rooted in the liberties that Britain had given to Canada. Presidents, even Roosevelt, might become dictators, and an American dictator would put an end to Canadian rights and freedoms. King, who did not have much of a sense of humour, tried to be funny on the point. Annexation would be bad for both countries, he remarked to Armour: "Certainly you have enough troubles of your own without wanting to add us to them."

In Canada itself, many already thought that King was soft on the United States. In such circles, as he himself recognized, the prime minister was called "the American." After all, he had spent much of his life in the United States: as a social worker at Jane Addams's Hull House in Chicago; as a student at Harvard and Chicago universities; and as a labour expert in the Rockefeller business empire during the First World War. Historian Donald Creighton picked up on this theme when he wrote that King was not so much a Canadian as a citizen of North America, a wholly negative politician who broke away from Britain without even trying to found a distinct and independent country. In effect, says Creighton, King prepared Canada for eventual absorption by the United States. Journalist Charles Lynch's similar opinion was that King ripped Canadians from the security of the British mother's bosom and landed them in the hard lap of the American uncle.

King did his best to avoid that criticism. He carefully pointed out that he was interested in trade and good relations with other countries, Great Britain most of all, and explained that forthcoming elections in Britain made commercial negotiations with that country difficult just then. Even so, some were bound to misunderstand or deliberately misinterpret his motives. So be it. He knew his own mind, and was confident that the majority knew it as well.

King's real objectives in seeking rapid agreement on a trade deal were a judicious combination of peace, politics, and prosperity. He was doing his bit for international goodwill by showing the world what constructive relations between friendly nations could produce. If things went wrong in the world, it would not be his fault. In addition, he was consolidating links, in the context of a devastating economic depression, with Canada's best trading partner. The United States already received 40.3 percent of Canadian exports and provided 58.1 percent of Canadian imports. And King had got something for every part of Canada: for British Columbia and for the Maritimes, the halving of U.S. lumber and timber duties, and reductions on fish; cuts in duties on livestock and farm products for the Prairies; and for Ontario and Quebec, help with lumber, cattle, dairy cows, and maple sugar. In addition, consumers across the country would gain by the downward revision of Canadian tariffs on American products, King claimed, without sacrificing any vital interest. The 1935 Canada–U.S. trade deal was less than the ministers of the previous government had demanded, but King had achieved agreement where the Conservatives had not.

It is impossible to measure exactly the economic impact of the agreement, or the one that would follow in 1938. The value of both Canadian and American exports did increase impressively after 1935. U.S. exports to Canada went from $303 million in 1935 to $487 million in 1938, while exports from Canada to the United States rose from $304 million in 1935 to $435 million in 1937 and $423 million in 1938. Tempting as it is to give the credit to the lower tariffs, there was a complex of reasons for these better numbers, not least the recovery of the two economies as they gradually emerged from the Depression. Canadian–American trade had in fact been improving since 1933. The figures for the late 1930s, even so, came nowhere near the strong performances for most of the pre-Depression years of the 1920s.

THE RISE OF CO-OPERATION

One thing was sure. Canadian–American co-operation was on the rise. James T. Shotwell, an Ontario-born academic who migrated south to Columbia University in New York City, was one of the driving forces behind a series of conferences designed to highlight the intimacy of the relationship and to improve understanding of Canada–U.S. relations in all their complexity. Shotwell initiated the first meeting in 1935 by saying that it was indicative of a new attitude and a new maturity in the relationship, and a new sense that problems ought to be dealt with on their own terms rather than on the basis of traditional grievances and prejudices.

The gathering attracted academics, entrepreneurs, public servants, lawyers, and soldiers. It dealt with tariffs, the flow of capital, radio, transportation, politics, foreign policy, education, public opinion, and, lest the delegates forget, history. There was no denial of differences and problems—quite the contrary—but J.W. Dafoe, the influential editor of the *Winnipeg Free Press*, captured the underlying spirit of optimism and co-operation: "I think Canada and the United States constitute in large measure what you might call a moral or an intellectual unity, and that in that fact we shall find the solvent for these minor difficulties. I am not sure that a few years ago one could have said that such fundamental unity existed."

Like Dafoe, Shotwell was a crusader for world peace and international co-operation, and he frequently wrote about Canadian–American relations as a superior form of the art. In his *The Heritage of Freedom: The United States and Canada in the Community of Nations* (1934), Shotwell celebrated the way in which the two countries, apart yet side by side, had evolved uniquely North American freedoms and methods of solving problems. He applied this argument on a grand scale when he and John Bartlet Brebner, another Canadian professor who taught in the United States, devised an ambitious series of scholarly books under the auspices of the Carnegie Endowment for International Peace. Twenty-five volumes on Canada–U.S. relations were published between 1936 and 1945, providing invaluable information about the infinite variety of continental links, from industry and transportation to the movements of population and ideas.

Academics were not the only group of co-operators. Dentists, doctors, merchants, engineers, lawyers, and bankers talked across the border. Workers were joining American trade unions in unprecedented numbers; in fact, Canadians played a vital role in building the U.S. union movement. Top bureaucrats too were beginning to exchange ideas and information regularly. The trade negotiations of 1935 and later of 1938 brought Canadian and U.S. public servants together in unprecedented ways.

The most prominent Canadian public servant of the time, O.D. Skelton, promoted the trade agreements as a way of removing Canada from the trap of its British, imperial, and European connections. These connections distracted his compatriots from concentrating on their real job of building a nation on the North American continent, and from time to time threatened to suck them into a faraway war that was none of their business. It was essential for Canada's future, said Skelton, to develop a "North American mind" which would be resistant to the call of blood and tradition.

Skelton's main ally on the American side was Jack D. Hickerson, a Texan who was emerging as the State Department's resident expert on

Canada. Hickerson had served at the American Consulate General in Ottawa in the mid-1920s, where he had encountered and become extremely friendly with Skelton, newly ensconced as undersecretary of state for external affairs. From Skelton and from Colonel Foster, who had been consul general in Ottawa for more than two decades, Hickerson imbibed lessons about the Canadian–American past and present. The 1911 election and the defeat of freer trade, he was told and came to believe, had been a disaster, a triumph of Canadian nationalism over good sense. Still, it demonstrated the extraordinary sensitivities of the northern citizens of the continent where the southern giant was concerned, and showed how tenacious was the Canadian desire for independence from the United States.

Hickerson realized that Canada and the United States must develop separately, but he wanted them to do so as colleagues, friends, and allies. He was America's key Canada–U.S. trade negotiator in the late 1930s, and those sessions only reinforced his conviction that the two countries and their officials belonged together. More and more his view was reciprocated. Even the pro-British Norman Robertson, the bright Skelton recruit who frequently found himself across the negotiating table from Hickerson, learned from experience that he could get on with the Americans "a damn sight more easily" than with "God's Englishmen," who assumed "inescapable moral ascendancy over us lesser breeds." A network of informal Canadian–American bureaucratic ties was beginning to take shape, and its importance can scarcely be overestimated.

There was one prominent public servant who did not fit into the new mould. Knowing that his position would be untenable under King, William Herridge had immediately resigned from his diplomatic post in Washington upon R.B. Bennett's defeat. The grandly named Sir Herbert Meredith Marler was transferred from the legation in Japan to succeed Herridge as Ottawa's minister plenipotentiary and envoy extraordinary to the United States. Marler's preoccupation was the British Empire and Canada's place in it. London, not Washington or Ottawa, was his spiritual capital. He liked to say that Canada ought to be contributing to the upkeep of the Royal Navy and British diplomatic corps, "having regard to the benefits which they confer on the dominions and on Canadians in foreign lands."

Marler's predecessors had been, each in their own way, impressive, successful, genuinely respected ministers. Marler was not. Sent to Washington because he had the essential qualifications of wealth, social standing, and Liberal political connections, he quickly became the butt of jokes by his colleagues and staff. He loved the ring of his full diplomatic title, even though it amounted to considerably less than true ambassadorial rank, and he thrilled to the words "your excellency." A story was even told of his insistence that his son be called "your little excellency." Another of Canada's fledgling diplomats who worked under Marler in the late 1930s, Charles Ritchie, wrote that Sir Herbert was "an impressively preserved specimen of old mercantile Anglo-Saxon Montreal. He looks like a painstakingly pompous portrait of himself painted to hang in a boardroom. He is not a quick-minded man—indeed one of my fellow secretaries at the Legation says that he is 'ivory from the neck up.' Nevertheless he has acquired a handsome fortune and his successful career has been crowned with the diplomatic posts of Tokyo and Washington and with a knighthood."

The British, as might be expected, took a more sympathetic view of Marler. They saw that he was voluble and not of very strong character, but he was thorough, determined, and could see the humour of his own mistakes. He improved upon the knowing, and no amount of trouble was too much for the loyal Marler to take in defence of a British Empire that he thought must be seen to be strong and unified in purpose, especially in vital—and rival—centres such as Washington. British diplomats in the United States, however, acknowledged that the important events in Canadian–American relations passed Marler by. His government paid him little attention and did its business in the United States either through emissaries, at the Cabinet level, or through the U.S. Legation in Ottawa. This tendency became all the more pronounced in the later 1930s, when Marler had a series of strokes at the same time that the international situation worsened.

But Marler's admiration of the values, power, and statesmanship of Great Britain was not unique to him. It represented a powerful strain in many Canadians, Prime Minister Mackenzie King among them. Canadian–American co-operation was important, King thought, but North America was not sufficient as a future for Canada. In fact, a Canada alone in the world with the United States was a Canada endangered. For King and even for Canadians who did not feel the tug of tradition and emotion quite so strongly, the connection with Great Britain was indispensable to national survival on the North American continent.

Mackenzie King's North Atlantic Triangle

Ottawa's politicians and diplomats preferred not to choose between Great Britain and the United States. Canadians had always felt vulnerable when the two pieces of their international personality were not in unison. Their mental health was best when the two great powers were

on a common course in world affairs. In the last volume of the Carnegie
series on Canadian–American relations, J.B. Brebner would coin the
phrase "the North Atlantic Triangle," which came to be thought of as a
happy place where the British and Americans, through the honest bro-
kering of Canada, got along as they must if the world was to be right for
Canadians.

In his exchanges with the Americans after regaining power in 1935,
King declared that he wanted to be a helpful fixer in Anglo-American
relations. He had a background in healing labour disputes, which he
believed easily translated into an understanding of international affairs,
and he could dredge up moments down the years when he believed he
had facilitated agreement between Great Britain and the United States.
King's whole career was an effort in conciliation, arising from the deepest
reaches of his anxious-to-please and eager-to-serve personality. Both in
domestic and foreign policy he saw his role as one of consensus building
and peacemaking. At home his watchwords were national unity, a term
he applied especially to his desire to keep English and French Canada
from colliding. Abroad he wished to be, as he confided to his diary, "a
medium to work for better relations among mankind" and a "midwife of
the creative forces of progress." Perhaps he could constitute that small
but crucial difference, "the dust in the balance," to help swing the international scales in favour of peace. That would have the pleasing advantage
of meeting all of King's aims, including the not incidental one of keeping
him in power by avoiding a conflict overseas which would divide
Canada between those who wanted to fight if England fought and those
who wanted to have nothing to do with the Old World and its problems.

Roosevelt was anxious to make use of King's desire for a trans-
Atlantic community of interests and ideals to set against the growing
threat of violence and dictatorship. On the last day of July 1936, the
American president met King and the Canadian governor general, Lord
Tweedsmuir, in Quebec City. The three discussed summoning a conference of heads of government to deal with the world's ills. Roosevelt
added a characteristically theatrical touch, saying that a meeting on
board a battleship at sea would isolate the great men, concentrate their
minds, and force them to solutions. Despite reservations, King took the
idea to the British in the fall, assuring them of the purity of American
intentions: at least Roosevelt was making a start at extracting the U.S.
from its isolationism.

The prime minister met Roosevelt again in March of 1937, this time
in Washington. King and Roosevelt played variations on the world conference theme, the Canadian pushing for a more universal and peaceful
version of the League of Nations, which would search for answers to

"My old friend:" Mackenzie King and Franklin Roosevelt, Quebec City, 1936. (National Archives of Canada/PA 16768)

the big economic and social questions that plagued humanity. The president spoke strongly about the need to lower trade barriers everywhere, a belief we know King passionately shared. More specifically, an Anglo-American trade agreement was in Roosevelt's mind, as the next stage in Secretary of State Hull's program of economic disarmament. Trade was the arena in which co-operation between Great Britain and the United States seemed most likely, because there was such strong opposition in the U.S. to political commitments that might suggest too much involvement in the dirty business of international affairs.

Once back home, the Canadian wrote effusively to both Roosevelt and Hull. He told the secretary of state, "It will mean much to the British government as well as to myself for me to have the North American background so clearly defined in my own mind." Nevertheless, when word of the meeting filtered back to the British Foreign Office, its permanent head, Sir Robert Vansittart, had little good to say about the political leaders of North America. The hopelessly naïve prime minister of Canada seemed to have lost rather than gained in intelligence. He was simply a minor and less effective echo of Roosevelt. All they seemed capable of were words, and often dangerously misleading words at that, unsupported by any resolve to *do* anything.

Not knowing that he was held in such low esteem in the unsympathetic precincts of London's Whitehall, Mackenzie King proudly sallied forth to the capital of the British Empire in the early summer of 1937 for the coronation of King George VI and the Imperial Conference that would follow. King again tried to interpret the constructive intent of the United States to British government officials, and he vigorously argued for a trade agreement between the two countries. On that depended American goodwill, which "was strong for Britain today but might be for another country tomorrow." The British, although suspicious of the U.S., were interested in an Anglo–American agreement for precisely the reason that King suggested. In the unfortunate condition of the world, American friendship might make all the difference in the great world struggle that many believed was inevitable.

CANADA IN THE MIDDLE: THE 1938 TRADE AGREEMENT

Canada now became part of the problem. The way to a trade deal lay through King, but Canada and the United States were competitors to sell British consumers many of the same products, such as apples and lumber. If there was to be an agreement between the U.S. and Great Britain, the King government would have to give up some of Canada's advantages in the British market, hard won at the Ottawa conference in 1932 and in an Anglo-Canadian trade agreement struck in 1937. Having contributed warm words on behalf of a British–American trade deal, and having promised a "big and generous" attitude on his government's part, King balked when asked for concrete support. Canada would demand direct participation and compensation, he said; otherwise, "we would be thought simpletons." In the months after the Imperial Conference of 1937, King insisted that separate Canadian–American negotiations be linked to any Anglo-American talks. This was his price for the vital concessions that would make an accord possible between the two great powers. He got his way. The year 1938 saw an unprecedented effort in triangular give-and-take, resulting in an Anglo-American and a new Canadian–American trade agreement. Both were signed on 17 November.

The 1938 Canadian–American trade agreement built upon and extended the 1935 deal. Canada made commitments on several hundred

American products, sometimes reducing the duty charged and sometimes simply promising not to increase rates. Some 60 percent of U.S. exports northwards were affected. Canada also dropped a particularly irksome 3 percent excise tax. The United States lowered its tariff on 202 items, including lumber products, livestock, fish, certain grains, metals, and many lines of manufacture. There was even a benefit for food potatoes this time, Roosevelt no longer having a burning political interest in protecting this item. Maine and Vermont alone of the forty-eight states had voted against him in the last presidential election. A Roosevelt adviser joked about a new electoral formula: "As Maine goes, so goes Vermont." So complete was the president's dominance that after the 1936 election someone had hung a sign on the Salmon Falls River bridge leading from New Hampshire into Maine, saying YOU ARE NOW LEAVING THE UNITED STATES.

If there had been doubt that Canadian negotiators had done well in 1935, there was none in 1938. Led by Norman Robertson, the Canadians were a formidable team that gained and kept American trust and goodwill. The reductions they won covered more than 80 percent of Canadian sales to the U.S., and the maximum concession possible, 50 percent, had been granted to goods representing about half of all dutiable exports to the United States. All of the advantages gained under the previous agreement were retained and quotas, where they were in place, were either increased or eliminated entirely. Because Canada held most-favoured nation status in the United States, it also derived benefits from changes in U.S. duties under the Anglo-American agreement. In his tight-lipped memoirs, one of the Canadian negotiators contrasted the 1935 and 1938 agreements. In 1935, Dana Wilgress said, "many people" thought the trade deal more favourable to the United States. In 1938, for the first time, there was an exchange of comprehensive tariff concessions. For the first time, the real barriers to trade with the U.S. had been breached. Sadly, the war intervened less than ten months after the agreement of November 1938. We cannot calculate just how much the patterns of Canadian–American trade might have been altered once the full weight of the agreement had been felt.

PRESIDENT AND PRIME MINISTER

Mackenzie King travelled to Washington to sign the Canadian–American agreement. For the third time since returning to power, he stayed at the White House with the president, revelling in their shared North American egalitarianism. The prime minister was pleased to hear it said that the Canadians had fought hard for their rights in the trade negotiations but that they and their American colleagues had dealt with each other frankly and harmoniously, aware somehow that they were in a grand enterprise together. King traded comments with Roosevelt about the artificiality of the British system of privilege and reflected that sending the titled Sir Herbert Marler as minister to the U.S. had probably been a mistake. Being only too human, he was at the same time pleased by the recognition and respect that his own exalted rank demanded: "Darkey messengers, porters, as well as members of the staff, all seemed to know one and give me the right of way, without any notice." We have already explored some of King's pragmatic motives in courting the American president. To these should be added that he found it exhilarating to be noticed and thought important. He loved the proximity of the rich, famous, and powerful. Roosevelt was all three.

Theirs was becoming, by any standards, a most remarkable relationship: there would be eighteen meetings over the ten years from 1935 to 1945. King had been extremely suspicious of Roosevelt in the early New Deal years after 1932, but his misgivings were melted by the president's right thinking on Canadian issues—and his respectful embrace of the prime minister himself. King was extremely insecure, and Roosevelt was so much easier to talk to than British politicians and officials were. There was none of the cold condescension or loftiness that he encountered so often in London. "The manner of these damn Englishmen," he wrote on one occasion, "in the self-satisfied way in which they take everything as a matter of course is most exasperating."

Roosevelt, by contrast, was so evidently the embodiment of the cheerful boy next door that he swept aside any sense of the great imbalance in the standing of the two countries. King derived great emotional and (he probably also hoped) political sustenance from the warm glow of the sunny American president. The Canadian was an uninspiring and on the whole unpopular leader, without the gift to communicate his goals and desires effectively. Roosevelt was the opposite, and he was better regarded in Canada than any American in memory. A close association with him, if not pushed too far, would have obvious domestic appeal.

Was it a real friendship? It seems unlikely. The Canadian was too much the sycophant, and he never overcame his awe and reserve. He wanted to call "the President" by his first name, but King could seldom force himself to be so bold. On the few occasions when he brought himself over the brink, the use of Franklin was exceptional enough to make headlines in his diary. Nor did he point out to Roosevelt, who called him Mackenzie, that *his* intimates addressed him as Rex. The president never troubled to sniff out that small but important detail. Roosevelt, it is true, could not have been a more winning companion. His charm was one of his great political weapons, and it was completely natural. Roosevelt liked people, hated to disappoint, and could say "my old friend" cheerily in eleven languages. But he was essentially superficial. Even though he had only met King once before November 1935—at Harvard University, from which they had both graduated—he almost immediately remarked that they had been close "almost since we were boys." Roosevelt admittedly could talk frankly and expansively to King, trying out his ideas. They were both politicians to their fingertips, and no doubt the prime minister's relationship with important Americans such as the Rockefellers gave him some credentials in dealing with the president. If Roosevelt actually liked the solemn and stuffy prime minis-ter, however, he was one of the few.

Whatever the exact nature of his relationship with King, Roosevelt was attuned to Canada as no other president before or since. His feeling for the country had undoubtedly taken root at his family's cavernous summer home on Campobello Island, New Brunswick. The president had spent much of his youth on the island. It was also there at the age of thirty-seven that he contracted the polio that crippled him for the rest of his life, and though he did not go back for more than a decade after the illness struck, his warm memories of the place were not extinguished. He began visiting again soon after becoming president. The sailor in him explored the Canadian coastline, where he could see the land's vastness and its untapped potential. He became reacquainted with ordi-nary New Brunswickers. Roosevelt knew that Canadians had distinct points of view—his memories included discussions of the 1911 reciproc-ity debates—but weren't North Americans basically the same in the ways that counted? Didn't they share the same values and fears?

GOOD NEIGHBOURHOOD, AMERICAN STYLE

Roosevelt's warmth played a role in his policies. He was inclined to per-sonalize foreign affairs, to express diplomatic relationships in the language of community. In 1933, in his first speech to the American public as presi-dent, he dedicated his nation "to the policy of the good neighbor—the neighbor who resolutely respects himself and, because he does so, respects the rights of others—the neighbor who respects his obligations and respects the sanctity of his agreements in and with a world of neighbors."

The "good neighbor" phrase stuck, coming to be applied specifi-cally to Rooseveltian diplomacy towards Latin America. As the fascist powers marched in the 1930s, it was attractive to think that Hitler and his friends could be repulsed by hemispheric solidarity. The Roosevelt administration led the diplomatic efforts that resulted in the 1938 Declaration of Lima, pledging the United States and the republics of Latin America to co-operate against any "foreign intervention or activity that might threaten them."

The folksy imagery of good neighbours had definite limits. Roosevelt talked sympathetically to the Latin nations and pulled the U.S. military out of Central America and the Caribbean—the Panama Canal excepted—but the United States still sought to control the region. In the Dominican Republic, for example, that was accomplished through the brutal strongman, Rafael Trujillo, who was kept in business by U.S. cash and arms from the 1930s to the early 1960s. "He may be an S.O.B.," said Roosevelt, "but he is our S.O.B." That summed up the hard realities underlying the policy of the good neighbour.

Canada was too sophisticated, too developed, too stable, ever to accept or require such an approach—or so we might hope. Nonetheless, there was some of the same condescension and the same desire for control apparent in U.S. policy towards Canada. There was also a recognition of Canada's fundamental importance to the United States. It only made sense for Washington's hemispheric thinkers to cast their eyes northwards as well as southwards. Roosevelt himself clearly did so. He sometimes referred to Canada in his descriptions of the good neighbour policy, and when the triangular trade negotiations of 1938 seemed in peril, he was far more concerned by the possibility that the Canadian agreement would be snatched away than by the potential loss of a British accord. One of his closest foreign policy advisors was former minister to Canada William Phillips, while Roosevelt's personal choice for the post in the late 1930s was Daniel C. Roper, the secretary of commerce who advocated an economic "Greater America" in the hemisphere. The president told Roper that Ottawa was "really among the top two or three of our diplomatic posts."

"OUR GATES WIDE OPEN": CONTINENTAL AND NATIONAL DEFENCE

The defence of North America was an obvious hemispheric concern, and not only for the U.S. The Canadian armed forces no longer worried about the threat of an out-and-out American attack. Canada's territorial integrity was much more likely to need protection in the event of a conflict between two rivals that seemed on a collision course: the United States and the Empire of Japan. Whether or not the British Empire and the U.S. were allies in such an eventuality, the acid test of sovereignty would be Canada's capacity to defend itself, particularly on the precarious west coast. The chief of the naval staff, Walter Hose, had warned the government in the 1920s that if Japan and the U.S. went to war, "the geographical position of our territory on the Pacific Ocean seaboard, placed between the United States main naval bases and her Alaskan territory where advance bases would, of necessity, be established, offers unique opportunities for un-neutral acts by either belligerent." The failure "to provide the requisite naval forces would render our territorial waters a most serious menace to both Canadian and United States trade. . . . [I]f it were found that our unprotected territorial waters were a menace to the United States or her commerce, ground would be given for demands on their part either during or after a war which would raise serious difficulties between us." Inaction would place Canadian defence "entirely in the hands of the friendly neighbour," in other words, and was a recipe for disaster.

The American military did fret about the vast undefended reaches of Canada and the abject condition of its armed forces. Strategic genius was not necessary to come to the conclusion, as the military intelligence division of the U.S. army's general staff regularly did, that Canada had few military resources, little munitions production, and practically no independent capacity for combat effectiveness. Canada itself presented no military challenge to the Americans, but it might be over-run by an enemy of the United States and used as a base for an attack against the republic. The famous U.S. air force general Billy Mitchell had visited Canada early in the 1920s, and he reported that "the Canadian frontier from Quebec to Camp Borden dominates our whole area contained in the North East States, Pennsylvania, West Virginia, Ohio, Indiana, and part of Illinois. Hostile aircraft, operating from this line, can render any cities or localities within the above area incapable of use."

In the 1930s, the two countries entered into reciprocal agreements to allow military overflights of one another's territory. These arrangements, however, in no way solved the problem of Canada's vulnerability from the air, because they had a distinctly limited aim: to make routes more direct for the two air forces. On Canada's west coast, Ottawa cautiously allowed overflights on a case-by-case basis only, the rationale being (as Hose had suggested) that this area was too sensitive from the standpoint of national sovereignty and security to concede to any general agreement.

U.S. army air corps officers publicly contemplated the possibility of an attack via Canadian territory in testimony before a Congressional committee in 1935. If there should be a conflict involving the United States, the argument ran, Canada might be a neutral, a hapless ally or, unlikely as it seemed, "involved on the side of a hostile coalition." The threat in each case, given rapidly developing military technologies, could be substantial. New airfields ought to be constructed in the threatened regions of the country, so that defensive bomber operations could be mounted and an enemy fended off. Senior American air officers, wanting one of these bases to be located in the Great Lakes area very near the frontier, suggested camouflaging it as a civilian field in order to avoid "passing away from the century-old principle that our Canadian border needs no defence." Word of the committee's deliberations leaked out, and President Roosevelt felt compelled to issue a soothing statement to Canadians. The military did not speak for the government. Canada was the best of neighbours.

The *Ottawa Evening Citizen* took these developments in stride. There was nothing surprising about American apprehensions or their air force's suggestions. Nations had to look after their own interests. Even within the Canadian armed forces, a member of the militia staff reacted matter-of-factly. He took no umbrage at the 1935 Congressional hearings and recommended that no one else do so. The United States had to protect itself against attack not from Canada but via Canada. "Publicity has simply been given to the fact that it is known to the world of Canada's impotence with regard to anti-air defence. Not only are our gates wide open but we have not even the semblance of a fence and our neighbour is, in consequence, obliged to provide against our lack of provision." The writer's boss, however, was not so sanguine. General A.G.L. McNaughton, the chief of the general staff, declared that the American military was convinced of "a direct menace to their own security," caused by the inadequacy of Canada's defences. They would not hesitate to invade Canada if they thought it necessary in order to defend their own nation, McNaughton wrote, and Canadian independence was in jeopardy. The logic of the Congressional committee's work was in the direction of "the institution of an American protectorate over this country."

An American proposal for a highway linking the United States to Alaska by way of British Columbia raised further concerns. In 1935, the U.S. Congress set aside $2 000 000 for the purpose and authorized the president to take up the question with the Canadian government. By 1937, the premier of British Columbia was enthusiastically seeking support for the project both in Canada and the United States, as a way to create jobs and bolster northern development. He even bearded the president in his New York home at Hyde Park to solicit American funding. Ottawa was not pleased by this exercise in provincial diplomacy, or by the idea of "mortgaging our independence" to U.S. financiers or the American government. The prime minister feared the "penetration" of American capital. His leading minister, Ernest Lapointe, thought financial "invasion" an apter description. Skelton of External Affairs suggested that the United States "was certainly not going to spend money abroad without a very definite *quid pro quo*," namely an understanding that the highway could be used in wartime—whether or not Canada was a belligerent—by the U.S. armed forces. The chiefs of Canada's military underlined these implications for national sovereignty. The existence of an Alaskan highway, particularly one that had been bought and paid for by Americans, would be a strong inducement for the United States to ignore Canada's right to make independent decisions. The truth was, however, that the U.S. army had little or no interest in such a highway, doubting its military value. Only the Second World War and Pearl Harbor would change that.

SEEKING SOLIDARITY

The United States commander-in-chief took much more cognizance of the country to the north than did his armed forces: its military importance, and its many military weaknesses. Canada, President Roosevelt knew from his own experience, was a huge and vulnerable land. A few days after his summer 1936 meeting with King at Quebec City, he issued a declaration in Chautauqua, New York, a short distance across Lake Erie from Canada: "Our closest neighbors are good neighbors. If there are remoter nations that wish us not good but ill, they know that we are strong; and they know that we can and will defend ourselves and defend our neighborhood." This was a warning against exterior aggression, but he was also putting Canada on notice about the lamentable state of its defences. The president sought solidarity with Canadians and their prime minister, expecting them to do their part in keeping North America, in the words of his 1938 Kingston speech, a "strong citadel wherein civilization can flourish unimpaired." He would do the rest.

The dignitaries arrive for the signing of the Canada–United States trade agreement, Washington, 1938. From left to right: Mackenzie King, Cordell Hull, O.D. Skelton. (National Archives of Canada/C 38741)

Roosevelt made defence an issue in Canadian–American relations, bringing it up in every encounter with King from their meeting in Quebec City until the outbreak of war in Europe. At Quebec the president told a pointed anecdote about "leading" senators who told him that the U.S. would have to "go in and help" if a virtually defenceless British Columbia were attacked by Japan. In March 1937 at the White House, the president raised the question of an Alaskan highway, which he said "would be of a great advantage for military purposes, in the event of trouble with Japan." He was also blunt about the deficiencies of western Canadian coastal defences, a point that was reinforced for him when he sailed in a destroyer to Victoria, B.C., during September 1937, as part of a visit to the nearby state of Washington. Roosevelt was shocked by the condition of Canada's Pacific naval forces and coast defences. The implications for the United States were grave because, as he put it, "the British Columbia coast had to be regarded in reality as a link between the United States and Alaska." It was clear that "his people would have to do a great deal there."

By his own recollection, the Victoria trip set Roosevelt to considering Canadian–American defence co-operation as he had not considered it before. The president now took a highly personal initiative in arranging talks between senior military officers of Canada and the United States in January 1938. This was a comical affair, conducted in utmost secrecy, with the chief of the Canadian general staff sneaking off to Washington in civilian clothes one day, the head of the navy travelling separately the next day. The visit caught the American military completely by surprise and they had neither an agenda nor any information "as to the reason or cause of our meeting." Only the minister at the Canadian Legation, where the talks took place, was aware that the military men were in their midst, and the high-ranking soldiers and sailors sequestered themselves in the building for the duration, coming out only for walks along fashionable Massachusetts Avenue. The discussion focussed on west coast defences. The U.S. army chief of staff, Major General Malin Craig, suggested that his responsibility be extended to include Canada's coastline to Alaska. The offer was politely declined. Though informal and improvised, the meeting was the first occasion in the peacetime history of Canadian–American relations that the top brass of the two countries had directly shared military intelligence.

The president's famous "the people of the United States will not stand idly by" bombshell in Kingston followed in August 1938. That November and the following June, Roosevelt talked at King again about defence. In the summer of 1939 Roosevelt took a cruise in Canadian waters off the Atlantic coast. The press release said that he was on holiday but he later admitted to the prime minister that he had come there, just as he had come to Victoria two years before, because of "his concern with the problem of coastal defence." He wanted, he said, to see what the naval and air defence of the east coast and Newfoundland involved, having found to his surprise that none of his naval officers had been in those waters or knew anything about them. He took along some of his senior military staff so that they could "spy out the land," and perhaps spot some of the bays or inlets where unfriendly submarines might lurk. The president also let it be known in this last summer of peace that he wished the American navy to have use of the port facilities at Halifax, Nova Scotia.

There was a danger here, and King knew it well. Part of the problem was political: the danger of being seen to be intimate with the Americans, and accused of allowing the imperial ties valued by so many Canadians to slacken in the process. Fifty percent of the population was still of British stock; a politician cosied up too close to the United States at his peril. King understood this instinctively because he was part of the 50 percent. Admiration, respect, awe of the Americans and their president did not alter, and frequently reinforced, the desire of Canadians to hold to the British connection in order to avoid being swallowed whole. For that reason King was careful not to overdo things with Roosevelt. There was a North American perspective, the prime minister told Sir Herbert Marler, but only "up to a certain point." It should not be permitted "to run counter to the advantages which come from belonging to the British Commonwealth." Time and time again politicians and officials resisted closer public ties with their U.S. counterparts because they thought that the Canadian public would not stand for it. There was never any permanent military liaison or joint planning before the start of the Second World War, for example.

As well as its potential effect on Canadian public opinion, too close a tie with the United States was regarded as a danger to Canadian sovereignty. The government took this very seriously, as can be seen by King's immediate response to Roosevelt's Kingston speech. The prime minister had the remarks he made at Woodbridge two days later on "our obligations as a good friendly neighbour" done up in a Canadian government booklet, which also contained the president's address, under the title, "Reciprocity in Defence." The desire to assert the rights and responsibilities of a self-respecting nation also lay behind the substantial increase in military spending undertaken by the government after 1935, much of it applied to coastal defence, and more particularly to the west coast.

King described Canada in the House of Commons as the most secure and fortunate of countries: rich in resources; separated by vast oceans from Europe and Asia; partners in the British Commonwealth; unthreatened to the north; and having the best of neighbours to the south. He asked members of Parliament whether they were prepared to surrender "the whole of our obligation in the matter of protection against foreign aggression" to the Americans. Was it likely that Canada would be able "to maintain friendly relations with the United States if we do nothing to defend our own coasts but simply take the attitude that we shall look to them for our defence?" Could neutrality be preserved if an enemy base operated against the United States from Canadian territory? The Canadian armed forces, as we have seen, had already given the government private answers to those questions. If Canada could not do the job, the United States would. If neutrality was not enforced by Canadians in a Japanese–American war, U.S. forces would be sure to occupy British Columbia. The Canadian army's planning document, Defence Scheme No. 2, was designed precisely to safeguard sovereignty against the threat of both Japan and the United States should those two great nations go to war. The plan received final government approval in May 1938.

THE APPROACH OF ANOTHER WAR

By 1938 the greatest immediate threat came from Germany, its "union" with Austria complete and its takeover bid of Czechoslovakia underway. The Canadian and American governments cautiously turned their attention to the defence of the Atlantic while keeping a close eye on the substantial isolationist segments of North American public opinion. King was a one-man polling company, keeping especially close watch on his political base, Quebec. He and his defence minister emphasized that they were rearming for Canada's sake, not the empire's. "The defence of our shores and the preservation of our neutrality—these are the cardinal principles of our policy."

In September 1938 came the Munich Crisis, however, when Hitler demanded that the great powers give him the Sudetenland—Czechoslovakia's German-speaking border region—or he would take it by force. King, who controlled foreign policy with an iron grip, made his real views known to the Cabinet. If Britain went to war over Czechoslovakia, Canada would have to as well. It was that simple. "I made it clear . . . that I would stand for Canada doing all she possibly could to destroy those Powers which are basing their action on *might*

Lower tariffs seemed the 1930s path to national riches. *(Winnipeg Free Press)*

and not on *right*, and that I would not consider being neutral in this situation for a moment." King's stance was not pure principle. Canada needed the mother country. Once the British were beaten in a world war, "the only future left for Canada would be absorption by the U.S., if we were to be saved from an enemy aggressor." The problem was temporarily solved by the expedient of capitulation. Hitler got what he wanted in return for saying he would take no more. Mackenzie King's passionate statement to Cabinet was never made public. He could continue to avoid for a little bit longer the issue of what to do in the event of a war involving Britain.

During the Czechoslovak crisis, Canadian air force planners realized the deficiencies of their Atlantic defences, and this led them to make an emergency foray to Washington. The Royal Canadian Air

Force was given a special spending warrant of $5 million—a huge amount of money, given total defence expenditure in that year of about $35 million—and instructed to buy as many aircraft as possible. Since the only planes available on such short notice were those already in production, the U.S. army air corps agreed to hand over some of its own orders. The crisis soon passed, however, and the money quickly dried up. Even so, this was another first: the Canadian armed forces, almost completely British in outlook, training, and equipment, had turned to the United States for a major weapon purchase. The government would again look south for aircraft in August 1939, on the eve of the Second World War. This time purchases were made, and King's only regret was that he had not acted sooner.

Like Roosevelt's promise to defend Canada from domination, the American air corps' generosity in offering to give up some of its orders was unlikely to be criticized in the United States. It was self-interested to assist in the defence of the continent and the hemisphere. There was strong opposition, however, to involvement with the big, bad world beyond North America, with Europe most of all. The tribal quarrels of the Old World had caused the First World War, and Europeans seemed set on yet more violent conflict. The bankers and arms makers, whom the neutralists believed had helped to inveigle the U.S. into war in 1917, would do their awful work again if allowed to—strictly for profit. Neutrality Acts were passed by Congress in 1935, 1936, 1937, and 1939 to prevent business transactions, most notably arms sales, with warring countries. There were anti-Europe, anti-business, and anti-war sentiments in Canada too. But neutralism was a genuine movement in the United States, and it was a far more serious restraint on Roosevelt's policies than it ever was on King's.

In March 1939, the downwards slide to war in Europe accelerated. Hitler gulped more territory, occupying Prague and the rest of Czechoslovakia, and the British guaranteed the territorial integrity of Poland, another of Germany's neighbours. A German invasion of that country would bring an armed response from Britain. Mackenzie King and Roosevelt, cautious politicians fighting difficult battles with various foes at home, reacted warily. But they did react. King began to voice support for Great Britain, although in such deliberately ambiguous terms that no one still quite knew where he stood. The American president denounced the dictators and inched towards material assistance for the British and their French colleagues. When he sought to revise the neutrality laws and end the arms embargo, however, the isolationists in Congress stopped him cold. The Germans rejoiced in the defeat of the "warmongering" U.S. leader. It is doubtful that they noticed Mackenzie King at all, despite his private warning to Hitler that Canada would be with Britain if the old country was attacked.

Not long after Hitler's trek into Prague, North Americans welcomed King George VI and the Queen Consort, Elizabeth, in an orgy of enthusiasm and escapism. Never before had a reigning British monarch visited Canada or the United States. Mackenzie King was at the royal couple's side almost every moment of the journey, even in the U.S. An incurable romantic where the monarchy was concerned—"I was prepared to lay my life at their feet"—he was in his glory. Roosevelt was only slightly less starry-eyed. They made a great many of the detailed arrangements personally, including Roosevelt's provision of hot dogs and beer for a picnic at his home in Hyde Park. King George and Queen Elizabeth arrived on 17 May in Quebec City aboard the ocean liner, *Empress of Australia*. They were two days late because of bad weather, causing errors in dozens of already prepared plaques and cornerstones ready to be deployed across the country. The King's first act of state in Canada was to welcome Daniel Roper as the new U.S. minister, leading the prime minister to remind everyone available of the perhaps not so evident symbolism. King was the grandson of a rebel who had escaped to the United States one hundred years before with a price on his head; the Americans themselves had gone against the Crown during the American Revolution; now they were all friends and allies.

The King and Queen traversed Canada westwards to Victoria in a specially designed and outfitted blue and gold royal train. They then made their way back to Niagara Falls, Ontario, where they crossed over into the United States. At that point they had not yet gone to the Maritimes; even so, the *New York Times* estimated that more than half of the Canadian population of eleven million had seen them in person. Huge crowds also lined their routes in the United States: seven hundred thousand in Washington and over three million in New York, a throng that rivalled the 1927 turnout to greet Charles Lindbergh, fresh from his trans-Atlantic solo flight. The cartoonist of the New York *Daily Mirror* showed a bewildered British prime minister, Neville Chamberlain, asking, "I say, just whose King *is* he?"

Both Roosevelt and King were overjoyed by the King's reception, and hoped that it would diminish the distance from Britain's plight felt by many North Americans. When the King, the prime minister, and the president spoke at Hyde Park at the end of George VI's time in the U.S., Roosevelt promised all the assistance he could give "short of actual participation in war." In fact, he said, the United States would "come in" if the Nazis bombed London. Later on in the summer, the president briefly contemplated the use of Canada as a way station for sending arms to his friends in Europe. Nevertheless, when Germany attacked Poland on 1 September 1939, and Chamberlain declared war two days later, Canada came to Britain's side and the United States did not. Roosevelt could not, for now.

C H Five E R

FORGED IN WAR

1 9 3 9 — 1 9 4 5

Pierrepont Moffat could feel the current of opinion shifting. The new U.S. minister to Canada had been in the legation in Ottawa only since June 1940 but he had no doubt about what he was to write to the acting secretary of state, Sumner Welles, in Washington. "Ever since I have been here, but more particularly in the last two or three weeks," Moffat noted on 14 August 1940, "there has been growing a public demand throughout Canada for the conclusion of some form of defence under-standing with the United States." That was true even of "elements which in the past have been least well disposed toward us, such as the Toronto public and the English-speaking sections of Montreal." A defence understanding seemed "a reasonable reinsurance policy" if Great Britain suffered further military reverses in the desperate period after the fall of France and the evacuation of British and allied troops from Dunkirk. In this new military situation, Moffat estimated, "the old fear that co-operation with the United States would tend to weaken Canada's ties with Great Britain has almost entirely disappeared. Instead, Canada believes that such co-operation would tend to bring Britain and the United States closer together, rather than to force Britain and Canada apart."

The patrician Moffat, an able professional diplomat with the best of connections in neutral Washington and already well on his way to estab-lishing links of friendship and trust with politicians and bureaucrats in Mackenzie King's Ottawa, was precisely right. The triumphs of Hitler and the *Wehrmacht* had been stunning, and Canadians were not immune to the fears that were gripping the world. The haughty condescension towards the Yankees, that staple of Canadian table talk for more than a century, had been replaced by concern and even fear for survival. If Britain was invaded—in August 1940 it seemed more a question of when—and if the Royal Navy fell into Hitler's hands, then North America would be open to attack. In such an event, Canada would have no choice but to throw in its lot with the United States and to fight for the survival of democracy in the New World. Surely it was only good sense to plan and to join together to ward off that evil day, no matter how many ancient shibboleths had to be violated in the process. Canada's relations with the United States, to this time ordinarily slow paced, were now to change. Urgent questions demanded solutions, and the tempo altered dramatically.

WAR COMES TO CANADA

The beginning of the Second World War initially caused remarkably few interruptions in the normal flow of business, tourism, and ideas over the Canadian–American boundary. The United States soon began to require passports for Canadians going south, and currency controls were slapped on by Canada's newly established Foreign Exchange Control Board (FECB) in September 1939. The FECB controls, however, were very mild, and throughout the war Ottawa tried to operate them in such a way as to avoid antagonizing business. The British high commissioner in Ottawa, Sir Gerald Campbell, noted on 20 September that "the frontier . . . remains entirely open and hundreds of tourists are passing everyday between the two countries. The consequent interchange of views which thus inevitably takes place cannot fail, in my judgment, to influence the mind of the average citizen of the United States to a far greater extent than any form of organised propaganda could do."

For the moment at least, there seemed to be a relative harmony of views between many in the neutral United States and the majority in a belligerent Canada. Roosevelt had told Americans that the United States was neutral, but he had added, "I do not ask you to be neutral in your heart." That warmed Canadians. Even so, the Neutrality Act came into force in the United States to cut off the supply of war matériel to belligerents. Because Canada was officially and legally neutral until

George VI declared war at the request of the Parliament of Canada, however, there was a week-long constitutional loophole. Roosevelt called King on 5 September to confirm this, and although legal opinion in Washington argued the contrary, the president authorized some supplies to be shipped north. A few military aircraft were literally dragged across the border in the days before Canada went to war.

All this was appreciated and understood in Canada, though the fact of American neutrality was secretly and bitterly resented by those Canadians who were wholeheartedly in the war. The popular view in certain quarters in Anglo-Canada was that the Americans, as in 1914, were shirking their duty to democracy. Even the prime minister, never the most bellicose of men, wrote in his diary that he felt "an almost profound disgust" after hearing the president issue the neutrality proclamation. "It was all words, words, words. America keeping out of this great issue, which affects the destiny of mankind. And professing to do so in the name of peace." For King, at least, his own prewar hesitations were forgotten and the issue, which a short time before he had seen as little more than an eastern European conflict of only passing interest to Canada, had been turned into a fight to the death between evil and democracy.

But no one in an official position breathed a hint of these feelings to American representatives. Ottawa bureaucrats exercised great care to keep the Americans happy and to consult them about the minor irritations inevitably produced in wartime conditions. Early in 1940, for example, when discussions with Washington about the construction of the long-sought St. Lawrence Seaway were bogged down over the division of costs, King pressed his finance minister to be accommodating: "The importance of keeping the goodwill of the United States at this time, and to co-operate with them on a matter which the President had so greatly at heart . . . was a strong reason why we should not take a stand which might risk all this goodwill and lead the U.S. to become more nationalistic and self-dependent than ever."

The goodwill of the Americans could sometimes be sorely tested. When the erratic Liberal Premier Mitch Hepburn of Ontario raised concerns in his province by claiming that there was a Nazi fifth column in the United States simply waiting for orders to invade Canada, government representatives in both Canada and the U.S. were quick to throw cold water on the charges. Postmaster general Chubby Power told the press "that Mitch Hepburn is crazy." In Washington, General George C. Marshall, chief of staff of the army, said that Hepburn was "fishing in thin air. . . . [D]oes the premier think anybody of this ilk could organize a strong force in the U.S. without the government knowing about it?" That ended the flurry of interest and concern.

What truly troubled President Roosevelt, as we have already seen, was the state of Canadian defences. When King visited him in April 1940, just after the general election in Canada had returned the Liberals to power and just before the Phony War in Europe ended, the president took pains to stress again, as King recorded, "that he felt a real concern about the inadequacy of the protection to our Canadian coasts. . . . He knew exactly from personal observation . . . much about the nature of the coasts." The prime minister got the point, noting the president's observation that "our inadequacy of defence represented a real danger to the United States." All he could offer in return was that "we were doing the best we could," but that was scarcely sufficient for the American leader. Events would soon make this a pressing and fateful matter.

THE LINCHPIN

The stunning defeats suffered by Britain and France in May and June of 1940 altered the balance of world power. North America had been virtually impregnable, separated as it was from Europe and Asia by broad sweeps of sea and protected by the Royal and United States navies. But now Hitler's Nazis were supreme on the continent, and there was every prospect that Britain would be invaded and subjugated. In such an event, the fate of the British fleet was a matter of immediate and vital concern for all North Americans, and President Roosevelt was quick to react.

At King's instruction, Hugh Keenleyside of the Department of External Affairs arrived in the president's office on 19 May 1940 to seek aircraft to keep the British Commonwealth Air Training Plan functioning. London was now obliged to keep every craft that could get off the ground for home defence. After making sympathetic noises, Roosevelt promptly showed that he had other matters on his mind: "certain possible eventualities which could not be mentioned aloud." Roosevelt told Keenleyside to whisper the words "British Fleet" to Mackenzie King, and the official added his own gloss that Roosevelt "was anxious to have an understanding that the British Fleet would be transferred to this side of the ocean" if Britain was defeated. That was an understandable concern, and King saw its point at once. But he was also being pressed by the new British leader, Winston Churchill, to urge the Americans to give all available assistance immediately. The Canadian believed, correctly, that such demands would not be appreciated in Washington. Roosevelt later told Keenleyside that he "felt there was, behind the argument, an implied—in fact, almost an explicit—threat. This might be expressed in these terms: 'If you don't help us at once we will let the Germans have the Fleet and you can go to Hell.'" That, the president maintained, was not helpful.

How helpful Roosevelt could be or was prepared to be was another question. His analysis, as offered to Keenleyside, was that Britain was unlikely to be able to resist the Nazi air assault. But Britain must fight to the end and disperse the fleet to the empire, even if that saw England destroyed the way Poland had been. By then, the United States would be ready to offer aid, and the navy would have escaped to shelter in American ports. In this way the U.S. navy could control the Pacific and the Royal Navy would still control the Atlantic. If the British fleet fell into German hands, the American navy would have to be concentrated in the Atlantic, Japan would dominate the Pacific, and Germany and Italy could swallow British colonies everywhere but in the western hemisphere.

King was horrified at this cold, *realpolitik* analysis and at Roosevelt's request that it be conveyed to Churchill. For a moment, King wrote, "it seemed to me that the United States was seeking to save itself at the expense of Britain. . . . I instinctively revolted against such a thought. My reaction was that I would rather die than do aught to save ourselves or any part of this continent at the expense of Britain." Still, after much agonizing and after sending Keenleyside to Washington once more, King did what Roosevelt asked. His telegram was duly dispatched on 31 May and Churchill gave his reply, King believed, in his magnificent address on 4 June. "We shall never surrender," Churchill told the House of Commons, "and even if, which I do not for a moment believe, this island or a large part of it were subjugated and starving, then our Empire beyond the seas, armed and guarded by the British Fleet, would carry on the struggle until in God's good time, the New World, with all its power and might, steps forth to the rescue and liberation of the old." Privately, Churchill warned King the next day "not to let the Americans view too complacently [the] prospect of a British collapse, out of which they would get the British Fleet and the guardianship of the British Empire." If Britain were defeated, Churchill said, he could not guarantee what a pro-German administration might do.

The British prime minister's message left Roosevelt most unhappy, and King sent off yet another cable to London. This time he urged that the U.S. be given bases in Iceland, Greenland, the West Indies, and

Newfoundland, and he asked that Canada's role be determined against the day when disaster struck and the Royal Navy had to be dispersed. Angry at what he believed to be North American timidity, Churchill roared back that he saw no reason to prepare for any transfer of the fleet. "I shall never myself enter into any peace negotiations with Hitler, but obviously I cannot bind a future government which, if it were deserted by the United States and beaten down here, might very easily be a kind of Quisling affair ready to accept German overlordship and protection. It would be a help if you could impress this danger on the President." A deeply troubled King was finding that it was not easy trying to play the role of linchpin, however much the prewar, postprandial rhetoric had stressed Canada's position as the interpreter between Britain and the United States.

THE GRIM BUSINESS OF JOINT DEFENCE

Mackenzie King's primary task now was to ensure that Canada could defend itself and survive if Britain fell. In June 1940, he began to press Pierrepont Moffat for a fresh round of military discussions between Canada and the U.S., and his legation in Washington delivered the same message there. Astonishingly, these feelers took almost a month to produce results. Military talks, the first serious and detailed ones to take place between the two countries, were finally held in complete secrecy in Washington on 11 July. There were no commitments, but the discussions, as the American minister later noted, "at least had the result that American aid would be effective" in the event of any attack on Canada.

In the same period, the idea of stronger continental links was beginning to be canvassed by academics and bureaucrats in both countries. In mid-July, a group of younger activists in the Canadian Institute of International Affairs produced "A Program of Immediate Canadian Action," which looked to Canada's economic plight if overseas markets were lost, and simultaneously called for a continental defence plan. And in Washington, Adolf Berle, the able and rambunctious assistant secretary of state, was drawing up plans for "the new American Empire" that called for a consolidation of the two countries and their futures. After speaking confidentially to the American official, Vancouver journalist Bruce Hutchison wrote "He has been working on the re-organization of the economy of all North and South America, the new hemispheric con-

cept." In Berle's plans, Canada would be required to make major adjust-
ments to its agricultural and industrial policies.

Keenleyside in External Affairs was meanwhile studying the potentially worrying implications of the war's course for Canada's relations
with the U.S. The Americans, he wrote, would not be prepared to protect
Canada indefinitely without a measure of active co-operation in return.
"It is a reasonable assumption that the United States will expect, and if
necessary demand, Canadian assistance in the defence of this continent
and this Hemisphere." Concrete steps that the Americans thought in
order included the construction of the Alaskan Highway, the defensive
development of the Pacific coast and the Maritime provinces, and the co-
ordination of Canadian and U.S. war matériel. "If the United States is
forced to defend the Americas against encroachments from across either
Ocean," Keenleyside concluded, "Canada will be expected to participate;
thus the negotiation of a specific offensive–defensive alliance is likely to
become inevitable." So it seemed, and Mackenzie King could scarcely
have been surprised when on 16 August Roosevelt asked to meet him
the next day at Ogdensburg, New York. The president, who was running
for re-election for an unprecedented third term, was combining some
politicking in his home state with an inspection of troops in the area.

A few days earlier, Roosevelt had chatted with Loring Christie, the
Canadian minister to the United States. The president had said that he
was thinking of sending staff officers to Ottawa to discuss the defences
of the east coast. As Christie reported to Ottawa, Roosevelt "had in mind
their surveying [the] situation from Bay of Fundy around to the Gulf of
St. Lawrence. They might explore [the] question of base facilities for
United States use, including [the] possible desire to make such facilities
available at say Chester or Louisbourg [Nova Scotia]." Roosevelt had
also said that he might telephone King soon. The next day the president
met some of his key advisers, including treasury secretary Henry
Morgenthau, Jr., to discuss the best way to handle the announcement
that negotiations for a defence deal with Britain were underway. Sites for
military bases that the U.S. forces wanted on Britain's island possessions
in the Caribbean and western Atlantic were to be traded for fifty U.S.
destroyers urgently required by Britain's Royal Navy. Everyone agreed
that the announcement should be made immediately and that it should
be cast in terms of what the U.S. was to receive from the U.K. Canada
was clearly implicated in Roosevelt's plan. As part of his announcement,
the president told the press that he was carrying on conversations with
Canada on the defence of the coasts. He then called Mackenzie King to
tell him what he had said and to invite him to meet the next evening. As

King recorded it, the president had said that they could "talk over the defence matters between Canada and the United States together. . . . I thanked him and said I would be very pleased to accept the invitation."

The next day, before leaving Ottawa, the prime minister briefly met Colonel Ralston, his new minister of national defence, and received a list of the equipment that Canada sought from the United States. Apparently, that was his only briefing prior to the meeting with Roosevelt and King took no advisers with him. Accompanied only by Pierrepont Moffat, the prime minister drove to Ogdensburg, arriving at the president's railway car at 7 P.M.

FDR and Mackenzie King at Ogdensburg, New York, 1940. *(Globe and Mail)*

What Roosevelt wanted was to set up a joint civil–military defence board between Canada and the United States, a body that would prepare plans for mutual assistance in the defence of North America. As important, he wanted this board, subsequently called the Permanent Joint Board on Defence (PJBD), to last beyond the present emergency. There is no indication that this disturbed King. The creation of the PJBD was dealt with quickly, and King agreed to it with eagerness, instantly seeing that he had secured military protection for Canada in a way that posed the least threat of American domination and allowed his country to continue to do its utmost for Britain.

The prime minister was not so accommodating when Roosevelt raised the question of the American bases in Newfoundland that were to be granted to the U.S. as part of the destroyers-for-bases deal. King explained that "as we had undertaken protection of Newfoundland and were spending money there, the British Government would probably want our Government to co-operate in that part" of the Anglo-American agreement. Canada, in his view, had present and future rights in Newfoundland, then being governed as a virtual Crown colony by a Commission of Government appointed in London. King had no intention of seeing the United States take control of the island. In a telegram to Churchill, the prime minister made the same point: "As you are aware, [the] Canadian Government is already assisting in defence of Newfoundland and is, at the moment, contemplating additional large expenditure for developments there. There will probably be necessity for co-operation between the three governments in matters pertaining to that island."

Perhaps King's protection of Canadian "rights" in Newfoundland got under Roosevelt's skin. King explained "that we would not wish to sell or lease any sites in Canada" for long-term occupation by U.S. forces but that Canada "would be ready to work out matters of facilities" that American units might use for specific purposes during the war only. To this Roosevelt replied that "he had mostly in mind the need, if Canada were invaded, for getting troops quickly into Canada." Of course, that was "all right," as far as King was concerned; so too were annual manoeuvres on each other's soil. But then Roosevelt remarked, King remembered, that he had told British ambassador Lord Lothian that he could not understand why Britain had hesitated about leasing West Indian bases, "that as a matter of fact, if war developed with Germany and he felt it necessary to seize them to protect the United States, he would do that in any event. That it was much better to have a friendly agreement in advance."

There was an implicit threat and a warning there, a Rooseveltian iron fist draped in the velvet of warmest good friendship, though one presented wholly in a British–American context. If King, ordinarily a man of great shrewdness and perception, recognized the implication of FDR's words, he gave no indication in his diary or papers then or later. The president had brought up the issue of bases in Canada with Loring Christie on 15 August, and he had done so a second time with the prime minister. King had rejected any such idea quite firmly. Roosevelt responded by placing the prime minister on notice: to ensure the safety of the United States in the western hemisphere, to be certain that Canada's lamentably weak defences on the Atlantic and Pacific did not put his country in jeopardy, he would do whatever he judged necessary. To put it in its most extreme form, for example, if necessity required the seizure of facilities in Halifax or Saint John, so be it. A "friendly agreement in advance" was the president's preference, and with the PJBD he had taken a long step towards its achievement, just as he had with the destroyers-for-bases deal.

There was a clear sign of United States determination in the autumn of 1940, when the military members of the PJBD produced the Joint Canadian–United States Basic Defence Plan. This plan for the defence of North America dealt with the possibility of Britain being overrun and the Royal Navy lost, and it gave strategic control of the Canadian forces to the United States, subject only to consultation with the Canadian chiefs of staff. In such dire circumstances as the defeat of the United Kingdom, the Canadian government obviously considered that this provision made sense. The next spring, however, after Britain had continued to fight and after hope of ultimate victory had begun to revive in Canada, the Board produced its second plan, ABC-22, to take effect if and when the United States joined the Allies against the Axis Powers. When the American members again tried to secure strategic control of the Canadian forces (something the Canadians now interpreted as including tactical command as well), and to integrate much of eastern Canada and all of Newfoundland into their Northeast Defence Command and all of British Columbia into the Northwest Defence Command, Ottawa resisted fiercely. The American PJBD chair, Mayor Fiorello LaGuardia of New York City, actually wrote to his counterpart to complain that the Canadian fears "would be all right in normal times, if we were arranging a joint celebration" but not when "we are engaged in the grim business of joint defense against a possible strong and ruthless enemy."

Canada eventually won its point. In Newfoundland, Canadian army commanders dealt gingerly with generals of the United States Army, who clearly had their eye on taking over responsibility for all the defences of the island. Some Canadians feared that Washington intended to make its role in Newfoundland a permanent one, possibly even absorbing the former dominion as a state of the Union and thus blocking any possibility that it would one day be incorporated into Confederation. Though he was usually portrayed as completely spineless by his legion of contemporary critics, Mackenzie King had backbone when he needed it, and the United States retreated from its demands and aspirations in the interests of amity with Canada. All that Canada conceded was the "co-ordination of the military effort" of the two countries "to be effected by mutual co-operation," that is, by consultation between U.S. and Canadian commanders, each of whom would retain full control over their own national forces. The Canadian military and civilian members of the PJBD had, with King's support, succeeded in projecting the principle upon which the body had been founded—consultation between nations as equals rather than domination of the weaker by the stronger—into the decisive question of control of armed forces. On this crucial issue, perhaps more than any other, the PJBD proved its worth.

The creation of the PJBD—the Ogdensburg Agreement, as it came to be known—was almost universally hailed in Canada and the U.S. Approval even came from elements like the Montreal *Gazette*, as King pointed out to Moffat, "which represented a point of view that a few years ago would not have liked a Canadian–American rapprochement." Yet there were some who fretted over the implications of the agreement. As Senator Arthur Meighen wrote, "I lost my breakfast when I read the account this morning and gazed on the disgusting picture of these potentates posing like monkeys in the very middle of the blackest crisis of this Empire." Meighen clearly saw the PJBD as yet another effort by King to give over Canada to the United States, an attempt to abandon Britain in its hour of need. But the Meighens of the nation were a small minority in a country that collectively breathed a sigh of relief after the Ogdensburg Agreement.

Meighen and his imperialist friends had missed the point of Ogdensburg. Canada had been forced to turn to the United States because of Britain's weakness after Dunkirk. Every military action and every ounce of economic assistance to help keep Britain in the war weakened Canada further. A private soldier or a pilot or a dollar's worth of munitions sent to Britain was one that would certainly be lost if Britain were invaded; and if Britain fell, then North America was in peril. Aid to Britain, in other words, while absolutely necessary, nonetheless weakened Canada. A militarily and economically diminished Canada had only one place to look for protection and help. As Frank Scott of McGill University put it in 1941, "We are in the curious position that the more we do to assist Great Britain . . . the more we are obliged to co-operate with the United States. . . . We help Great Britain, and therefore we must be more closely associated with the United States." Mackenzie King wanted to protect Canada and to help Great Britain as much as possible, and he understood and accepted that this obliged him to seek even closer relations with Roosevelt's America.

ECONOMIC DEFENCE

Meanwhile, in 1940, the war had begun to pull the Canadian economy out of the slough of depression. War factories had gone into production, especially after the fall of France, leading the British and Canadian governments to place orders in massive quantities for everything imaginable. As Canadian exports boomed, so too did imports to fuel the expanding economy and help construct some of the products for export: when a Canadian factory built a military truck for export to Britain, for example, certain parts and components or certain specialty steels might have to be imported from the United States. The flood of imports from the south was increasing almost daily, and Canada's holdings of the American dollars needed to pay for the goods were running out. In peacetime Canada ordinarily had a balance of payments deficit with the U.S., but this was usually balanced by the surplus in trade with Britain. In effect, the sterling earned in the U.K. was turned into American dollars on the free exchange market. But after 1939, Britain made its currency inconvertible, with the result that Canada had a large and growing surplus in London that it could no longer use to freely cover its expanding debt with the United States. The problem was compounded by the fact that belligerent Canada could not borrow in the money market of the neutral United States. Nor had Canadian exports to the United States been greatly assisted by the pegging of the Canadian dollar at ninety cents U.S.

Ottawa had been aware of this problem since the spring of 1940. In June, Norman Robertson, the Department of External Affairs expert on trade and tariffs, and Graham Towers, the governor of the Bank of Canada, had travelled to Washington to explain their situation. "Our normal export trade to the United States was unlikely to expand and the prospects of our securing the large credit from tourist expenditures which our balance of payments required, had become extremely uncertain." As a result, the government had decided that it had to impose a 10 percent War Exchange Tax on all imports except those from the group of countries, dominated by Britain, whose foreign exchange reserves were mainly or completely in sterling. The Americans were unhappy at the damage Canada was doing to the 1938 trade agreement, but they understood.

The new tax had little effect. By the fall, Ottawa was searching for new ways to save dollars. Travellers to the U.S. were soon told that they could not exchange Canadian for American dollars, a measure that cut the flow of visitors to the south. Ottawa was beginning to contemplate rationing imports of U.S. fruits and vegetables but that, as Pierrepont Moffat told his Ottawa friends, simply would not be acceptable. Whole industries in Florida and California depended on the Canadian market, senators and members of Congress would be outraged, and "it would be a shame if restriction begetting restriction we ended up with the loss of our Trade Agreement and an embitterment of feeling." But what could Ottawa do? The balance of trade deficit with the United States was now running at almost $300 million a year, a very large amount. Washington protested so strongly that the federal government backed away and confined itself only to controls on non-essential imports. Finance minister J.L. Ilsley admitted this in Parliament when he explained why no measures to check the import of fruits and vegetables would be introduced: "We had to weigh . . . the inevitable public reaction there would be in many of the agricultural districts of the United States . . . and the danger which would ensue . . . to our own trade relations with the United States."

The problem of the shortage of American dollars did not go away, however. In fact, it got worse. In January 1941, the Roosevelt administration introduced the Lend-Lease Bill in Congress. This measure removed the dollar sign from war trade between Britain and the United States. Once the act became law, the U.S. could "sell, transfer title to, exchange, lend, lease, or otherwise dispose of" any defence equipment "for the government of any country whose defense the President deems vital to the defense of the United States." The lend-lease appropriation was $7 billion, a sum larger than the Canadian gross national product.

Nonetheless, lend-lease posed a difficulty for Canada. Britain had been paying for the war matériel and supplies it acquired in Canada, but if goods could be secured free of charge in the United States, why should London pay sterling and scarce dollars to Canada? The British understood the strong hand the American measure suddenly gave them. They pressed Canada to accept the advantages of lend-lease for itself and, if necessary, to sell off Canadian investments in the United

States, as Britain had been doing with its own investments, to demonstrate poverty to Washington. This was not Ottawa's response, however, nor could it be. The Americans were the hard-pressed Allies' best friends, but Britain had the Atlantic separating it from the U.S. Canada shared a continent with the Americans, and it would not do to be so beholden to Washington. King noted in his diary in March 1941, "We do not intend to avail ourselves of the Lend-Lease Bill but to allow its advances wholly to Britain. There is, of course, a bigger obligation because of it all than appears on the face of it. I have no doubt the U.S. would undoubtedly keep the obligations arising under the Lend-Lease Bill hanging pretty much over . . . [Britain's] head to be used to compel open markets or return of materials, etc. It is a terrible position for Britain to be in." It would not be one that Canada would find itself in if King and his government had anything to do with it.

Canada needed some way to get the benefits of lend-lease and to solve her exchange problems without paying a present or future price for them. The solution, after some important preliminary negotiation, was left to Mackenzie King, who trundled off to visit President Roosevelt at his home in Hyde Park, New York, on 20 April 1941. It was a Sunday, and playing the role of the perfect host, the president was relaxed, friendly, and expansive, the conversation roaming widely over the events of the war. After dinner, the two got down to business. As Grant Dexter of the *Winnipeg Free Press*, the journalist with the best connections in Ottawa, later reported that King had told him,

> Roosevelt had said to King that he didn't know much about the exchange situation: that he would like King to tell him about it and outline the policy which Roosevelt should follow. King hadn't bothered about the economics of it. He told Roosevelt that if he were in his place, he would have regarded only . . . the neighbourly phase of it. What the U.S. and Britain had done was one thing. Canada as the neighbour on this continent, the only one that really mattered, was another proposition entirely. If the U.S. insisted upon taking from Canada the few possessions she had in the U.S. it would only give voice to anti-U.S. sentiments in this country. Why not buy from Canada as much as Canada is buying from the U.S.—just balance the accounts. Roosevelt thought this was a swell idea.

The president was not quite the naïf he was painted in Dexter's unpublished and confidential account, but certainly Roosevelt had accepted the basic outlines of the Canadian's plan. Mackenzie King's years spent in the deferential cultivation of the president had perhaps paid off.

The Hyde Park Declaration, which had in fact been the subject of prior negotiation between the two countries, said that "in mobilizing the resources of this continent each country should provide the other with the defense articles it is best able to produce." The expectation was that Canada could supply the U.S. with "between $200 000 000 and $300 000 000 worth of such defense articles" and thus "materially assist Canada in meeting part of the cost of Canadian defense purchases in the United States." Where "Canadian defense purchases in the United States consist of component parts to be used in equipment and munitions which Canada is producing for Great Britain, it was also agreed that Great Britain will obtain these parts under the Lend-Lease Act and forward them to Canada for inclusion in the finished articles."

This was a triumph for King. At a stroke on that "grand Sunday," as Roosevelt termed it, he had solved many of Canada's financial problems. The Americans would increase purchases in Canada, thus helping industry and going a substantial distance to easing balance-of-trade difficulties. And the components intended for inclusion in munitions destined for the U.K. would now be charged not to Canada but to Britain's lend-lease account. That too materially helped the exchange shortage. As the jubilant prime minister told Parliament, "the Hyde Park declaration will have a permanent significance in the relations between Canada and the United States. It involves nothing less than a common plan for the economic defence of the western hemisphere" and "the enduring foundations of a new world order."

There was more to come. In December 1941, a few days after the Japanese attack on Pearl Harbor at last brought the United States into the war, the president and the prime minister released a declaration proclaiming that "the production and resources of both countries should be effectively integrated and directed towards a common program of requirements for the total war effort." The two leaders promised to work to overcome "legislative and administrative barriers, including tariffs, import duties, customs and other regulations or restrictions of any character which prohibit, prevent, delay or otherwise impede the free flow of necessary munitions and war supplies between the two countries." The promises of Hyde Park were now to be fully implemented.

Exaggerations about Hyde Park were understandable enough at the time. The Canadian government's relief was palpable. But Hyde Park was not absolutely indispensable to Canada, nor did it land the country firmly in the American economic lap, as so many commentators (the present authors included) have stated. It did, however, greatly assist the Canadian government to the tune of $1187 Hyde Park dollars spent by the U.S. in Canada from 1941 to 1945. Once the United States entered the war, of course, its economy grew by leaps and bounds, and Canadian exports to the U.S. increased several fold as a consequence.

Washington's New Insensitivity

When Europe was collapsing in the summer of 1940, the American gaze was focussed on North America first. In those circumstances, Canada was very important, a nation worthy of attention at the highest levels. Hence, Ogdensburg and Hyde Park. But once the British seemed likely to survive and fight on, and especially after the United States entered the war in December 1941, Washington's eye turned inevitably to global issues. It was Britain, the Soviet Union, and the strategy of the Grand Alliance that now mattered. Canada was suddenly a minor player, a fit subject only for low- or middle-ranking bureaucrats. The president and the prime minister would still meet, the ease was still there, but Mackenzie King would never again act as a conduit for messages that might affect the fate of the world. Reality had intervened. The North Atlantic Triangle was not really as important as it had seemed.

What did this mean for Canadian policy? Just after Pearl Harbor, Norman Robertson began to consider the problem. Only thirty-seven, a tall, stoop-shouldered man with a large, balding head, Robertson had been picked by King to succeed Dr. O.D. Skelton, the long-time undersecretary of state for external affairs, who had died of a heart attack at the wheel of his car in January 1941. Robertson was cerebral and hard working, if almost as disorganized as Skelton had been. He had the prime minister's ear and had quickly gained his complete confidence. The undersecretary wrote that Canadians "have tended to take it for granted" that Washington "will always regard Canadian interests as a close second to their own and appreciably ahead of those of any third country." That was no longer true. Instead, as an inevitable consequence of the U.S. having taken the leadership of the democracies, the president now had much less time to spend on Canadian concerns. Now that the war was truly global, "the United States is, not unnaturally, inclined to take Canadian concurrence and support entirely for granted." The "special relationship in which Canada . . . [had] hitherto stood with regard to the United States" was no more, and that fact would have to shape Canadian policy.

There were clear signs of this attitude in every sphere. In the late spring of 1941, for example, the Cabinet became concerned that, the PJBD notwithstanding, Canada was not learning enough about American military plans and the secret discussions under way between Britain and the U.S. One way to learn more would be to send a military mission to Washington headed by a senior officer. This seemed a simple request to make, but to Ottawa's surprise both the Americans and, when they learned of it, the British, were reluctant. London made the traditional if outmoded argument that everyone would be far better off if the Commonwealth spoke as one and through them. Moreover, surely Canada did not have an experienced officer to spare for Washington. The Americans weighed in on the British side. The PJBD and the military attachés posted to the Canadian Legation were quite enough. It took a year of tenacious arguing before the Canadian Joint Staff Mission in Washington was reluctantly accepted.

Another crisis arose over the tiny islands of St. Pierre and Miquelon off the coast of Newfoundland. Within days of writing his memorandum, Robertson saw first-hand what American obduracy could do. St. Pierre and Miquelon were French possessions located very near to the convoy routes to Britain, and Hitler's puppet government at Vichy controlled the administration of the islands. There were fears, bolstered by the interception of messages between Vichy and the French Legation in Ottawa, that information about convoy sailings might have been passed on to the Germans. In the summer of 1941, plans were made in Ottawa to seize the islands and rally their population to the Free French of General Charles de Gaulle, but these were dropped for fear of the American reaction. Then there were suggestions that the Free French do the job themselves, a course opposed by the U.S. State Department, which was both unfriendly to de Gaulle and concerned that the seizure of the islands could violate the Monroe Doctrine. By this time, Canadian officials, notably Robertson, were becoming exasperated. In mid-December 1941 Admiral Muselier, one of de Gaulle's officers, visited Ottawa for discussions on the fate of the islands. According to most accounts, he was warned against taking military action. According to others, the Canadians, fed to the teeth with Washington's interference and failure to realize that there was a war on and that ships might be lost if the islands passed information on to Berlin, gave Muselier the go-ahead on the quiet. In any case, though they were assigned to work under the Canadian naval command in Newfoundland, Muselier and his Free French fleet of four vessels seized the islands on 24 December.

Christmas Day saw furious activity in Washington and Ottawa. The prime minister learned that Cordell Hull, the American secretary of state, was "very disturbed." He wished "Canada to order the Free French forces away." An angry Pierrepont Moffat ruined his own and many Canadian officials' Christmas dinner with demands that some formula be found that would satisfy Washington. Robertson understood the message all too clearly, but he was determined not to do anything that would be seen as disavowing de Gaulle. Washington then released a press statement. Canada, it flatly stated, had been asked "as to the steps that Government is prepared to take to restore the *status quo* of these islands" and to expel "the so-called Free French." Lester Pearson, recently returned from England to be assistant undersecretary at External Affairs, characterized the statement as "entirely inexcusable."

The crucial decision on Canadian action—or inaction—came on a train to Washington. Mackenzie King, several of his ministers, Robertson, and King's secretary, J.W. Pickersgill, were among the passengers. As Pickersgill remembered, King might have done what Hull wanted, "but Norman and I were so opposed to the American attitude. . . . We said that Canada cannot disturb the occupation. . . . It has happened and that is that." Stiffened by this, King refused to do anything. De Gaulle, characteristically, also refused to budge. That effectively ended the crisis, though there was still much shouting in Washington and a deep enmity towards de Gaulle that would endure. The Americans could be irrational and bullying, but the affair demonstrated that a firm position could withstand Washington's pressure.

There were examples of similar American insensitivity on the military side. The Royal Canadian Navy (RCN) had spent almost two years escorting convoys and fighting U-boats on the North Atlantic. The RCN had yet to become skilful at this difficult task by mid-1941, something understandable because of its tiny prewar strength and because its ships were fitted with obsolescent equipment. But although the United States was not yet in the war, its navy took control of the western Atlantic in September 1941 and the RCN ships committed to the protection of offshore shipping were placed under its overall command. That hurt, as did an attempt to send advisers to teach the RCN in March 1943. "Your people," Admiral Ernie King, commander-in-chief of the U.S. fleet, wrote condescendingly to Canada's chief of naval staff, "have as yet had little opportunity to conduct the work involved on the scale required." Rear-Admiral L.W. Murray, in command of the Canadian Atlantic coastal area, raged at this. His ships had by this time been doing the job for three and a half years, and the Americans had no operational experience that could compare.

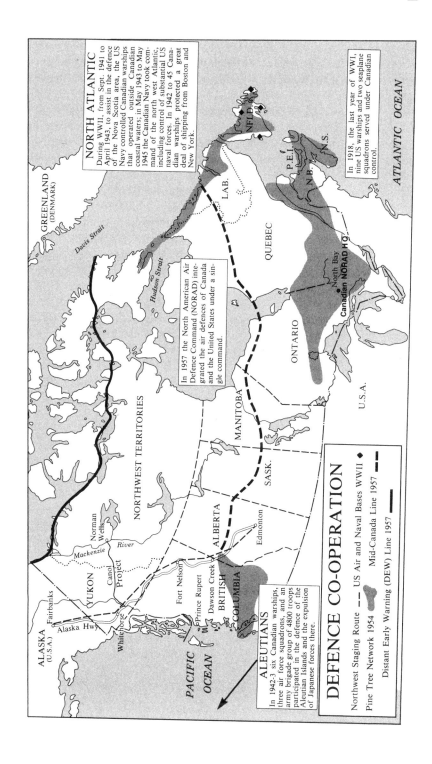

DEFENCE CO-OPERATION

Northwest Staging Route — —
US Air and Naval Bases WWII ◆

Pine Tree Network 1954
Mid-Canada Line 1957 – – –

Distant Early Warning (DEW) Line 1957 ——

NORTH ATLANTIC

During WWII, from Sept. 1941 to April 1943, to assist in the defence of the Nova Scotia area, the US Navy controlled Canadian warships that operated outside Canadian coastal waters; in May 1943 to May 1945 the Canadian Navy took command of the north west Atlantic, including control of substantial US naval forces. In 1942 to 45 Canadian warships protected a great deal of shipping from Boston and New York.

In 1918, the last year of WWI, nine US warships and two seaplane squadrons served under Canadian control.

In 1957 the North American Air Defence Command (NORAD) integrated the air defences of Canada and the United States under a single command.

ALEUTIANS

In 1942-3 six Canadian warships, three air force squadrons, and an army brigade group of 4800 troops participated in the defence of the Aleutian Islands and the expulsion of Japanese forces there.

The Canadian argument that they were the ones with hard-won experience, in fact, shortly brought the release of the RCN's east coast commands from American control. On 30 April 1943, Murray became commander-in-chief, Canadian northwest Atlantic, with supreme authority over shipping defence operations from the waters south of Nova Scotia to the ocean routes east of Newfoundland.

A new and nationalist thrust began to take hold of Canadian policy early in 1942 as the government's resentment at being cut out of allied grand strategy grew. When the British and Americans devised a series of combined boards to allocate resources, food, and war production, the reaction in Ottawa amounted to outrage. Canada, a nation that produced far more food than Britain, was being shut out of a board set up to allocate foodstuffs. The case was strong, so that Hume Wrong, the brightest of the senior officers of the Department of External Affairs, was able to develop an argument expressing Canada's desire that its substantial contribution to the war effort receive appropriate recognition. As eventually presented in Parliament by the prime minister after intensive departmental discussion, this was the functional principle: "Authority in international affairs must not be concentrated exclusively in the largest powers. . . . A number of new international organizations are likely to be set up as a result of the war. In the view of the government, effective representations on these bodies should neither be restricted to the largest states nor necessarily extended to all states. Representation should be determined on a functional basis which will admit to full membership those countries, large or small, which have the greatest contribution to make to the particular object in question." In other words, Canada did not claim the right to be represented on every allied body. It made little sense, for example, for the country to try to get a seat on the Combined Chiefs of Staff, the senior military commanders of the alliance. But the Food Board or the Combined Production and Resources Board was a different matter.

London's position on the Canadian demands was predictable—the United Kingdom could be trusted to represent its dominion's interests. When Ottawa objected, the response was that if Canada got a seat, then Australia would demand one, to which Ottawa said, quite sharply, that when Australia produced as much as Canada it would be entitled to one. The Americans fidgeted and hoped the problem would go away. Maybe London could resolve it; that was what they had always said they could do. But the Canadians would not be put off. The result was that Canada, alone among the smaller powers, eventually got seats on the Food Board and the Production and Resources Board, a minor triumph for Canadian policy.

BIG BROTHER ON CANADIAN SOIL

The country needed those triumphs. Events were forcing relations with the United States to the forefront. After Pearl Harbor, the defence of the Pacific coast became a major question. The Americans had grumpily tolerated the lackadaisical Canadian approach to this subject until then, but they were unwilling to accept it after they were forced into the war.

The first victims of the new urgency were Japanese-Canadians. About 23 000 lived in Canada, all but a thousand or so along the B.C. coastline. The great majority were engaged in fishing or market gardening or lumbering, ordinary enough trades. But because they inhabited locations of strategic importance, and because they were the long-standing subject of both suspicion and prejudice, the Japanese-Canadians concerned planners and politicians in Ottawa. As early as 1937 and 1938, interdepartmental committees had been studying what to do with them should Japan attack. In November 1941, the Canadian and American representatives on the PJBD had agreed to co-ordinate action against their Japanese residents in the event of war. After Pearl Harbor, the public pressure against the Japanese minorities in both countries mounted dramatically. By February 1942, after the Allies suffered stunning defeats in Hong Kong, Singapore, the Philippines, and the Dutch East Indies, the demand reached a crescendo. On 20 February, the American government announced that Japanese-Americans would be moved inland; four days later, the Canadian government took the same action.

Another area of concern was Alaska, where the Japanese occupied islands in the Aleutian chain in June 1942. This was American territory on the North American continent, and the psychological impact of such a move was serious. The idea of an overland route through Canada to Alaska, as we have seen, had been in the air since the 1930s. Canada had hitherto been reluctant, but Norman Robertson had told a visiting U.S. delegation in August 1941 that, from Canada's point of view, "there was only one prevailing consideration, namely that of national defence. If it could be shown that the armed services of the two countries gave [the] project a high priority rating Canada would be able to agree with the United States on terms of construction in a very few days." That turned out to be exactly true. On 13 February 1942, Moffat told Robertson that the war and navy departments believed the road was "imperative," and Canadian concurrence came almost at once. Within weeks, American can do spirit had generated seven engineer regiments totalling, with civilians, 11 000 workers. There was some heartburn in the "white man's country" that was then Canada about the black construction workers employed at carving the road northwards over the barrens. The road, rudimentary though it may have been, was completed from Dawson Creek, B.C., to Big Delta, Alaska, a distance of 1428 miles, by October 1942. The cost was just under $150 million. In addition, the U.S. army, concerned about a secure supply of oil for its Alaskan forces, spearheaded the drive to develop the Canol pipeline to exploit the oil fields at Norman Wells, Northwest Territories.

The Alaska Highway project was facilitated by the existence of rough airstrips, the North West Staging Route, linking northern Alberta with Alaska via northern British Columbia and the Yukon. An idea originating with the Canadian Department of Transport in the 1930s, this route was used during the war by the U.S. army air forces to ferry military aircraft to Alaska. Soviet pilots picked them up there for final delivery to the USSR. U.S. officials also pushed for the construction of

The faraway Alaska Highway. (National Archives of Canada/PA 121715)

airfields and weather stations in the central and eastern Arctic. The North East Staging Route (or Crimson Project) was designed to funnel newly built short-range bombers and fighters to Europe by short hops over the Great Circle Route. Though not in the end heavily used during the war and never fully completed, this network of facilities provided an important infrastructure for postwar northern development. By 1943, there were 33 000 American military and civilians working in the North.

Fiorello LaGuardia, the American chairman of the PJBD, found all these developments exciting. He wrote to the president that the scheme for the airfields was "so gigantic and dramatic. It took our Canadian colleagues by surprise." Then LaGuardia noted that the Americans might encounter "the usual difficulties because of pride and the little brother attitude with which you are familiar." In fact, once the plans were firm in Washington, Canada quickly agreed. But inevitably there were incidents in this sparsely settled area that troubled Canadians. At one point, the U.S. army actually built airstrips in the Northwest Territories without authority. One popular joke told it all: the U.S. army's northwest command headquarters switchboard in Edmonton was said to answer its telephone with a cheerful "Army of Occupation." Curiously, Ottawa did little to counter this impression until Malcolm MacDonald, the British high commissioner in Canada, reported on a visit to the North in March 1943.

MacDonald had earlier been told by Mackenzie King that the Alaska Highway "was less intended for protection against the Japanese than as one of the fingers of the hand which America is placing more or less over the whole of the Western hemisphere," so he was probably primed for what he found. On his return to Ottawa, the high commissioner spoke to King, appeared before the Cabinet War Committee, and prepared a major report. In it, he warned about

> the danger of so much initiative and decision belonging to our American allies. Admittedly it is highly important from the point of view of the vigorous prosecution of the war that these roads and routes should be built forthwith, and they will in any case be of immense value to Canada after the war. But it is surely unfortunate that the Canadian authorities have little real say as to, for example, the exact placing of these airfields, and the exact route of these roads on Canadian soil. The Americans decide these according to what they consider American interests . . . [and] they are designing those works also to be of particular value for (a)commercial aviation and transport after the war and (b)waging war against the Russians in the next world crisis.

Informed of MacDonald's report, Norman Robertson told the prime minister that "for most practical purposes, the Canadian Government's representative in local contacts with the American forces in the Northwest . . . [had been] the Secretary of the Alberta Chamber of Commerce and Mines." This was clearly a dangerous situation. The diplomatic precautions that could be taken in Ottawa, Robertson warned, "to make sure that American operations in this area are purely for war purposes and terminable at the close of hostilities" would amount to little without an effective Canadian presence on the scene. Robertson recommended the appointment of a special commissioner to keep Ottawa informed. In May 1943, General W.W. Foster was named to the post, provided with an aircraft and a large flag to hang out of the cockpit window, and charged to ensure that "the natural resources of the area shall be utilized to provide the maximum benefit for the Canadian people and to ensure that no commitments are to be made and no situation allowed to develop as a result of which the full Canadian control of the area would be in any way prejudiced or endangered."

That was one step. Another came in December 1943, when the federal government announced that the United States was to be paid in full for all permanent military installations it had built in Canada. If Washington did have intentions of capitalizing on its investments in Canada, they had now been blocked. After agreements were negotiated in 1944 and 1945, Ottawa paid $123.5 million for twenty-eight airfields, fifty-six weather stations, and a variety of other facilities, many of which had no immediate utility after the war. As King told the House of Commons, "it is thought undesirable that any other country should have financial investment in improvements of permanent value such as civil aviation facilities for peacetime use in this country." The Norman Wells oil fields were similarly handled on terms that fully protected Canadian sovereignty.

Canada had been initially lax, and astonishingly so, in its too-easy turning over to the Americans of the keys to the national attic. Yet once the problem was grasped, thanks largely to MacDonald's intervention, Ottawa acted with toughness and skill to protect the national interest.

The problems between Canada and its neighbour ought not to obscure the genuine co-operation that ordinarily existed. The PJBD was the show-piece of the military relationship, and its mandate extended to both coasts and, as we have seen, into the North. Its recommendations, not binding on the two governments but ordinarily accepted, were sometimes very specific: "15 November 1940: That an aerodrome be constructed at Ucluelet (Vancouver Island)." Some were less so: "29 July

1941: In view of Far Eastern situation, completion of both Canadian and U.S. sections of an airway to Alaska now of extreme importance." The Board was undoubtedly most important when the United States was a neutral; then it served not only to co-ordinate North American defence but to help bind the Americans to the Allied cause. But throughout the war, the PJBD provided a forum for discussion and the exchange of information. The good will was genuine.

In the period after Pearl Harbor, while Americans were helping with the defences of Prince Rupert, B.C., Canadian air and ground units moved into Alaska to help protect the giant territory. This co-operation increased after the Japanese occupied islands in the Aleutians, and RCAF squadrons flew regular operations against enemy forces on Attu and Kiska. The sole Japanese aircraft shot down by an RCAF pilot came on one of those sorties. In 1943, when the Americans were ready to re-take the Aleutians, suggestions emanating from Washington that Canada join in were eagerly picked up by General George Pearkes, commanding on the west coast. Reluctantly, Ottawa was persuaded to agree and the 13th Infantry Brigade was assigned to the job. The troops trained for the invasion, acquired some American weapons, equipment, and vehicles, and sailed on 12 July. After some further training at Adak under a marine corps officer skilled at amphibious operations, the Canadian and American forces stormed ashore at Kiska on 15 August. Unfortunately for the troops, who were reported to be eager for action, the Japanese had staged a secret withdrawal eighteen days before. There was no opposition.

TOWARDS THE PEACE

The Canadian government was also prepared, again with some reluc-tance, to play its part in the great offensive directed at Japan. From the beginning of 1944, Ottawa had been giving consideration to how it should participate. The RCN had ambitious plans for fleet work, escort duty, and landing craft; the RCAF considered the dispatch of up to sixty squadrons of fighters, bombers, and transports, and the army was pre-pared to provide one division. In September 1944, the Cabinet War Committee reached its decision: the army contribution would go as planned but both the navy and air contributions would be slashed. The RCN would now provide 13 000 sailors aboard two heavy cruisers and some forty additional vessels; two aircraft carriers and some destroyers would be provided later; and the RCAF was to provide twenty-two squadrons. The Canadian Army Pacific Force, almost 16 000 strong, was to use American equipment, except for uniforms, and follow U.S. army organization. The 6th Canadian Division, commanded by Major-General Bert Hoffmeister, who had served with great distinction in Italy and northwest Europe, was expected to participate in the invasion of Japan in 1946. Its personnel, drawn in part from men who had been attached to U.S. marine and army divisions through some of the fiercest battles of the Pacific war, were in training when the atomic bombs on Hiroshima and Nagasaki forced Japan's capitulation. Canada's national interest and prestige had required a contribution to the war against Japan. The war ended, however, before the country had to pay any further price in blood.

The national interest also demanded that the legation in Washington be upgraded to embassy status. The flow of business between the two countries was so great, the daily negotiations on a host of issues so far reaching, that it was ludicrous to see tiny Latin American nations with full-fledged embassies while Canada remained with its representation one peg below. In 1943, Leighton McCarthy, the minister to the United States, was transformed into the ambassador, the first Canadian diplomat to hold that rank. In Ottawa, Pierrepont Moffat's successor, Ray Atherton, took the same title. This was a mainly symbolic move to be sure, but one that signified both a new Canadian status and the vital nature of the relations between the two countries. In 1945, Lester Pearson, McCarthy's senior official and the man who did all the work that mattered, became ambassador.

It was an important post. As early as December 1941, the undersecretary of state for external affairs had complained to the prime minister that it was difficult to co-ordinate the Canadian position in Washington because direct contacts between boards, agencies, and departments of the two countries had multiplied so greatly. The Department of Munitions and Supply dealt with its counterpart, for example, and even the Canada Shipping Board had an official permanently stationed in Washington. The Wartime Prices and Trade Board had to deal directly with the Office of Price Administration, and in addition to the PJBD, there were other joint organizations such as the Materials Co-ordination Committee. Four years later, that list had expanded enormously. Canadian–American wartime relations were big business.

The prospect of peace showed few signs of reversing the growth in Canadian–American links. By 1943 both nations had already begun to look towards the postwar world. That involved Canada in ultimately fruitless attempts to persuade the Big Three powers (the U.S., the U.K., and the USSR) that a strong Canadian presence should be accepted in

The Big Two flank Canada, Quebec Conference, 1943. Roosevelt is at the left, Winston Churchill is at the right. (National Archives of Canada/C 31186)

the newly founded United Nations (UN). There was some bitterness in Ottawa about this, a feeling that Canada's very substantial efforts in the war were not being properly recognized.

Although there was concern about the great powers' intentions in the new UN, the Canadian government nevertheless decided to follow the U.S. lead on the postwar world. Canada had produced its own draft charter for the establishment of the International Monetary Fund, but it went along—as it had to— with the American plan that prevailed. The same was true of the long and difficult negotiations that created the International Civil Aviation Organization, designed to regulate civil air transportation. Nor were matters very different in the area of trade policy. The Americans wanted to see a world of multilateral trade with the lowest possible tariff barriers and an end to the imperial preferences that had so often embittered trade negotiations between Canada and the United States. Norman Robertson noted in 1944 that "Canada would be willing to wipe out the preferences in many cases and in some cases to make the rate free to all." The country was for free trade if possible, a logical position as the war came to a close. Nations such as Canada and the U.S. were in the strongest position and ready to flood the devastated nations of Europe and Asia with manufactured goods and raw materials. Even so, the new Canadian, and American, interest in what was described as "multilateral horizontal" tariff cuts was a contrast to the protectionism of the 1930s. Hard negotiations lay ahead before these attitudes could be transformed into legislation.

Cultural affairs continued to illustrate the differences between the two countries. New organizations such as the Canadian Committee had come into existence to lobby for increased government support for the arts, something very difficult to come by while munitions were swallowing all the available funds. Walter Herbert, an amateur playwright and executive secretary of the committee, organized the Canada Foundation as a co-ordinating agency to stimulate the arts. Herbert sought advice from American foundations that supported the arts, since there were precious few of those in Canada. But the Canada Foundation had no intention, Herbert said, of "scurrying across the world's largest undefended border to beg assistance from our American cousins." Although he managed to scrape $45 000 together by 1947, there was to be little success in securing private funding. In the U.S., the wealthy supported museums, symphonies, and the like, apparently only too willing to pay to see their names enshrined on a gallery or a pavilion; in Canada, there was no such desire, at least not yet.

THE "ALL-PERVASIVE FRIENDSHIP"

The war had irrevocably altered Canada's relations with its great neighbour. The U.S. was now indisputably the greatest financial and military power in the world, and few Canadians were unaware of this. However much they might admire gallant little Britain's very large share in the victory over Hitler, they had to know that the mother country's power and prestige were on the wane. And they had to know what that meant for relations between Canada and the U.S.

In May 1945, the Canadian Institute of International Affairs (CIIA) had its annual meeting at Kingston, Ontario. The CIIA numbered among its members virtually everyone with an interest in foreign policy: the academic, the journalist, entrepreneur, bureaucrat, and politician. The British High Commission dispatched one of its officers while the State Department in Washington sent one of its Canadian experts, J. Graham Parsons. The British diplomat reported back that after Parsons had spoken, "There was a high degree of acceptance of the proposition that Canada's future political alignment would be with the United States, and only secondarily with the British Commonwealth. . . . [Parsons] said that Canada's views and wishes exerted an influence on the United States out of all proportion to Canadian power, and added that on commercial policy Canada already enjoyed a consideration accorded to great powers alone. The enormous gratitude of the company at this remark could not be concealed." Undoubtedly there was a substantial dollop of persiflage in Parsons' words, but there was an element of truth in them too. Canada counted in some areas, not least trade, in which the cross-border flow of goods was the single most important aspect of each country's total exports. Two Canadian officials who had spent much of the war representing their country in Washington wrote in an academic article about the co-operation they had found. "There has been the open exchange of confidence," A.F.W. Plumptre and Sydney Pierce said, "the warm welcome, the freedom from formality, the plain speaking, and the all-pervasive friendship" derived from "our common background of language and culture," and the close trade and industrial relationship. "In part, it is due to the fact that our approach to problems is similar."

Another, more casual sign of the happy similarities was a mock note that Mike Pearson drafted in September 1941 to set out the rules for a Washington softball game between the U.S. Legation staff and officials from External Affairs. "It is suggested," Pearson wrote, "that the bases be leased . . . , the baselines be unguarded, for 3000 miles . . . that the bats and balls be lease-lended to the United States authorities." After the game, Pearson reported home that the contest, "which did not go the full nine innings because of the torn muscles and creaking limbs of the participants, was won by your Department by the handsome score of 40–18." At the end of the sixth inning it had been seventeen all. The External Affairs team, inspired by the introduction of undersecretary Robertson (who was notoriously unathletic) into the game as a base runner, "made a magnificent rally which produced 21 runs and was only ended by approaching darkness." The relaxed ease of the officials as they played and laughed together said something. Canadians were not unaware of the potential for danger in the relationship, especially now that Britain was in decline, but they and their American friends were going through a searing experience in which the differences seemed far less—and far less important—than the values and interests held in common. The Second World War made Canada more North American.

C H A P T E R   S I X

COLD WAR AND WARM HEARTS

1 9 4 5 – 1 9 5 7

In 1944, the Canadian government's Post Hostilities Planning Committee, a body composed of bureaucrats and military officers, produced a paper on the form that the postwar Canadian–American defence relationship would take. Allied victory was becoming certain, but already there was concern over the shape of the new world order and the possible hostility between the Americans and the Russians. One of the first bodies in the Canadian government ever to try to anticipate the future, the committee recognized that because Canada lay on the air and overland routes between the Soviet Union and the United States, the Americans were bound to take a greater interest in Canadian defence preparations than before the war. Roosevelt had, after all, insisted on calling his Ogdensburg creation the *Permanent* Joint Board on Defence, and it would continue after the end of the war. Conscious of the size of the American bases in the North and their tendency to expand without permission, the committee stated bluntly that the U.S. would not be permitted "to provide and maintain defence installations in Canadian territory." That was one lesson of the war. More important, however, nobody in Ottawa doubted that if the Soviet Union and the United States ever went to war, Canada would be involved from the outset and on the American side. This realization would inform the direction of postwar Canadian–American relations.

THE DOLLAR PROBLEM

As the war ended, the threat of another war seemed no bigger than a cloud the size of a fist on the far horizon. The peace had arrived, the boys were home from overseas, and optimism was the rule of the day.

On 21 May 1945, Canada and the United States had pledged to "consider and deal with the problems of the transition from war to peace in the same spirit that was manifested in the Hyde Park Declaration," a paper promise that nonetheless had some effects. When the war was almost over, for example, the U.S. War Production Board decided, that "to the extent consistent with the avoidance of general unemployment in the United States, military contracts with the Canadian producers should be cut back on the same basis as the reduction of contracts with domestic producers." That was a gesture of American friendship. More would soon be required.

Like that of the United States, the Canadian economy that emerged from the war bore scant resemblance to that of 1939. The Gross National Product had more than doubled, and both imports and exports had boomed. The government had put in place the foundations of the welfare state: every mother received a baby bonus cheque each month, and the jobless now had unemployment insurance to fall back on. And the Canadian people generally had emerged from ten years of depression and six years of war into the sun of prosperity. Years of wartime overtime had left Canadians with money in the bank and the itch to spend it. They wanted holidays, new furniture and appliances, plentiful food and drink, and the good life.

Canadian firms scurried to convert their factory production lines from Bren guns to washing machines. But American factories seemed quicker off the mark, and imports from the U.S. boomed. In 1945, they amounted to $1.2 billion; the next year, they were $1.4 billion; and the next year, $2 billion. Exports, by contrast, fell from $1.2 billion in 1945 to $884 million in 1946 and inched up again to $1 billion in 1947. The trade deficit was worrying because it meant a decline in Canada's holdings of American dollars. The drop was accelerated as a result of the Canadian decision in July 1946 to move the dollar to parity with its American counterpart: one Canadian dollar now equalled 100 cents U.S. Instantly, Canadian exports cost more and imports were cheaper.

There was another trade problem, too. With most of Britain's, France's, and the Netherlands' money going into reconstruction, Canada had to help with loans and grants if its goods were to be sold abroad. Taking courage in its hands, Ottawa put up almost $2 billion for Britain and other trading partners to buy Canadian goods. The British loan alone was $1.25 billion, about one-quarter of Canada's prewar GNP and a sum that compared more than favourably with the $3.75 billion offered Britain by the United States.

Thus the dimensions of Canada's problem were clear. The country had a large and growing dollar deficit with the United States. This was scarcely unusual, but until 1939 it had been balanced by earnings else-where in the world that could be readily converted to American dollars. Now Canada itself had to put up the cash to get European states to buy Canadian goods. Worse, most countries kept their currencies under tight control. Notably, Britain kept such tight rein that a pound sterling could not be turned into dollars. Moreover, American dollars, almost the sole hard currency in a world ravaged by war, were scarce every-where. Everyone owed the United States money; everyone needed American goods that could be paid for only in U.S. dollars; and no one knew where to get the currency so desperately needed. Countries like Britain faced economic collapse while their citizens groaned under the bread and meat rationing that persisted into the peace. So huge was the problem that between 1946 and 1953, the American trade surplus was $49 billion—and in those years a billion amounted to real money.

By the beginning of 1947, Ottawa knew that Canada faced a crisis. Graham Towers, the austere, dry-as-a-stick governor of the Bank of Canada, noted correctly, "Canada cannot continue indefinitely to sell on credit in overseas markets while she is incurring a substantial cash deficit in her balance of payments with the United States." In a sense, this was like the situation that had existed in 1941. Hyde Park had helped Canada then, but what was to be done this time? During the winter, bureaucrats began to consider the imposition of controls on American goods as a way to save scarce dollars, and Mackenzie King, still prime minister at the age of seventy-three, took the message to President Harry Truman when they met in Washington in April. King suggested that one way to ease matters, just as in 1941, was to increase exports of raw materials, and especially aluminum. Interesting, the tough, homespun president replied, but unfortunately the American aluminum industry was already running on reduced hours. Ah, King replied, the real difficulty was the worldwide shortage of U.S. dollars, and he hoped that some could be made available to western Europe to get them through the reconstruction period. Truman gave only a dusty reply, presumably understanding King's hope that dollars in British and French pockets would find their way to Canada to pay for wheat, lum-ber, and rye whiskey.

Still, King had in effect told the president that Canada would soon be faced with the necessity of putting import restrictions in place. In late May, the Canadians again put their case to American officials. The "intolerable drain in our reserves" was going to force restrictions on imports and pleasure travel and worse unless the United States bought more in Canada. As Towers said flatly, there was no satisfactory solution for Canada as long as Britain and western Europe were impoverished by their shortage of dollars. The difficulty, the Americans replied, was with Congress. It was not what was economically possible but what could be done politically: the Democratic President Truman was very unpopular and the Republicans were in control of Congress. Lester Pearson, now the undersecretary of state for external affairs, told King that time was running out: "Once again, weaknesses of the United States political and constitutional structure stand in the way of strong action by the United States." In June 1947, nevertheless, Secretary of State George C. Marshall told a convocation audience at Harvard University that the European countries should get together, plan for reconstruction, and put a proposal for massive economic assistance before the United States. The Marshall Plan, as it came to be called, had been born.

Norman Robertson, now high commissioner in London, pointed out that while the Marshall Plan could help speed Europe on the road to economic co-operation, it might shut Canadian exports out of Europe.

President Truman visits an uncommonly happy Mackenzie King, Ottawa, 1947. (Bill and Jean Newton/National Archives of Canada/PA 164723)

Canada could also be forced into the impoverished sterling area, obliged to confine the bulk of its trade to Britain and its ramshackle empire. There was little future there, even though London, at American urging, had made the pound sterling freely convertible in July 1947. Another option, this wisest of Canadian diplomats said, was closer continental integration with the United States, his preferred choice if a choice had to be made. In fact, he asked, shouldn't Canada be thinking "of a real reciprocity agreement with the United States which would strengthen our dollar position in the short term, and in the long run, ensure us against too great a dependence, relative to the United States, on the European market"? "It might be possible," he added, "to work out a scheme for a graduated approach to reciprocal free trade in a good many commodities on a continental basis." Certainly that course would be preferable to a defensive and discriminatory policy against American exports.

Robertson's idea sat on the table while the clock ticked and Canada's dollars disappeared. In July 1947, the Foreign Exchange Control Board in Ottawa estimated Canada's dollar deficit for the year at $1.041 billion, an increase of $250 million from the prediction at the beginning of the year. The impending disaster loomed nearer while Congress continued to dither. In August, the British faced a run on sterling and had to re-impose their rules against convertibility, and there was therefore small prospect of any American dollars coming to Canada from London.

At the same time, Ottawa began to put out feelers for a $750 million loan from the U.S. The idea was almost immediately shot down. As one U.S. official put it, "$750 000 000 is not to be had for the asking in Washington. The loan would have to be authorized by Congress." That was just not possible. The next month, the deputy minister of finance, Clifford Clark, went to Washington to make one last pitch to the key State Department officials. Clark was a former Queen's University academic and a man who had made and lost a fortune in the American property markets in the 1920s. In 1932, Prime Minister Bennett had brought him to Ottawa on O.D. Skelton's recommendation, and Clark in turn had recruited the able economists who now worked with him. The deputy minister told the Americans of Canada's position: the dollar reserves were dropping fast, and the trade deficit with the U.S. would wipe them out. What could be done? Clark said that the government did not want to impose trade restrictions because they would hurt the global trade negotiations at Geneva, which were soon expected to produce a General Agreement on Tariffs and Trade. Canada, he said, "had staked a great deal on a world of comparatively free trade and interchangeable currencies. If such a world was not to be, Canada would have to consider fundamental and drastic changes in her economy."

The Americans were sympathetic and concerned, but they had nothing to offer. No one could predict when—or even if—the Marshall Plan would pass the House of Representatives and the Senate. Nor was there any guarantee that there would be anything in the plan for Canada, not even the country's inclusion as a place in which Europe's Marshall dollars could be spent on supplies. That simply was not good enough, and Clark indicated bluntly that import restrictions were now certain. As the deputy noted after he came back to Ottawa, "we will have to impose severe restrictions before the Americans will believe that there is anything in our problem." The Canadian ambassador in the U.S., Hume Wrong, picking up on this cue, told his American friends that the coming restrictions would be "savage."

That was clear when the Canadians returned to Washington one last time on 28 October 1947. Clark and Towers brought with them two plans to deal with the gap between the $300 million Canada could expect to earn in the United Kingdom and the $1.2 billion deficit with the United States. Plan A was horrific: rationing on pleasure travel to save up to $40 million; import restrictions to save up to $446 million that would ban every consumer item from the U.S. other than citrus fruits, prunes, cabbages, carrots, and textiles, all of which would be under tight quotas; diversion of exports to net $50 million; and a loan from Washington's Export–Import Bank of $350 million. Plan B was marginally softer: the same ban on pleasure travel; import restrictions to save $175 million; long-term measures to see Canada become a Marshall Plan source of supply and possibly create a new trade treaty; and a loan of $500 million.

The Americans were appalled by Plan A, but at last they were seized of the Canadian problem. For the first time, they indicated that Canada could probably be used as a source for what was being called Marshall Plan "off-shore purchasing." They were also receptive to a new trade agreement. But the loan would be difficult to arrange for a host of reasons peculiar to the Export–Import Bank. Even so, by 4 November, the obstacles had been overcome, and four days later a stand-by credit, if not a loan, of $300 million had been arranged. With these assurances in hand, Plan A was scrapped. The Cabinet accepted Plan B on 13 November, and the trade restrictions were announced on 17 November, a date carefully chosen to minimize criticism in the media. In Geneva that day, Canada signed the General Agreement on Tariffs and Trade (GATT), committing itself to work for a world of lower tariffs. In London, Princess Elizabeth married Lieutenant Philip Mountbatten in a burst of postwar pageantry that had Britons on the streets and Canadians glued to their radios. And from Ottawa, the Canadian people had Minister of Finance Douglas Abbott to tell them that they could no longer go south for holidays and that many imported goods would be scarce for the next year or so.

Why had the United States come to Ottawa's rescue? American self-interest was certainly in large measure responsible. A Canada that verged on economic disaster would have to cut imports from the south, and economic interests in every part of the Union were at stake. Secondly, as Canadians proudly and often condescendingly thought, Canada was the only other country in the western hemisphere to be worth anything. The Americans actually seemed to agree that the democracy to their north was a special case. The third reason, one only rarely verbalized in Washington, was that aid to Canada drove a wedge into the heart of the British Empire and into the Ottawa system of preferential tariffs. That had been a long-standing American goal.

Intimations of this were to be found in the American Embassy in Ottawa, where there was restrained glee at the gratitude of Canadian ministers and officials about U.S. assistance. Julian Harrington, the number two at the embassy, reported on a conversation he had had with the finance minister. Abbott had been very grateful for Washington's assistance, said Harrington, and had confessed that "the success of his plans . . . [was] very largely dependent upon still further assistance from the U.S. He admitted to me that Canada is part and parcel of our economic orbit and hoped that we would continue to be helpful." Harrington added, "We have long recognized the inevitability of Canada becoming closely integrated into the American economic sphere, but it was encouraging to hear Abbott's frank admission of it."

Harrington's superior, Ambassador Lawrence Steinhardt, said much the same thing in a report a year later. American aims had been realized dramatically in the last dozen years, so much so that long-held fears of Canada strengthening its imperial orientation were now as dead and gone as the British Empire. Steinhardt reported that the Canadians had instituted changes "to strengthen Canadian military integration with the United States," although the trend was by no means complete. The Canadian government was asking for joint production programs and thus "promoting the integration of military resources." In economic matters, the movement had been the same, "closer integration" and "a growing commercial orientation towards the United States." The Commonwealth link, the ambassador concluded, "is still a cherished heritage for many but as Great Britain's economic and military power declines in relation to that of the United States the Canadian government has . . . tended to turn more to the latter as a source of economic welfare and military security." Moreover, improved communications "have made the full impact of U.S. culture felt in Canada so that in this regard as well a shift in orientation is discernible."

FREE TRADE?

Some Canadian and American officials were positively eager to speed the process of integration. During the wearying discussions over Canada's dollar shortage, Canadian negotiators had suggested a new trade agreement. The aim, as John Deutsch of the finance department said, was to achieve "a better balance in the one-way trade associated with our branch plants." Millions of dollars in components and parts flowed into Canada each year as American parent companies supplied their manufacturing subsidiaries; very little of the finished product went south and most branch plants served only the Canadian, or in some cases the Commonwealth, market. Hector McKinnon, the chair of the Canadian Tariff Board, added that the Canadians had been authorized by Cabinet to explore "the possibility of concluding a comprehensive agreement involving, wherever possible, the complete elimination of duties." According to the American summary of the subsequent talks, McKinnon added that Canada was prepared for an agreement "even if it necessitated a major readjustment and reorientation of Canada's international economic relations." Officials in Canada felt that the country "must either integrate her economy more closely with that of the United States or be forced into discriminatory restrictive policies involving greater self-sufficiency, bilateral trade bargaining and an orientation toward Europe with corresponding danger of friction with the United States, if not economic warfare."

Those were striking statements made by two powerful and competent officials who spoke with the blessing of the government. McKinnon had been in government service for years, and had played a major role in negotiating the trade agreements of the 1930s between Canada and the U.S. Much younger, Deutsch was the child of dirt-poor German immigrants to Saskatchewan, and had risen through sheer grit and ability to work for the Bank of Canada, External Affairs, and finance. Both men were by instinct free traders; both had been involved in the long struggle to negotiate the GATT agreements. Neither had any desire to see Canada forced into the kind of restrictive, beggar-thy-neighbour policies towards which war and reconstruction had pushed Europe. Deutsch, for one, said, "We have the choice between two kinds of worlds—a relatively free enterprise world with the highest existing standard of living and a government-controlled world with a lower standard of living." Deutsch was convinced that "meshing our economy with that of the United States would ensure the Canadian future."

Deutsch and McKinnon and their like-minded friends in the bureaucracy knew the political implications of that "meshing" of economies. Deutsch, who had briefly worked for the *Winnipeg Free Press* at the end of the war, told a journalist friend, "The price of a customs union with the U.S. is the loss of political independence in the sense that we would no longer be in effective control of our national policies. Things have changed since the reciprocity campaign of 1911. Then reciprocity simply broadened the area of trade . . . [but now] . . . we would inherit a vast structure of American government policy. . . . Policy would be shaped in Washington. A customs union . . . may be a fine thing. . . . But let us not blink at the price." Whether Canada was prepared to pay that price remained to be determined.

The Americans had little to lose in moving ahead with such an arrangement. Europe and Asia were unreliable mendicants, while Canada, short of American dollars though it might be, was a democracy, a proven ally, a storehouse of vast mineral resources, and a like-minded nation. Yet American officials (most notably the young and able Paul Nitze of the State Department) realized that a trade agreement had little chance of passing a protectionist Congress. What was needed instead was "some plan sufficiently bold and striking to fire the imagination of the people and force favorable action by Congress." A "special form of customs union" might do the trick, one that would produce free trade between the two countries while allowing each to have individual tariffs against third parties. "As Canada would retain tariff autonomy," Nitze argued, "there would be less grounds for fearing political absorption by the United States." The American idea was presented to Deutsch at a private dinner party on New Year's Eve. He immediately responded that this was "political dynamite" and promised to indicate within two weeks if there was any possibility of Canada agreeing to such an arrangement.

Back in Ottawa, Deutsch found divided opinions. Some officials were cool, but C.D. Howe, the powerful minister of trade and commerce, and Douglas Abbott, the able, relaxed finance minister, were very interested. More to the point, and much to Deutsch's surprise, the prime minister indicated strong approval. As King wrote in his diary, "It is clear to me that the Americans are losing no opportunity to make their relations as close as possible with our country." Deutsch had the green light.

All through January and February 1948, studies and discussions in both countries proceeded in secrecy. Analyses were made, technical details sorted through. Woodbury Willoughby, director of commercial policy at the U.S. State Department, was a convinced advocate, and in a paper on 22 January he dealt with the implications for Canada and the U.S. as he saw them. Such an agreement would be a "momentous decision" for Canadians, he said, one that would "radically alter the pattern of her foreign trade from a predominantly East–West to a predominantly North–South movement." There would be major industrial ramifications. Even so, Canadian officials were convinced that they were headed in the right direction. "They tend to the view that Canada's ultimate destiny is inevitably linked to ours and that the integration of the economies which was effected during the war should be continued and developed further." An agreement would create opportunity for the U.S., Willoughby argued, and the costs were small. Imports from Canada threatened few American producers, and only such industries as wheat, flour, zinc, cheese, frozen blueberries, and silver fox furs faced tough competition from Canada.

After a long series of talks that began on 18 February, Deutsch, Willoughby, and their colleagues had a deal. All duties would immediately be removed by both nations. There would be no quantitative restrictions on imports after five years other than in a few areas. Each country could impose "absolute transitional (5-year period) quotas" on certain sensitive products. Joint consultation would be required, especially to work out agricultural marketing agreements. Finally, "consideration ... [was] given to a clause ensuring, in the event one country ... [was] subject to military attack, continued free access to the products of the other." That last clause acted as a reminder that in early 1948 the Cold War was on with a vengeance. The Soviet Union was considered a menace of frightening proportions.

The Americans believed they had an ideal arrangement. It was simple and dramatic, and it would wipe out Commonwealth preferences. And the time was ripe, Willoughby argued: "There has never been a time when conditions in Canada, both economic and political, were more favorable." Americans, too, would like the plan "on both economic and strategic grounds. ... The widespread popular concern over Russian policy will undoubtedly lead to an acceptance of the international political and strategic implications," which would override any economic objections.

Deutsch was as committed to the plan as Willoughby. In a memorandum to ministers and key officials, the negotiator put forth the benefits that would come to Canada. The transitional period offered genuine protection to Canada, and Canadian industry and agriculture would have the immediate benefit of virtually free access to the giant American market. Deutsch admitted that greater economic integration would ensue, but suggested that it would have been forced on Canada in any case by the economic chaos in Europe and Asia. Either Canada negotiated as a self-sufficient nation now, he concluded, or as a supplicant later. He said nothing of the political impact. The initial soundings in Ottawa were favourable, and Washington was advised of this. The timing, however, was crucial. Canada would almost certainly need a general election on the issue of free trade with the United States, and the issue would probably be so emotional that a government victory was far from certain. Nineteen forty-eight was an election year in the United States, and a good deal would hinge on the Republican and Democratic conventions and candidates. If they were opposed to it, free trade was unlikely to pass Congress.

The key figure in Canada was Mackenzie King. As late as 25 March, Deutsch was under the impression that the prime minister continued to be favourable to the deal, though Deutsch told Willoughby that King wanted at least two more weeks to make certain he could "swing the deal politically." In fact, King had begun to wobble as early as the middle of the month. A copy of *Life* magazine had come across his desk with an editorial calling on Canada and the U.S. to forge a customs union. King did not admire the American owner of *Time* and *Life*, Henry Luce, and support from him, especially for an agreement that had been negotiated in secrecy, was not what the prime minister wanted to hear. Then, on the 22nd, King talked with Clifford Clark and Deutsch. He came away completely worn out. The old man, after more than twenty years in power, was finally running out of steam: "I was really so depressed and weary in my head that I wanted to get away from everything. What has been suggested to me today is almost the largest proposal short of war any leader of a government has been looked to to undertake. Its possibilities are so far-reaching for good on one hand, but possible disaster if project were defeated that I find it necessary to reflect a good deal before attempting a final decision."

Two days later, King reached up on his bookshelf and, again apparently by chance, hauled down a copy of Sir Richard Jebb's *Studies in*

Colonial Nationalism. The page fell open on a chapter entitled "The Soul of Empire." Instantly, King saw its message. Free trade would destroy both the unity of the empire and the regard in which King was held in Canada. The Tories would be sure to paint his last act in power as a capitulation to the Americans and an abandonment of Canada's proud British tradition. And then King said, "I would no more think of at my time of life and at this stage of my career attempting any movement of the kind than I would of flying to the South pole."

There were additional discussions, but the customs union with the United States was now dead. The prime minister was still, in such important matters, all-powerful. King was a mystic, a spiritualist, a curious, lonely man made up of equal parts of suspicion and ambition. He was also a superb political strategist and tactician, a master of the swift stroke. The idea that King killed free trade in 1948 because of a near-mystical experience brought on by a chance encounter with an obscure book fits the image. King already had doubts about the Deutsch–Willoughby scheme, however, and he was deeply concerned about how the opposition parties could campaign against it. The flag of Anglo-Canadian nationalism would be waved just as furiously as it had been in 1911, and King, who had lost his own seat in Parliament in that election, feared the worst. He had in fact been concerned since the war about American intentions in Canada. He had resisted those intentions; could he do less now?

Characteristically, King held out one way in which the negotiations could be resumed. As Ambassador Wrong told the Americans on 1 April, "It is thought that trade discussions might begin again if and when a satisfactory North Atlantic Security Pact is signed. It would be natural for the trade discussions to be related to the pact, since they are concerned with measures for economic defence against aggression." The defence of Canada, North America, and western Europe had become the important issue, and free trade with the United States and possibly with all the North Atlantic nations could only be achieved within the context of a North Atlantic Treaty. Much of the bureaucratic drive towards free trade was lost, moreover, after the 3 April 1948 passage of the Marshall Plan in Washington. The great aid scheme did include the promised provision to cover off-shore purchases, and Canada was quick to take advantage of this. The British used some of their Marshall Plan dollars to pay for previously contracted deliveries of Canadian wheat, and other recipient nations steered some of their dollars to Canada. The results were astonishing. In the period from the second quarter of 1948 to the second quarter of 1950, the Marshall Plan put

U.S. $1.155 billion into Canada, a vast sum that was more than enough to restore Canada's dollar holdings. The heat was off the Canadian economy, and the trade restrictions put in place in November 1947 soon disappeared.

On the other hand, there was a new danger looming. Canada was in the American camp, economically as well as militarily. Canadian trade with the United States had burgeoned dramatically after the war. In 1946, Canadian exports to the U.S. had been $884 million and imports from the U.S. $1.387 billion. By 1949, exports to the south were $1.5 billion (or just half of all of Canada's exports) and imports from the United States $1.9 billion. A very substantial portion of Canadian trade with Europe had in effect been subsidized by the U.S. through the Marshall Plan. The great American aid scheme might speed European recovery, which might in turn eventually let some of Canada's traditional trading partners pay their own bills. Maybe. But no one could bank on that, and in the circumstances, C.D. Howe, the trade and commerce minister, bent every effort towards entrenching Canada's position in the U.S. market—the one stable, booming economy in the world. But his efforts would have to be without free trade.

THE SOVIETS AND A PAX AMERICANA

Canadians and Americans were both worrying about more than trade after the war. The hostility of the Soviet Union dominated Canadian and American thinking about the postwar world. Stalin's Communist regime was apparently strong and powerful; his armies had proved that, having borne the lion's share of the war against Hitler. The USSR had liberated Eastern Europe and its tank armies sat menacingly in the formerly independent states to ensure that only friendly governments took office. The Soviets were ensconced in Manchuria; they occupied islands off Japan; they were pressing into Iran; and they were supporting Greek guerillas and Mao's Chinese Communists.

Canada's introduction to the Cold War came at the beginning of September 1945. A cipher clerk named Igor Gouzenko left the Soviet Embassy on Charlotte Street in Ottawa with a sheaf of documents proving that Moscow had run spy rings of civil servants and military officers in Canada. The Soviets had been trying to learn about the development of the atomic bomb, which had brought British, French, and Canadian scientists to work in Canada and to co-operate with nuclear research under way in the United States. There was every indication that the spies had secured the desired information. Gouzenko's documents and the verbal evidence he could offer also pointed to espionage in high places in the United States' departments of state and the treasury. The Gouzenko case forced Mackenzie King into secret discussions with British Prime Minister Clement Attlee and President Truman, and the secret services in all three countries quickly renewed their wartime cooperation. The Soviets' obduracy at the United Nations and their use or threatened use of the veto to block Security Council action again squeezed the Americans, Canadians, and British together.

To a substantial extent, however, neither Canada nor the United States was yet overwhelmingly concerned with the military threat posed by the Communist state. The Americans, after all, had the bomb, and the Soviets did not. The speed with which the armed forces were demobilized in Canada proves how limited concern really was. The Canadian force of a million men and women recruited between 1939 and 1945 quickly dwindled away. In 1945, the chiefs of staff had prepared plans for compulsory service and an army of 55 000, an RCAF of 30 000, and a navy of 20 000. The government snorted, reduced the proposed budget by almost half, and cut the personnel projections in like manner. There would be no big battalions in postwar Canada.

Yet as planners had realized during the war, the very presence of the Soviet Union across the North Pole and the simple fact that Canada was sandwiched between the U.S. and the USSR had significant defence implications. As early as July 1945, an American member on the Permanent Joint Board on Defence raised the question of "the continental defence value of the Canadian Northwest"; in November of that year, the Americans proposed updating ABC-22, the continental defence plan prepared in 1941, when Germany had been the enemy. By 1946, the PJBD had essentially agreed on the desirability of "close cooperation" between the two countries' armed forces. That meant exchange of personnel, standardization of equipment to the greatest extent possible, and reciprocal provision of military facilities. At the same time, a joint staff study had produced an "Appreciation of the Requirements for Canadian–U.S. Security." This appraisal did not see a serious threat of invasion for "at least several years," but there was the possibility of small lodgments in the North. That threat later led Lester Pearson, a man with a quick wit, to suggest that Canada's defence in the North would be based on "scorched ice." The planners declared the need for an effective air defence system and they also produced a "Basic Security Plan" as a replacement for ABC-22.

King and Truman discussed defence questions during the prime minister's visit to Washington in October 1946, and Truman followed up by sending a strong message to King on the need for action. First the Cabinet Defence Committee and then the whole Cabinet had to consider how the government should respond. There was serious concern at the scale and cost of the American proposals. It was easy to contemplate the closest possible co-operation with the Americans in defence; everyone was for that. It was another thing entirely to pay large sums of money to do so. As a result, only a joint Canadian–American public statement emerged on 12 February 1947, with no specific policy to give it teeth. Each nation agreed that "its national defence establishment shall, to the extent authorized by law, continue to collaborate for joint security purposes. The collaboration will necessarily be limited." It was so limited, in fact, that the statement said bluntly, "No treaty, executive agreement or contractual obligation has been entered into. Each country will determine the extent of its practical collaboration in respect of each and all of the foregoing principles. Either country may at any time discontinue collaboration." Co-operation if necessary, but not necessarily co-operation was the order of the day as long as Mackenzie King ruled the roost in Ottawa.

More would soon be necessary. The increasing danger of Soviet aggression in Europe, as well as the very real possibility that Communists might take power through the electoral system in France and Italy, sent a shiver through western capitals in 1947 and 1948. A Communist coup in Czechoslovakia in early 1948 increased the tension, as did Soviet pressures on the Allied garrisons in Berlin and the imposition of a blockade to cut road and rail communication between the former German capital and the Allied occupation zones to the west. North Americans watched these events with feelings akin to dread; no one wanted another war before the wounds from 1939–45 had healed. The Canadian government, which drew much of its confidential information about events from British diplomatic sources, and more recently from American ones, had already given public indications that the like-minded democracies might have to band together for self-defence. Thus, when Great Britain proposed in March 1948 that Canada and the United States join it in secret discussions about a mutual assistance pact, nobody hesitated over participating, not even Mackenzie King. For the next year, discussions took place in secrecy in Washington, and eventually broadened to include the other western European democracies. The result, signed on 4 April 1949, was a document creating the North Atlantic Treaty Organization, or NATO.

In the discussions leading to the treaty, Canada had several aims. It wished to ensure that the United States came into the alliance from the beginning. American isolationism was still strong in the late 1940s and the Congress was full of senators and representatives who considered all foreigners to be after two things only: American money and American soldiers to rescue them from their follies once more. Those who remembered how costly American isolationism had been to the world in the pre-1941 period were worried about its recurrence. The Truman administration, which recognized the threat, had used every form of persuasion, including scare tactics, to push the Marshall Plan through Congress in the spring of 1948; similar methods were employed with the North Atlantic Treaty, and again they were successful.

Secondly, Canada wished to promote the idea of freer trade. In scuppering the customs union proposal, King had held out the prospect of liberalized trade being tied to defence. The ministers and officials in Ottawa who wanted free trade were essentially the same ones who wanted the security pact, and their efforts were concentrated on Article 2 of the treaty, which called for attention to the economic and cultural dimensions of western unity. This Canadian clause had initially been resisted bitterly by the Americans, who believed that it would be difficult enough to get a straight military assistance treaty through Congress, let alone one with economic clauses. The clause did find its way into the treaty, however, and it bound the twelve signatories to "seek to eliminate conflict in their international economic policies and . . . [to] encourage economic collaboration between any or all of them." But if its purpose was to promote free trade, Article 2 was destined to have no success. In fact, judged from any perspective (except perhaps Canadian domestic politics), Article 2 was a bust.

Thirdly there was a pair of related reasons for Canadian support for the Atlantic alliance. Wartime experience had taught Canada that there was safety in numbers when dealing with the Americans. NATO seemed to provide this. As well, Canada had been left out of the great power decision making in the last war, and a treaty of mutual defence seemed to ensure that Canadians would be involved in decisions from the outset in the event of another conflict. The alliance created a Pax Americana, to be sure, but it also enmeshed the United States in obligations that could help control its tendency, as Canadians and many others saw it, to run wild. In any case, for those who objected to a Pax Americana, there was always Norman Robertson's seriously intended quip, "Better a Pax Americana than no Pax at all."

Above all, the North Atlantic Treaty marked an historic change of course for both North American nations. For years, the Americans had sheltered behind their Monroe Doctrine, wary of foreign entanglements; they had entered the two world wars belatedly and only after the Allied cause was in serious danger. Canada had been present in both wars from the outset, though the official policy before and after was "no commitments" and "Parliament will decide." Parliament and Congress would still decide, but both countries had committed themselves in advance to the defence of western Europe against the Soviet Union, and done so in peacetime. That was a highly significant break with the past.

Defending Korea, Defending North America

For more than a year NATO was simply a paper commitment for Canada. The country had no troops in Europe, and growth in the defence budget was small. Matters changed dramatically, however, after the forces of Communist North Korea invaded the South on 25 June 1950. The Americans had only a small military mission in South Korea, but they had troops nearby in Japan. With the Soviet Union by chance boycotting sessions of the United Nations Security Council in protest at the failure of the world organization to admit the Communist government of China, the UN was prevailed upon by Washington to authorize the use of force to resist aggression. Within days of the attack, largely untrained American forces were suffering heavy casualties and defeats in action. It was officially a UN war, the first of its kind, but it was really Washington's war and the U.S. very quickly began exerting diplomatic pressure on its friends to send troops to help stop the Communist advance.

The initial response in Ottawa seemed cool. Prime Minister Louis St. Laurent, called in from vacation to talk to reporters, responded to the first question by saying casually, "I hope to be out fishing again the day after tomorrow." In other words, Korea was a long way away. Canada did answer the call for assistance, but initially with only three RCN destroyers. American officials were annoyed at this "token" response. When Canadians objected that three destroyers were not a token, a State Department official offered the rejoinder, "Okay, let's call it three tokens." Soon, RCAF transports were also on their way to Japan to ferry troops and equipment between North America and the Far East, but Asia was not a sphere of much interest to Canada, and the last time the country had sent troops to that part of the world—Hong Kong in 1941—they had all been killed or captured. Moreover, the Canadian armed forces were again, as they had been in the 1930s, few, ill equipped, and not very well trained. Apart from the welfare of a handful of missionaries, Canadians neither cared about Korea nor seemed passionately concerned about fighting for the UN. General Maurice Pope, a senior army planner and diplomat, once said of the commitments to collective security in the UN Charter, "Our people instinctively believe the chickens subscribed to by fifty nations are unlikely to come home to roost."

Cabinet delayed its decision on committing ground troops to Korea. The opportunity to discuss the question came after the funeral of Mackenzie King, who died on 22 July 1950, and was buried in Toronto. On the return journey to Ottawa, the ministers finally sat down to discuss Korea. Understandably enough under the circumstances, several ministers asked "What would Mr. King do?" but St. Laurent, who had become prime minister in the autumn of 1948, indicated that he favoured a commitment. For a prime minister, a French-speaking prime minister, to favour the dispatch of Canadian soldiers to a war in Korea fought by the United Nations was unheard of. Mackenzie King and his

From left to right: Henry Cabot Lodge, Dwight Eisenhower, Louis St. Laurent and C.D. Howe. (National Film Board/National Archives of Canada C 53459)

policies were dead and buried now, but many of his former colleagues lived on. There was sharp opposition to sending troops from ministers such as C.D. Howe of Trade and Commerce and Jimmy Gardiner of the Department of Agriculture. Before a final decision was taken, emissaries secretly set off for Washington to get the American view.

Lester Pearson, who had left the diplomatic corps in 1948 to become secretary of state for external affairs, saw Dean Acheson, the secretary of state in the Truman administration. Korea, the American said, was just a phase of the general conflict between the capitalist and communist worlds. By itself, he admitted, Korea was not important, but the challenge had to "be met by the free peoples; they must call a halt to communist aggressive tactics." Moreover, and most important, now that the Soviets were permitting satellite countries to carry out military aggression, "the most significant deduction to be made from the Korean attack was the necessity for strengthening as rapidly as possible the forces of the free world to meet aggression elsewhere." Elsewhere could be Europe or North America or both.

Pearson was convinced by this analysis, and believed firmly that Canada had to participate in Korea. By 7 August, Cabinet had agreed to send a brigade of troops to Korea; soon thereafter, the decision was taken to station a second brigade and an air division of fighter aircraft in Europe with NATO. The brigades were not grouped with the U.S. military, but with British forces in Europe and Commonwealth forces in Korea. Ottawa's world view had altered quickly, and Canada's defence spending, just 2.2 percent of the GNP in 1949, rose to 5.5 percent in 1951, and 7.6 percent in 1953. In dollar terms, the increase from $361 million in 1949 to $1.9 billion in 1953 was staggering for what was still peacetime, and indicated just how seriously Ottawa took the Communist threat in both Europe and, secondarily, Asia. The lessons of the 1930s had been well learned in Ottawa. Aggression must be nipped in the bud.

Inevitably the new emphasis on defence drew North Americans closer together again. The Joint U.S.–Canadian Industrial Mobilization Planning Committee (JIMPC) had been created in 1949. By August 1950, under the impact of Korea, it was hard at work. From Canada's point of view, its main task was to draw up principles to recognize that indigenous industries were full partners on what was described by the business press as "the defence manufacuring team." The public announcement of the JIMPC principles came on 26 October 1950, making clear that something approximating integration of the two mobilization efforts had been achieved. The document contained repeated use of words such as "co-ordinated," "mutually consistent," and "consultation," and although the accord did not bind the Americans to purchase specific amounts of Canadian materials, it nonetheless took a long step towards complete military integration. Canada had the JIMPC principles as a lever to get its goods and minerals into the U.S. defence market and that would help earn dollars and balance the trade flows. The Americans, exquisitely conscious of their vulnerability in not possessing a domestic supply of certain scarce minerals and metals, now had an argument to put behind their investment in Canadian mining. One component of the overall rearmament program greatly favoured the Americans. In 1951 and 1952, the U.S. bought $300 million worth of defence equipment in Canada. As Canadians rearmed, however, they had to spend $857 million in the United States.

Some Canadian officials had differed with the prevailing view of an aggressive and expansionist Soviet Union right up to 1949 or even 1950. In the months immediately after the beginning of the Korean War, however, opinion in Ottawa was at one with the hard-line views of Washington. The old days of "Parliament will decide" and the evasion of responsibility were apparently gone forever.

Characteristically, North American unanimity did not last long, and certainly not over Korea. Canada had done its part by sending troops to participate in the American-led United Nations War, but there were soon difficulties. As 1950 ended, China sent hundreds of thousands of troops southwards after General Douglas MacArthur's UN troops drove into North Korea and neared the Yalu River that separated Chinese Manchuria from Korea. The Canadians at the UN had argued, not too strenuously, that the UN should liberate South Korea but not press into the North. When Ottawa pressed Pearson to try harder to block the Americans' desire to eliminate North Korea as a threat, his reply was revealing: "You have no idea what the pressure is like down here. I can't."

The intervention of the People's Republic proved that Canadians' concerns had been correct, that challenge had met response, but this made them more, not less, unpopular in Washington. "I told you so" is never a line with which to win friends and influence people, and Pearson and his officials from External Affairs quickly developed a reputation for being fair-weather friends, more interested, in political scientist Denis Stairs's apt phrase, in playing the "diplomacy of constraint" than in helping to crush Communist aggression. Canada began to use its influence to twist arms in Washington and New York to press for an armistice, in order to stop the fighting before the war spread into a general conflagration in Asia. Constraint was a difficult balancing act. As one of Pearson's key assistants, Escott Reid, put it, "If you consider that the United States is proposing to do something unwise and dangerous . . . , how far do you go in standing up to them and opposing them in public? You have to make this assessment, day after day, as you have to ask yourself: 'Is the cost of opposition truly in the national interest of Canada?'"

That was a hard question, day after day and year after year. If Canada opposed American wishes in Korea, would this have an echo on tariff policy that might put people out of work in Moosonee or Moose Jaw? If Canada opposed American wishes in Korea, what would the impact be on the strategic interests of Canada and on the broader questions of peace and war? Pearson, as Canada's foreign minister, was certainly aware of the disadvantages that might result, but keeping the Korean War limited and bringing it to an end as soon as possible were important enough to run the risk of American anger. So he proceeded and was in the forefront of the efforts at seeking an armistice, so much so that his earlier close relationship with such Americans as Dean Acheson began to fall apart under the strain. Sarcastic, brilliant, a tough-minded defender of America's global interests and, moreover, the son of a Canadian, Acheson could get powerfully scornful of the constant Canadian preaching about restraint and peace. He was more than willing to point out that American taxpayers were paying the bills and that American troops, not Canadian, were carrying the burden in Korea and suffering the high casualties. (As the official Canadian army historian noted drily, Canadian casualties in almost three years of fighting were about the same as in a year's carnage on the highways.) It was about time, Acheson later wrote, for Canadians to stop playing the role of "the stern daughter of the voice of God." Stop hectoring us, in other words.

To his credit, Pearson did not stop. In his dispatches he was quite prepared to complain about American "impatience and tactlessness, and the absence of any clear-cut sense of direction." Other Canadians also found much about the American management of the war to make them unhappy. Brooke Claxton, the minister of national defence, visited the front in 1951 and later wrote of how American staff officers "had all got in the habit of receiving and lying to Congressmen and they put on a similar show for us. Their estimates of military possibilities, ammunition expenditures, casualties, etc., were fantastic. . . . In the greatest detail and with the utmost seriousness they reported the number of Chinese killed, wounded and missing, the number of bridges, engines and trucks destroyed. There wasn't a word of truth in it." Moreover, "American expenditures of lives and ammunition are high according to our standards, higher than our people would be willing to accept." Claxton's views were unquestionably shared by the Canadian military, and they may have helped push Pearson along in his continued efforts to get the Americans and their allies to accept armistice discussions. In the summer of 1951, peace talks began. It took more than two years and cost tens of thousands of casualties before those talks bore fruit.

If there was a new testiness in the relationship, it failed to affect the fundamentals. Although Pearson said, "We don't agree with this tactic of the Americans, and I'll go on record as saying I don't agree," he went on to add that it was important for the Soviets and their friends not to misunderstand. The Americans were "our leader and we stick with them and we'll be solid and don't get any ideas you're splitting us."

There must be no mistaking, then, that the Soviets were the enemy and that America was Canada's friend. That assessment lay behind the unabated drive to close co-operation in defence and major new military initiatives. The vulnerability of the Arctic had to be considered seriously for the first time in the face of Soviet hostility; a bomber attack across the pole was believed to be a real possibility. As early as 1947, the Royal Canadian Air Force had supported the development of a Canadian interceptor specially designed to operate over the huge distances of the North. In 1951, under the spur of rearmament and the fear of a Soviet nuclear attack against North America, defence minister Claxton announced that nine air defence squadrons would be equipped with the new interceptor, the CF-100, and that greater emphasis would be placed on radar to give early warning of bomber attack. By 1954, the Pinetree Line of thirty-four radar stations was in place, running roughly along the fiftieth parallel. The Line cost $450 million, and two-thirds of the bill was paid by the United States, which also provided just over half the operating and maintenance personnel. The Pinetree Line was too far south to provide much warning time, however, and in 1955 the Mid-Canada Line, its ninety-eight unstaffed radars to be located along the fifty-fourth parallel, was begun.

But again bomber technology was advancing by leaps and bounds. American defence officials and scientists called for yet more warning time, and it was decided to build a Distant Early Warning Line in the High Arctic. The cost for the seventy-eight stations of the DEW Line along the seventieth parallel was enormous and Ottawa was correspondingly nervous. The result was a compromise: Canada would assume full costs for the Mid-Canada Line if the Americans picked up the tab for the DEW Line. That seemed to be a bargain. It became less so when American security regulations were put in force at DEW Line sites and Canadians, even members of Parliament, had to apply through Washington for permission to visit the radar stations.

THE SEAWAY AT LAST

The anti-Americanism that such Pentagon insensitivity fostered was relatively mild. The Cold War demanded sacrifices from everyone, and Canadians considered themselves very fortunate to have the United States as a partner. The U.S. was lucky too, because Canada always put a very high premium on promoting co-operation. That was apparent when the question of the St. Lawrence Seaway was finally resolved.

The seaway was a gigantic construction project that would allow ocean-going ships to get around the rapids on the St. Lawrence and hence into the Great Lakes, and simultaneously create huge resources of hydro-electric power. If the seaway was in place, the newly accessible iron ore of Labrador, for example, would be able to reach the rolling mills of Ohio, thereby helping Canadian development and, Canadian officials and American steel manufacturers argued, advancing U.S. security. But what was good for the goose was not always good for the gander. Those operating on the east and west coasts who benefited from ship traffic, and the railways and trucking firms that carried goods inland, stood to lose. After yet another victory for regional interests and a defeat for the seaway in Congress, Prime Minister St. Laurent told the House of Commons in 1949 that if the Americans did not want to participate, Canada would do the job itself.

The need for St. Lawrence River power forced Canada to act. The costs of the project were so large, however, that this had about it the smell of a bluff. Nonetheless, the Canadian government played its cards well and finally in January 1954, thanks to strong support from an Eisenhower administration very anxious to prevent unilateral action from the north, Congress agreed that the United States should participate. General A.G.L. McNaughton, chair of the Canadian section of the Permanent Joint Board on Defence and a longtime seaway advocate, said that Canada had given away nothing to get the U.S. aboard. "Our friends across the border could come in with us if they wanted to, but it would be on our own terms. . . . [W]e had taken over the diplomatic initiative." The seaway, capable of handling ships up to 222 metres long, 23 metres wide, and with 8 metres of draft, was opened in 1959. It was run by two national seaway authorities, which harmonized their activities.

Gordon Stewart has rightly pointed out that the St. Lawrence Seaway agreement was a high watermark in Canadian–American relations. Canada had laboured hard to get the U.S. on side so that costs would be shared and to ensure the success of the enterprise. Yet, Stewart argues, "public fanfare about good neighborliness should not obscure the reality that the United States had acted to gain readier access to Canadian raw materials, to prevent Canada from pursuing an autonomous, nationalist policy on seaway matters, and to confirm physically, as it were, the complementary nature of the two economies. The seaway was like a huge economic zipper knitting these countries together."

COMFORTABLE, AND YET...

By 1957, Canada and the United States were both riding the crest of what seemed to be a permanent postwar boom. There was a car in every garage and a chicken in every pot for both Canadians and Americans, and pervasive prosperity had done much to ease strain across the border. Few Americans had many concerns about Canada. President Eisenhower and Prime Minister St. Laurent were of similar age, and though Ike had been a soldier and Uncle Louis a corporate lawyer, their view of the world was not very different. North America was a favoured part of the globe, with a responsibility to keep the godless Communists from taking over all of Europe and Asia. The two countries spoke the same language (even the French-Canadian St. Laurent) and thought the same thoughts. That explained the co-operation on defence and economics and the participation in Korea and in NATO. Of course, there were differences, but to most Canadians they seemed to be just family squabbles. As the distinguished commentator on Canadian foreign policy, John Holmes, put it, in the early 1950s Canadians were more relaxed in alliance than they had ever been.

Canadians *were* more comfortable than they had been, but they still looked on the relationship a little differently than the Americans did. Yes, there was agreement and friendship, but Americans were also insensitive to Canadian concerns. Yes, the two nation's world views were generally the same, but enough difference existed on broad issues of principle (as in Korea) to give pause.

There had been a nasty fight at the United Nations in the fall of 1955, for example. Paul Martin, the minister of national health and welfare, was leading the Canadian delegation at the General Assembly, and he launched a major effort to break the Cold War deadlock that had prevented the admission of new members to the world body. The Americans bitterly opposed the Canadian plan, arguing that some of the proposed states, Outer Mongolia usually being mentioned, were not "peace-loving." But Martin persisted, finding friends where he could, and subtly using the great powers' domination of the UN as a device to strengthen support. In Washington, Secretary of State John Foster Dulles called in a Canadian diplomat and angrily told him that "in view of the relations between the two countries, he would have expected a more co-operative attitude. . . . [T]he neighbourly relationship which normally existed had not obtained in the case of the new members question."

Canada, in other words, wasn't doing what it was told. Henry Cabot Lodge, the American UN delegate, blasted Martin in private meetings, even asserting that Canadian Liberals had trouble dealing with a Republican administration in Washington. Later, there were threats about possible changes in a deal that had seen Canadian oil guaranteed access into the U.S. After the UN vote had been won, adding sixteen members to the organization, including Ireland, Italy, Portugal, Romania, and Spain, the Canadian ambassador in Washington called on the State Department to express Canada's anger over this shoddy treatment. Dulles's rough words, the ambassador was told, were a sign of the close Canada–U.S. relationship—he would not have spoken so frankly to the British ambassador! As Paul Martin noted in his memoirs, "this reference was, of course, double-edged." So it was. The close relationship posed problems for both countries, but especially for Canada.

Strains: The Pipeline, Suez, and Herbert Norman

Most Canadians knew little about the details of the UN fight, but everyone could see the increasing Americanization of the country. In 1956, a perfect example of this echoed through the country like a thunderclap. The issue was the construction of a pipeline to carry natural gas from Alberta eastwards. The pipeline would be all Canadian in route and purpose, but the firm created to carry out the work had a temporary preponderance of American business people and money. C.D. Howe, the dynamic minister of trade and commerce, pushed the House of Commons hard for a loan so that work on the project could begin immediately. Central to the public and parliamentary response was that Howe, always denigrated by opposition critics as "American-born," wanted to use government money to help an American-controlled company. When that was packaged with a strong dose of Liberal government arrogance, the effect was devastating. The Liberal government, in office for so long, was in difficulty, and anti-Americanism was on the rise.

Other factors compounded the new mood of nationalism. Canada's trade was with the United States, overwhelmingly so, and her foreign investment increasingly came from south of the border. In 1950 American investment amounted to 76 percent of all foreign investment in Canada and totalled $6.5 billion; by 1955 the total was $10.3 billion, with the biggest increases in oil, mineral, and mining sectors. That worried people like the Liberal stalwart Walter Gordon, a Toronto investor and chartered accountant. Gordon was appointed in 1955 to head a royal commission on Canada's economic prospects. The extent of American penetration and control of virtually every sector of the economy shook him. His interim report, issued just before the Canadian election of 1957, sounded a warning cry. Canada had somehow jumped squarely into the American bed.

Growing concern about American influence was fuelled by the Suez Crisis of October–November 1956. The combined Israeli–British–French invasion of President Nasser's Egypt had stirred passions around the world and not least in Canada. President Nasser was painted as a Hitler in the making, but the St. Laurent government was furious at Britain for using military force, and it used the United Nations to work for a solution. The subsequent creation of the United Nations Emergency Force (UNEF), the work for which Lester Pearson, then external affairs minister, won a Nobel Peace Prize, was seen by Ottawa as a way of rescuing Britain from the consequences of its folly. But not in some parts of Anglo-Canada, which viewed UNEF as a way to throw Britain to the dogs of the Third World and Pearson as a slave to Washington's policy. ("I think you have done a wonderful thing," Eisenhower exclaimed to St. Laurent after Canada had secured UN support for the resolution that created the Emergency Force.) The Suez Crisis was almost the last gasp of British imperialism in Canada, though in 1956 few realized that. The anti-government reaction, focussed through the opposition Progressive Conservative and Co-operative Commonwealth Federation parties, suggested serious unease about just how close Canada had got to Washington and how far it had drifted from London.

Yet another issue centred Canadian attention on the United States in the months after the Suez Crisis. Early in 1957, the Canadian ambassador to Egypt, Herbert Norman, committed suicide by jumping from the roof of an apartment building in Cairo. A distinguished student of Japan, a member of the Department of External Affairs since just before the outbreak of war in 1939, Norman had come under attack in a

Congressional committee in Washington for alleged Communist party membership. Under the strain of coping with this charge, the diplomat took his own life. The outcry in Canada was fierce, both government and opposition leaders denouncing the United States harshly. In truth, as we now know, Norman had been an active Communist during his time at Cambridge University in the 1930s. Whether he was formally a party member or not remains unclear, as does his subsequent connection (if any) to Communist activities. In 1950, his department brought him back from Japan, where he had served on General MacArthur's staff and as the head of the Canadian mission. An investigation followed, though not a very thorough one; according to transcripts of his questioning, recently released to researchers, Norman had lied about his youthful enthusiasm for Communism. Cleared of all suspicion, Norman was made head of the department's American desk, a sensitive post during the Korean War, and then sent to New Zealand as high commissioner. Shortly before the Suez Crisis, he had been made ambassador to Egypt, and by every account he performed well there, helping to persuade President Nasser to accept Canadian troops as part of the United Nations Emergency Force.

Norman's suicide caused a major, though brief, crisis between Canada and the United States. Many felt that he had been hounded to death by irresponsible allegations before uncontrollable Congressional committees. American apologies, including those made by President Eisenhower, were perfunctory at best. It was McCarthyism, many charged, referring to the outrageous activities of the Communist-hunting Wisconsin senator. But the Americans had valid reasons to be concerned about Norman. Many British "moles" had already been uncovered or had defected to the Soviet Union, and there was a clear link from his Cambridge days between Norman and some of those defectors. Moreover, because of the close military, political, and economic relations between Canada and the U.S., Norman might have been privy to the many American "secrets" known to officials in Ottawa. In other words, Canada could not claim a total independence as long as Canada had needed and wanted inside information on American planning and policies; as long as Canada was tied to Washington, the Americans had a legitimate concern, though it was, of course, Canada's responsibility to vet its own public servants. The rights or wrongs of the Norman case remain murky, despite two books on the matter. (Roger Bowen finds him innocent while James Barros declares him to have been a Soviet agent.) A government investigation by a retired foreign service officer and political science professor, completed in 1990, exonerated Norman but left many questions unanswered. What is certain is that Canada by 1957 was so thoroughly linked with the United States that such regrettable incidents were almost inevitable.

CANADIANIZING CULTURE

As always, American influences were most noticeable in the area of culture. The Royal Commission on National Development in the Arts, Letters, and Sciences reported in 1951. The commission was chaired by Vincent Massey, former minister to the U.S. and high commissioner to Britain, and its report in 1951 bemoaned the struggle that Canada's culture had to survive in the face of American books, magazines, radio, movies, and now television. *Time* and *Reader's Digest* dominated the magazine racks and took the lion's share of advertising; Hollywood films flooded into Canada, while Canada produced almost no movies except the documentaries of the National Film Board. The Canadian Co-operation Project, a Hollywood–Ottawa concoction of the late 1940s and early 1950s, promised (as Pierre Berton has shown in *Hollywood's Canada*) more Canadian film production, but all it delivered was a sprinkling of deliberate references to Canada in American films—this calculated to attract droves of U.S. tourists! The Canadian Broadcasting Commission produced radio entertainment with skill, but its too earnest and too intellectual efforts sank in the tide of low- and middle-brow productions from NBC, ABC, and CBS. When TV came to Canada in a major way in 1952, years after Canadians in cities close to the border had erected aerials to bring in television signals from Burlington, Buffalo, Detroit, Fargo, and Portland, the CBC found itself virtually forced to air U.S. sitcoms and quiz shows to generate the advertising revenue it needed to mount occasional Canadian dramas and news shows. The 1957 Fowler Royal Commission on broadcasting lamented the violence and commercialism of some American TV shows, but added that it "would be difficult to justify a Canadian policy that sought to protect Canadian viewers from poor American programmes." Rather, the good taste of the people would have to be relied upon, and indigenous programming would have to be developed to create a "separate Canadian consciousness and sense of identity." Fowler was short, however, on specifics to execute this unobjectionable recommendation.

Massey's commission recommended establishing the Canada Council, to stimulate the arts and culture. In 1956, the St. Laurent government seized this idea and funded the new council with inheritance taxes collected from the estates of two Canadian multimillionaires, Sir James Dunn and Isaac Walton Killam. The council poured millions into symphony orchestras, ballet companies, and universities; it funded historians and sociologists and painters and poets; and it largely created the basis of a Canadian cultural industry. It did not, because it could not, stop the flow of American ideas and pop culture northwards.

Canada's mistrust of the United States had already put down roots during this period: concern about the defence relationship and foreign investment; fear that Britain had been marginalized in Canadian life and policy; and worry over the Americanization of culture. All that was needed was the right person to exploit these latent tensions. In 1957, John Diefenbaker burst upon the scene.

CHAPTER

THE CRISIS YEARS

1 9 5 7 — 1 9 6 3

The prime minister was angry. The young president had come to Canada on his first official visit abroad and he had failed to show proper deference to his older, more experienced host. That rankled. Worse yet, after a difficult and blunt meeting he had found a one-page memorandum by a presidential aide stuffed between the cushions of a couch. On it was laid out "What We Want from Ottawa Trip," including three points on which the president should "push" the Canadian leader. The Canadian was infuriated: how dare the Americans talk about pushing him!

For months, the memorandum ate away at the prime minister. Ten months after the single page had been found, he told his ambassador to the United States that he had not yet made use of the paper but "when the proper time came," he would not hesitate to do so. The ambassador, horrified at this conversation, wrote in his diary that "I have rarely if ever been so disturbed by a conversation with the head of the Can. govt." Inevitably, word of the misplaced memorandum reached the president and the secretary of state. It was unforgivable, the latter said. "Diefenbaker should have returned it or burned it. It was a disguised attempt at blackmail." The president's response was unprintable.

Canada's relations with the United States had reached their nadir. Trust had been completely destroyed by the clash of personalities and by disagreement over issues that went straight to heart of the bilateral relationship. Prime Minister John G. Diefenbaker and President John F. Kennedy had obviously not been destined to be good neighbours.

DIEF THE CHIEF

Born in 1895 in rural Ontario, John Diefenbaker moved to Saskatchewan with his parents as a young child. He grew up on a farm and later, in Saskatoon. His university years were interrupted by the Great War, in which he was injured during a training accident. Diefenbaker never forgave the Americans for waiting until 1917 to come into the war. Called to the provincial bar in 1919, he began a successful career in the law, most often as a defence attorney. He made several attempts for municipal, provincial, and federal office, all without success. In 1940, Diefenbaker was finally elected as a Conservative member of Parliament from Lake Centre, Saskatchewan.

The new MP soon established a reputation for fiery oratory. He was strongly pro-British, perhaps in compensation for his German name, which had subjected him to abuse in both wars. His Germanic background also prompted him to support the concept of unhyphenated Canadianism, although this position led Québécois to conclude that he was unsympathetic to their aspirations. In the postwar years, he came out against the increasing economic, cultural, and military influence that the United States was exercising in Canada. Diefenbaker, in other words, combined many of the traditional attributes of Canadian Toryism with a strong nationalism, and when that message was delivered with striking oratory in an almost biblical fervour, he made a considerable impression. In 1956, his party selected him as its leader in a national convention. The next year, Diefenbaker took to the hustings in a general election.

He was sure to be beaten. Despite the great pipeline debate of 1956, no one gave the Conservatives a chance. The Liberals had been in power for twenty-two years straight. Louis St. Laurent, though obviously showing his age, was highly regarded and his Cabinet still seemed strong. But Diefenbaker galvanized the nation, denouncing the government for selling out Britain at Suez, excoriating the Liberals for their arrogance and their dependence on American capital to develop the country, and pledging change. "One Canada!" he cried, promising the country "a vision of our nation's destiny." Northern, national, even imperial, certainly that destiny was not continental. The voters heard, even if the media continued to be blissfully unaware of what was happening, and on 11 June 1957 the Canadian people put John Diefenbaker into power with a minority government. Early the next year, after a campaign marked by the same fervour and the same arguments, the electors gave Diefenbaker's Progressive Conservatives the largest majority in Canadian history to that time. The Chief was in power. The now awed media spoke of "the Conservative century" that was to come.

Diefenbaker's anti-American nationalism was powerful, and it troubled the United States government. Although opinion polls in 1956 had shown that only 27 percent of Canadians thought the United States had too much influence in Canada, the Americans watched anxiously as Diefenbaker, fired with old-style British Empire patriotism, went to London within days of his election to attend a Commonwealth prime ministers conference and to meet the Queen. In a fit of enthusiasm on his return to Ottawa, the new leader pledged his government to increase trade with Britain, a move that flew directly in the face of American policy for Canada; indeed, the prime minister stated his "planned intention" to switch 15 percent of Canadian trade from the United States to Britain. This idea had not been canvassed through the Ottawa bureaucracy before his announcement, and it was simply impossible to achieve. Britain's trade foothold in Canada had been shrinking year by year while American exports to Canada had risen annually until they made up three-quarters of the total in 1956. Moreover, many British goods (Scotch whisky excepted) were simply not suited for the North American market. The bureaucrats duly produced their analyses the ministers read them in horror, and the government blamed the whole episode on a misunderstanding exaggerated by the press.

The U.S. ambassador to Canada, Livingston Merchant, was not worried. In 1957, this consummate professional diplomat had told fretful State Department officials that the newly elected Canadian ministers would continue "as sound and reliable colleagues. Support for NATO is truly non-partisan. In general they tend to see the world through our eyes. They appreciate the geographical realities of their defense situation. They believe in free enterprise and we need have no fear they will abandon us." At the same time, suggested Merchant, rhetoric under Diefenbaker would be "higher pitched, shriller . . . than we have been used to." The ambassador's assessment was probably correct for 1957, but the nationalist rhetoric was not without its impact. By 1958, Merchant noted that Canadians had become extraordinarily sensitive because of "their position of inferiority in power in relation to us." The last year had seen the development of a "strident, almost truculent nationalism."

Alvin Hamilton, the Saskatchewan minister of northern affairs in Diefenbaker's Cabinet, embodied that truculence. Soon after he took office, Hamilton visited a DEW Line radar site run by a United States Air Force colonel. "The colonel came running out and told me, 'You can't land here!' I said, 'I can and I did. I'm the minister of northern affairs. I'm in charge now and I run all this. You don't.'" Hamilton then added, "I was shocked to see an American flag flying over the base, but no Canadian flag. I told him, 'You get that flag down or I'll pull it down. You are not in Georgia here.'" The officer did as he was told. Hamilton almost certainly exaggerated that story in the re-telling, but it illustrated the new Canadian nationalism very neatly. It was Diefenbaker who had fostered that mood, but other Canadians were beginning, just beginning, to ask the same questions he did about American power and influence.

Surprisingly, there were few serious difficulties in the prime minister's initial years in office. The reason was Dwight Eisenhower. The president was genial and unthreatening, and he handled Diefenbaker perfectly. It was Ike and John, and that cordiality greatly pleased Diefenbaker. The prime minister looked on Eisenhower, the wartime general who had led the victorious Allied armies, as a genuine hero. For his part, the president treated the prime minister without condescension and with patience, overlooking his idiosyncrasies for the sake of harmony. Eisenhower had dealt with difficult people before—Field Marshal Bernard Montgomery and General Charles de Gaulle were only two examples—and he knew how to get what he wanted. Essentially, he flattered and charmed Diefenbaker out of any hostility. "This fellow Eisenhower is an American," Diefenbaker told one of his ministers, "but he's not so bad." Later, echoing Eisenhower's campaign slogan, he added, "I like Ike," probably because the president's administration did not treat Canada as "a forty-ninth state composed of Mounted Police, eskimos and summer vacationers." Considering the issues on the bargaining table, Diefenbaker's determination not to fight with the United States was the greatest tribute to Eisenhower's political skills.

ARROWS, BOMARCS, AND NUKES

Most contentious Canadian–American issues during the late 1950s and early 1960s concerned defence. When Diefenbaker took office, a joint air defence agreement between the two North American nations was in its final stages of negotiation. The idea of combining air defences had a clear logic to it because a Soviet bomber attack would threaten both countries, and could best be met by using warning and fighter resources in unison. In December 1956, Canadian and American military chiefs had accepted the North American Air Defence agreement (NORAD), and American political approval followed quickly. General Charles Foulkes, the chair of the Chiefs of Staff Committee and the most powerful military bureaucrat in Canadian history, promised his friends in Washington that Ottawa's decision would be made by mid-June 1957. That promise was left unkept because of the election that tossed out the St. Laurent government. From the moment the new government took office, Foulkes put the pressure on Diefenbaker's defence minister,

Soulmates: President Eisenhower (left) and John Diefenbaker, New York, 1960. (National Archives of Canada/PA 122743)

George Pearkes. Pearkes was a Victoria Cross winner in the Great War and a major-general in the Second World War. He and Foulkes had served together. The agreement had to be signed, Foulkes argued, and Pearkes recalled that he had the impression "it was all tied up by the Liberal government, that promises had been made. . . . I do know that [the Canadian military was] under almost daily pressure from the military in the United States." Pearkes went to see the prime minister and in a brief conversation persuaded him to sign the agreement. On his copy, Pearkes wrote "Discussed with the Prime Minister and approved 24 July, 1957." The Cabinet was not informed; neither was the Department of External Affairs.

Almost at once the government was in hot water. Was NORAD part of NATO? Yes and no, Diefenbaker tried to reply, falling on his face and annoying External Affairs, the Americans, and NATO, all of whom knew that NORAD had nothing to do with NATO. Why had the decision been made in such haste and without Cabinet committee scrutiny? Why had the government let General Foulkes ram it through? Humbug, Diefenbaker grumpily said later: "To suggest that we were stampeded in the early weeks of our government is to suggest that I, as Prime Minister, and more particularly, Major General George Pearkes, V.C., the Minister of National Defence, had no appreciation of the requirements of North American defence."

Diefenbaker had indeed been stampeded by Foulkes, who in turn had been pushed by the American military, and he had entered into a major defence agreement without understanding what was involved. Once bitten, twice shy, and Diefenbaker developed a complete mistrust for the advice of generals, just as he had for the rest of the public service. (In External Affairs, they were all "Pearsonalities," the Chief grumbled.) NORAD also reinforced his simmering anger at the take-Canada-for-granted attitude of some parts of the American bureaucracy. The next issue to arise did nothing to change his views.

The Royal Canadian Air Force flew CF-100s, now increasingly obsolescent, on its NORAD duties. The previous Liberal government had pressed A.V. Roe Co. to design and build a new supersonic interceptor, the CF-105 or, as it was better known, the Arrow. The Arrow was designed to be very fast and well armed; it was also destined to be very expensive, in substantial part because much of its technology was new and had to be built from scratch in Canada. The Liberals might very well have jettisoned the Arrow, but the election of 1957 intervened and left the decision to the Conservatives. For months, Diefenbaker tried to avoid the inevitable. Salespeople and diplomats fanned around the globe trying to sell the aircraft and so increase production and cut the unit cost. There were no takers. The Americans argued that their new F-101B and F-102 aircraft were just as good, able to use the Semi-Automatic Ground Environment (SAGE) system of computers as the Arrow could not, and cost about one-sixth the Arrow's price of $12 million a copy. Contrary to popular demonology, the Americans did not force Canada to scrap the Arrow. In fact, the Americans even considered paying for a few squadrons' worth to help out the Canadian government and the RCAF, a service very close to their own air force. In February 1959, however, the government screwed up its courage and abandoned the project. Unfortunately, the announcement was clumsily handled, and the bitter management of A.V. Roe responded by putting its workers out on the street the same day. Many of the skilled engineers laid off that day eventually found work in U.S. aircraft plants and with the National Aeronautics and Space Administration (NASA).

The truly important part of this unhappy episode was Diefenbaker's announcement coupling the Arrow's demise with other decisions on air defence. The government, he told Parliament, intended to secure "Bomarc B" anti-aircraft missiles from the United States, weapons that were effective only when armed with nuclear warheads. Canada would pay the full cost of building the Bomarc bases and the extensive SAGE system required to fire them, but the United States, planning to build thirty Bomarc bases of its own in the U.S., agreed to provide the missiles themselves to Canada without cost.

A few months later, the government announced that it had selected the American F-104 aircraft for service with Canada's air force squadrons in NATO. Two hundred of these were to be built in Canada with certain modifications and to be called the CF-104. In accordance with the NATO decision to rely on nuclear weapons to counter the Warsaw Pact's superior number of troops, the CF-104s were to take on a strike-reconnaissance role. This required them to use nuclear weapons to hit specified targets behind the front lines, possibly including military concentrations or even urban centres in East Germany or Czechoslovakia. A battery of Honest Johns, American-made tactical missiles with a battlefield range of some twenty miles, would be acquired for the Canadian army in Europe. These again were effective only with nuclear warheads. In other words, Diefenbaker had moved ahead quickly to equip the armed forces for the 1960s; Bomarcs, CF-104s, and Honest Johns demonstrated Canada's commitment to the Western alliance and to nuclear weapons.

Or did they? Delivery of these complex weapons systems had a long lead time. Bomarcs ordered in 1959 would not be operational until

1963, for example. Moreover, after the Soviet Union had put *Sputnik*, the first satellite, into space in October 1957, it seemed apparent that the era of the intercontinental ballistic missile was just over the horizon. The day of piloted bombers such as the CF-104s was strictly limited. There was therefore both reason and time for second thoughts, and there were second thoughts aplenty—most notably after Howard Green became secretary of state for external affairs.

Green was a Vancouver MP, first elected in 1935. Genial, engaging, a thoroughly decent man, the new external affairs minister had a simplistic view of the world. In his first twenty-five years in Ottawa, Green had remained a straight-out imperialist, loyal to Britain, and suspicious of the Americans. But under the tutelage of Norman Robertson, his undersecretary of state, Green had come to a different view of international developments. Most significantly, he had begun to understand that nuclear weapons were a threat to all human life. Why should Canada have these wretched things, he asked? Why should Canada not try to eliminate them? Those were good questions, the right questions. But they clashed with the views of Douglas Harkness, the Calgary parliamentarian who succeeded George Pearkes as defence minister in 1960. A dour, decorated Second World War colonel, Harkness wanted his troops to have the best available weapons and, in a world in which other countries had nuclear weapons, Canada would have to have them too. What is more, Canada had agreed to buy weapons that needed nuclear warheads and, if the weapons were not armed, large gaps might result in Allied defences. In North America, for example, the two Bomarc stations at North Bay, Ontario, and La Macaza, Quebec, were important for the defence not only of the industrial heartland of Canada, but also of Cleveland, Pittsburgh, Philadelphia, and New York. The Americans would be furious if Canada reneged now.

And so they were when U.S. Embassy officials in Ottawa saw the government beginning to waver. Diefenbaker had already established a reputation for indecision on a range of political and economic issues, but to see him torn between the pro- and anti-nuclear views of Harkness and Green worried the Americans greatly. On one day, the prime minister would put off a Cabinet decision about the warheads until the U.S. presented a justification for their installation in Canada; the next day, he would tell his ambassador in Washington that the early conclusion of a nuclear agreement was desirable to determine American rights and responsibilities for the warheads they would provide.

This was the situation when President John F. Kennedy came to Ottawa for his official visit in May 1961. Only forty-four years old, the handsome and engaging president had a crusader's zeal about America's mission in the world, something that did not sell well in the Cabinet chamber in Ottawa. He did not know much about Canada, but he shared the usual benevolent attitude to "our neighbours to the north." As a Massachusetts senator, he had spoken and voted for the construction of the St. Lawrence Seaway in 1952, though lobbyists warned that this would hurt his state's port and rail concerns. But his interest in Canada did not withstand the shock of meeting the prime minister. The president completely failed to hit it off with Diefenbaker. His wife, Jacqueline, had even less in common with Diefenbaker's often acerbic and anti-American wife, Olive. Mme. Vanier, wife of the governor general, was a lovely women, Mrs. Kennedy said after the visit. Of Olive, she wisely said nothing at all. Kennedy's briefings had told him that the Canadian prime minister was anti-American, extremely nationalistic, and afraid to make hard decisions. Many of his ministers were similarly characterized, and especially Howard Green, who was described as "naïve and almost parochial." In this light, the purloined memo with its request that Kennedy "push" Diefenbaker is easy to explain.

For his part, Diefenbaker had formed a negative view of the new president simply from watching his performance during the 1960 election campaign. Diefenbaker had deemed Republican candidate Richard Nixon, whom he had met as vice-president during the Eisenhower administration, to be a man of quality and experience. In contrast, Kennedy was a mere stripling, too young and inexperienced for the job of leading the free world. One might be forgiven for thinking that Diefenbaker also envied Kennedy his good looks and the magnetism that made him so attractive as a political leader. Diefenbaker had had the adulation of the crowd but by 1961, when Kennedy took office, the prime minister all too often heard only the jeers of protesters.

None of the auguries were favourable, and especially not after the prime minister sensed that Kennedy found him a stick-in-the-mud, slow to act and cool to the aggressive new American power that Kennedy embodied. The contrary Chief, who had spent his life opposing things, never did respond well to pushing, and when the two leaders talked about nuclear weapons, Diefenbaker was markedly unforthcoming. As Canadian missions abroad learned, the prime minister "said that in view of public opinion in Canada it would be impossible politically at [the] moment for [the country] to accept nuclear weapons." Kennedy was not amused, and the chill of dislike lingered over relations between the two leaders.

Although negotiations with the United States continued and construction of CF-104 aircraft and of the Bomarc bases in Canada went ahead, no progress was made in determining the conditions under

The enormously popular Kennedys come to Canada: Parliament Hill, Ottawa, 1961. (Duncan Cameron/National Archives of Canada/112430)

which Canada would take the warheads. Indeed, government spokes-people largely denied that there was any *commitment* to take them, though they could scarcely deny that Canada had purchased the weapon systems requiring the warheads. Through 1961 there was little movement at all.

In 1962, the nuclear question remained suspended, as Diefenbaker took his party to the polls and nearly lost an election on economic issues. The government, on the advice of the governor of the Bank of Canada, James Coyne, had followed policies that managed to upset business, economists, and the public. That was bad enough, but when Coyne launched a crusade against the "foreign domination" exercised in Canada by American investment, the Americans and Toronto's Bay Street were apoplectic. The governor denounced the "unimpeded inflow of foreign capital on the part of foreign companies and investors who thought they saw golden opportunities to undertake various projects in Canada or to buy up existing companies." Coyne was messily sacked by the Cabinet in 1961, but the next year, the country faced a run on the dollar that decimated Canada's reserves of U.S. currency. Critics blamed this directly on the Tories' faltering hand on the economic tiller. The dollar crisis forced the government to peg the dollar at 92.5 cents U.S. in the middle of the election campaign, shaking confidence in Diefenbaker dramatically. The outcome was both a Conservative minority government and an economic crisis. The prime minister was left at the head of a weakened administration dependent on the support of Social Credit MPs from Alberta and Créditiste MPs from Quebec. The economic situation forced massive retrenchment in government spending and an appeal, answered at once, to the United States for a standby credit: in effect a loan that could be drawn on as needed.

There ought to have been some gratitude in Ottawa for Washington's ready assistance, but none of it spilled over to the nuclear question. There matters remained in stasis. Ministers and departments dug their positions ever deeper, public opinion grew more divided (though a two-to-one majority still supported acquisition of the warheads), and the Americans grew ever more exasperated.

THE CUBAN MISSILE CRISIS

This was the state of affairs when the Cuban missile crisis erupted in October 1962. The Eisenhower and Kennedy administrations had been frustrated with Canada's refusal to cut ties with Fidel Castro's regime, and there had been several sharp confrontations between ministers and officials of the two countries, the Canadians invariably arguing that to isolate Cuba economically was to force it ever tighter into Moscow's grasp. The United States had even used its Trading with the Enemy Act to prevent American-owned Ford of Canada from selling trucks to Cuba, though such a sale in no way clashed with Canadian government policy. Canadians were outraged that an American law could be made to assume precedence over Canadian wishes.

The American response was invariably that the hemisphere had to be free of Communist regimes. This view motivated President Kennedy to sponsor an abortive invasion by Cuban exiles at the Bay of Pigs in April 1961. Castro's easy crushing of that laughable attempt did not ease matters. Then in the early fall of 1962, American spy aircraft discovered that the Soviet Union was installing missiles on Cuban bases. The missiles had a range capable of reaching most of the United States, and Kennedy, naturally enough, saw this as a threat to American security. In deep secrecy, he prepared to act. His plan was to mount a naval blockade around the Caribbean island and to demand that Soviet leader Nikita Khrushchev remove the weapons forthwith. Kennedy's emissaries flew to Paris, London, Ottawa, and other capitals just prior to the president's national TV address on the crisis; they carried photos of the missile installations and other evidence, and they sought Allied support. In London and Paris, the answer was prompt and affirmative.

In Ottawa, the message was very different. Although the prime minister told Kennedy's envoy, Livingston Merchant, that "in the event of a missile attack on the United States from Cuba, Canada would live up to its responsibilities under the NATO and NORAD agreements," the next day he refused to allow Harkness to put Canada's NORAD aircraft on alert to match the action of the U.S. forces. The defence minister sought out Diefenbaker and found him "loath" to act because "it should be a Cabinet decision." A day later, Harkness told the Cabinet why the alert was necessary, but external affairs minister Green argued that if Canada went along with the Americans now "we'll be their vassals forever." The prime minister, Harkness remembered, then "argued against it on the ground that an alert would unduly alarm the people, that we should wait and see what happened, etc." The Cabinet, led by the Chief, decided to do nothing.

Angry and frustrated at this failure to allow him to put the Canadian forces at the "Alert State for Military Vigilance," the equivalent of the Americans' DEFCON 3, Harkness returned to his office and on his own authority effectively ordered the alert "in as quiet and unobtrusive a

way as possible." The service chiefs had been made fully aware of the
seriousness of the crisis in the Caribbean through their links with their
counterparts in the Pentagon and at NORAD headquarters in Colorado
Springs, a perfect example of what political scientists call transnational
and transgovernmental activity. The generals, air marshals, and admi-
rals were delighted and relieved at Harkness's decision, and orders
went out quietly through unofficial channels to the commanders in the
field and at sea. The army went to full alert, ships and aircraft put to sea
to track Soviet nuclear submarines and sink them if necessary, and the
RCAF armed its fighter aircraft with their conventional weapons. The
Bomarcs, still incomplete, sat useless at their bases. The Canadian military had been mortified at their inability to act in support of their allies;
now, at last, they could hold their heads up around the NORAD and
NATO tables. The armed forces were as ready as they could be, but the
political delays scarcely reassured either the American administration
and military or the other NATO allies that Canada's government was
prepared to fight.

Then Diefenbaker worsened matters. Pursuing a foolish idea from
External Affairs, the prime minister suggested in Parliament that the
United Nations might send a mission to Cuba made up of the "eight
nations comprising the unaligned members of the eighteen-nation disarmament committee . . . to ascertain what the facts are." The prime
minister added to the press, "In that way the truth will be revealed."
Well-meaning though the suggestion was, it did seem to imply that
Kennedy's photographs of the missile bases were either faked or inconclusive.

Officials in Washington were now livid, not least the president.
Kennedy had telephoned Diefenbaker to urge him to put the NORAD
forces on alert, and the prime minister, shouting at "the young man,"
had refused: "No, we can't possibly do that." Diefenbaker was just as
angry as Kennedy, arguing that the terms of the NORAD agreement
entitled Canada to be fully consulted before the forces went on alert.
Diefenbaker almost certainly never knew of Harkness's decision to go to
DEFCON 3.

Finally on 24 October, as the world hovered on the brink of nuclear
war, Diefenbaker responded to Harkness's pleas and authorized the
Canadian forces to move to DEFCON 2, an alert status that foresaw
imminent war. Fortunately, war was averted, the Soviets withdrew their
missiles, and the crisis blew over. But the Americans would not forget
Diefenbaker's wobbling. Nor did Canadians. Though the public was not
privy to the secret details, there was no doubt that Canadians supported

Kennedy's action and thought Canada's role had been inglorious. One official in Ottawa, assessing opinion polls that showed 80 percent support for Kennedy's actions, observed that Canadians felt "a fundamental alliance with the United States that is often covered over but never seriously threatened." The real lesson, he said, was "that when the U.S. President chooses to psychologically mobilize the American people . . . the Canadian people will be drawn up in the process also." Canadians had wanted and expected their government to stand shoulder to shoulder with Kennedy, and though Diefenbaker said publicly that "there never was any question as to where Canada stood," they were appalled that their country had hung back. The Chief had lost the last measure of public sympathy and his government was now living on borrowed time. In the circumstances, there was little surprise when the Conservative government fell on the nuclear issue with a little push from its friends south of the border.

The Fall of the Diefenbaker Government

The nuclear issue was front and centre on the political agenda by the end of 1962. The New Democratic Party, successor to the social-democratic Co-operative Commonwealth Federation, had no doubts about where it stood: no nukes for Canada. The Liberals had more difficulty with the question. Party leader Lester B. Pearson had opposed Canada's acquisition of the warheads and his wife, Maryon, was a member of the ardently anti-nuclear organization, the Voice of Women. Nevertheless, many Liberals thought the anti-nuclear stand was wrong and more still believed that the Conservative government was failing to honour its commitments and, in the process, blackening Canada's good name in Washington and other NATO capitals. In November 1962, two of Pearson's MPs, Paul Hellyer and Judy LaMarsh, visited NATO headquarters to talk with the American general Lauris Norstad, the supreme Allied commander. Canada, they heard, was not meeting its obligations to the alliance. On their return to Ottawa, the two apparently threatened to resign if Liberal policy was not changed.

Before this could occur, General Norstad came to Ottawa on a farewell tour of NATO capitals. At a press conference on 3 January 1963, the officer was asked if "Canada has committed itself to provide its Starfighter [CF-104] squadrons in Europe with tactical nuclear weapons." His reply was clear: "We established a NATO requirement for a certain number of strike squadrons. This includes tactical atomic strike squadrons, and Canada committed some of its force to meet this NATO-established requirement. And this we depend upon." Did that mean, a reporter asked, that if Canada did not accept nuclear weapons for the CF-104s, it would not be fulfilling its NATO commitment? "I believe that's right," Norstad replied. For the first time, someone in a position to know had said that Canada had promised to take nuclear weapons. The Norstad visit apparently prompted Pearson to change Liberal policy, and in a Toronto speech on 12 January, the opposition leader was straightforward:

> I am ashamed if we accept commitments and then refuse to discharge them. . . . [Canada] should end at once its evasion of responsibility by discharging the commitments it has already accepted. . . . It can only do this by accepting nuclear warheads, for those defensive tactical weapons which cannot effectively be used without them but which we have agreed to use. . . . [A] new Liberal government would put Canada's armed forces in the position to discharge fully commitments undertaken for Canada by its predecessor.

Opinion polls in November 1962 had shown that substantial majorities wanted Canada to have nuclear weapons. In his memoirs, Pearson wryly admitted that "these factors certainly did not inhibit me."

Now the Conservative government was up against it on the issue. So long as the opposition parties were united against the acquisition of nuclear weapons, Diefenbaker had felt relatively safe. The situation had changed, however, and a final decision could not long be put off. On 21 January, defence minister Harkness urged that a decision be taken, but Diefenbaker continued to argue, astonishingly, for delay until after another election, something that everyone could see looming ahead. The next day, the prime minister agreed to create a Cabinet committee to find a solution that would reconcile the positions of Harkness and Green, a task roughly equivalent to squaring the circle.

The ministers on the committee pored over the records and agreed that the government had made definite commitments about nuclear weapons. That was progress. Their one-page report stated that if NATO reaffirmed the necessity to acquire nuclear weapons, then the country must fulfill its obligations. As for nuclear warheads for the NORAD forces, the ministers agreed that the desultory negotiations with the United States should be continued "with a view to reaching agreement to secure the highest degree of availability to Canada." Earlier talks had explored a Canadian idea to have the Bomarcs ready to fire except for one missing part, which would be flown to the bases in the event of a crisis. This scheme, designed to maintain Canada's nuclear virginity, was rendered foolish by the unpredictability of winter weather. Yet despite their concerns that hasty installation might actually trigger a nuclear explosion, the Americans seemed willing to store the warheads if they could be deployed without delay when necessary. In truth, however, the Pentagon could not figure out how this could be practically handled.

The ministerial committee's consensus was dashed by Diefenbaker amid scenes of confusion and threatened resignations. When he rose to speak in the House of Commons on 25 January, none of his ministers knew what the prime minister would say. For a time, his words seemed to imply that he was rejecting nuclear weapons totally and stressing the necessity for and virtues of conventional weaponry. That was designed to satisfy Green. Yet in the next breath, he revealed the secret Bomarc talks with the United States and stated that the Cabinet committee's recommendations were government policy. That satisfied Harkness. Few others were content, however, and the press was completely confused. So muddled did matters seem after Diefenbaker's address that Harkness issued a clarification, emphasizing the committee recommendations as "the definite policy of the Government." That infuriated Diefenbaker: "This is terrible—you've ruined everything."

Further ruination was just days away. At 6:15 P.M. on 30 January, the U.S. State Department issued a press release. The statement detailed the weapons that had been put into Canada, noted the inconclusive negotiations about arming them, briefly corrected some of Diefenbaker's statements in the House, and then said bluntly and with devastating effect that "the Canadian Government has not as yet proposed any arrangement sufficiently practical to contribute effectively to North American defense." The prime minister had been called a liar and worse.

The State Department's announcement had been drafted at the urging of the American ambassador in Canada, Walton Butterworth. Quick-tempered, aggressive, sometimes rude, and always impatient, Butterworth had been holding private briefing sessions on the nuclear issue for Canadian journalists in his embassy. Efforts to shape public opinion quietly having failed, Butterworth now suggested that his government go public and correct Diefenbaker's misstatements. At the State Department, the officials huddled and concluded that Butterworth was right. "We felt we just had to say something public," Willis Armstrong, the senior official with responsibility for Canada, said later. "Diefenbaker had made an erroneous statement on a major, important subject. . . . Unless we issued a public statement, we would never catch up. You couldn't just let it pass." At root, the Americans were simply fed up with Diefenbaker: "We were tired of the fuzz from Diefenbaker that surrounded the whole issue," Armstrong recollected. "We hoped it would force Diefenbaker to get off his duff and decide." The draft of the press release went before George Ball, the undersecretary who was then acting as secretary of state, and then to McGeorge Bundy, Kennedy's national security adviser at the White House. The busy president did not see the release, but it was issued nonetheless on Bundy's simple "Go ahead." After the fact, Kennedy tore a strip off Bundy. The American media excoriated the administration for what Arthur Krock in the *New York Times* called its "hamhanded, ill-conceived and undiplomatic" intervention.

In Ottawa, initially, there was only a stunned silence. The predictable explosion came soon enough. The prime minister recalled Canada's ambassador from Washington as a sign of his displeasure. ("No one will miss me," Charles Ritchie wrote in his diary.) Although all parties deplored the State Department's intervention, the Liberals and New Democrats privately had no doubt that the complaints were accurate enough. The prime minister, on the other hand, now believed that he should reject the Cabinet committee agreement that he had announced in Parliament. Moreover, as he told his colleagues, he wanted to dissolve the House of Commons and fight the election on the issue of American intervention. "He was convinced he could win an election on an anti-U.S. appeal," the defence minister noted, "and this to him, was all that mattered." After confusing Cabinet meetings that saw Diefenbaker threaten to leave and ministers try to topple him, Harkness departed the administration, resigning on a question of principle.

"ME AGAINST THE AMERICANS": THE 1963 CAMPAIGN

In Parliament, the Liberals scented power and moved want of confidence in the government. On 5 February 1963 the Liberal motion came to a vote. The prime minister stood in the House to say, "I cannot accept the fear of those who believe we must be subservient in order to be a good ally of any country in the world. . . . I believe in the maintenance in spirit and in fact of Canada's identity, with the right to determine her own policy without extramural assistance." Powerful words and the right principles, but they were not enough after six years of indecision. Diefenbaker fell from power on a vote of 142 to 111. David Lewis of the NDP, who opposed the acquisition of nuclear weapons, still voted for the Tories' ouster: "It wasn't a government worth supporting any more. The issue didn't count. It was a carcass; it wasn't a government." Further resignations from the Cabinet followed.

Diefenbaker's Progressive Conservative party seemed destined to be totally crushed in the election scheduled for 8 April. The nuclear weapons question, the ostensible cause of the parliamentary defeat, had undoubtedly been bungled, and the polls continued to show substantial support for their acquisition. The economic policy of the government had been confused, and Diefenbaker himself, hailed as the nation's saviour in 1957 and 1958, was now painted as a dithering boob, especially in the urban media. The Chief was a superb campaigner, however, and never better than when his back was to the wall. He retained the support of the Prairies and of rural Canada, and he had the Americans' overt intrusion into Canadian politics to use as a powerful electoral weapon. Use it he did. "It's me against the Americans, fighting for the little guy," he exulted as his campaign got rolling. At rallies all across the country, the prime minister shouted that the United States could not accuse Canada of failing to do its duty, not after the Americans had stayed neutral in the Great War until 1917 and in the Second World War until December 1941. "We don't need any lessons as to what Canada should do after that record of service in two world wars."

This attack disturbed many Conservatives, but the prime minister would not be dissuaded. After one minister complained that he would not participate in an anti-American campaign, Diefenbaker stormed, "I will do whatever I bloody well like and I don't care whether I have your resignation or not." Then luck played its part. In late March, a letter purporting to be from Ambassador Butterworth to Lester Pearson fell into Tory hands. The letter congratulated the Liberal leader on his nuclear policy and offered assistance: "At the first opportune moment, I would like to discuss with you how we could be useful to you in the future. You can always count on our support." The letter was branded a forgery by both the embassy and Pearson—subsequent investigation confirmed this—but Diefenbaker allowed rumours of its existence to be leaked nevertheless. Then, in the tense atmosphere of the campaign, Kennedy used the services of a Canadian journalist as an intermediary to offer Pearson his unspecified support. Pearson's response was quick:

"For God's sake, tell the President not to say anything. I don't want any help from him. This would be awful."

Pearson was certainly correct. Any overt assistance to the Liberals would have played directly into the Conservatives' hands. As it was, Diefenbaker repeatedly referred to the purported close links between Pearson and Kennedy and made lightly veiled allusions to the memorandum he had found in May 1961, sometimes letting his aides suggest that it had contained a pencil note by Kennedy referring to the prime minister as an "s.o.b." Kennedy, told of this, denied it flatly. "At the

"Somebody up there doesn't like us." (Reprinted by permission—Toronto Star Syndicate.)

time, I didn't think Diefenbaker was a son of a bitch," he said to a friend, "I thought he was a prick." The prime minister also made good use of a cover story in the American magazine *Newsweek*, which denounced him in ringing terms and featured a large black and white photo that made him look positively satanic. The Conservatives mailed out the photograph and story in the tens of thousands to shore up support for their party.

There was more. During the campaign, hitherto secret Congressional testimony by Kennedy's secretary of defence, Robert McNamara, was released in Washington. The Americans had begun to doubt the effectiveness of the Bomarc, and they were reducing the number of sites in the United States. As for the Bomarcs in Canada, McNamara seemed to have said, they were useful only because they would attract Soviet firepower onto Canadian targets. That, at any rate, was Diefenbaker's interpretation of the secretary's words. Conveniently forgetting that his government had bought and installed Bomarcs in Canada, he claimed that the missiles were worthless. The *Toronto Star*, a Liberal supporter, complained that the Chief was like "some alcoholic patriot in a tavern," and the *Montreal Star* denounced the Tories for behaving "like the outraged citizens of some banana republic." It made no difference what the big city papers said, however. The Liberals, in the lead but on the defensive, were floundering.

There could be no doubt that the American question, always a touchy one even for those Canadians who had strong positive feelings towards the U.S., had turned sure defeat for the Tories into an election cliff-hanger. The campaign had been one of the most extraordinary in years. Not since the reciprocity election of 1911 had the major issue been the relations between Canada and the United States; not since 1911 had the rhetoric of anti-Americanism been so powerfully deployed. The Liberals won 129 seats, the Conservatives 95. With the smaller parties holding 41 seats, Pearson had failed to win a majority, and Diefenbaker had snatched a moral victory from the gaping jaws of defeat.

What are we to make of Diefenbaker, that extraordinary man? As an administrator, he was a disaster, a weak leader with no idea how to run a government. As a campaigner, he was the nonpareil of twentieth-century Canadian politics, a spellbinding, table-thumping orator who shook Canadians and gave them pride in themselves and their country. Most would probably agree with these judgments, but further conclusions become contentious.

There should be no question that Diefenbaker's government secured weapons from the United States and made commitments to the Americans and to NATO to arm them with nuclear warheads. Similarly, there should be no doubt that Diefenbaker, troubled by the divisions between his defence and external affairs ministers, then dithered about whether or not to accept the warheads. The onset of the age of the intercontinental ballistic missile partly justified his hesitation, it is true. Still, those commitments to share in the NATO and NORAD defences were real ones and they were, if not broken, at least badly bent. For a small country, especially one in a strategic position between the super-powers, to pick a fight with its neighbour, friend, and ally was utter folly. Diefenbaker ought to have been aware of that. That he was not, that his defects of personality and hubris blinded him to reality, eventually destroyed his government and ruined his career. The blatant anti-Americanism with which he fought the 1963 election was simply a scandal.

On the other hand, the United States government had played its controlling hand with the utmost arrogance. Eisenhower had understood how to jolly Diefenbaker along, but Kennedy, young and conscious of his and his country's awesome power, had no time to waste on the Canadian. It was almost as if the president had decided to teach Diefenbaker a lesson on how to deal with the power of the American empire. Moreover, though the world situation was delicate in the early 1960s, there was little to be lost by allowing Canada's government time to decide about the warheads in its own way. The simple fact of unarmed Bomarcs, CF-104s, and Honest Johns would probably have forced the government to act; if it did not, the opposition and media would have had a field day in denouncing the enormous sums wasted on unusable military equipment. The State Department's press release was an unacceptable intrusion into the affairs of a friendly sovereign state. Worse, from the point of view of U.S. interests, it was an inexcusable blunder that almost allowed Diefenbaker to retain power. No one, either in the Canadian or the United States governments, emerged from this long and messy affair with much credit.

Lester Pearson and the Liberals were now in power. The party was committed to accepting nuclear weapons and restoring harmony with the Kennedy administration. The Americans were delighted. The election, Ambassador Butterworth wrote in a private letter from Ottawa, had been about fundamental questions. "That is why facing up to them was so very serious and why the Pearson victory . . . was so significant." Canada's place in the world and on the continent were at the core of the election, the ambassador said, and that place had been resolved for the present and immediate future. "At any rate, the outcome holds salutary lessons which will not be overlooked by future aspirants to political office in Canada." American columnist Richard Starnes said much the same thing as Butterworth, though more colloquially. "Adroit statecraft by the American State Department brought down the bumbling, crypto anti-Yankee government of John Diefenbaker. . . . Canadians turned their backs on him just as the State Department knew they would. The American intervention was coldly calculated to do precisely what it did—and it was a brilliant success."

John Diefenbaker himself could not have analysed events from the American perspective more clearly. The only point he would have quarrelled with was the description of himself as "a crypto anti-Yankee." Crypto nothing, Diefenbaker was by then openly anti-Yankee.

CHAPTER eight

"YOU SCREWED US"

1 9 6 3 — 1 9 6 8

"What did you think of my speech?" Prime Minister Lester Pearson asked President Lyndon Johnson. The two men were eating lunch on 3 April 1965 at Camp David, the president's cozy mountain retreat near Washington, and Pearson's question referred to his address of the day before at Temple University in Philadelphia. There he had urged the United States to pause in its bombing of North Vietnam in an effort to get peace talks under way. "What did I think of your speech?" the earthy Texan glowered, leaning closer to the prime minister, and then taking him by the arm and leading him outside and onto the terrace. "Awful." "What followed," noted Canadian Ambassador Charles Ritchie, who had accompanied Pearson, "I witnessed mainly in pantomime, although from time to time the President's voice reached us in expletive adjuration." As Johnson "strode the terrace, he sawed the air with his arms, with upraised fist he drove home the verbal hammer blows. He talked and talked . . . expostulating, upbraiding, reasoning, persuading." Pearson tried to get the occasional word in, "only to have it swept away on the tide."

The president was angry both because of what the prime minister had said and where he had said it. The Americans were fighting a costly war in Vietnam, defending freedom and democracy against communism, or so they saw it. And what was Canada doing? Carping at U.S. policy and refusing to assist in the war in any way that might be really helpful. Johnson termed spurious the argument that Canada's role on the International Control Commissions, created by the 1954 Geneva Conference to move the former French colonies in Indochina towards peace, forbade any support for the belligerent Americans. For Pearson to come into the United States to attack American policy was, Johnson claimed, simply outrageous; not to consult Johnson before giving the speech was unforgivable. What if the president had come to Saskatoon and made a speech attacking Canada's treatment of native peoples? What would Pearson have thought of that?

The tirade went on and on, the aides from both countries watching in mingled horror and fascination. The drama, Ritchie scribbled in his diary, "seemed to be approaching a climax of physical violence. Mike,

Camp David, 1965: LBJ and a beleaguered LBP. (Reprinted with permission— Toronto Star Syndicate.)

only half seated, half leaning on the terrace balustrade, was now completely silent. The President strode up to him and seized him by the lapel of his coat at the same time raising his other arm to the heavens." Ritchie clearly thought he should intervene to stop the verbal and physical attack, but Mac Bundy, Johnson's national security adviser as he had been Kennedy's, smiled. "It will be all right now," he said, "once the President has got *it* off his chest." The departure from Camp David was marked by genial handshaking, but Pearson was badly shaken and things were never quite the same again between the two leaders.

Pearson ought not to have been surprised at LBJ's outburst. His own secretary of state for external affairs claimed to have had threatened resignation if Pearson persisted in giving the speech as originally drafted. From Washington, Ambassador Ritchie had warned of the likely reaction, and Pearson in response had instructed his ambassador not to pass the text to the State Department before it was delivered. The prime minister must have been unnerved by the force of the denunciations, but all he wrote in his own diary was, "The President is tired, under great and continuing pressure, and . . . beginning to show it."

The Camp David incident, later magnified by reporters to suggest that Pearson had literally been picked up by his lapels, helps to demonstrate the differences between the two leaders and their countries. The United States had global responsibilities and interests and the capacity to exercise its power anywhere. Its leaders had to wrestle with that burden, recognize that their actions might cost American lives and treasure, and still get elected and re-elected. The strain was fierce. Canadian prime ministers were raised within a system of genteel compromise in a country with little power and few responsibilities. While their burdens could not be dismissed, they were far fewer than any president's.

MIKE AND JFK: BINDING THE WOUNDS

Relations between Pearson and Kennedy had been very different in tone if not in substance. When Pearson's Liberals took power in April 1963, the bad blood between Kennedy and John Diefenbaker had brought the interaction of the two countries to its lowest point. Kennedy and Pearson had the immediate intention of seeking a rapprochement between their countries. They had met several times before, they liked each other, and they shared a delicious wit. Kennedy believed in the "quality of individuals," one of his aides said, and "Pearson was a man of evident quality." Another added that the American administration "simply preferred Pearson" to Diefenbaker. On election evening, Kennedy had sent a warm message to Pearson, saying, "Early establishment of close relations between your administration and ours is a matter of great importance to me." As for Pearson, he admired Kennedy's style, if not always his hardline anti-communist rhetoric, but that was beside the point. The U.S. was too important to let personalities get in the way. Diefenbaker's anti-Americanism and anti-JFK stance had been deeply irresponsible. He and his country had to get on with Kennedy and his.

Pearson was a diplomat by trade and training. He was adept at finessing issues and coaxing individuals to accept the best possible arrangement in the circumstances of a given moment. Pearson—his nickname "Mike" capturing his breezy style—believed at his core that every issue could be resolved, and his own skill in pressing people into compromise and conciliation was his greatest asset. Time and again he was able to find a way out of a morass that had bogged others down. "Mike is like Houdini," his friend and colleague Hume Wrong once said, " put him in the middle of a crisis and he will get himself out of the mess, and in the process will help others to get out of it too."

Those diplomatic talents were also useful in Canadian politics and although Pearson's political skills have sometimes been denigrated by critics, they were as good as those of any recent Canadian practitioner. Mike Pearson had after all led his Liberal party back from the ruins of the 1958 election, gradually and surely destroying Diefenbaker's credibility, or, more correctly, ensuring that the public knew just how the Chief was destroying his own. He had nearly won the 1962 election, and he had come to power, though without a majority, in April 1963. That was a real achievement: Diefenbaker, as we have seen, was a formidable orator and campaigner; Pearson lisped through his speeches and was greatly embarrassed by the necessity of asking for votes. His outspoken wife, Maryon, frequently had her own commentary on political life—"if I am served one more cup of coffee, I shall vomit"—which heightened the impression that Pearson was not entirely comfortable with political trappings.

Pearson's task was to repair the schism with the United States. In 1963, maintaining North American and NATO defence was crucial for Kennedy and his military, and Pearson understood this. Even though he had not believed in the utility of the Bomarcs, even though he feared the proliferation of nuclear weapons, Pearson accepted the realities of the power balance. The new Canadian prime minister realized that his country simply could not win a one-on-one fight with the United States on an issue so important to the more powerful nation. For its part, the Kennedy administration did not want to push Pearson, passing word to the new government that it was content to have the Canadians initiate the nuclear discussions. The Americans did not have long to wait. Pearson flew to Hyannisport, Massachusetts, the Kennedy family vacation compound, for talks on 10 and 11 May 1963. Some of the conversation was about baseball, a topic Pearson, who had played semi-professionally, knew well. His encyclopedic knowledge reportedly impressed the Kennedy entourage, perhaps as much as his Nobel Peace Prize. The subject of nuclear weapons was at any rate quickly dispatched: the Bomarcs, Honest Johns, and CF-104s would get their warheads at last. There was some risk for the minority Liberal government in this course because the motion to take the warheads might be defeated in the House of Commons, but Pearson told Kennedy that he "was prepared to stand or fall" on the issue. The government squeaked through.

With one question resolved, another sprang up at once. In his conversations with Kennedy, Pearson had indicated that his government might bring in some nationalist economic measures to deal with the huge influx of American foreign investment. The Canadian government "did not wish to discourage the inflow of United States capital," Pearson said, "but nonetheless it had to be recognized that the effect of United States investment in Canada constituted a political problem." Kennedy asked Pearson how he was going to handle the problem, and the prime minister answered that "there were means of encouraging Canadian control by informal methods"—for example, "by persuading United States companies of the importance of putting Canadians in management positions and also by resisting any tendency to make United States regulations and laws apply to Canadian companies in Canada." Pearson added that the government would establish a "Canadian development corporation, one purpose of which would be to help Canadians to buy into industrial companies in such a way as not to invite legitimate United States criticism." Kennedy said nothing to indicate disagreement.

REMINDERS OF DEPENDENCE

Walter Gordon, a close friend of the prime minister and a campaign backer, was also his finance minister. Gordon had been the chair of the 1955 royal commission that had identified the foreign investment problem. He understood business, he believed, and he recognized the

Binding the wounds: Pearson and Kennedy, Hyannisport, 1963. (AP/Wide World Photos)

benefits that investment brought to Canada in the form of jobs and new technologies and techniques. But there could sometimes be too much of a good thing: Gordon feared that the country was on the verge of becoming an economic dependant, with "no future except the hope of eventual absorption." The extraterritorial application of U.S. laws offended him, notably the Trading with the Enemy Act, which forbade American firms and their Canadian branch plants to conduct commerce with Cuba, China, North Korea, and other countries, even though such sales were legal in Canadian law. Gordon condemned the prosecution of American companies by the anti-trust division of the U.S. Department of Justice when their Canadian subsidiaries entered into agreements, perfectly legal in Canada, that violated American law and practice. Gordon wanted to change the country's economic setting, rally the people, and capture control over Canada's destiny. It was a grand, not to say grandiose, dream.

The first Gordon budget, hurriedly prepared so that it could be presented during the promised "Sixty Days of Decision," was presented to the House of Commons on 14 June 1963. There was to be a 30 percent takeover tax on sales of shares in Canadian companies to non-residents, while the 15 percent withholding tax on dividends paid to non-residents was revised to favour shareholders in companies that retained substantial Canadian ownership. Also included were favourable changes to depreciation allowances for companies with at least 25 percent Canadian ownership.

These measures produced an enormous storm, and mainly from within Canada. Montreal Stock Exchange president Eric Kierans, the heads of large corporations, and the editorialists of the major newspapers all denounced Gordon for interfering with the free flow of capital. Though Gordon had unaccountably missed this fact, they were saying, Canadian corporations were hooked into a continental economy. There were warnings from the governor of the Bank of Canada that the withholding tax could produce "massive attempts at liquidation" of American investment and another exchange crisis. For their part, U.S. government officials let Ottawa know that the taxes angered them. "Frankly," the assistant secretary of state told the Canadian chargé d'affaires in Washington, "these features . . . [have] come as a real surprise. While Prime Minister Pearson had indicated at Hyannisport that consideration was being given to some measures regarding investment, we were not under the impression that any measures were contemplated which would affect United States investment so directly."

When Washington's complaints were combined with the outraged and vicious protests of Canadian business, the precise, aristocratic

Gordon was suddenly transformed from a supremely confident finance minister into a man under siege. "A tab collar Castro," one Canadian publisher called him, while E.P. Taylor, the country's most famous businessman, denounced one of the minister's measures as "absolute nonsense, contrary to good business principles, unnatural and monstrous." On 19 June, he withdrew the takeover tax and, the criticism mounting, offered his resignation the next day. Although Pearson refused to accept it, Gordon's humiliation became complete when, early in July, the United States, itself concerned about the outflow of gold and capital, created an "interest equalization tax" and slapped restrictions on foreign borrowings.

For all their concern about American investment, Gordon and his officials realized that Canadian business was dependent on money borrowed on Wall Street. The finance minister had to dispatch his officials south to plead for an exemption for Canada, an appeal that the Kennedy administration accepted, though not before using the occasion to make a few telling points to the Canadian supplicants. The U.S. undersecretary of state told the Canadian ambassador that "there was no element of retaliation or discrimination in the development of these measures." Of course, the American official could not refrain from adding that "the United States had shown much restraint in reacting to the Canadian budget measures." United States assistance to the Canadian government during the 1962 balance of payments crisis was also mentioned. Kennedy liked Pearson and he liked Canada, but JFK's administration was not averse to playing hardball with his friends. And the Canadians got the message, one finance department official telling a meeting of officials from both countries that Canadians had been "seriously disturbed by this reminder of dependence on the U.S.A."

"CONTINENTAL WATERBOY": THE COLUMBIA RIVER DISPUTE

So many and varied were the links across the border, however, that it seemed impossible for everything to go badly all at the same time. Something positive was bound to happen soon. Unfortunately, the next important issue between the two countries did not break the cycle. Just at the time that Gordon's fiscal measures were so upsetting Washington, the Liberal government was bringing to a close the long-drawn out negotiations for the development of the Columbia River's hydro potential, a solution to the enormous growth in demand for power in the Pacific Northwest. The Eisenhower and Diefenbaker administrations had signed a treaty in 1961 calling for generating plants in the United States and three huge water storage dams in British Columbia. The treaty, to last sixty years, would give Canada half the power generated downstream in the U.S., permit the diversion of Kootenay water into the Columbia in order to generate some power in Canada, and set aside $64 million for the flood control benefits the Americans would gain. Substantial flooding would have to occur in the Arrow Lakes region of southern British Columbia, however, and that produced enormous protest. Although it had been consulted during the treaty negotiation, the B.C. Social Credit government of W.A.C. Bennett was also unhappy, but not about the flooding in its province. Bennett was proposing to develop the power of the Peace River, and he began to fight Ottawa over who would pay how much of the Columbia project's costs. In fact, "Wacky" Bennett's plan was to develop both the Peace and the Columbia and to sell the Americans the downstream benefits of the latter for twenty years for cash instead of bringing them back into B.C. as cheap power.

In this complicated situation, marked by Bennett's takeover of the B.C. Electric Co. and the Peace River Development Co., the Diefenbaker government promised the Americans that the treaty would be ratified. The Americans, their need for power always growing, continued to press Ottawa, but Diefenbaker was driven from office before the matter was resolved. It fell to the Pearson government to conclude the Columbia arrangements in July 1963. British Columbia got its way. Bennett would sell the downstream benefits to the United States, and use the proceeds to finance Peace River power. To many Canadians, most notably General A.G.L. McNaughton, the fiery former chair of the International Joint Commission, this was a virtual sell-out of the Canadian national interest, a point the Liberal government scarcely contested. Bennett boasted of his great political victory over Ottawa, but his citizens, as the authors of *Canada Since 1945* noted, would receive "expensive hydro power from the Peace, not cheap power from the Columbia." Washington had made "a swap of money for energy, a trade that the U.S. government was only too eager to make." *Continental Waterboy*, the title of Donald Waterfield's passionate book about the controversy, seemed an appropriate label for Bennett. The primary benefit for Canada was simply that at least one nagging issue had been removed from the agenda of Canadian–American relations.

President Kennedy had hoped that relations with Canada would be better with Pearson in office, and the Columbia treaty resolution perhaps demonstrated from the president's standpoint that they could be. Still, the Gordon budget had demonstrated that serious troubles remained. The Americans still felt it was necessary to apply political power from time to time, as they had when Diefenbaker ruled the roost. Kennedy did not want to be obliged to worry about Canada, but the country next door came to occupy more and more of his time. In mid-November 1963, in fact, McGeorge Bundy sent a memorandum to Cabinet members to note that "all aspects of Canadian–American relations are of intense interest and concern to the President himself." For that reason, Bundy directed, "the President desires that the White House be fully informed of all significant negotiations or plans for negotiations with the Government of Canada."

LBJ AND THE AUTO PACT

But Kennedy was soon gone, his meteoric career abruptly halted by an assassin's bullet on 22 November 1963 in Dallas, Texas. There was genuine grief in Canada at the American tragedy, and some concern at the accession to power of Vice-President Lyndon Baines Johnson, the former senator from Texas and power broker extraordinaire. Johnson was rough where Kennedy had been smooth. He was crude, earthy, a giant of a man given to slapping people on the back as he spoke to them and picking up his dogs by the ears with the comment, "I like to hear them yelp." When Johnson flew back to Washington to take up the office he had sought all his political life, one of those who greeted him at the airport was Charles Ritchie, the Canadian ambassador. "Pearson," LBJ said. "Your Prime Minister. My best friend. Of all the heads of Government, my best friend."

For a time, it seemed to be true. In the spring of 1964, Canada had played a large role in putting together a United Nations peacekeeping force for Cyprus, thus preventing a war between Greece and Turkey, two NATO members. Paul Martin, the secretary of state for external affairs, had worked the telephones incessantly, as only he could, lining up commitments in Scandinavia and Ireland. He and Pearson had sent Canadian troops off to the Mediterranean island even before the UN force was authorized. Johnson, appalled at the consequences that a

Greco-Turkish war might produce, was grateful. "You'll never know what this has meant," he told Pearson over the phone. "Now, what can I do for you?" Person-to-person dealings like that—a quid for every quo—summed up Johnson's view of the world. What can I do for you, and what have you done for me—lately?

Pearson did not ask to be repaid, but he must have remembered LBJ's sense of obligation. The Canadian government was particularly upset by one aspect of the trade imbalance with the United States: the enormous deficit in automobiles and auto parts. In 1962, for example, Canada had imported $642 million in autos and parts from the U.S. and exported only $62 million, and the difference amounted to more than two-thirds of Canada's total trade deficit with the United States in that year. Canadian officials argued that their compatriots bought about 7.5 percent of North American auto production, but the Ontario plants at Oshawa, Oakville, and Windsor produced only 4 percent. Ottawa wanted to bring those numbers into balance. The Liberal government's solution, announced in the summer of 1963, was to set up an export incentive scheme that allowed plants in Canada to import more parts duty-free as they increased their exports. The Studebaker company promptly shut down its American operations and relocated in Canada, a mixed blessing for workers as the company soon folded. The American administration objected to Pearson's plan, threatening to slap countervailing duties on Canadian exports if it was deemed to be a bonus or an export subsidy. U.S. leaders of the United Auto Workers feared that the American worker was being forgotten in the race to pro-tect the Canadian one, but no one else wanted a fight. The two countries soon agreed to a broad negotiation that would head in the direction of continental free trade in autos and auto parts.

The talks began in July 1964, and from the outset the Americans flatly refused to give the Canadian auto plants a fixed share of the market. Then the Canadian government entered into agreements with Ford, Chrysler, and General Motors of Canada to bind them to output targets similar to those Ottawa had hoped to achieve through the export incentives. The arrangement was to be linked to some sort of free trade agreement for automobiles and parts. The United States agreed with both parts of the Canadian plan, and the outline of a deal was in place. Nevertheless, Ottawa was still deeply concerned about one important point: if the American negotiators struck a deal, could they guarantee Congressional acceptance? As so often before in Canadian–American relations, an unruly, hard-to-manage Congress was the potential fly in the ointment. Administrations could propose but senators and representatives disposed. LBJ knew how to manipulate Congress, however, and in this case the White House lent its considerable muscle to the effort at persuasion. The draft agreement was accepted. The final text was signed by Pearson and Secretary of State for External Affairs Paul Martin, and Johnson and U.S. Secretary of State Dean Rusk, at the LBJ ranch in Texas early in 1965. Johnson slipped and called the prime minister "Mr. Wilson" in a brief ceremony on his arrival, apparently confusing Pearson with the then British leader, Harold Wilson. Pearson was equal to the challenge. "Think nothing of it, Senator Goldwater," he shot back in a reference to the Republican presidential candidate swamped by Johnson in November 1964.

"It was all very homey and unpresidential," Pearson wrote of his two days with Johnson, "perhaps a little too much so, even for a ranch." It was "quite unlike anything that could have happened at any other place in any other meeting between the leaders of government." The friendliness, the wild drives over the president's vast acreage, the drinking, barbecues, rodeos, the constant telephone conversations and passing of secret messages from Vietnam across the table for Canadians to see—it was all "a reflection of the special relationship we have" and of the quintessential Johnson. Yet, Pearson mused, there was danger in "a possibility you are taken pretty much for granted because you are so close-treated." Nevertheless, the Canadian had got what he came for and the Auto Pact, as it was always called, was now signed, sealed, and delivered.

The pact appeared to be a Canadian victory. At a stroke, duties were eliminated on Canadian cars, trucks, and buses, auto parts, and accessories entering the U.S. and on similar American vehicles and parts entering Canada—the latter so long as a certain minimum level of production and sales took place in Canada. Because of the higher costs and prices of cars in Canada, only manufacturers meeting designated criteria were to be allowed to import free of duty. In other words, a private citizen could not bring an automobile purchased in Detroit at the lower American price into Canada without paying a duty. That provision guaranteed that the auto industry in Canada would expand and the trade deficit would narrow. The Auto Pact had a negative aspect, however, as the entire continental market was rationalized on the U.S. model. "I did not like this in principle," said Walter Gordon later, "but as three companies dominated the industry on both sides of the border, this acceptance merely acknowledged the existing fact."

The results of the deal were extraordinarily favourable for Canada in the first few years. American data in June 1967 demonstrated that autos and parts were the largest single item in cross-border trade, thus "statistically ending," as business historian Michael Bliss neatly put it, "the myth of the Dominion as [a] hewer of wood and drawer of water." American automobile and parts exports to Canada rose from $660 million to $1.3 billion and U.S. imports from $75 million to $900 million between 1964 and 1966. New investment in the Canadian industry was some $500 million. Vehicle production in Canada had risen by 35 percent and employment in the industry by 27 percent. Fully half of the cars and trucks produced in Canada by 1967 were being sold in the U.S. So beneficial to Canada was the Auto Pact that President Johnson resentfully complained about it to Ambassador Ritchie in a speech at a diplomatic gathering. Canadians generally agreed that this was one deal on which they had gained something, though to avoid having the Americans notice few crowed about it very loudly. In 1968, Canada had a small surplus in the auto trade and four years later a very large one, but the numbers bounced around and there were as many bad years as good. Some Canadians came to wonder about the merits of the deal, although most considered it a success story.

The concern that American unionized autoworkers had expressed over the Auto Pact demonstrated that jobs were often scarce in both the U.S. and Canada. The United Auto Workers had strong locals in both countries but it was headed from the United States. Indeed, all the international unions had a tension within them: however strong they were in Canada, they were stronger in the United States and most of the power resided there. After the unions in the Canadian Labour Congress affiliated with the American Federation of Labour–Congress of Industrial Organizations in 1965, dues paid by 982 000 Canadian workers went south in large monthly sums. Some nationalists fretted over this, while the government worried that both the new outflow of dues and the profits earned by American subsidiaries added to the trade deficit, but the leadership of the union movement seemed generally happy with the status quo and would remain so for another decade.

One man who was unhappy in the mid-1960s was Hal Banks, the U.S.-born head of the Canadian district of an American union, the Seafarers' International Union (SIU). Banks had come to Canada in 1949 to break the stranglehold exerted on Great Lakes and deep sea shipping by the Communist-led Canadian Seaman's Union. He had used strong-arm methods to establish a personal fiefdom and it was rumoured that he occasionally lent muscle or money to assist Liberal party candidates in Quebec. In 1954 Banks was ordered deported, but the decision was quashed by a Liberal cabinet minister under questionable circumstances.

Hand across the border. (Merle Tingley)

The stink of corruption grew as Banks attempted to extend control over collective bargaining rights in the transportation industry and seamen opponents who called for a clean union and an end to Banks's terrorism were roughed up. An inquiry into the labour situation in the shipping industry implicated Banks in 1963, and this was followed by his conviction for conspiracy to assault. He fled into hiding in the U.S., where Dean Rusk of the State Department refused Canadian government requests for his extradition. It was subsequently revealed, undoubtedly to the embarrassment of the secretary of state, that the SIU had been a heavy contributor to the Democratic party coffers.

The Banks affair had an important impact on the Canadian trade union movement. In an era of rising nationalism, as law professor William Kaplan points out in his book, *Everything That Floats*, this American leader of an American-based union had gone too far in depriving legitimate rights to his Canadian members and those of other labour organizations. A serious crisis was precipitated, finally forcing the Canadian Labour Congress to take action against Banks and the SIU. The result was a diminution in the influence of American-organized labour in Canada.

THE VIETNAM MORASS

By 1966, Vietnam was *the* topic in American politics, in international affairs, and in Canadian–American relations. Canadians were caught up in the concern of many Americans that U.S. involvement was deepening, with no end in sight and the issues and values at stake becoming murkier by the day.

The United States had first become involved in Vietnam in the 1950s, and the Americans were already providing aid to the South Vietnamese by the time of the Geneva conference in 1954, called to ease French withdrawal from Indochina and to create independent successor states in Laos, Cambodia, and Vietnam. Canada, too, was involved. To monitor the withdrawal, the exchange of prisoners, and the transfer of peoples, the conference created the International Control Commissions (ICCs), made up of soldiers and diplomats from Canada, Poland, and India. In Laos and Cambodia, the ICCs did their work quickly and well. In Vietnam, however, the Communist North and the "democratic" South were at loggerheads, and though there were some successes, notably in the peaceful transfer from North to South of tens of thousands of refugees, a guerilla war raged unchecked. The Soviets and Chinese backed the North, the Americans the South, and the ICC, paralyzed by its western–communist–neutral make-up, hovered uneasily in the middle.

The ICC teams had access to the North, and Canadian diplomats and officers collected intelligence information and passed it on to the Americans. Later on, diplomats passed messages to the North Vietnamese leaders, mixing tough talk and sweet promises from Washington. The Canadians, both soldiers and diplomats, apparently assumed that this was normal. After all, they were on the ICC explicitly as a western representative. Moreover, the cruelty of the Communist regime and the atrocities committed by the Viet Cong guerillas in the South were such as to make virtually all the Canadians who served in Vietnam into convinced opponents of the Communists. It was not that the South was democratic; the North was a brutal dictatorship. Still, the passing of information and the carrying of messages caused excruciating embarrassment in Canada when they became known after the theft and publication of secret, high level U.S. official documents in the *Pentagon Papers* in 1972.

In the early 1960s, the North stepped up its infiltration of the South and the tempo of the war increased dramatically. President Kennedy had sent in military advisers in large numbers and connived to topple the South Vietnamese government that blocked "democratization" and a more effective war-fighting policy. Johnson, who seemed to believe that if Vietnam was lost, Red hordes would land in California the next week, stepped up the war by sending in United States marines and army units, and by flying B-52 bombers, with their huge bomb loads, over the North. The U.S. launched its "Rolling Thunder" bombing campaign against the North in the spring of 1965. The Vietnam War was very soon a massive conflict. The United States had committed upwards of a half million soldiers, and began asking its allies to assist. The South Koreans, the Australians, and others responded to the appeal. Canada flatly refused, arguing that its ICC membership, hitherto a burden but now a blessing in disguise, made an active role in the war impossible. That was plausible enough, though neither the Canadian government nor Canadian firms had qualms about selling large quantities of munitions and supplies to feed the American war machine: $1.3 billion between 1959 and 1966, including napalm and chemical explosives.

What should Canada do? When he had talked with Kennedy at Hyannisport in May 1963, Pearson was asked what he thought the president should do about Vietnam. He had answered that he thought the U.S. should get out. "Any fool knows that," Kennedy replied, "The question is how." So it was, and no one knew the answer. The Pearson government was most concerned by the possibility that the war might expand into a general Asian or world war, or might lead to American use of nuclear weapons. That would be catastrophic, so every effort to move the belligerents towards peace was worth the effort. The odds were long, however. The Ho Chi Minh government in the North was implacable, confident that it could prevail against the Americans, and confident too of the support of its Soviet and Chinese allies. The United

States government tried desperately to prop up its ally in the South, but all the will and resolution seemed confined to the North. What is more, Johnson's policy, though still favoured by the majority in opinion polls, was increasingly under attack. "Hey, hey, LBJ, how many kids did you kill today?" chanted American—and Canadian—youths as the toll of dead GIs and marines mounted. For Pearson, Vietnam really did seem to be the wrong war in the wrong place, fought for the wrong reasons.

Pearson nonetheless saw no point at all in condemning the United States. That would achieve nothing other than to anger President Johnson. Still, perhaps a Canadian nudge in the right direction could lead the Americans to rethink their position. In that frame of mind, Pearson went to Temple University on 2 April 1965. "There are many factors which I am not in a position to weigh," he admitted, "but there does appear to be at least a possibility that a suspension of such air strikes against North Vietnam, at the right time, might provide the Hanoi authorities with the opportunity, if they wish to take it, to inject some flexibility into their policy without appearing to do so as the direct result of military pressure." That was a modest proposal, to be sure, but it might better have been made in Canada. Johnson was livid, as we have seen, and every Canadian visitor to the White House thereafter received the same message from the president: "Give Lester my best . . . and tell him that if he's got any more speeches to make on Viet Nam, to please make them outside the United States." Pearson had violated Johnson's cardinal rule that you did not cause trouble for another politician on his own turf. LBJ, who loved dogs and salty language, likened this to "pissing on my rug."

There was some punishment for Canada after the Temple speech. At one lunch that included the Canadian and West German ambassadors, the president was full of praise for the Germans who "have always been our allies," and scornful of the "so clever" Canadians who "can come down here to teach us how to run the war in Vietnam. You screwed us on the Auto Pact—oh, yes, you Canadians are *so* clever." Charles Ritchie described the situation: "They are still civil in the government offices—civil and chilly—but give them a drink or two after dinner and it all comes out with rough frankness. Your government has erred and strayed from the way and the sheep-dogs are at your heels barking you back into line. Disagreeable it is at times—even offensive." Of course, Ritchie said, even when Johnson "consulted" allies, he never really listened. "The phrase 'consultation with allies' is apt to mean, in United States terms, briefing allies, lecturing allies, sometimes pressuring allies or sounding out allies to see if they are sound. The idea of anything from allies seems strange to official Washington thinking. The word comes from Washington and is home-made."

Pearson's Temple University speech, the only one he would make on Vietnam in the U.S., was a product of his own unease. Although polls demonstrated that most Canadians supported LBJ's war, the articulate and the politically committed were beginning to have doubts. American draft resisters and deserters would be welcomed into Canada and organizations would spring up to care for and comfort them. Most of the estimated 50 000 who came would remain in Canada after the war and after President Jimmy Carter's amnesty on his first day of office in 1977. Doug Fetherling, a writer who came to Canada in 1967 not to escape the draft but because he opposed American policy, recalled an uncomfortable meeting in Winnipeg with his brother, also a journalist but a veteran too, and still a U.S. resident. "Is there anything I can send you from the States?" the brother asked. "I'm afraid it's the other way around," Fetherling said. "We trade with Hanoi, Peking, Havana, remember?" Which one was the exile, Fetherling asked himself.

Anti-war "teach-ins" took place on virtually every Canadian university campus, usually initiated by faculty members who had just been hired from the United States to staff Canada's expanding post-secondary institutions. Canada, after all, was just like the United States to many of these young Ph.D.s, and few stopped to think that it might be improper to organize demonstrations against American policy in Canada or, for that matter, to teach sociology from American texts, or literature courses that ignored Canadian authors. "There's no radicalism in Canada," the American profs said, overlooking in their ignorance the existence of successful socialist parties and Quebec separatists. And Vietnam spawned a radicalism of its own. Even if Canadian soldiers were not dying there, television brought the war into every home each and every night in a completely unprecedented way. No war is ever pretty; Vietnam seemed all the more ugly for being readily available on the small screen.

Canada could do little, however. Pearson and Paul Martin, his foreign secretary, did what they could to propel the belligerents to the conference table, but no one paid much attention. Pearson tried to be as polite and supportive as possible of the American position, but in September 1966 he came out in favour of a unilateral bombing halt, the first time in fifteen months that he had taken so unequivocal a position. There was no change in U.S. policy, only further frostiness from the increasingly isolated LBJ, and in 1967 Pearson told the House of Commons that all his government could do was to bring "our worries and anxieties to the notice of those who are more immediately and directly involved in the hope that our advice and counsel will be of some help to them." Johnson's Washington was not apt to listen, especially after Pearson's Temple speech. Even Johnson's visit to Montreal's Expo '67 on 25 May 1967, intended to be a formal state visit to mark the centennial of Confederation, was announced on one day's notice and lasted the briefest time compatible with the stiff protocol of such occasions.

General Lyndon Baines Johnson. (Reprinted with permission—
Toronto Star Syndicate.)

PRINCIPLES FOR PARTNERSHIP
(OR SUBORDINATION)

The Temple speech was symptomatic. A long list of clashes between U.S. and Canadian interests and values had replaced the relative calm and consensus of the ten years after the end of the Second World War. In January 1964, before Vietnam had exploded into a major struggle, President Johnson and Prime Minister Pearson had met in Washington and as their communiqué reported, "discussed at some length the practicability and desirability of working out acceptable principles which would make it easier to avoid divergencies in economic and other policies of interest to each other." The next month, Livingston Merchant, twice ambassador to Canada, and Arnold Heeney, twice ambassador to the United States, were named to a working party to produce the "acceptable principles."

Friends of long standing, the two men set to work at once, agreeing that they alone would constitute the group. "We were, perhaps, the smallest task force on record," Heeney wrote. They agreed that the central problem between the nations was "consultation," which had to mean more than something other than advice and automatic consent. "We both understood that if agreement upon mutually satisfactory solutions or accommodations could not be reached, each government should be free to follow its own course, without recrimination." Their report, *Canada and the United States: Principles for Partnership*, was given to Pearson and Johnson at the end of June 1965 and released to the public the next month.

The American media scarcely noticed the document, but the Canadian press and informed public went wild. Though there was much that was sensible, even anodyne, in the report, one paragraph had ventured this suggestion: "It is in the abiding interest of both countries that, wherever possible, divergent views between the two governments should be expressed and if possible resolved in private, through diplomatic channels." Canadians ought to feel confident "that the practice of quiet diplomacy is not only neighbourly and convenient to the United States but that it is in fact more effective than the alternative of raising a row and being unpleasant in public." This perfectly expressed the idea of "quiet diplomacy." Professionals could and should fix up problems themselves and in private.

Many Canadians failed to see the virtues in this approach. Quiet diplomacy was taken to be a shorthand phrase to describe what could only be the gagging of the Canadian government and public opinion.

Keep quiet, one journalist said, summing up the response in Canada, and "hope for the lollipops which are dished out only to good boys." Because it was issued only a few months after Pearson's Temple University address, the Heeney–Merchant report was interpreted by some as a response to the prime minister's criticism of Johnson's Vietnam policy. As a result, poor Heeney was charged with having been "conned" by Merchant, and Charles Lynch, a powerful columnist, remarked, "If the Heeney–Merchant doctrine catches on, it seems certain to confirm our lackey status." Only a few commentators recognized that the report had been designed to enhance Canadian independence, not constrain it; no small country could ever win a shouting match with a superpower. Blair Fraser, the able *Maclean's* writer, wrote that persuasion in private had advantages and did not mean that Canadians were barred from speaking out against the policies of friendly nations. Rather, "such speaking out" was "a sign that persuasion had failed."

Heeney was unmoved by the criticism. As he put it in his memoirs, "The desire of Canadians for an independent foreign policy for Canada is understandable in the sense that all nations would like to be untrammelled. . . . The trick is to achieve and maintain that sufficiency of freedom of action which will enable the nation, and the individual, to contribute best to its own and to world society." With that few could disagree, but Heeney's next words were more debatable: "In the Canadian situation there is no alternative to partnership with the United States, provided always that the terms of the partnership give the necessary minimum protection for Canadian independence and that the international policy of the United States, not in detail but in general, is not hostile to Canadian national objectives."

A FAR BETTER PLACE TO BE

Heeney's bland explanation met a critical response because it clashed with a new nationalism in Canada. The causes of the new mood were many and various and difficult to nail down with precision. The United States was still the richest and most powerful nation on the globe, but the American dream too often became the American nightmare. The assassination of Kennedy (and later Martin Luther King and JFK's brother Robert), guns in the street, the appalling ghettoes of the big cities, the unbridled greed of corporations, the dreadful, never-ending war in

Vietnam, and the absence of American social services all gave Canadians pause. They were led to think that their country was a far better place to be, slower paced though it was, unencumbered with compulsory military service, and protected with unemployment insurance, family allowances, and, soon, national medicare.

Anti-Americanism had become the Canadian national sport. Frank Underhill, the historian, once joked that a Canadian was the model anti-American, the ideal anti-American, the anti-American as conceived by the mind of God. There had always been some truth in that, but in the 1960s the tone became shrill. In *The New Romans*, a critical anthology of Canadian reactions to the United States, published in 1968, poet Raymond Souster captured the majority view with his offering, "Death Chant for Mr. Johnson's America":

> America
> you seem to be dying . . .
> wafting inshore from off the Great
> Lakes the same unmistakable stink, so unlike the
> usual putrefaction of these waters . . .

Canada had all the benefits of North American life with few of the disadvantages, and, now more than ever, Canadians felt pleased with their lot.

The centennial of Confederation in 1967 was the manifestation of this national pleasure, celebrated in virtually every city and town across the land. Canadians had made a country out of their sprawling land, and they were proud of their achievements. The new maple leaf flag, adopted only in 1965, was suddenly flying everywhere in a country that had never before been flag-conscious. Canadians showed their pride, with the centennial train, its whistle tootling the first bars of "O Canada"; with Expo '67, the extraordinarily successful world's fair in Montreal; and with centennial arenas and parks in cities big and small. The fact that some French Canadians were seeking independence for Quebec and receiving support from President Charles de Gaulle of France merely intensified the nationalism of the great majority, French- and English-speaking alike.

CULTURE: "PURE AMONG THE BEAVER"

Culture to some extent reflected the change. The creation of the Canada Council had led to extraordinary developments in the arts. The Montreal and Toronto symphonies, for example, became very good indeed, thanks to the council's subventions. Stratford's Shakespearean festival and the Shaw Festival at Niagara-on-the-Lake offered superb theatre, and the National Ballet, the Royal Winnipeg Ballet, and Les Grands Ballets Canadiens took their place among the great companies. Painters such as Jack Bush and Jean-Paul Riopelle, poets like Irving Layton and Leonard Cohen, novelists like Margaret Laurence and Marie-Claire Blais, and short story writers such as Mavis Gallant attracted notice at home and frequently abroad. It was a far cry from only a few decades before, when the arts had lingered in the backwater of colonial doldrums, when to escape to New York or Los Angeles was the object of every talented Canadian girl or boy.

Of course, American culture, especially popular culture, was still to be found everywhere. Hollywood movies dominated the screen, though now there were at least a few Canadian feature films. Television was still a wasteland of sitcoms and game shows, though again Canadian productions were more professional and more noticeable than a few years before. Canadian networks knew well that one hour of American TV could be purchased for about 10 percent of the cost of producing an hour from scratch in Canada. The pressures for both the CBC and the CTV network to save money by buying American were almost irresistible. Moreover, the simple truth, however unpalatable, was that the public wanted to watch American shows. The medium may have been the message, as Toronto guru of communications Marshall McLuhan put it to worldwide acclaim in the 1960s, but Canadians turned the dial first to the message offered on American stations. In the first week of March 1963, for example, seven of the top ten shows on the CBC TV network were American-made. There were differences between Canadian and American TV tastes, however, most notably in the consistent appetite of Canadians for information programming. In 1965, the American networks devoted only 3 percent of air time to information shows, while the Toronto CBC station had 24 percent and Montreal's French-language CBC station had 43 percent. The success of Canadian news and investigative journalism programs, in other words, demonstrated that the public wanted information about their own country or with a distinctively national perspective.

That seemed less true in periodical publishing. American magazines still took the lion's share of readership and advertising revenues, and the Canadian government struggled to find a policy that would give domestic magazines a level playing field on which to operate. In 1965 finance minister Gordon took away income tax deductions for advertising in non-Canadian newspapers and magazines. But *Time* and

Reader's Digest, creaming off most of the advertising revenue, were exempted, the Pearson government in effect giving the two magazines the status of honorary Canadian citizenship. Critics remained unhappy and continued to demand tougher action. Gordon explained that Canada could not have gotten the Auto Pact if he had hit *Time* and *Reader's Digest* hard, such was the magazines' support in Washington.

To some critics, junk was junk whether it was American or Canadian. The American political columnist Richard Rovere was surely correct when he asked, "What would happen in Canada if full sovereignty were invoked and the southern border were sealed tight against American mass culture—if the airwaves were jammed, if all our comic books were embargoed, if only the purest and most uplifting of American cultural commodities were allowed entry?" The answer? "Native industries would take over, obviously, and produce junk of their own." Frank Scott, the distinguished constitutional lawyer, nationalist, and poet summed up the naïveté of the cultural Canada Firsters in a poem called "The Call of the Wild":

> Make me over, Mother Nature,
> Take the knowledge from my eyes,
> Put me back among the pine trees
> Where the simple are the wise.
>
> Clear away all evil influence
> That can hurt me from the States
> Keep me pure among the beaver
> With un-Freudian loves and hates,
>
> Where my Conrads are not Aiken
> Where John Bishop's Peales don't sound,
> Where the Ransoms are not Crowing
> And the Ezras do not Pound.

The Agenda of the New Nationalism

As Scott suggested, there was as ever a strong component of simple-minded anti-Americanism built into Canadian nationalism. The way Kennedy had intervened to topple John Diefenbaker from power fed this anti-U.S. fervour. Diefenbaker was still around, forced out as

Conservative leader only in September 1967, and there were already enough warts on the Kennedy legend to lend credence to the Chief's grumbles that "they" had done him in. As a "living legend," Dief was a rallying point for a certain kind of know-nothing nationalism, one that harked back to a mythical simpler age when Britain ruled the waves and the fondest desire of every Canadian was the monarch's favour.

More seriously, Canadians looked as never before at the statistics that demonstrated their economic subordination to the United States. By 1967, the United States sent $7.9 billion worth of goods into Canada, compared with only $619 million received from Britain. In the same year, Canada exported $7.1 billion to the U.S. and only $1.2 billion to the United Kingdom. Of $34.7 billion in foreign investment in Canada, 81 percent was American, and 10 percent British. Those numbers were staggering, and by 1967 polls showed that two-thirds of Canadians believed Ottawa had to take action to reduce foreign control of Canadian industry.

The same poll revealed that almost as many Canadians thought their country did not demonstrate enough independence in its dealings with the United States. To most Canadians, that almost certainly meant nothing more than speaking up in Washington and at NATO and UN sessions. But an articulate few, mainly in the universities and the media, sought another agenda: Canada should get out of NATO or at the very least bring home the soldiers sent overseas at the beginning of the 1950s to help Europe until it got on its feet again; should get out of NORAD on the grounds that the bomber threat was effectively finished; should recognize the Beijing government of China and break ties with Chiang Kai-shek's Taiwan regime; and should begin to wholeheartedly criticize America's war in Vietnam. James Eayrs, an articulate, pro-American Cold Warrior in the 1950s turned nationalist crusader for Canadian independence and diplomatic purity in the 1960s, symbolized the drastic shift in mood.

Every point on that agenda clashed with Washington's view of the world. There, the threat from the USSR was considered real and ever present. NATO was, and would remain for almost another quarter century, the centrepiece of America's European policy. Taiwan represented an article of faith and the Chinese "Reds" an object of detestation, not least for the support they offered North Vietnam in a war that was proving extremely costly in lives, money, and public morale. If Ottawa set off in the direction suggested by Canadian critics, there were certain to be costs that might make LBJ's thunderous anger after the Temple University speech seem like a mere rain squall. Canada's actions, its leaders had discovered, had consequences.

The Canadian government felt obliged at least to consider the points raised in the nationalist critique. Foreign policy, like everything else in the 1960s, would have to be shaken up and re-thought. One of the first efforts at "re-appraisal" was undertaken by Norman Robertson, retired from External Affairs and in ill health. Twice undersecretary, twice high commissioner in London, a former ambassador in Washington, and a clerk of the Privy Council, Robertson was the most senior professional diplomat in the country. He surveyed the whole policy spectrum, and his conclusions were typically sensible and straightforward. "The chief restraints on Canadian foreign policy are the lack of a clear sense of national identity and the need to preserve tolerably friendly relations with the U.S.A." There could be no arguing with that, nor with his conclusion that there was almost no possibility for independent freewheeling in the face of the "essential need to maintain mutual confidence and respect in our relations with the United States," despite "all the dilemmas which that relationship poses for us." More contentiously, Robertson went on to defend quiet diplomacy, assert the "integrity" of the American position in Vietnam, and declare "fundamental agreement with the United States on the essentials of the Western strategic position in the prevailing international situation." For good measure, he lambasted the critics of Canadian policy for their "emotional and at times ill-informed rhetoric." Robertson's report was never published, though its contents were leaked to the press and used as a debating tool by several of the ministers in Pearson's Cabinet who sought to succeed him as Liberal leader after his 1968 resignation. The report made little impact on the eventual winner, Pierre Trudeau, who set himself to turn Canadian foreign policy in completely new directions.

Lester Pearson had been the pre-eminent Canadian of the years since the war. He was a nationalist, though not one of the stridently anti-American variety. He recognized, just as did Robertson's report and the Heeney–Merchant one before it, that there were limits on Canadian independence. It was simply impossible to share the continent with the United States and to pretend that the superpower was not there or did not care what Canada did. Realism, in other words, had to take precedence, and for Pearson it did.

C H A P T E R

THE FAILED REVOLUTION

1 9 6 8 – 1 9 7 6

Revolution and unrest were in the air in 1968. In France, student protests in Paris almost led to the ouster of President Charles de Gaulle. In Czechoslovakia, in a foretaste of what would come twenty years later, crowds urged their government to move towards socialism with a human face, a gallant effort that was crushed when Moscow ordered in the tanks. In the United States, unrest took the form of black riots in Detroit, Washington, and other large cities, as tens of thousands protested the assassination of Martin Luther King and vicious police actions on the streets of Chicago during the Democratic party convention. Upheaval in the U.S. led not to fundamental change but to backlash, contributing to the election of a "law and order" president, Richard Nixon, in November. A former congressman, senator, and vice-president, Nixon had lost the 1960 election to John F. Kennedy. Admired on the right for his fierce anti-communism, despised on the left for sometimes unspeakable tactics, Nixon was shrewd and able, a quick study, and unafraid of using American power.

TRUDEAU THE REVOLUTIONARY

In Canada, a very different man—an apparent revolutionary—came to power. Pierre Trudeau had first run for Parliament only in 1965, becoming justice minister in Pearson's Cabinet the next year, and now he emerged to captivate a public that sought a change from the long string of grey-faced leaders who had ruled Canada for a half century. Though he was forty-nine years old, he was a physically fit bachelor with charisma that shone through on television, even if his set-piece orations were usually dreary. Everywhere he went during the Liberal leadership race he was mobbed like a rock star. The same crowd scenes occurred during the election campaign that Trudeau called within days of taking power. At last, Canada had a leader of its very own who exuded Kennedy-like star quality.

But there were differences. Kennedy had been elected in 1960 by talking tough about Cuba, the USSR, and missiles. Trudeau's appeal in English Canada was largely a product of his strong federalist position, but when he touched on foreign policy he sounded very different from his prime ministerial predecessors. First, he wanted to recognize China, a country he had visited and one whose exclusion from world councils he found absurd. Then, Trudeau complained that instead of a Canadian defence policy shaped by foreign policy, "Canada's foreign policy was largely its policy in NATO, through NATO." Did we really need troops in Europe twenty-three years after the end of the war? Did we need to think like a great power, sending troops abroad when Canada's task was to defend its territory first and to help in the defence of North America as an afterthought?

Those questions were not original, though it was certainly unusual to hear a prime minister raise them. Academics and journalists had been saying much the same things for a decade. The simple truth was that Canada was not very important militarily any more. In the early 1950s, when Europe had still felt the effects of the war, the brigade group and air division amounted to a very substantial contribution to NATO's strength. That was not so anymore; the fate of the smaller nations was certain to be determined not by Canadian efforts but by Soviet and American strategic nuclear arsenals. Now, with the cities south of the border burning, Trudeau was concerned about North America. As he told one external affairs officer, he wasn't sure "it was right for us to be thinking so much about the European threat. Perhaps we should be worried much more about civil war in North America. . . . He did not want in ten years time to look back on the present and have to say, 'Why in God's name did we not realize what was happening on our own door step?'"

Just as important as unrest in the United States was the trouble in Canada. In 1968, Quebec was restive. Terrorists in the Front de Libération du Québec were setting off explosions at the offices of federal agencies and at the homes of "collaborators." Legitimate separatists began to coalesce around the charismatic former Quebec Liberal minister, René

Lévesque. Pro-Canada forces seemed in disarray. Trudeau was a convinced federalist, a hard-line anti-*nationaliste*, and in power in Ottawa. His priority, his very reason for being in politics, was to keep Canada together. Everything else, to him, was secondary.

This attitude led Trudeau to order a sweeping review of defence and foreign policy. Repeatedly, the departments of national defence and external affairs sent papers to the Cabinet concluding sagely that the status quo was best. Repeatedly, Trudeau sent them back demanding a review from first principles. All the options had to be studied, from neutrality to full engagement in NATO. At the end of March 1969, the Cabinet spent two extraordinary days in a Trudeau-led seminar—a former university professor, Trudeau was ever the intellectual—before deciding on a "planned and phased reduction" of the contribution to NATO that would ultimately halve the country's forces in Europe. In descending order of importance Canada now had as its aims sovereignty, North American defence, NATO, and peacekeeping. The defence budget was frozen at $1.8 billion, and the ships and aircraft on hand, already starting to run down, were not to be replaced with newer equipment. Trudeau, in other words, seemed more interested in cutting back defence than in backing his new priorities with troops and equipment.

This was evident when the defence department issued a White Paper in August 1971 to provide a rationale for the decisions Trudeau had imposed. The paper, approved by Cabinet but drafted by national defence minister Donald Macdonald and only one aide, devoted substantial attention to North American air defence. The Bomarcs, Diefenbaker's nemesis, were to be retired, but air defence within NORAD would continue to be provided by CF-101 Voodoo aircraft, purchased in 1961 and armed with air-to-air nuclear missiles. Ominously for the air force, the paper noted that the government was "not prepared to devote substantial sums to new equipment or facilities for use only for active anti-bomber defences." Indeed, the policy of the government in 1973, when the air defence agreement with the United States was due for renewal, would depend on "the strategic situation extant. "

TRUDEAU AND NIXON

None of this sat very well with the new Nixon administration. Trudeau had made some incautious but sensible remarks about Nixon's proposals for an anti-ICBM (intercontinental ballistic missile) defence system that might have seen exploded missiles and their radioactive contents falling on Canadian soil. The White House had also received warnings, including one from a former Harvard professor of Trudeau's, that the stylish prime minister with a rose in his lapel was pushing Canada towards neutralism.

The two leaders met for the first time in March 1969, when Trudeau visited the White House. There was undoubtedly some curiosity in each direction: they were highly intelligent men, though in very different ways. Certainly they did not become close. Henry Kissinger, Nixon's national security adviser and later his secretary of state, recollected that "it cannot be said that Trudeau and Nixon were ideally suited for one another," and Nixon a few years later referred to the prime minister as "that asshole Trudeau" on one of the famous Watergate tapes. In their meetings, however, Nixon treated Trudeau with attention and respect. For his part, Trudeau was probably more fascinated by Kissinger than by Nixon. The former he found physically and intellectually impressive; Nixon, Trudeau later said, was "a complex man, full of self-doubts. . . . Very strange." Yet even without Kissinger, "he would have had a shrewd appraisal of world politics." To the press and other observers Trudeau's demeanour in Washington was one of awe to be near a man exercising such power. The prime minister actually said to Nixon that he looked forward to getting "the information and wisdom" that would be forthcoming.

Despite the unease in Washington about Trudeau, it is significant that he did not receive any lectures on the need to stand tough against the Soviets. Nor did he denounce the Americans' ABM plans. Nixon was a realist, and he had probably assessed Canada's importance just as astutely as he assessed global forces: nothing that Ottawa did mattered very much, and pushing too hard would get Canadian backs up. Trudeau was fully aware of Canada's global significance as well: "We may be excused, I hope, if we fail to take too seriously the suggestion of some of our friends . . . that our acts—or our failure to act—this or that way will have profound consequences or will lead to widespread undesirable results." Canada was not a great power and Trudeau, in the process of turning the country inwards, did not see anything wrong with that.

The president said that he hoped Canada would not cut its NATO commitment. He spoke to no avail, as the announcement of the reduction came a few days later. As for China, Canada was on the verge of moving to recognition, and though the Americans did not like this course of action, it did not upset them terribly. In fact, soon after Canada and China agreed to exchange diplomats in October 1970 as part of a formula that saw Canada break its formal links with Taiwan, the United States itself acknowledged the Beijing regime's existence.

The results of the Canadian government's long-lasting foreign policy review were finally released in late June 1970. Characteristically, for the Trudeau government, *Foreign Policy for Canadians* appeared in a trendy six-booklet format with slipcase and dripping with jargon-laden prose. Canadian–American relations were scarcely touched upon. The relations were so apparently complex, so all-embracing, so intractable that they defied description and capsulization. Humbug, critics said. As long as Canada had no defined policy statement, no basic position towards the United States, it would always be outmanoeuvered by the Yankees.

In Washington, the American government looked at Ottawa's efforts to define foreign policy with sympathy and some amusement. Incoming presidents usually undertook their own reviews of foreign affairs, but policy only rarely changed course. As far as Canadian–American relations went, official Washington was quite content. It wanted U.S. capital to have the freest access possible to Canada—no more Walter Gordons, please. At this point, Trudeau did not seem to be an economic nationalist, or a nationalist of any kind, so few worried. The U.S. also needed Canada to maintain at least a minimum defence of its airspace. The prime minister had not much interest in defence questions generally, but though he had cut back in NATO, he sounded much more concerned about North American defence. Those two matters, in other words, seemed in hand at the beginning of the 1970s.

THE *MANHATTAN* AFFAIR

Nonetheless, nationalist clouds on the Canadian horizon caused small *frissons* of concern in Washington. In the fall of 1969, the United States announced plans to test a nuclear device on the Aleutian island of Amchitka. The whole area was prone to earthquakes and there were fears about sympathetic quakes or tidal waves. British Columbian, Canadian, and Alaskan protests were vehement, but the Nixon administration proceeded, fortunately without the anticipated effects. Then in the same autumn, a large Humble Oil Company tanker, the SS *Manhattan*, made a voyage westwards through the Northwest Passage. Though it had to be specially reinforced to handle the ice and though it required assistance from Canadian icebreakers, the *Manhattan* trip seemed to demonstrate that commercial tankers might be able to carry the oil from Alaska's North Slope to market. In Canada, however, the tanker's voyage was seen by nationalists and others as an American challenge to Canadian sovereignty in the North: it was long-standing U.S. policy that all straits were international waters open to any nation's ships. The Northwest Passage, encased in ice, had never before been thought to be navigable, though American, Soviet, and probably British nuclear submarines frequently patrolled beneath. Now, if tankers could sail the Passage, the United States government might mount a major assault in international law against Canada's hold on its North.

There was another side to the story, too. Oil tankers ran aground or broke up close inshore with monotonous regularity. Each time, beaches were fouled with the thick black sludge, and sea birds and fish died in the tens of thousands. The ecology of the Arctic, as Canadians had belatedly realized, was especially delicate. To send heavily laden tankers through ice-filled water did not seem either safe or responsible. What would happen to the narwhals and fish of the Arctic Ocean? What about the Inuit who lived in harmony with their environment despite snowmobiles, televisions, and other modern appliances? Environmental concerns combined with nationalist nervousness to force Ottawa to take action by establishing its control over the waters of the Arctic seas. The method chosen was the Arctic Waters Pollution Prevention bill, introduced in Parliament in April 1970. The Arctic was pristine still and therefore special, the government maintained, and to prevent its pollution, the federal government must assert control over all commercial shipping in the North. Lest the United States or any other power disagree with Canada's right to so act, the Canadian government said bluntly that on this issue it would refuse to accept the jurisdiction of the International Court of Justice. This was despite disagreements in Cabinet, notably from those ministers who were proud that hitherto Canada had always accepted the Hague court's decisions.

The Americans were unhappy at what they saw as this interference with their sovereign right to sail wherever they wished, so much so that they tried to organize a conference to create a multilateral Arctic regime and thus prevent Canada and other states from imposing national control over Arctic waters. But Ottawa sent emissaries to other Arctic nations and brought them on side, not least the Soviet Union, which was quite pleased to tweak the eagle's tail feathers. The Canadian position prevailed, and when the *Manhattan* tried the Passage once more, it did so only after its owners accepted Canadian standards on safety and responsibility for pollution. Washington grumbled, but it could do little more. As it turned out, the second *Manhattan* voyage was the last; presumably there were easier ways to get oil and gas to market.

"NO MORE UNCLE SUGAR": THE 1971 SHOCK

What did Canada want from the United States in this new era? As in previous eras, trade. In a speech at the National Press Club during a visit to the U.S., Trudeau pointed out that Canada was America's biggest source of imports and largest customer. Canada bought more American goods than Japan, Britain, Germany, and France, the next four largest purchasers, combined. That posed problems for Canada, Trudeau said, for it was difficult to be so dependent on one market. Canadians had been singing this refrain for a long time, but Trudeau put it unforgettably: "Living next to you is in some ways like sleeping with an elephant: no matter how friendly and even-tempered the beast, one is affected by every twitch and grunt." American policy, global in its thrust, could hurt Canada in myriad ways, either intentionally or not. A small American measure aimed at bringing Japan into line on some trade matter or reducing the outflow of gold brought on by the war in Vietnam could cause enormous damage in Ottawa. When Washington coughed, Ottawa was in danger of catching double pneumonia. That was a fact of life, however hard to swallow.

In 1971, the elephant rolled over. The United States, long the dominant economic power in the world, suddenly realized that it could no longer set the terms of trade for the world. On 15 August, therefore, the president decided, in his own words, that it was "no more Uncle Sugar" and that he had to tackle the growing American balance of payments deficit. Appearing on nation-wide TV, he announced a wage–price freeze to fight inflation, tax credits to stimulate industry, the end of the convertibility of the dollar into gold, measures to encourage U.S. multinationals to do their exporting from their American, not foreign, factories, and a 10 percent surcharge on dutiable imports. The last two measures, sprung on friendly nations without prior consultation, made headlines all over the world. A reeling Japan saw its press call the news a "Nixon shokku."

But no country was more stunned than Canada at seeing its exports suddenly cost more in the United States. If the U.S. treasury got its way and also forced Canada to raise its dollar above par, Canadian goods were almost certain to be priced out of the American market. The time-honoured practice that Canada would be exempted from such measures had been thrown in the garbage. As Trudeau's foreign policy assistant,

Ivan Head, noted in *Foreign Affairs*, the August measures had "brutally broken the custom of according special treatment to Canada." There was no doubt, in either Washington or Ottawa, that this was deliberate.

Canadians did not know how close they had come to an even more serious blow. The man behind the 15 August measures was the treasury secretary, John Connally, a tough Texan Democrat who had been riding in John Kennedy's automobile that terrible day in November 1963 and had himself been seriously wounded. Now serving Nixon, Connally wanted to lash out at the freeloaders who had sponged off Uncle Sam for too long, and his eye lit on the Auto Pact of 1965. Canada had made too much out of this agreement, a pact that had never been intended to be permanent. Scrap it, Connally ordered, in the run up to 15 August. Happily for Canada, a State Department official saw the press release before it was issued and, talking fast, persuaded the secretary of state to intervene. The agreement, after all, had been properly and duly negotiated and if it was cancelled unilaterally, the Canadians would be justifiably outraged. Moreover, as just under one-third of Canada's exports to the U.S. were covered under the terms of the Auto Pact, its annulment would cause enormous disruption to Canada. The State Department prevailed and Canada was spared.

No one in Ottawa knew that the Auto Pact had even been in jeopardy. The Nixon administration's other unilateral measures were bad enough. As the largest trading partner of the United States, sending almost 70 percent of its exports south, Canada stood to be hit harder than any other country by the import surcharge. Ottawa scrambled to react, hampered by the absence of Trudeau and his finance minister on a European holiday. A government delegation flew to Washington to see Connally for a testy meeting. The secretary got matters off on the wrong foot by mistakenly reading from a brief intended for Japan, and the deputy minister of finance, Simon Reisman, who could shout just as loudly and talk just as bluntly as any Texan, repeatedly interrupted Connally's comments to correct errors of fact. There were even stories that an angry Reisman had butted his cigar on the secretary's desk at the meeting's end. There was to be no exemption for Canada from the American measures, even though there was every prospect of a loss of $300 million in exports, factory shut-downs, rising unemployment, and the necessity for Ottawa to pump money into affected industries to keep them in operation.

Negotiations went on, increasingly heated, and Trudeau said that the Americans did not "know much or care much about Canada." The prime minister added later that Washington's policies were simply unfair: "Are you saying that your economic system is leading you to buy up as much of the world as possible?" If Canada couldn't trade to earn American dollars, that would be the result. And if the Americans simply wanted Canada to provide natural resources and purchase manufactured products, then, Trudeau said bluntly, "we will have to reassess fundamentally our relations with them—trading, political and otherwise."

Finally, in December, Trudeau flew to Washington to talk with Nixon. The president was unhappy about some comments Trudeau had made during a visit to the Soviet Union in May 1971. The prime minister had appeared to suggest that "the danger to . . . [the Canadian] identity from a cultural, economic and perhaps even military point of view" was greater from the United States than from the Soviet Union. Those kinds of remarks were unwise if Canada expected special consideration from the Americans a few months later. Cynics might with some justice say, however, that Nixon's August measures demonstrated the truth of Trudeau's complaint.

"Now, as for press statements on our talks—here's yours." (Reprinted with permission—Toronto Star Syndicate.)

Officials on both sides met to thrash over the economic details in yet another unpleasant session. Yet Trudeau and Nixon, accompanied by only a few aides, talked pleasantly, and Trudeau offered the American leader an explanation of economics, Canadian style. Had Nixon's government taken a conscious decision that Canada's trade balance could never be in surplus with the U.S.? If so, Ottawa would have to protect itself and implement restrictionist and nationalist policies that would hurt American interests. One example Trudeau could have employed, but did not, was that Canadian sun-seekers left half a billion dollars in Florida each year; if restrictions were slapped on tourist travel or on the exchange of Canadian into American dollars, that sum could be greatly reduced. The reaction of hotel keepers and restaurant owners in Miami and Key West could be imagined.

While the president merely suggested that it had never been his intention to damage Canadian interests, Henry Kissinger intervened to say that the Canadians had to be accommodated. The emergency surcharges would soon be lifted and Canada's floating dollar exchange rate passed unchallenged. Trudeau positively bubbled when he later reported the president's remark, "'we don't want to gobble you up' . . . . This to me was a fantastically new statement in the mouth of the President of the United States, and it was said with utmost simplicity and not at all in a grudging way." As the prime minister's gushing phrasing made clear, it seemed to have been a good day for Canada, holding out the prospect that the country could manoeuvre without fear of being squashed by the United States, although within narrow confines.

Nixon paid his first presidential visit to Canada on 13 April 1972. In a speech to which he had paid personal attention, Nixon told Parliament and all Canadians that it was time to move away from the sentimental rhetoric and clichés about the undefended border that had been the staples of the past. "It is time for us to recognize that we have very separate identities; that we have significant differences; and that nobody's interests are furthered when these realities are obscured." His policy towards Canada was based on the assumption "that mature partners must have autonomous independent policies; each nation must define the nature of its own interests; each nation must decide the requirements of its own security; each nation must determine the path of its own progress." The special relationship, Nixon seemed to be saying, was over. Canada's position in the American future would be less certain.

The end of the special relationship: Trudeau and Nixon, House of
Commons, Ottawa, 1972. Secretary of State William Rogers and External
Affairs Secretary Mitchell Sharp (far right) share the bench with Nixon.
(Ted Grant/National Archives of Canada/PA 155408)

THE THIRD OPTION

The 1972 election was the first time that Canadians had the opportunity
to pass judgment on Pierre Trudeau's stewardship of their country. In
the four and a half years since he first came to power, Trudeau had been
the recipient of enormous praise and near unanimous approval, even
when he used the draconian powers of the War Measures Act to crush
the terrorists of the Front de Libération du Québec during the October
Crisis of 1970. But Trudeau had angered the people for his perceived
arrogance, his unwillingness to listen to protest over his policies, and

t for dismissive phrases. "Where's Biafra?" he had said to tnose demanding a more sympathetic approach to the Ibos fighting a civil war in Nigeria. "Why should I sell your wheat?" he had told farmers protesting a lacklustre grain marketing policy. Cutting comments like those had hurt the Liberals in the opinion polls, and the election was too close to call.

Perhaps that explains why few Canadians noticed when the Department of External Affairs released a special issue of its magazine, *International Perspectives*, a few days before the polls opened on 30 October. "Canada–U.S. Relations: Options for the Future" had been written under the personal scrutiny of the minister of external affairs, Mitchell Sharp, and of some of the ablest minds in the department. It set out three choices for Canada: "Canada can seek to maintain more or less its present relationship with the United States . . . ; Canada can move deliberately toward closer integration with the United States; . . . [or] Canada can pursue a comprehensive long-term strategy to develop and strengthen the Canadian economy and other aspects of its national life and . . . reduce the present Canadian vulnerability."

Stated like that, the third option was obviously the preferred course, and in fact it had already been grudgingly accepted by the Cabinet. The government had indicated that Canada had become too close to the Americans, too susceptible to policies set in Washington. Relations abroad had to be strengthened both economically and politically and the Third Option, henceforth always capitalized in government statements, was the chosen path. This was a daring *geste*, a bold move to reverse the course of Canadian economic and political history, and it would be splendid if it succeeded.

Within months, Canadian ministers and officials began to pay more attention to Europe and Japan in an effort to enhance and solidify ties abroad. Even NATO suddenly began to seem more important to Trudeau. There should be no doubt that the government was deliberately turning away from the United States. As one external affairs paper put it in the spring of 1972, "If it is to make sense and be feasible," the Third Option "must be conceived as seeking important but limited relative changes in some dimensions of our relationship with the United States, which continues to involve extensive interdependence." Domestic measures had to be taken to reduce the necessity for imports of American capital and goods; efforts were needed to expand sales of goods abroad. Although the ministers of industry, trade and commerce, and of finance were unpersuaded that Canada could or should move consciously away from the United States, the prime minister and the Cabinet agreed with

External Affairs. "Theatrical, mystical, idealistic," deputy minister of finance Simon Reisman said of the Third Option. "You know, we're a North American country."

There were a few successes. By the mid-1970s, Canada had struck contractual links with Japan and the Common Market, both achievements a tribute to Trudeau's efforts at selling his concept of Canada overseas. But the country's exporters found the Japanese market hard to crack. It had extraordinarily high standards and serious barriers of language and culture. Europe was little easier: what sold in Germany would not necessarily sell in Britain or Italy. The American market was a known quantity, and Canadians spoke the language and understood the problems and opportunities implicitly. The proclaimed shift away from the United States, greeted by officers in the American Embassy in Ottawa with a sardonic "lots of luck, Canada," soon petered out. According to opinion polls, the Canadian public seemed to prefer the familiar to the unknown in foreign policy. Trade increased in primary products with Japan, but Tokyo had no interest in Canadian manufactured goods. Europe wanted Canada's uranium and timber, not its machine tools. As the American political scientist Charles Doran noted, Ottawa had made the error of thinking that "the Europeans and the Japanese were in the least interested" in acting as counterweights to American influence "when all they wanted from Canada was cheap resources." Perhaps most significantly, the Trudeau government made no effort to draft a coherent industrial strategy to back up the Third Option, and without that essential prop the plan had no real chance of success. The Third Option may have been a gallant effort to reverse the course of modern Canadian history, but it foundered on the incapacity of Canada's business community to sell abroad, on the reluctance of Europe and Japan to buy what Canada most wanted to sell, and on Ottawa's inability to grapple with industrial strategy. The indispensability of the United States had been demonstrated.

THE WAR IN VIETNAM

Richard Nixon had come to power in January 1969 on the strength of his election promise to find a way out of the Southeast Asian quagmire. He cut back American troops from 542 000 in January 1969 to 45 000 in July 1972, and ordered the heaviest bombings of the war in early 1972. Peace talks in Paris went on through the air attacks and then there was a pause, but after Nixon won re-election in a landslide in November 1972, he almost immediately resumed the bombing more fiercely than ever. The Trudeau government had said little through the early stages of the air offensive, but after the close Canadian election of 30 October 1972, the Liberals had only a minority hold on government and the New Democrats, opposed to Nixon's war, held the balance of power. Thus in early January 1973, the Trudeau government sponsored a resolution in Parliament condemning the prolongation of hostilities in Vietnam. Nixon shouted abuse and Kissinger claimed that the Canadian action was reprehensible. The Americans were unmollified by explanations about the delicate balance in the House of Commons. A draft peace agreement was reached on 13 January in Paris, and Canadian officials found themselves frozen out everywhere in the U.S. capital. Phone calls were not returned, meetings were cancelled, and the ambassador, Marcel Cadieux, found only a chill wherever he went.

But the Americans needed Canada to take part in a new International Commission of Control and Supervision, to supervise the Vietnam truce. Canadians were experienced peacekeepers and were acceptable to both North and South Vietnamese. As we have seen, Canada had been involved in the earlier ICC that had begun operations in 1954 and finally collapsed in acrimony in 1972. That had been a frustrating experience and one Ottawa did not want to repeat, but it was impossible to say no to U.S. pressure and to a chance for peace in a long, costly war. Ottawa agreed to participate in the four-nation ICCS (Hungary, Poland, Indonesia, and Canada) but this time there were conditions. Canada would stay in Vietnam only as long as the commission functioned well; the country's initial period of commitment was a mere sixty days, which would be extended only if there was tangible evidence of success. To make sure that there was no doubt about Canada's position, the Canadian ambassador to the ICCS was explicitly told to adopt an "open mouth" policy, pointing out violations to the truce and, if necessary, attacking the obstructions thrown in front of the ICCS by the Hungarians and Poles.

The Canadian fears were almost entirely justified. The ICCS did arrange exchanges of prisoners of war, a matter of enormous importance to the United States, which had thousands of officers and soldiers in North Vietnamese hands. But elsewhere, the "peace" was a transparent fraud, and the ambassador shrieked whenever one of the parties violated the agreement. Usually it was the North Vietnamese. The external affairs minister, Mitchell Sharp, visited Vietnam to study matters himself, and though he saw little to be pleased with, he did agree to extend the term of service of the 290 Canadian diplomats and officers by another 90 days. That greatly gratified the United States. In May, when Canada had to decide again whether to stay or go, Washington pushed hard for Ottawa to stay. Canadian–American relations had been happier recently, the American Embassy in Ottawa said quietly, but matters could get unpleasant if the Canadians broke up the ICCS. Kissinger himself called Ottawa to ask for a renewed term. Ottawa decided to remain for one month longer before withdrawal, but there would be no retreat from that decision. By the end of July 1973, Canada was out of the ICCS and thus was spared the ignomy of trying to make the commission function while the North Vietnamese overran South Vietnam and finally brought the wretched war to its conclusion in April 1975.

OIL AND GAS

Trudeau's Canada had tried to do a good turn for the Nixon administration in Vietnam, a hard enough task. It won scant gratitude in Washington, however. Other forces were at work. Canada was in another nationalist mood in the early 1970s, and Richard Nixon never had been and never would be popular in Canada. The Watergate affair that eventually brought him down stirred few regrets north of the border.

The nationalism that swirled through the media and the universities struck few responsive chords with the prime minister. All nationalisms, not just Quebec's, struck him as dangerous and irrational. Still, he was a politician and the Liberal party had always had a strong nationalist streak running through it. Moreover, as one of his closest Cabinet colleagues and friends, Gérard Pelletier, said, "Foreign ownership wasn't a bother in itself. It is a fact of life that Canada's standard of living depends on foreign investment. But the constant preoccupation in the mind of anyone sitting around the cabinet table is, how long can a country remain master of its political decisions if the economic decisions that really affect it are made somewhere else?" In other words, he added, "Is the Canadian government really governing or is it just the cherry on the cake?" Such considerations had lain behind the creation in 1971 of the Canada Development Corporation, an idea first bruited by Walter Gordon, to direct investment towards Canadian enterprises.

Concern about the impact of American investment was also reflected in the Gray Report, named after Herb Gray, the minister of national revenue who was its sponsor in Cabinet. The report, leaked to the small, venerable journal *Canadian Forum* in 1971, called for interventionist measures and regulations to force the review of takeovers of existing Canadian firms, the establishment of new foreign-owned firms, and licensing, franchising, and investments by multinational corporations and existing foreign-owned companies. As a result of the report, the Trudeau minority government decided to establish the Foreign Investment Review Agency (FIRA), as a device to screen foreign money and to ensure that any foreign ownership in Canada had benefits for the nation. FIRA turned out to be a feeble instrument; the great majority of cases that came before it were decided in favour of the foreign investor. Its very existence, however, angered American and other investors, who believed that capital knew no boundaries and who resented the delays the agency usually produced.

Oil and gas came to be an especially sore point between the two countries. Canada had had practically no production in this area until the Leduc oil field was tapped in Alberta in 1947; from that point on new reserves were discovered and wealth gushed from the ground. Much of the oil and gas production went to the States, thanks to lenient policies established by the National Energy Board in Ottawa, and thanks too to skilful lobbying in the 1950s and 1960s that persuaded the Americans, scarcely contemplating shortages in their own domestic supply, to admit Canadian imports into their market. Canadian diplomats sold the idea of an oil and gas supply as politically secure as Texas. The prairie provinces were happy. Oil producers there wanted to export the maximum possible, and as easily accessible American supplies began to tail off in the 1970s, barriers in the United States to Canadian imported oil and gas began to break down.

At the same time, Alaskan oil and gas was discovered in vast quantity on the North Slope. The *Manhattan* voyages had demonstrated that it was technically feasible to transport crude by tanker through the Northwest Passage, but Canada's pollution legislation posed political problems. Might it not be easier and safer to send the oil and natural gas south through Canada by pipeline? Indeed, since there was almost certainly oil and gas under the Canadian Arctic seas, both countries could use the pipeline. From Ottawa's point of view, all this made sense. Canada's oil and gas, as well as Alaska's, could go via pipeline, and Canadian construction firms would derive many of the benefits involved in such a huge project. The logic of a continental energy policy began to be felt in Ottawa and Washington by the beginning of the 1970s.

While the two countries negotiated sporadically with each other over building a pipeline, and the possible location of it, oil and gas consumption continued to increase. Meanwhile the Arab nations, as the primary producers, were interested in boosting returns from their only marketable natural resource and in breaking the stranglehold exercised upon them by the "seven sisters," the big international oil companies. The revolution in Libya that had toppled the compliant King Idris and put Colonel Qaddafi in power was one sign of this new nationalism. The 1973 transformation of the Organization of Petroleum Exporting Countries (OPEC) into a cartel of the major producing countries was another. When the United States supported Israel against Egypt and friends in the Yom Kippur War of October 1973, the Arab members of OPEC turned off the tap and cut supplies to the Americans and other unfriendly states. At the same time, OPEC raised prices dramatically. By the end of 1973, a barrel of Middle East oil cost $11.65, four times the price just twelve months earlier. Suddenly, oil was a scarce and high-priced commodity.

Canada had a problem. Albertan oil and gas supplied the country west of the Ottawa River, while imported supplies served the east. Much of that imported gas came from Venezuela and the U.S., but some came from the Middle East; all of it was now expensive, and there were concerns that American companies, faced with shortages and long line-ups at the pumps throughout the U.S., might feel obliged to break their Canadian contracts.

Ottawa moved quickly to meet the need. It established a nationally owned oil company, Petro-Canada, to arrange imports of oil into Canada, to develop the Alberta tar sands, and to explore for oil and gas. Even before the Arab–Israeli War, the government had frozen domestic oil prices at $4 a barrel and slapped an export tax on every barrel going south. The theory was that oil exported to the U.S., sold at the world price, would help to subsidize eastern Canada. It seemed a brilliant solution: the Americans would pick up the cost for the Canadian consumer. Ottawa also announced plans for the immediate construction of a pipeline from the West to Montreal in order to free eastern Canada from its dependence on imported oil. To ensure supply from the prairie fields that were already producing at or near capacity, the government added that over a decade it would gradually cease exporting oil to the U.S.

The Americans were outraged at every aspect of this policy. Petro-Canada was socialist and therefore unAmerican. The export tax to subsidize eastern Canada's oil costs was the deliberate gouging of a friend, something the U.S. continued to argue even after rising world prices forced Ottawa to unfreeze oil prices and make Maritimers carry the cost. Worst of all, the threatened gradual cut in Canadian exports left some parts of the northern U.S. without any secure source of supply. The pressure in Washington mounted, and it had its echo in Alberta.

The Progressive Conservative government of Peter Lougheed in Alberta had little ideological sympathy with Ottawa. Like the privately owned oil companies, it disliked Petro-Canada instinctively, and it resented Ottawa's ability to set export and pricing policies for oil and gas and to skim off about 10 percent of proceeds for itself. Most especially, it objected to the way Ottawa fixed the price of these commodities and prevented the oil companies and the province from getting the full economic benefit from a dwindling resource that rising prices offered. Ottawa countered, very quietly, that its policies were subsidizing the oil companies and, moreover, doing so at a time when their profits were exploding. The federal–provincial dispute raged on, but the Canadian–American one was more immediately worrying to the government.

Yet in December 1974 when Trudeau met President Gerald Ford, successor to the scandal-besmirched Nixon, matters had already been smoothed over. Trudeau was doing nothing to interfere with natural gas exports, most of which were already committed in long-term contracts. The Canadian government had also produced a program that offered special petroleum arrangements for the northern states. As a result, the Ford–Trudeau discussions were full of bonhomie, and the U.S. eventually accepted Canada's plan to phase out oil exports in due course. "We had a great visit," the prime minister said. "They make great coffee here." As the secretary of state for external affairs, Allan MacEachen, put it more formally, "USA irritation with our export policies" had been substantially reduced.

By the mid-1970s the National Energy Board in Ottawa was nevertheless beginning to foresee problems with Canada's own supplies of natural gas and oil. A mere half dozen years earlier, estimates were that Canada had fuel to burn; now shortages were proclaimed to be imminent. That made Arctic gas and a pipeline to get it to market all the more essential, or so Ottawa believed, and attention focussed on a route south through either the Mackenzie Valley or along the Alaska Highway. But this planning was scuppered by the burgeoning of the new Canadian environmentalism. In 1974, Ottawa had appointed Mr. Justice Tom Berger to assess the impact of a pipeline down the Mackenzie and after hearing the testimony of Métis and Dene leaders across the North, he finally reported in May 1977. The Berger Report recommended that no pipeline be built for at least a decade on both sociological and ecological grounds. The impact of pipeline construction on native peoples would, he said, be massive and irreversible, while the damage to the environment would be far reaching. The Alaska Highway route remained a possibility. Lengthy negotiations ensued with the Americans, producing agreement but no pipeline. The cost, a minimum of $12 to $14 billion, was one factor and Alaskan gas itself was too high priced. The big gas pipeline remains unbuilt.

A FORD, NOT A LINCOLN

The likeable new American president was given to pratfalls, verbal and physical. He fell out of cars and down airplane steps and had a habit of striking onlookers with errant golf shots. One of his more endearing remarks, uttered in the face of a difficult problem, was "If Abe Lincoln were alive today, he'd roll over in his grave." Gerald Ford had been a long-serving Michigan congressman of right-of-centre political hue. Not a creative thinker, never a man of ideas, although a hard and earnest worker, he had been picked by Nixon as Spiro Agnew's replacement after the vice-president's forced resignation. Wags suggested that Nixon had chosen Ford because the possibility of his succession to the presidency would help to keep the Watergate-beleaguered president in power. The cover-up of the bugging of the Democratic party's Watergate headquarters drove Nixon out of power, however, and in 1974 Ford became president of the United States. From the Canadian point of view, he had two main virtues. First, he came from a border state and had a benign, if unfocussed, attitude of friendliness towards "our great neighbor to the north." Second, he had wisely retained Henry Kissinger as his secretary of state. Kissinger had established a mystique about himself and a reputation for near-wizardry in resolving crises and negotiating agreements with friend and foe alike. One magazine cover pictured him as a Clark Kent of diplomacy: "Super-K." Kissinger understood Canada, even if it did not bulk large in his view of the world. His memoirs scarcely mention Canada, but the words he does write are among the most perceptive ever offered by an outsider about Canada's place in the world. Canada, he said in *White House Years*, was "beset by ambivalences" that created great complexities for its politicians and officials.

> [The country] required both close economic relations with the United States and an occasional gesture of strident independence. Concretely, this meant that its need for American markets was in constant tension with its temptation to impose

discriminatory economic measures; its instinct in favor of common defense conflicted with the temptation to stay above the battle as a kind of international arbiter. Convinced of the necessity of co-operation, impelled by domestic imperatives towards confrontation, Canadian leaders had a narrow margin for maneuver that they utilized with extraordinary skill.

On a personal level, relations between Trudeau and Ford were surprisingly good. The two men were athletic and they shared a passion for skiing. Ford was open and friendly, and the whiff of sleaziness and untrustworthiness that had always clung to Nixon was simply not present. Though he was infinitely the president's superior in intelligence, Trudeau accommodated himself to the new American leader and de-

Canadian Moral Superiority. (Reprinted with permission—Toronto Star Syndicate.)

ferred to the power Ford exercised. Perhaps that was the most sensible course. Trudeau desperately wanted Canada to be a member nation of the western summits, the first of which was scheduled to take place in France in 1974. The French were unpersuaded, though Kissinger tried hard to get Canada accepted. "Canada is no longer a minor partner," Kissinger said on a visit to Ottawa, "but a country which rightfully takes its place in the economic and political councils of the world." The next year, the summit was scheduled to meet in the United States. With Ford deciding who was to be invited, Canada and Italy were added.

The North American nations still had disagreements aplenty. The Foreign Investment Review Agency roiled the waters. The tensions over oil and gas had upset many Americans, who were apt to condemn both Canadians and Arabs as intransigent. Canadian cultural nationalists regularly denounced the U.S. and its film, TV, and literary output with such vehemence that visiting Americans were almost always taken aback. The icon for the Canadian literati was Margaret Atwood, who in 1972 wrote *Survival*, arguing that the central image of Canadian culture was that of a collective victim struggling for survival against a hostile natural environment and a continuing colonial history. Atwood argued that Canada as a whole was "a victim, or an 'oppressed minority'. Let us suppose in short that Canada is a colony . . . a place from which a profit is made, but *not by the people who live there.*" One of Atwood's epigraphs, a poem by John Newlove, put it well: "I'm starting . . . to feel like a Canadian/only when kissing someone else's bum." Exaggerated and selective *Survival* certainly was, but its instant acceptance by the public demonstrated the Canadian need for an explanation of the national condition. It was all part of what Northrop Frye in *The Bush Garden* had called "the famous Canadian problem of identity." If the Canadian looked south, "he becomes either hypnotized or repelled by the United States; either he tries to think up unconvincing reasons for being different and somehow superior to Americans or he accepts being 'swallowed up by' the United States as inevitable." The great critic went on to call the problem of the Canadian identity "a rationalized, self-pitying or made-up problem to those who have never had to meet it," but "the creative instinct has a great deal to do with the assertion of territorial rights."

The owners of television stations in such border cities as Spokane, Fargo, Buffalo, Plattsburgh, and Portland understood that too. They were furious that Canadian legislation, aiming to funnel advertising dollars going to Canadian stations, blocked them from running Canadian advertising. Indeed, the nationalist Canadian Radio and Television Commission

(CRTC), claiming the right to regulate cable transmissions too, allowed Canadian stations to block out parts of American simultaneous transmissions so that Canadian ads could be run in place of those emanating from CBS, ABC, and NBC. As well, Canadian content regulations stated that 60 percent of prime-time TV production had to be Canadian-made; that no more than 30 percent of the remainder could come from any one country; and that 30 percent of all music played on the radio had to be Canadian. The Americans, used to easier regulation in their own marketplace, were at once perplexed and annoyed.

And then there was *Time*, the American newsmagazine that had long published a Canadian edition, with a perfunctory opening few pages devoted to Canada, and a boatload of advertisements from Canadian companies. In 1961, the Royal Commission on Publications had recommended that *Time* lose its privileged tax status as a medium for advertising. The Diefenbaker and Pearson governments had succumbed to American pressure and allowed *Time* to continue but in 1976 the Trudeau government decided that Canadian ads in the Canadian edition would no longer be tax-deductible. The American government was unhappy, and *Time* scrapped its Canadian edition. *Reader's Digest*, though also American-controlled, played its political cards with more skill and managed to keep its status as a special case. The same act of Parliament that did in *Time* also forbade Canadian advertisers on American TV stations from writing off their costs, and that provision caused enormous bitterness that had ripples in Congress.

All of these high-handed actions and irritations were ordinarily tolerated, if resented, in Washington. Brent Scowcroft, President Ford's national security adviser, characterized them by saying, "Well, there go the Canadians again." The departing ambassador in Ottawa, William Porter, did let fly at Canadian policy at an on-record cocktail party for the media. Porter was duly snubbed by the prime minister and denied the traditional farewell interview before his departure, demonstrating that Canadian leaders too could aspire to great power status in their pettiness.

What truly upset President Ford, however, was Trudeau's decision regarding Taiwanese athletes at the 1976 Olympics in Montreal. The Taiwan government wanted to use the name of the Republic of China, and that was the sticking point for Ottawa and the People's Republic of China. Trudeau agreed that only China should be able to call itself China; and the exiled nationalist government would have to parade its athletes under the banner of Taiwan. Taipei refused to accommodate itself to the host government's rules and withdrew from the games. The

Americans were outraged. Nixon had regularized American relations with Beijing, but the U.S. link to Taiwan remained strong. The White House seriously considered asking American athletes to withdraw and, if the games were cancelled, offering to stage them in the U.S. on forty-eight hours' notice. The president himself wrote of his anger that "political concerns [had] interfered in the conduct of the current Olympiad" and denounced the "narrow political interests" that had shaped the Canadian government's decision. The summer of 1976 was a time of political campaigning in the United States and perhaps that explained the extraordinary American reaction.

For all Porter's shouting and Ford's unhappiness, relations remained friendly and close between the two governments and between citizens of the two countries. The end of the war in Vietnam had finally eliminated one persistent source of governmental and popular grievance, and Kissinger's policies were generally applauded in Ottawa. Trudeau and Ford, even after the Olympics row, continued their friendly relations. Gerry Ford was not a great president, to be sure, but he had allowed the United States and the world to forget about Vietnam and Richard Nixon. Those were no mean accomplishments, but the American voters narrowly chose someone else to lead them in November 1976.

By the end of 1976, the Third Option that was to have heralded Canada's new relations with the United States was demonstrably not working. Europe and Japan refused to become more interested in Canada, and Canadians for their part remained transfixed by the United States. The Americans were the dominant factor in Canadian national life, and on a host of issues from oil to culture, the friendliness and co-operation that had always been the necessary concomitant of the trans-border relationship remained. So too did the friction.

CHAPTER

COLD WAR, ENERGY, AND PEACE

1 9 7 7 – 1 9 8 4

Ten days before Christmas 1983, Pierre Trudeau flew to Washington to meet President Ronald Reagan. The world was in a tense mood, with the Soviet Union fighting guerillas in Afghanistan and western opinion still outraged by the Soviet destruction of a Korean airliner. The American administration had been especially bellicose, and Trudeau, launched on a peace initiative that had already taken him around the world to see Communist, western, and neutral leaders, hoped to ease matters. But how to appeal to Reagan, a Mr. Feelgood president whose views of the world were noticeably and notably simplistic? The ideologies of the president and the prime minister had almost nothing in common, their leadership styles were as different as could be, and the relations between their two countries were caught up yet again in a period of crisis. But Trudeau had to talk to Reagan, had to reach him with the warning that the world was threatened by nuclear war. Some advisers insisted that the prime minister had to give exactly the same message to Reagan that he had to other leaders; otherwise, he would lose credibility abroad. But Allan Gotlieb, the ambassador in Washington, differed. Such an approach was certain to fail. Instead, he urged Trudeau to seize the high ground and speak directly to Reagan's kinder side. Trudeau agreed.

Taking this soft approach, the prime minister had leaned towards the older man and said, "Mr. President, your intentions are good and I agree with them wholly. You are a man of peace. You want peace through strength. Because of your policies, the U.S. has regained its strength and self-confidence." Then Trudeau paused. "But, Mr. President, your message is not getting through. The people think you want strength for its own sake, and that you are ready to accept the risks of war. That must change, Mr. President. You must communicate what you really believe in." At least one American official found Trudeau's approach offensive, seeing that the prime minister took "a condescending view of the President as a simpleton in international affairs." Certainly Trudeau saw no point in arguing about missile throw-weights, a subject he himself knew little about, with a man who understood far less. Reagan's comment as the prime minister left the White House was "Godspeed," which struck many as dismissive. The peace initiative, cobbled together in haste, did nothing to move the world away from the possibility of war and nothing to change opinion in the U.S. A third-ranking official in the State Department remarked that the prime minister's peace efforts resembled nothing so much as those of "a leftist high on pot." Even so, the Reagan rhetoric cooled slightly in the coming weeks, and Trudeau and his closest aides took such comfort as they could in that.

THE GEORGIA PEACH

Trudeau's relations with President Jimmy Carter, a liberal, southern Democrat, had been different—very warm, and especially so at the beginning of the former Georgia governor's term in January 1977. Canadian Liberals have a natural affinity for American Democrats, believing since the days of King and Roosevelt in a special community of interests and liberal values.

Canada itself was at issue in early 1977. In November 1976, René Lévesque had been elected premier of Quebec with a large majority in the National Assembly for his separatist Parti Québécois. Canada was certain to face a time of trial, and the support and understanding of the United States was essential. Thus when Trudeau went to Washington to visit Carter early in the new administration, he came as a supplicant. Canada needed help. There could also be no doubt that the American national interest would be best served if Canada stayed in one piece. An independent Quebec, especially one governed by the social-democratic Parti Québécois, might be as nationalist in its economic and strategic policies as in its linguistic ones. It had declared itself neutralist and clearly might not wish to be part of NATO and NORAD, a development

Georgia Peach: Jimmy Carter and Pierre Trudeau in Washington.
(AP/Wide World Photos)

that would weaken western and North American defence. The certain-
ties of dealing with Canada, difficult and touchy as the country often
was, would evaporate. And no government, and especially no great
power, enjoys uncertainty. As a State Department paper, "The Quebec
Situation: Outlook and Implications," summed it up in August 1977,
"The U.S. preference . . . is a united Canada. This is clearly in our
national interest, considering the importance of Canada to U.S. interests
in defense, trade, investments, environmental questions, and world
affairs. It is also understandable because we have developed a good system of managing our relations with the present Canada, a known quantity."

Not every indication pointed to American support for the federal
government. Carter's national security adviser was Zbigniew Brzezinski,

the son of the prewar Polish consul general in Montreal. Brzezinski had received a B.A. and M.A. from McGill University and had gone on to Harvard for his doctorate. He had established a substantial reputation as an academic specialist on the Soviet Union and its policies. His major interest was in seeing that American policy to the USSR followed the proper line, but as a one-time Montrealer he had an interest in and views on Quebec. To Zbig, as he was known, Quebec nationalism was likely to prevail and the United States should be prepared to accommodate itself to it. His views were probably based more on intuition and a desire to see nationalist sentiment triumph in his family's homeland and other Soviet-controlled territories than on any deep understanding of the climate of the mid-1970s. In any event, he was overridden in Carter's immediate circle by the strongly contrary advice from the embassy in Ottawa, "that we comport ourselves in such a way as to leave no doubt of any possible support to Quebec."

Carter did what he could to set Trudeau's mind at ease at their first meeting. He arranged for Trudeau to address a joint session of Congress, thus giving the prime minister the best of platforms from which to state his convictions about Canada's future and to reassure American public and business opinion. In their private talks, the president asked Trudeau for his assessment of Canada's prospects, and the prime minister replied honestly that his government and country were in a real jam for the short term at least. The crisis over separatism would last for some time, but he remained confident that in the end federalism would triumph. Using an analogy that the southerner Carter would be sure to understand, Trudeau suggested that Canada would emerge stronger from the ordeal, much as the United States had done in the aftermath of the Civil War. Impressed by Trudeau's candour, Carter told the press that while Canada's constitution was its own affair, "if I were the one to make the decision a confederation would be my preference." The statement was perhaps limp, but it was nonetheless policy. The State Department certainly took it as such.

For his part, Premier Lévesque also sought to reassure American opinion about his aims and intentions. On 25 January, he went to New York to address the Economic Club, an influential group of business people and investors. Quebec, the premier argued, was simply following the American lead of two hundred years before by making a revolution, and to try to illustrate his point he offered a potted history of Quebec's rising nationalism. The speech "laid an egg," as the *Baltimore Sun* observed, and Trudeau's Canada had won Round One in the United States. Once seized by the federal government, that initiative was never lost. The separatist government of Quebec continued to receive short shrift in the United States, and the Parti Québécois began to adapt its platform as a result. In 1979, the neutralist orientation was dropped. Henceforth, the new Quebec would have a foreign policy much like Canada's, and membership in NATO and NORAD would be sought. Indeed, Lévesque himself suggested that many in his province would prefer to see Ottawa manage foreign policy for an independent Quebec. Perhaps that turnaround helped in Washington but if so there was no sign of it. Quebec's only gains in the United States came from the scholarly works of a few academics who, generously subsidized by Quebec City, produced studies demonstrating the indissoluble links between Quebec and the United States. None made much scholarly or public impact.

Because Canada needed the United States at this time, the Trudeau government tended to take a softer and less nationalistic line in its policy making during most of the Carter presidency. Besides, the secretary of state for external affairs, Don Jamieson of Newfoundland, was "the most pro-American minister of external affairs in History," or so one account argued. He had wanted Newfoundland to join the United States in 1948–49, for example, not Canada. His senior colleagues, Jean Chrétien in the Department of Finance and Jack Horner, the Alberta Tory who had crossed the floor to sit with the Liberals in 1977 and had been rewarded with the industry, trade and commerce portfolio, were similarly friendly to the United States. The Trudeau government, if it had ever warranted the label "anti-American," could not have been so characterized late in the 1970s.

There were still problems, and most notably those surrounding the vexed question of Canada's declining fishing industry. As a defensive tactic, Canada proclaimed a 200-mile economic zone in 1977 as an addition to the 12-mile territorial limit, which both countries had put in place in 1970. The U.S. and Canada also codified long-standing fishing rights in each other's waters, first in 1970 and then with a modified agreement in 1977. Now the task was to conclude an agreement to cover other contentious fisheries issues, maritime boundaries in the Georges Bank in the Gulf of Maine, south of Nova Scotia, and the management of offshore oil and gas resources.

The negotiations were extraordinarily complex, and as they were taking place fishers from both countries fought on their boats and in the courts. The situation became so tense that each country formally closed its waters to fishers from the other. Both governments fervently hoped that the result of the talks would prove acceptable lest the fishing war lead to loss of life. Four agreements were presented to the public in March 1979: the Pacific fishery was dealt with, to almost no one's satisfaction, in two documents; and the Atlantic fishery was dealt with in the third and fourth. The thorny question of sharing hydrocarbon resources was left unresolved and the boundary question was referred to the International Court of Justice for arbitration. The court's decision, rendered in 1984, divided the Georges Bank between the two countries. A disappointed U.S. had wanted the entire area. Canada had asked for one-third of the bank, and got about a quarter, but a quarter very rich in both fish and oil.

The east coast agreement defined the share of and access to the fishing grounds that each country could have, and American fishing interests shouted that they had been robbed. Most independent observers seemed to agree that Canada had got the best of the negotiation and that Marcel Cadieux, Canada's negotiator, had taken the pants off Lloyd Cutler, his American counterpart. The settlement was duly recommended by the Carter administration as "in the best interests of the United States," but it had to be ratified by the Senate, and there the senators from New England had their chance. Understandably responsive to the economic interests of their constituents, they stalled and shouted. Just because Canada was a friend, one senator said, the U.S. should not ignore its own interests. Not for the first time, Canada discovered that the Senate could unmake the efforts of international negotiators and diplomats. The Carter administration tried to move the matter along, but here as elsewhere its handling of Congress was inept and produced little. After the 1980 election, the Reagan administration, not unhappy to kick the ousted Democrats or to give the by-then uppity Canadians a slap, withdrew the initiative. It was an unhappy end to a long and arduous negotiation.

JOE CLARK AND THE CANADIAN CAPER

In Canada, however, fish and boundaries took a back seat to other forms of politicking. The Trudeau government, re-elected with a comfortable majority in 1974, had become increasingly unpopular at home for a variety of reasons. The public disliked Liberal economic policy, were unhappy over official bilingualism, and had developed a deep and abiding resentment at the arrogance of the prime minister. In May 1979, the Canadian people gave a minority mandate to the Progressive Conservatives, led by

"Heal . . . ! " Jimmy Carter's high-minded view of America's role in the world.
(Reprinted with permission—Toronto Star Syndicate.)

Joe Clark, a forty-year-old Albertan MP who had surprisingly been
selected party leader in 1976. Clark was not an impressive figure physically, especially when compared to the still-dynamic sexagenarian
Trudeau. Intelligent and earnest though he was, and a quick master of
short memos and oral briefings, he would soon be defeated in Parliament
and at the polls. His tenure lasted just over six months.

The Clark government, in trouble from the time it took office, had
little time to shape a coherent policy towards the United States. Clark
and Carter got on well when they met at a Tokyo summit meeting, but

the opportunity for a new course in relations with Washington, if it had been intended, did not arise. The one notable event in the Canadian–American relations of Clark's time came after the downfall of the Shah of Iran and in the midst of the 1980 federal election campaign. On 4 November 1979, Iranian mobs had stormed the American Embassy, the bastion of the Great Satan, as the U.S. was ordinarily referred to in Tehran, and seized the staff as hostages. A few Americans managed to find their way to temporary safety, and on 9 November, Ottawa was asked by Canadian ambassador Ken Taylor if he could offer them shelter. There were obvious risks involved, but the secretary of state for external affairs, Flora Macdonald, and the prime minister agreed at once. Five Americans were taken in on 10 November and a sixth arrived on the 22nd. For more than two months, they lived in some discomfort but in relative safety. Rumours were flying, however, and the secret was getting out; at least one Canadian journalist had almost the whole story. It was important to get the Americans out of Iran. Early in the new year, false passports were prepared. On 28 January, the diplomats made their escape without incident and with them the Canadian Embassy staff.

The next day, the story broke in Canada, probably leaked to help the Clark government in its faltering re-election efforts. The response in Canada was one of surprise and quiet national pleasure; of course, Canadians would help Americans in such circumstances. In the U.S., however, the response was passionate. The heartfelt thanks were so fervent that they were almost embarrassing. Ordinary Americans wrote to Ottawa in the thousands; the president beamed and Congressional resolutions of thanks were adopted; and Ambassador Taylor was lionized, cheered at dinners, football games, and in parades. (External Affairs soon appointed him consul general in New York City, in order to get the maximum advantage from his celebrity status.) It was almost as if Americans had come to expect nothing but abuse and more abuse from friends and enemies alike, so extraordinary was the gratitude for Canadian assistance to their hunted and harassed diplomats in Iran.

MORE GAS: THE NEP

"The Canadian caper," as it was quickly dubbed, failed to help the Conservatives, who went down to defeat on 18 February 1980. Amazingly, Pierre Trudeau was back in power, though only a few months before he had resigned the party leadership. When the Clark government fell he had been persuaded, without much difficulty, to return to head the Liberal opposition in the election. "Welcome to the 1980s," the exuberant re-crowned king had said at the Liberal victory celebration.

The U.S. brought in the 1980s with a dynamic leader of its own, the charismatic and camera-wise former movie actor and California governor Ronald Reagan. He defeated Jimmy Carter, who had been painted as weak and ineffectual, in some part because of his inability to free the hostages held in Iran. The new president was the oldest chief executive in American history, and certainly the most conservative and militantly anti-communist in decades. His critics maintained that he was incapable of understanding even simple issues, relying on a grab bag of *Reader's Digest* clippings and shopworn, clichéd individualist nostrums. Whether that was so or not, Reagan had superb abilities as a communicator and he was, according to every report, a thoroughly pleasant individual. In his vague, offhand way, he purported to like Canada and Canadians. In 1979, when he announced his candidacy, he had talked vaguely about a North American accord that would unite Mexico and Canada with his country. Almost immediately, both Trudeau and the Mexican president had denounced the idea, which would not "serve the best interests of their countries." Perhaps that was not a good augury for the Trudeau–Reagan years.

Certainly by the time Reagan assumed office in January 1981 Canadian relations with Washington had perceptibly chilled. The National Energy Program (NEP), announced in the Liberal government's budget of 28 October 1980, drew a pall over Canada–U.S. interactions. The Liberals had made a perfunctory attempt to strike a revenue-sharing arrangement with the oil- and gas-producing provinces, but when this failed, with shouting and recriminations, they were determined to act unilaterally. The NEP was the government's comprehensive attempt to ensure security of supply, control prices, and alter the distribution of oil and gas income. The program had been created entirely within the Ottawa bureaucracy, by-passing consultation with the oil industry, the provinces, and the United States government. Ottawa set a "blended oil pricing regime" to produce domestic prices below international levels. After the Iranian revolution and the onset of war between Iran and Iraq, prices abroad were running at more than U.S. $26 a barrel and rising, but Canadian consumption was also going up, by almost 1 percent a year. The government wanted the people to switch from oil to natural gas for heating, and a pipeline to carry gas into the Maritimes was declared essential. Trudeau and his energy minister, Marc Lalonde, wished to reduce dependence on imported supplies, and they sought a bigger cut of the oil and gas revenues. To that end, a Petroleum and Gas Revenue Tax (PGRT) of 16 percent was imposed on gross revenue earned by the oil and gas companies. The PGRT was not deductible for income tax purposes, an unprecedented move that amounted to double taxation. The federal government would thus increase its take from oil and gas production from 10 to 24 percent of profits while industry's proportion would decline from 45 to 33 percent. The provincial governments' share would drop from 45 to 43 percent.

The NEP also created the Petroleum Incentives Program, to encourage northern exploration and favour Canadian-owned firms. As well, a "back-in" provision in the NEP legislation implemented a retroactive and future expropriation of a 25 percent interest in oil and gas discovered on the so-called Canada Lands owned by the federal government and located primarily in the North. Only companies at least half-owned by Canadians, furthermore, could explore the Canadian Lands. Finally, the government wanted to see the oil and gas industry in the hands of Canadians, and aimed at 50 percent Canadian ownership of the oil industry by 1990. The entire NEP was based on the premise that oil prices would continue to rise. Seeing themselves sheltered by the federal government from the worst effects of price hikes, the argument ran, Canadians would see the program's benefits.

Some already did so. The NEP fulfilled most of Canadian nationalists' dreams for the oil and gas sector. At last Ottawa would reclaim one of the most important areas of the economy for all Canadians. Nationalists were enormously surprised and pleased that Trudeau, emphatically anti-nationalist as he was, had introduced the NEP, but the political imperatives that had led him to this change in policy were many. Rising prices at the gas pump angered Canadians who knew that they had huge resources; oil company profits, most of them sent out of the country,were galloping and there were new pressures within the business community for action, especially from a generation of competent, aggressive oil and gas entrepeneurs. Finally, the Department of Energy, Mines and Resources employed an able crew of officials and a minister who had Trudeau's ear. All this came together to produce the NEP, which debuted to favourable opinion polls and ringing cheers in some important sections of the media and public.

Not all Canadians were happy, however. In Alberta, government and industry expressed utter outrage. Had the province had an army, they might have sent tanks to the provincial borders and to "Red Square," the derisive local name for the Calgary headquarters of Petro-

Canada. The Americans had tanks, of course, but happily their initial response in the dying days of the Carter administration was simply one of puzzlement. Why would any friendly and democratic nation act, as they saw it, so unfairly, by confiscating the capital of private corporations? To Washington, Canada seemed to be an industrial country that followed Third World policies.

That was an unfair characterization, but there could be no doubt that Canadians had a different attitude to the role of government than did their American cousins. Of the four hundred biggest industries in Canada, twenty-five were Crown corporations; of the top fifty industries ranked by sales, seven were wholly or partly controlled by the federal or provincial governments; and even financial institutions had heavy governmental involvement, nine of the top twenty-five being fully or partly controlled by government. Health care was also government-patrolled, and medicare programs offered every Canadian protection. The program was so popular that, as surveys regularly demonstrated, Canadians (and Americans too) perceived it as a fundamental characteristic of the Canadian identity. Canadians liked government involvement in such areas as medical care and business. One major reason that the Conservative government of Joe Clark lost the 1980 election, for example, was its pledge to sell Petro-Canada to the private sector. No similar affection for the role of the state existed in the United States, where the American Medical Association regularly denounced the "socialist" Canadian system for controlling patients' freedom and doctors' incomes.

The incoming Reagan administration certainly upheld traditional American principles in this regard. Reagan's officials and supporters saw the NEP as an attack on the free market values he cherished. The reaction from American oil companies with extensive interests in Canada was apoplectic: the Canadians were changing the rules—and cutting into profits. Some members of Congress even feared that Canadian oil companies, handed large advantages by the NEP, might try to get control of American corporations. Americans at the time were beginning to worry about too much foreign investment in their country: Japanese, Arab and, yes, Canadian too. After years of complaining about the dangers of precisely that phenomenon, Canadians now had the pleasure of watching Americans bewail the power of Canadian capital, and in the same rhetoric that Canadians had used. "Should we stand idle," said one American corporate leader threatened by a takeover bid, "and watch our economy come under the control of foreign investors? Should Congress permit American companies to stand vulnerable . . . ?"

The new secretary of state (who was a former Kissinger military aide, Nixon chief of staff, and NATO supreme commander), Alexander Haig, reacted to all these pressures by sending a note to Ottawa labelling the NEP "unnecessarily discriminatory" and demanding major changes. "Should the balance of concessions be disturbed, the United States would be obliged to consider how a new balance might be achieved." After protests from Ottawa and the Canadian Embassy the note was withdrawn because of its "tonal problem." And when the president paid his first visit to Ottawa in March 1981, neither he nor his entourage had much tough talk at this point.

That would come soon enough. The Washington bureaucracy had now studied the NEP in detail and liked it not at all. The American oil rigs were being pulled out of Alberta and back to the U.S., and critics pointed the finger of blame at the NEP. There was some truth in that argument, but the onset of a world recession and a decline in oil prices were primarily responsible. Washington was not finished with its complaints, however. The "back-in" provisions verged on confiscatory, the Americans argued, and Ottawa tactfully conceded the point in May 1981 by offering payment for its 25 percent interest. The Trudeau government also promised that it would examine proposals from American and Canadian companies with impartiality when tenders were presented for participation in oil megaprojects, such as the development of the Alberta tar sands or offshore oil fields. Yet Ottawa refused to make major alterations in its program. The idea of "Canadianization" of the oil industry was very popular, and even to some of its sharpest critics, the interventionist NEP seemed to be a success—not least in getting the Canadian public on side. Opinion polls in the spring of 1981 showed that an amazing 84 percent of Canadians supported the goals of the program. Once a new arrangement on sharing NEP revenues with Alberta was struck, even that provincial government's criticism died down.

That left the Americans. The new ambassador in Ottawa, a Reagan fund raiser and tough-talking hawk from Chicago named Paul Robinson, wanted change but not overt retaliation against Canada which might jeopardize his mission at its very beginning. "Finger-twisting," as one Washington official called it, was okay, but no massive retaliation. Robinson managed to argue successfully that the two countries were simply too interconnected, that punishment was certain to affect American interests as well as Canadian.

But the pressure kept up. The American secretary of state wrote to his counterpart in Ottawa of his fears "that our two countries are heading toward a confrontation," that the situation was "urgent and extremely serious." In October 1981, finally, Reagan's treasury secretary, Donald Regan, came to Ottawa for discussions. These too were a virtual failure; the Americans went home angry that the Canadians seemed unwilling to listen and Ottawa officials were affronted by the unending insistence from the Americans that the Trudeau government had to change *its* policy to suit *their* concerns. Still, the federal budget of November 1981 did offer another olive branch of sorts with a promise from finance minister Allan MacEachen that the NEP would not expand into other fields. Thank you very much, the Americans said. Now, about the Canadianization aspects of the NEP. . . . Through recession and falling prices and into the great oil glut of 1984, the government remained committed to the NEP. Not until Brian Mulroney led the Progressive Conservative party to victory in September 1984 would the program be consigned to the ashcan, to the great gratification of the Reagan administration.

INVESTMENT, TRADE, AND ACID RAIN, INGREDIENTS OF INTERDEPENDENCE

The NEP, however important it was, was not the sole issue between the Trudeau and Reagan governments. The May 1980 referendum in Quebec, producing a sixty–forty verdict in favour of federalism, had seemed to end the prospect of Quebec separatism and made the American government's support for a united Canada no longer as necessary as it had been. The Foreign Investment Review Agency, however, remained an issue. It continued to incense the Americans (and the Japanese and Europeans). Ambassador Robinson waxed eloquent about its violation of accepted practices for the treatment of American capital. The United States, which hoped to see Canada committed to the principle of non-discrimination against foreign capital, formally hauled its neighbour before a tribunal of the General Agreement on Tariffs and Trade in Geneva in March 1982 to vent its complaints, but unsuccessfully.

The shouting from Washington was difficult for Canadians to comprehend because the impact of FIRA seemed almost inconsequential. American investment in Canada remained enormous and continued to get bigger. In 1981, American direct investment was $48.7 billion and portfolio investment amounted to $38.2 billion; five years later, direct investment was $68.3 billion and portfolio $60.3 billion. Moreover, American direct investment in 1986 was 81 percent of all direct foreign investment in Canada. In several sectors of the economy, U.S. control lly complete by 1984: tobacco, 99 percent; rubber products, 92 percent; and chemicals, 69 percent. Trade between the two countries was similarly huge: in 1982, 70 percent of Canadian imports were from the U.S., or $47 billion worth; 69 percent of its exports went there or $58 billion in total. Two years later, exports to the U.S. were $85 billion, a stunning 76 percent of the total, while imports were $66 billion and 72 percent of everything Canadians brought into their country. Canadian trade amounted to about one-fifth of America's total imports and exports. The two countries were dependent on each other, to be sure, but the much smaller population and economy of Canada made its position extremely delicate. In that sense, for the Trudeau government to ruffle the eagle's feathers as it had been doing was either highly courageous or completely foolhardy, depending on one's perspective.

The Canadian predicament was highlighted by the lack of other refuges to seek, other countries with which to build strong relationships. Japan and the European Community were dynamic, booming economies, carefully protected by high walls of tariff and non-tariff barriers. Canada had tried to crack its way into those markets with the Third Option and contractual links negotiated with Japan and the Community, but the results had been far from spectacular.

The Republican administration, as indicated by candidate Reagan's prattlings about a North American accord, was philosophically in favour of free trade or at least liberalized trade. Given both the volume of Canada's trade with the U.S., and the president's inclinations perhaps that cause might be advanced. In the early 1980s, however, with the NEP poisoning relations, the Americans decided that "the timing was not appropriate." In Ottawa, bureaucrats were desperately seeking a way of keeping the economy going and preventing the isolation of Canada if, as seemed likely, Europe and Japan were going to remain all but closed to Canadian manufactured exports. The Third Option had passed away in failure, and a new trade strategy was published in the summer of 1983. *Trade Policy for the 1980s*, while not writing off Europe and the Pacific Rim, attracted notice primarily because it suggested that limited sectoral free trade arrangements might be negotiated with the United States. The Trudeau government was still paying lip service to multilateralism, but it now declared bilateral trade with the Americans as its goal.

The problems that affected Canada abroad had a similar impact on the U.S. Trade fights with Japan, which enjoyed an enormous surplus in its sales to the United States, were numerous and unending. The European Community's Common Agricultural Policy hurt American farmers just as much as Canadian ones. And the overall trade and budgetary deficits in the United States were dreadful and—under Reagan—getting worse. Even so, it was difficult to find those limited sectoral areas for free trade. Where would there be benefits for both countries? In February 1984, Canadian and American negotiators produced a list of four areas: government-procured mass transit equipment, steel, agricultural equipment, and computer services. While those were important, they did not represent more than a fraction of Canada–U.S. trade. It would take a new Canadian government to pick up the bureaucrats' proposals and press forward with a greatly expanded version of them.

The significance of all this was immediately clear, however. Though the NEP and FIRA were still in place, Ottawa had realized that its economic future seemed to be tied increasingly to that of the United States. This had to be seen as a harbinger of better and closer relations in the future.

But there were still enough disputes to make that halcyon future a long way off, and one of the most difficult concerned acid rain. Acid rain consists of industrially generated sulphuric and nitrous oxides borne on the wind and deposited on the ground as dust or in rain and snow. The deadly rain poisons lakes and kills trees. Some Canadians shouted angrily that it was all the fault of the steel mills of Pittsburgh and Ohio—but the smelter in Sudbury produced more pollutants than any other North American industry. The crucial Canadian argument, however, was that the country was at least trying to do something about its mess, but the Americans, who produced almost ten times as much, weren't. There was more truth in that claim, though Canadian anti-pollution legislation had ordinarily been just as toothless as American law. Still, there was an international problem here, and there could be no doubt, given the prevailing winds, that American pollutants were falling in Canada. Canadians and their government were angered that the United States was reluctant to do anything: there were too many jobs at stake in already hard-hit and depressed areas of the country and the costs of cleaning up were enormous. The Carter administration did sign a memorandum of intent in 1980 to negotiate a bilateral agreement to fight acid rain, but Ronald Reagan took a different view.

The president apparently believed that carbon dioxide emitted from trees caused pollution, and he argued that more research had to be undertaken before irrevocable decisions were made. His head-in-the-sand approach led thousands of Canadians to demonstrate to stop acid rain when Reagan visited Ottawa in March 1981, and the federal government to launch an almost unprecedented $1 million public relations campaign in the United States to publicize the damage being done.

Negotiations for an agreement on reducing the emissions that caused acid rain collapsed in June 1982 when the Americans refused to accept any target figures. The Canadians, moreover, complained that the Reagan administration had made "blatant efforts to manipulate the acid rain groups" that were undertaking scientific research. In 1983 two National Film Board productions on acid rain were declared by the U.S. Department of Justice to be "political propaganda": they therefore had to be registered under the Foreign Agents Registration Act, and the NFB was required to tell the U.S. Department of Justice who was making use of the films. By 1984, the Department of External Affairs was dispatching toughly worded notes to Washington, stating Canada's "deep disappointment" at the "unacceptable breach of USA commitment." There would be no joy in Canada on this issue, however, until Reagan left the presidency.

". . . however we may have a definite lead on what's causing your hair to rust . . . " (Roy Peterson, *Vancouver Sun*)

REAGAN'S BELLICOSITY AND TRUDEAU'S TOO?

The president, in fact, was viewed with something close to contempt by the prime minister. As one successful politician dealing with another, Trudeau accorded Reagan due respect in public; as the leader of the most powerful western nation, Reagan's every word merited close attention. But the Canadian had no respect for Reagan's mental capacity or his attempts in one-on-one meetings to tell bad jokes. At a press conference for summit leaders at Versailles in 1982, Reagan stumbled in answering a question, and Trudeau, sitting nearby, said *sotto voce,* "ask Al." Trudeau was referring to Secretary of State Al Haig, whose grasp of the issues was far surer than the president's. Such comments did neither Trudeau nor Canada much good with the American administration. On the other hand, in a world with nuclear weapons at the ready, the western alliance deperately needed a firm hand at the tiller, and Reagan's palsied grasp was apparently anything but that.

Canada was also disconcerted by the president's military policies. Reagan believed that America's prestige and power had waned, and he resolved to pump huge sums of money into rebuilding the United States' military strength. That would make America "stand tall" again. The massive effort was accompanied by heightened rhetoric, as the president railed against the Soviet Union as "the evil empire." Such slanging did nothing to improve relations between East and West, and Canadians and others were more than a little frightened by the bellicosity of the administration. The U.S. had shifted its policy from deterrence, which had accepted a quasi-equality between the superpowers' nuclear arsenals, to acceptance of the possibility of fighting and winning limited nuclear wars. Canada itself had no nuclear weapons on its soil—the last fifty-five nuclear warheads were removed in July 1984—though as a NATO and NORAD member, the country was associated with nuclear weapons indirectly. A defensive nuclear posture was one thing; it was quite another to be linked to a superpower that thought in terms of using them as a war-winning weapon.

The Trudeau government simply had no trust in Reagan's good sense or in his military policies. The U.S. was talking tough and playing aggressively all over the world, even in the western hemisphere. In October 1983, the States joined by six Caribbean nations sent troops into Grenada to topple a puny but vicious military regime that had seized power from the Marxist Maurice Bishop. The invasion troubled the Trudeau government, not least because neither the United States nor the

Caribbean Commonwealth nations, to which Canada had thought itself close, had informed Ottawa about the scheme. If the Americans were ready to attack in this way, who was next? Anything seemed possible. The situation was especially anxious for Canada because the armed forces had been allowed to run down during the Trudeau government's long tenure, to become in journalist Richard Gwyn's damning phrase, "a national joke." Now, with Washington rearming and putting pressure on its allies to do the same, Trudeau knew that he was about to be squeezed and squeezed hard. Canada had done the bare minimum for years. Canadian defence expenditures were ranked thirteenth out of the fourteen NATO countries with armed forces; to rise to the average, Canada would have to double its defence budget and virtually triple its military personnel. To counter this image, the Trudeau government in 1978 had pledged to increase defence expenditures by 3 percent a year after inflation. In fact, it did better than that and the budget rose from $4.3 billion in 1980 to $6 billion in 1982 and $7.9 billion in 1984. That was still inadequate, critics claimed.

Nonetheless, the NORAD agreement was regularly renewed, and Canada continued to operate the old Voodoo fighters that helped protect the American Strategic Air Command and the nuclear deterrent. In NATO, Canada maintained its troops at a level slightly above that established in 1970. Because Trudeau had sought West Germany's assistance when the Third Option policy was in full cry, the Canadian NATO contingent had even acquired $200 million worth of new, German-made tanks. Canada had also purchased other weapons systems at high cost, including Aurora long-range patrol aircraft for $1.5 billion, and new F-18 interceptor aircraft from the United States for $2.3 billion. Still, the forces were tiny—just over 80 000—and generally ill equipped. The navy especially, though it retained a crucial anti-submarine role, had all but lost the capacity to carry it out, so antiquated were its few ships.

The Reagan administration began to put the heat on. Ambassador Robinson, who clearly believed that Canada conducted its defence policy as if it had no enemies, spoke out frequently to Canadian audiences about the nature of the Soviet threat and the weaknesses of Canada's military forces. The pro-American Conservative opposition in Parliament denounced the government for its destruction of Canada's military forces; and the complaint that Canada, by taking a "free ride," was abdicating its defence to the United States was heard more often. Thus in 1981, when Reagan's defence secretary, Caspar Weinberger, picked up on an idea first advanced at the Permanent Joint Board on Defence in 1980 and asked that the United States be allowed to test the cruise missile over Canada,

Trudeau was careful not to reject the proposal outright. In October, the Cabinet committee on priorities and planning decided that a testing agreement could be negotiated. Trudeau himself told the president in December 1981 that he "agreed in principle" with the tests. An exchange of notes between the two countries in February 1983 set out the terms for the testing of a number of weapons in Canada over a decade: a specific decision on cruise would be made later.

The cruise could be launched from a ship or an aircraft, and it flew low and slowly. The preferred method and route was for a B-52 bomber to launch a cruise over the North Pole. The missile, hugging the ground to avoid radar, would fly at subsonic speed until it hit its target 1500 miles away. Canada's vast northern expanse of lightly populated territory, very similar to that of the Soviet Union, was a good place to test the cruise in offensive operations and, equally, to practise interception techniques against the types of weapons that the Soviet Union had already deployed. In June 1983, the Americans formally asked for permission to test the cruise and, after a very sharp debate in Cabinet Trudeau agreed despite the reservations built up over a peaceful career. The missile, it was stipulated, would not be tested in Canada with a nuclear warhead.

Trudeau probably reckoned that he had few options; he had already done everything but promise the tests could go ahead. Moreover, making the decision in the face of public and some ministerial opposition might just win him some credit with President Reagan. To refuse would cause a major rupture with the American administration at a time when the government was trying to bind the wounds caused by the NEP and FIRA. At the very least, public anger in Canada let the prime minister tell the president that he had done his part—and at some political cost—for the western alliance. Trudeau's insistence at summit meetings that the West show some willingness to accommodate the Soviet Union had begun to annoy Reagan and British Prime Minister Margaret Thatcher, but now he had helped the alliance, saying "We must also show the Soviet Union that we can meet them gun for gun if necessary."

Trudeau's bellicosity, unlike Reagan's, was only lightly held. That became evident when the global confrontation between East and West intensified in the fall of 1983. On 30 August, Soviet interceptors shot down a Korean Airlines jumbo jet near Sakhalin Island with a huge loss of life. The immediate response in Ottawa was sharp, and the ambassador to the United Nations called the Soviet action "little short of murder." Canada joined the United States and other countries in slapping sanctions on the USSR. Trudeau's personal reaction was very different, however, for he feared that events could slip their leash. "We are at the brink of the abyss," he said, and when the war drums in the United States continued to beat against the Soviet Union, the prime minister refused to go along, declaring the incident a mistake. "I do not believe that the people in the Kremlin deliberately murdered some 200 or 300 passengers. . . . I do not believe that. I believe it was a tragic accident, an accident of war." Trudeau had based his comments on his reading of secret communications intelligence shared with Canada by the U.S. National Security Agency. "It was obvious to me very early in the game that the Reagan people were trying to create another bone of contention with the Soviets when they didn't have a leg to stand on. . . . [T]he Americans knew that it was an accident and the Soviets knew that the plane was not sent by the Americans. The two superpowers were talking past each other."

CONFRONTING A WHITE-HOT WORLD

After the KAL disaster, a superpower conflict, always a terrifying prospect, seemed more likely. "Comrades," one high-ranking Politburo official told a meeting in Leningrad, "the international situation at present is white hot, thoroughly white hot." Trudeau wanted to do what he could to defuse the tense atmosphere. In late September, he met with a small group of ministers and officials to discuss the need for a peace initiative. The prime minister was nearing the fourth year of his electoral mandate, and he almost certainly realized that the negative opinion polls, to say nothing of his own desire to be free to spend more time with his three young sons, meant that his time in power was limited. Should he say nothing until he left office, and then reveal himself as a crusader for peace? Or should he use the power that his position gave him to try to launch a crusade for world sanity? For Trudeau, an adventurer in politics, that was no choice at all. The initiative was launched with a major public speech on 27 October, and the prime minister proposed a ban on testing high-altitude weapons, a comprehensive test ban, a joint NATO–Warsaw Pact consultative process, and a five-power conference on nuclear arms control. Before long, Trudeau was on the road, first to western Europe, then to the Commonwealth meeting in New Delhi, then to Beijing, and finally to Washington and Moscow. There was frequently interest but no commitment.

The American response to this effort was anger. Trudeau had not done Washington the courtesy of consultation before he had set off on his globe-girdling travels. Of course he hadn't, Canadian officials said. If he had got American approval, the Soviets would simply have seen Trudeau as a stalking-horse for the United States. Besides the mood in Washington in the fall of 1983 was jingoistic. The invasion of Grenada a year earlier, the first successful U.S. military operation since the end of the Vietnam War, prompted a resurgence of pride in the military. The president's Strategic Defense Initiative, announced in March 1983, was being trumpeted as a way to shield America from nuclear attack. Reagan continued to soar in the opinion polls as his undoubted ability to make Americans feel good about themselves and their country worked its magic. The U.S. was in no mood for a deal on ending the Cold War.

Here was Trudeau peddling peace, while the Americans saw him as soft on communism. William Buckley's *National Review*, reportedly Reagan's favourite reading material, had said so, and the president had heard enough from the prime minister at their meetings to believe it. One Pentagon official, told of the peace initiative, said, "Oh God, Trudeau's at it again." But then Trudeau had little influence anyway, so why worry? The circumstances for the peace initiative were not propitious, and though Reagan heard Trudeau's pitch with attention, the results in Washington and elsewhere were minor.

Trudeau had been right to try to do something, anything he could, to ease international tensions. Certainly the Canadian people believed he was correct, and his standing in the polls shot up dramatically. But the most damning indictment of his peace efforts came from Robert A.D. Ford, the retired Canadian ambassador to the Soviet Union. Ford remarked that the initiative was "a total absurdity, and the Russians just laughed at it." Trudeau had no leverage in Washington and "no corresponding clout in Moscow. . . . [H]e had no credit in the banks of either place." Trudeau's government had alienated the United States with its policies on foreign investment, energy, and culture; and in Washington's opinion, Canada had not played the part of a good western ally. By not consulting the American government on the peace plan, the prime minister had given himself a purity of motive in his own eyes and in those of other Canadians; but by not consulting Washington, he had also doomed his initiative from the outset. As for the Soviets, there was no percentage in taking the Canadian seriously if he spoke only for himself. If he spoke for the U.S., he was even more suspect.

Pierre Trudeau announced his resignation as leader of the Liberal party after "a walk in the snow" in February 1984. A subsequent convention chose as his successor John Turner, a former senior minister in

Trudeau's government who had returned to private life. Turner took office as prime minister on 30 June and named his main rival for the leadership, Jean Chrétien, as his secretary of state for external affairs. Turner was believed to be pro-business and pro-American, a pragmatist who knew American politicians like Secretary of State George Shultz very well indeed. But what the new government might have done about Canadian relations with the United States, we shall never know. Turner announced an election on 9 July, and the result turned out to be a horrific Liberal disaster on 4 September 1984. Dealing with Washington would now be the task of Brian Mulroney and the Progressive Conservative party. The new leader, it quickly became clear, approached that task in a very different way from his predecessors.

AN ALTERNATIVE VISION

1 9 8 4 —

The Free Trade Agreement was central to Canada's future, the prime minister told the television audience watching the debate between the national party leaders on 25 October 1988. "I know that Canadians can compete and I know that Canadians can excel in the markets of the world and strengthen our identity as Canadians in the process." The leaders of the opposition parties, Brian Mulroney said in a refrain that was already too familiar to the voters, had a duty to explain their alternative. "They would tear up the Free Trade Agreement and then what?" Mulroney's analysis did not satisfy either John Turner or Ed Broadbent. The Liberal leader proclaimed the issue of the election to be nothing less than "the future of Canada," with the prime minister's real intent to turn Canada into a pale replica of the United States. Broadbent, the NDP leader, denounced both the Free Trade Agreement and Mulroney, accusing the prime minister of giving the Americans what they wanted in the agreement while failing to get what Canada needed. It was the same old stuff, three patently insincere politicians mouthing the predictable platitudes to a nation that believed the election was already decided in the Conservatives' favour. The leaders' debate was not going to change anyone's mind.

But the carefully scripted plans of the leaders, their handlers, and media advisers suddenly went awry during a segment of the debate that put John Turner head to head with Brian Mulroney. When one of the press panel asked whether jobs would stay in Canada if the agreement went ahead, Turner seized the opportunity to lambaste the prime minister. "I think the Canadian people have the right to know why, when your primary objective was to get unfettered and secure access into the American market, we did not get it; why you did not put clauses in to protect our social programs in this negotiation that we will have on the definition of subsidies. . . . Why did that not happen?" There was an inconclusive exchange, and then Turner, his face flushed and contorted, snapped, "I think the issues happen to be so important for the future of Canada. I happen to believe you have sold us out."

To this point, Mulroney had been cultivating a statesmanlike approach, speaking with his voice pitched low and in measured phrases. But Turner's "sell-out" charge was too much, and the prime minister huffed, "You do not have a monopoly on patriotism. I resent the fact of your implication that only you are a Canadian. I want to tell you that I come from a Canadian family and I love Canada and that's why I did it, to promote prosperity, and don't you impugn my motives."

"Once a country yields its economic levers," Turner interrupted. "Once a country yields its investment, once a country yields its energy . . . "

"We have not done it," Mulroney shouted.

"Once a country yields its agriculture . . . ," the Liberal went on.

"Wrong again!" Mulroney interjected.

"Once a country opens itself up to a subsidy war with the United States in terms of definitions," Turner tried to continue, as Mulroney once more interrupted him—"Wrong again"—"then the political ability of this country to [resist] the influence of the United States, to remain as an independent nation—that has gone forever, and that is the issue of this election."

Mulroney again intoned that he loved Canada, but Turner continued his attack by noting that for more than a century Canadians had built a country on an east–west axis. "For 120 years, we have done it. With one signature of a pen, you've reversed that, thrown us into the north–south influence of the United States, and will reduce us, will reduce us I am sure, to a colony of the United States, because when the economic levers go, the political independence is sure to follow."

"Mr. Turner," Mulroney rejoined, "it was a document that is cancellable on six months' notice. Be serious. Be serious."

"Cancellable? You're talking about our relationship with the United States."

"A commercial document that's cancellable on six months' notice."

"Commercial document?" Turner virtually shouted. "You're talking about . . . "

"That document is a commercial treaty," the prime minister went on.

"It relates to every facet of our life, it is far more important than . . . "

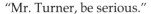

"Mr. Turner, be serious."

"Well, I'm serious," the Liberal chief said, "and I've never been more serious in my life!"

Those few minutes of gripping television at once encapsulated and galvanized the election campaign of 1988 and the national debate about the Free Trade Agreement that the Mulroney government had negotiated with the Reagan administration. The future course of the country was at stake: economically and psychologically, free trade with the United States represented a marked shift in direction. There had been reciprocity with the U.S. from 1854 to 1866, there had been a reciprocity agreement rejected by Canadian voters in the election of 1911, and there had been a succession of trade agreements, both bilateral and multilateral, in the years after 1935. But now, the Mulroney government had turned wholeheartedly to the south, and John Turner's impassioned declarations expressed the doubts and fears of countless Canadians.

"OPEN FOR BUSINESS AGAIN"

Brian Mulroney's benign view of the United States, as Richard Gwyn and others have pointed out, grew in part out of personal experience. Of Irish stock, he was born and raised in Baie Comeau, Quebec, a company town that had been built on the north shore of the St. Lawrence River by Colonel Robert McCormick of the *Chicago Tribune* and *New York Daily News* to supply his operations with cheap newsprint. Mulroney's father, an electrician who worked in the paper mill, had been one of the town's pioneers in the 1930s. The young Brian had sung Irish ballads and Quebec folksongs for the colonel and his friends at the Le Manoir hotel and had received five dollars as his reward. He took pride in that ever after, even though his detractors (quick to see a rich allegory of subservience to the Americans) gloated every time he told the story. Later, Mulroney encountered many Americans at St. Francis Xavier University in Antigonish, Nova Scotia, a small college noted for importing U.S. students. After law school at Laval and a successful career at the bar in Montreal, Mulroney became president of the Iron Ore Company of Canada, an American resource concern not unlike the one his father had laboured for.

Mulroney had the political bug, and even as a student his hard work and shrewd understanding of Quebec's politics made him a valuable aide and adviser to federal leader John Diefenbaker and his justice minister,

Davie Fulton. Mulroney was, like countless Canadians, enthralled by John F. Kennedy, and he patterned his political style after the Boston Irishman. Mulroney's speech at the Conservative leadership convention of 1976, his first attempt to capture the party's brass ring, was a conscious attempt, right down to the measured cadences, to capture the martyred president's appeal and oratory. The idiom of American politics came naturally: "It is a great country," Mulroney said, "where the son of an electrician can seek the highest office in the land."

It is crucial to understand that Mulroney did not feel threatened by the United States. In *The 49th Paradox*, Richard Gwyn astutely noted that

> Of all Canadian prime ministers, Mulroney is the most wholly North American. He likes Americans, he understands them, and he admires unstintingly the American dynamic of egalitarian individualism of which his own climb from Champlain Street in Baie Comeau to 24 Sussex by way of the presidency of Iron Ore of Canada amounts to a shining example. . . . None of this makes Mulroney less a Canadian in any respect. It does, however, make him a certain *kind* of Canadian. He is in a sense a Canadian of the 1950s, a product of the era of "Good Neighbours," when most Canadians aspired to be like Americans. The doubts about the nature of American society that many Canadians came to hold in the 1960s and 1970s never affected Mulroney.

Mulroney had captured the leadership of the Progressive Conservative party in 1983 after his long campaign in the backrooms had successfully undermined Joe Clark's hold on the loyalty of his troops. Then in September 1984, he crushed John Turner's Liberals, bringing the largest number of MPs in Canadian history with him to Parliament Hill. There were 211 Conservatives in a House of Commons of 282, and Mulroney's party had captured exactly half of the popular vote.

From the beginning, the prime minister placed "good relations, super relations" with the United States at the top of his foreign policy agenda. "Our message is clear," he told the Economic Club in New York on 10 December 1984 in his first major address in the United States, "Canada is open for business again." The Foreign Investment Review Agency, ineffectual though it was, was to be replaced by Investment Canada, an agency with the goal of welcoming American capital. In 1986, American investment in Canada amounted to $126.2 billion; one year later it was up to $134.7 billion, and, significantly, direct investment was increasing much faster than portfolio investment. At the same time, the National Energy Program, as hated in the U.S. (and Alberta) as FIRA, was to be altered as well. These initiatives were well received by American industrial and financial movers and shakers.

The prime minister was also well received by the president. Mulroney had trotted down to Washington in June 1984 while still leader of the opposition, and he paid another visit just eight days after his election victory in September. Things had gone smoothly in the U.S. capital, as the Tory leader had so ardently desired. He knew very little about foreign policy, but he knew what he liked, and there was a lot for Mulroney to like in Ronald Reagan—his panache, his oratory, his insistence that business values were the key to righting the economy. The president was no intellectual fireball, to be sure, but he enjoyed the blarney and camaraderie at which Mulroney was a master. The president and the new prime minister were both of Irish origins, and Reagan had telephoned Mulroney when he won the party leadership in 1983 to say that "it was nice to see another Irishman in there."

Reagan had never been comfortable in his dealings with Trudeau, whose mind did not work in either the same way or at the same speed as his own. By contrast, Mulroney adopted a winking, smiling, go-along-to-get-along style that was calculated to squeeze around rather than to confront differences between the two countries. He had been horrified at the Trudeau government's criticism of and carping at the Americans, which he believed had brought no benefits to Canada. Moreover, Mulroney believed in the maintenance of an essential North American loyalty and solidarity. During the United States' 1983 invasion of Grenada, an operation that was notably unpopular in Canada, Mulroney had supported Reagan: "If our friends need the benefit of the doubt from time to time, so be it."

Despite the complexities of Canadian–American affairs, individuals can still make a difference. For good or ill, this was clearly going to be the Age of Mulroney in the relationship, and the bond was going to be much closer than it had been. There was an almost audible sigh of relief from the White House that Canada was once more firmly on side.

Shrewdly, Mulroney gave the most prestigious (if no longer the most important) portfolio in the Cabinet to former prime minister Joe Clark. But the new secretary of state for external affairs was made aware of just who the boss was. In very public ways, Mulroney stipulated that foreign policy generally and Canadian–American relations specifically were ultimately a prime ministerial responsibility. The two junior ministers at External Affairs and the ministers of regional economic expansion and national defence were all staunch Mulroneyites. Clark had a distinctly shaky start in his job, a combination of bad luck and worse judgment that was in no way helped by Mulroney's public remonstrations. The former prime minister proved more durable than anyone might have anticipated, however, becoming one of Mulroney's most effective and articulate ministers. On Canadian–American issues, as on all others, there had not been the slightest public whiff of disloyalty or disagreement, even over free trade where Clark might have had private reservations. During the Persian Gulf crisis, which erupted in August 1990, Clark's bellicose support of the American position at times seemed even stronger than the prime minister's. There could be little doubt that that was just what Mulroney wanted.

Ronald Reagan and Joe Clark make foreign policy. (*The Leader Post*)

The foreign and domestic policies that Mulroney plumped for might justly be described as an alternative vision for Canada. Domestically, the government's policy was privatization—the selling of government assets to private business—and a frontal attack on the budget deficit (not, in the event, a very successful one) in an attempt to make the government more efficient and keep it out of business's way. Relations with Quebec and the provinces were also to be transformed, as Ottawa moved to accommodate Quebec City, disgruntled over Trudeau's failure to deliver constitutional reform of a type that satisfied *nationaliste* aspirations. The 1987 Meech Lake Accord was intended to give Quebec most of what it wanted, but to ease opposition elsewhere, it offered all the provinces the same powers. Essentially, this was a policy of decentralization, a divestiture of federal powers. As one Quebec journalist colourfully put it, the boys bellied up to the bar, and Mulroney obligingly filled their provincial glasses full.

The alternative Mulroney vision was nowhere more clearly or more uncompromisingly expressed than in the area of Canadian–American relations. The prime minister and his secretary of state for external affairs insisted that Canada was a confident, mature nation that could realistically confront "options that a few years ago produced emotional reflexes that made national discussion difficult." That was certainly a reference to Pierre Trudeau's Third Option policy which had aimed at reducing American economic and cultural penetration in order to allow Canadians and their institutions to develop more independently. The Tories believed that approach to be timid, unconstructive, and scarcely worth the attempt. Instead, they edged towards the Second Option— increased, not diminished continental integration—which Mitchell Sharp had canvassed and rejected in his 1972 "options" paper. "I am arguing," Clark said, "that we are better able to stand on our own than we have ever been. The modern purpose of Canadian nationalism is to express ourselves, not protect ourselves." Strengthened economic links with the U.S. could return big dividends: greater access to the American bonanza, a stronger economy, and a better chance that the world might heed Canadian pleas for trade liberalization. "So long as we are held back by our economy," Clark added, "we will not be as effective as we should be in our international activities or in our domestic policy. A strong economy builds respect, and allows initiative. Successful nations are listened to."

Mulroney had not been perfectly consistent in pursuing his vision. In 1983, when he was contesting the party leadership, Mulroney had opportunistically attacked John Crosbie, another candidate, for his call for free trade with the U.S. That issue, Mulroney then claimed, had been settled once and for all in 1911. "Free trade is terrific until the elephant twitches, and if it ever rolls over, you're a dead man. We will have none of it." That, he must have thought, was good politics, a traditional

Canadian rant. But in office, Mulroney sang a different tune, one much closer to his instinctive pro-Americanism. His trade minister, James Kelleher, soon began dropping hints about a comprehensive Canada–United States free trade area, and a discussion paper, issued in 1985 by Kelleher's department, pointed that way. "Good relations, super relations" would lead to more prosperity for Canadians—Mulroney's major election promise, after all, had been "jobs, jobs, jobs." In addition, and this probably did not hurt, the polls showed that free trade was becoming a popular issue.

The Shamrock Summit

The Reagan administration was determined to demonstrate that Mulroney's confidence in the United States and its president was justified. Reagan had put forward a vague plan for a Canadian–American–Mexican "alliance" in his first major speech of the 1980 campaign. In his memoirs, he says only that Canada "agreed" but adds nothing further because, in fact, Pierre Trudeau (and the Mexican president) scotched the idea at once. With Mulroney, however, Reagan found a sympathetic echo in Ottawa, and the president began to evince renewed interest in Canada. No other country, the White House told a Canadian journalist in 1985, "is more important to the United States than Canada, and we are blessed to have such a nation on our northern border. Canada is a friend, a neighbor and a trusted ally. We may have a larger population and a larger GNP, but we're also dependent on you." This was bound to be seductive for Canadians, who were used to being ignored by the U.S. or to being told that it was *they* who were dependent.

Rhetoric was transformed into policy. On the eve of Reagan's first visit to Canada to meet with the prime minister, *Maclean's* uncovered a U.S. administration assessment of "what Mulroney wants: 1. To be taken seriously—e.g. high level meetings. 2. To show his pro-U.S. tilt is paying off." *Maclean's* also reported that a "country review" was under way in Washington, "mobilizing almost every department and agency to come up with issues that would demonstrate that Mulroney's friendship with Washington was producing concrete political payoffs."

Reagan's trip to Canada was scheduled for Quebec City on St. Patrick's Day, 1985. The Shamrock Summit, as it was promptly dubbed, was an occasion. The presidency may not be quite as imperial as some critics have suggested, but when it is on parade in a foreign land it certainly seems that way. The pre-advance team descended on Quebec City, complete with a set of toy cars to ensure that backwards Canadians could grasp the order of battle for the presidential motorcade. Next came the advance group, sixty strong; then the advance-advance group arrived to take over the Château Frontenac, suddenly transformed, as the calling cards said, into the "Quebec City White House." Reagan came in their wake. Air Force One, the presidential Boeing 707, disgorged the president and his wife, Nancy, a core of senior staffers, and about half the cabinet. The president, wearing an Irish green tie, moved across the tarmac of Quebec's airport with the prime minister in tow to inspect a guard of honour provided by the Royal 22nd Regiment.

That night, at a gala concert, Mulroney led his wife and the Reagans on stage to lead the singing of "When Irish Eyes Are Smiling." The last few words, the prime minister crooned alone. It was, as *Time* said, pure hokum, but the Mulroney entourage was ecstatic. The Tories, Michel Gratton of the prime minister's press office remembered, "were proud of their boy. Most of them had heard stories of his vocal prowess; it turned out as advertised. I was beaming. We'd taken the round. Reagan had barely moved his lips. We'd beaten the Great Communicator at his own game—showmanship." Show biz and circuses had propelled Reagan's shallow but enormously successful political career, and Gratton (and likely Mulroney) believed that it made for success in Canada too. It did not. Mulroney never quite lived down this exercise in prime ministerial ego and bad taste.

The Shamrock Summit was full of pre-arranged achievements. Accords were signed to co-ordinate law enforcement, to end fifteen years of squabbling over the Pacific salmon harvest, to further joint work in space—Canada had previously designed and built the highly successful "Canadarm" for the American space shuttle program—and to concert efforts to attack global trade protectionism. The two countries also agreed to set up a North Warning System, a modernized version of the obsolete DEW Line that warned of attacks by Soviet bombers. The NWS was to consist of long- and short-range radars scattered across the Arctic, roughly along the seventieth parallel, supplemented by over-the-horizon backscatter radars along the east and west coasts. There was also to be a series of dispersal bases for airborne warning and control system aircraft. Initially, in pre-summit discussions, the Pentagon had indicated that it wanted to pay for and manage the entire system, one indication of its concern about the threat posed by Soviet cruise missiles. But eventually

Two Irishmen. (John Mahoney, *The Gazette*)

the U.S. generals had to agree that Canada would retain complete control of the radar system. Admittedly, Ottawa had to commit itself to lay
out $760 million for the privilege, but that allowed Mulroney and Clark
to underline their devotion to the protection of the country's sovereignty.

The president and the prime minister then appointed special
envoys, former Ontario premier William Davis and former U.S. transportation secretary Drew Lewis, to report on acid rain. This agreement,
like the others signed at Quebec City, amounted to a small victory for
Mulroney. The Davis–Lewis inquiry did not amount to much, but it was
the first time the Reagan administration acknowledged that acid rain
might be a problem that required governmental action. The Mulroney
approach had made some progress in an area of domestic importance.

The prime minister could be forgiven for believing that he was doing what Canadians wanted. A clear majority of delegates to the 1983 Conservative convention had favoured closer ties with Washington, and polls taken in 1984 demonstrated that many of their compatriots agreed. But the question of relations with the U.S. was always touchy. After the summit, the *Globe and Mail's* national affairs columnist Jeffrey Simpson attacked the prime minister for sacrificing Canadian independence by linking himself unquestioningly to the aims of American foreign policy. Simpson's criticism was reinforced by an inauspicious slip of the tongue by Reagan's defence secretary, Caspar Weinberger. Despite official American and Canadian assurances that Canada could make up its own mind whether or not to participate in the Strategic Defense Initiative, Reagan's beloved Star Wars scheme to provide a shield against nuclear attack, Weinberger had told Canadian TV interviewers that some SDI sites might be located in Canada. It all depended "on where is the most effective technical place for them to be put." That made it essential for Mulroney, if only for domestic political reasons, to make clear that there was a distinction between American and Canadian policies and interests. Obeisance to that distinction had always been the main ingredient in the recipe for Canadian survival. It was a tactic the prime minister would learn and practise over the next months.

DIFFICULTIES IN THE NORTH AND IN THE SKIES

The Strategic Defense Initiative created a difficult problem for the Mulroney government. SDI, proposed by President Reagan in March 1983, was an enormously costly effort to protect the United States from attack by nuclear missiles. Wholly new areas of research had to be pushed forward at top speed—the initial research budget was said to be $26 *billion*—and if they were successful and a viable SDI system resulted, there were serious implications for East–West relations, arms control, and the principle of deterrence on which the Cold War uneasily rested. For Canada, SDI offered the promise of protection from attack, if it could be made to work. But would the U.S. want Canada to participate in the research effort? Or as the site for SDI bases, as Weinberger had suggested? And what would happen to the general thrust of relations with Reagan's Washington if Canada declined to participate? Did the North Warning System, the papers for which had been signed at the Shamrock Summit, have implications for SDI?

In the face of contradictory statements from his ministers and from American officials, in April 1985 Mulroney named Arthur Kroeger, a senior Ottawa bureaucrat who had begun his career as a defence expert in External Affairs, to look at the question. Kroeger's report demonstrated that, like so much else in Reagan's America, SDI was full of hype. The research budget was padded enormously with already allocated funds. There was precious little chance that much research would be placed in Canada, even if Ottawa sought it: Kroeger's top estimate was about $30 million a year. Moreover, the Pentagon was convinced that American firms could handle the job all by themselves. That made Kroeger's recommendations easier: there was little money to be gained and little to be lost in terms of the broad spectrum of relations by saying "no thanks" to official governmental participation in SDI. A parliamentary committee, set up by Joe Clark to explore the issue, produced a similar recommendation. The way was clear, therefore, and on 7 September 1985 the prime minister declined a governmental role in SDI but promised to place no barriers in the way of private firms that sought contracts.

That decision was hailed by peace groups and by the large numbers of visceral anti-Americans in Canada. Just as well, too, for the government was simultaneously caught in another issue that stirred emotions to an extraordinary degree: a voyage from Greenland to Alaska through Canada's Arctic waters in August 1985 by a U.S. Coast Guard ship, the *Polar Sea*.

Canada claimed the Northwest Passage as internal waters, a position that the Americans had never recognized. To the United States, it was an international strait through which all nations had right of innocent passage. It made no difference if the waters were, in fact, ice for most of the year, for principles with world-wide implications were at stake. Curiously, almost no one in Washington or Ottawa was initially concerned by the *Polar Sea*'s voyage. Probably everyone had grown accustomed to the transit of the Passage by the United States Navy's nuclear submarines. The American Coast Guard had, as a courtesy, informed its Canadian sister service of the *Polar Sea*'s voyage, but the responsible government departments in Ottawa did not learn of U.S. plans until May 1985. This was followed by much bureaucratic scrambling in the Canadian capital, and an American agreement that Canadian officials could sail on board the ship. The U.S. also indicated its intention to abide by the government's Arctic Waters Pollution Act, passed in 1969 after the oil tanker *Manhattan* made its way through the Passage. That was a gain for Canada; on the other side, however, the United States refused to concede that Canadian permission was necessary for the *Polar Sea* to get underway. Inevitably, the voyage became public knowledge, and the politicians and press were soon in full cry. Liberal Jean Chrétien shouted that "The Americans are using their friendship with Mulroney to take away a piece of Canada," while the *Ottawa Citizen*'s Christopher Young said that the incident demonstrated "that sucking up doesn't pay." Mulroney had in so many ways done what Reagan wanted, and what was his reward?

In response to the criticism, Ottawa's first move was to announce that it was giving permission to the Coast Guard ship to make the voyage, even though Washington had not sought this. Then, the government decided not to take the issue to the International Court of Justice at The Hague. "From a legal perspective," Joe Clark said weakly, "we are better to respond to a challenge to our jurisdiction rather than ... cast doubt on our claims by taking the case there ourselves." The next day, 22 August, the prime minister toughened the position, saying that any suggestion that the Arctic was not Canada's was "an unfriendly act. ... It is ours. We assert sovereignty over it." In September, the government told Parliament that an order-in-council had been passed, formally setting out its claim in the Arctic archipelago. An increased military presence in the Arctic was promised, as well as the construction of a major-league icebreaker which could do its business the entire year. At the same time, talks were announced with the U.S. In January 1988 these resulted in an Agreement on Arctic Co-operation that, as External Affairs put it, "affirms the political will of the two countries to co-operate in advancing their shared interests in Arctic navigation, development and security." Prior consent now had to be secured from Canada before each and every transit through the Arctic archipelago by American government-owned or -operated vessels. The Americans had tested Canadian sovereignty with the *Polar Sea* and, after some hesitation, the Mulroney government had acted with a measure of force and dignity. However, domestic politics—the pressure not to be seen to cave in to the United States—was the determining factor.

The Department of National Defence later announced its intention to acquire nuclear submarines as, a 1987 government white paper on defence put it, "a vivid demonstration of Canadian determination to meet challenges." The nuclear subs, after an initial period of favour, ran into a hornet's nest of public opposition. What, after all, would Canadian submariners do if they detected an American (or a Soviet or a British) boat in Canadian waters in peacetime? Sink it? Canadian sovereignty had to be protected, but Canadians were not about to be gulled into allowing sovereignty to be a selling tactic for anything and everything. Besides, the issue was cast less in terms of sovereignty than in stark

Reaganesque Cold War rhetoric, an approach that few Canadians had patience with. The "vivid demonstration" of nuclear subs was soon just another abortive initiative, as was the Arctic icebreaker.

Canadians not only wanted to protect their sovereignty, they also sought to protect their forests and lakes from the ravages of acid rain. Half the acid rain falling in eastern Canada—in all, some 26 million tons of sulphur dioxide a year—was generated in the United States, and the issue had been on the political agenda since the beginning of the 1980s. In 1982, Trudeau's government had pledged it would enforce a 25 per-cent cut in Canadian sulphur dioxide emissions and promised to double that if the U.S. would agree to halve its emissions. The Reagan govern-ment refused, and the issue stayed largely dormant until after the Canadian and American elections in 1984. Mulroney had made some progress at the Shamrock Summit, getting Reagan's grudging consent to the Davis–Lewis study. "We did not work a miracle," Mulroney exulted, "but we did take a significant step forward."

In early January 1986, Lewis and Davis reported. They acknowl-edged that acid rain was a real problem and recommended that the U.S. spend $5 billion to "demonstrate emerging control technologies in a way that achieves some near-term reduction in transboundary pollution." That was more progress, but no targets were set for acid rain reduction. Still, Reagan that year committed his government to pursue a program to develop and demonstrate innovative control technologies, announc-ing his support at a 1986 summit meeting at Washington with Mulroney. Congress, however, was still reluctant to act, its concerns about the deficit and the potential loss of jobs in smokestack states outweighing environmental concerns. All that could be squeezed out was $725 million in "clean coal" technology research over two years. Further negotiations between Ottawa and Washington ran into roadblocks thrown up by the U.S. administration, though there were reasons for optimism by 1988 with the growing support for tough legislation among the Democratic leadership in the Senate. In the election campaign of 1988, moreover, George Bush indicated that the time for study had passed and the time for action had arrived. With his encouragement in 1990, the American Congress finally passed a tough piece of legislation to control acid rain. This was a victory for Mulroney and the hardworking lobby, the Canadian Coalition on Acid Rain, but also for American environmental groups.

There are severe limits, understandably enough, to what Canada can achieve in Washington without some help from its friends, and Mulroney, acting on an issue which was crucial to his domestic standing, found the limits of his relationship with Reagan. For all his vaunted close ties to the president, for all his desire to link Canada closely to the United States, he had been unable to secure effective action until after Reagan left office. Reagan, of course, also had restraints on him, but he was unwilling to exercise any real leadership on the issue of acid rain. Not even Mulroney's support for free trade had moved the president.

The "Leap of Faith": Free Trade

Free trade was *the* Canadian–American issue during the Mulroney government's time in power. There was more than a little logic behind raising the question in the mid-1980s. For Canadian officials and business people, the world was becoming an unfriendly place by the beginning of the decade. The "Third Option" had failed. Trade with the Europeans and Japanese increased, to be sure, but not as much as it did with the United States. What made matters worse was that the Common Market and Tokyo had mastered the application of non-tariff barriers as devices to keep out unwanted foreign goods. The United States was saddled with an enormous and growing trade deficit—$150 billion in 1985—and was facing trade difficulties of its own, and the reaction in Congress was to erect higher barriers to keep out the goods of those nations that would not give American products a fair shake.

The protectionist mood was global, and it terrified Ottawa. Alone and afraid in a world dominated by powerful trading blocs, Canada seemed to have nowhere to turn. A trade policy review in Trudeau's last term in office had considered the difficulties and produced an idea for sectoral free trade with the U.S. In fact, there already was a striking degree of free trade in North America, thanks to repeated negotiations since the Second World War under the aegis of the General Agreement on Tariffs and Trade. After the negotiations at the 1979 Tokyo Round of GATT, almost 85 percent of Canadian manufactured goods entered the United States without duty; and just over 60 percent of American manufactured goods entered Canada free of duty. Those percentages represented very large sums indeed: in 1986, Canada exported $94 billion worth of goods to the United States and imported $77 billion worth. Sectoral free trade seemed a way to build on areas of strength without opening Canada to a still greater flood of American products. But it ran into roadblocks in Ronald Reagan's Washington.

By the fall of 1984 Trudeau had retired and the new Liberal leader, John Turner, had been overwhelmingly defeated by Brian Mulroney in a general election. Free trade had not been an issue in the election campaign, but Canadians seemed to approve of the idea. Opinion polls in June 1984 showed that 78 percent of Canadians favoured free trade with the United States; a year later, 65 percent did so. Economists, led by the heavyweight Richard Lipsey of Queen's University, liked the idea both practically and theoretically. The Canadian corporate elite, troubled by the barriers thrown up at the U.S. border, cheered for free trade as a way out of their problems. And on 5 September 1985, the Royal Commission on the Economic Union and Development Prospects for Canada, appointed by Pierre Trudeau and chaired by Donald Macdonald, a longtime Liberal minister (and a fervent nationalist in his early years in Cabinet), issued its report. The Macdonald commission called for free trade: "The day of the apologetic Canadian is gone and there is no reason to suppose that our present confidence will be undermined by an arrangement designed only to secure a continuing exchange of goods and services with the United States." Macdonald admitted that free trade would not be an easy path. There would be problems aplenty for Canadian industry if it were to go head-to-head with the U.S. Free trade would be a "leap of faith," but it was a necessary one and would have a bracing effect on the Canadian economy.

The report was music to the prime minister's ears. Just three weeks after the Macdonald commission reported, Mulroney told the House of Commons that he had spoken that day with President Reagan "to express Canada's interests in pursuing a new trade agreement between our two countries." There was, Mulroney said, support for free trade from the provincial premiers and business, and while that was heartening, the prime minister added that he understood the concerns expressed by many Canadians about the potential impact of free trade on Canada. Any agreement, he promised, would not impinge on "political sovereignty, our system of social programs, our commitment to fight regional disparities, our unique cultural identity, our special linguistic character—these are the essence of Canada. They are not at issue in these negotiations." Mulroney added that he had told Reagan that he wanted to negotiate "the broadest possible package of mutually beneficial reductions in tariff and non-tariff barriers."

There was no doubt about the government's fundamental objective: to secure and enhance access to the American market. As one study prepared by the Trade Negotiations Office, the body created to handle negotiations with Washington, put it, "Canada requires an agreement that exempts our exports from U.S. protectionist measures aimed at reducing the imports of other countries." The prime minister reinforced that objective repeatedly. In Parliament on 16 March 1987, he stated that "Our highest priority is to have an agreement that ends the threat to Canadian industry from U.S. protectionists who harass and restrict our exports through the misuse of trade remedy laws. Let me leave no doubt that first, a new regime on trade remedy laws must be part of the agreement." Another objective was that any agreement had to contain a binding dispute resolution procedure, something that would tie both countries to a fair arbitration process.

For their part, the Americans wanted an agreement that would oblige Canada to open up its market once and for all to U.S. goods. They wanted to find a way to compel Ottawa to curb the variety of subsidies it offered an endless array of Canadian industries from fish to publishing. They wanted to see the abolition of all controls on American investment and to force Canadian governments at all levels to open up their purchasing to American suppliers. And the Americans wanted to see that American trade law and the remedies therein continued to apply to U.S. corporations in Canada.

The process of achieving those objectives was long and complex. The Canadian government devoted substantial resources to the effort, both of money ($10 million a year) and personnel (a staff of eighty-four). To head the negotiation, Mulroney called on Simon Reisman, a former deputy minister of finance and a long-time advocate of free trade. Tough-talking, blunt, and loud, the sixty-six-year-old Reisman was, as the creator of the 1965 Canada–U.S. Auto Pact, a skilled bargainer, a man used to getting what he wanted. The Americans by contrast put a relatively junior official, the boyish-looking thirty-nine-year-old Peter Murphy, in charge of their negotiation team.

The first round of talks took place in May 1986, after President Reagan had narrowly secured legislative approval to "fast-track" the negotiations, meaning that the Senate's Finance Committee could accept or reject a trade agreement but could not change it in any way. Just as the two trade ambassadors were getting acquainted, the U.S. slapped a 35 percent tariff on Canadian red cedar shakes and shingles. The Mulroney government fought back, and it looked like the free trade talks might be in jeopardy. But the prime minister felt strongly that this episode, and an ugly dispute over softwood lumber in late 1986, fully justified his commitment to finding a permanent mechanism to avoid the unpredictable application of American protectionism.

The free trade negotiations were conducted throughout the second half of 1986 and most of 1987. Repeatedly, they came near to the breaking

The perils of negotiation: free trade ambassadors
Simon Reisman (left) and Peter Murphy (right).
(Canada Wide)

point. Repeatedly, political intervention at the highest levels was needed
to get the talks back on track. The Americans found Reisman hard to
take, one official saying that "Instead of negotiating, he's constantly
telling us why he's right." The Canadians felt much the same about the
team across the table, the deputy chief negotiator, Gordon Ritchie, noting

that "I spent 2 1/2 years in a closed room getting beaten up by a bunch of ugly Americans." On 23 September 1987, with the negotiations deadline looming, Reisman suspended the discussions because of American intransigence on the terms of a binding dispute mechanism. Once again, the telephone wires burned between Ottawa and Washington, and the politicians got the talks going once more. Finally on 3 October, just prior to the midnight deadline at which the negotiations were to cease, officials from both countries wrung enough of a compromise out of each other to justify signing an agreement of intent. The final text was completed on 7 December and tabled in Parliament four days later. On 2 January 1988, the prime minister and the president, in separate ceremonies in the two capitals, put their names to the agreement. Canada and the United States had agreed on free trade.

The Free Trade Agreement (FTA) committed both countries to the elimination of cross-border tariffs by 31 December 1998. Some reductions were to occur at once while others were to be phased in over five or ten years. But secure, guaranteed access for Canadian products? The end of all forms of protectionism? These had not been achieved. The accord put in place a binational tribunal that was intended—theoretically—to reduce the harassment Canadian exporters of lumber and pork, for example, had had to contend with. Even FTA supporters, however, were unhappy about the weakness of this device because it could only decide whether each country was obeying its own trade laws. The agreement offered the United States non-discriminatory access to Canada's natural resources, including oil and gas; and if these were in short supply, the U.S. was entitled to receive a proportionate share of Canadian production. The FTA's provisions effectively eliminated Canada's ability to set a made-in-Canada price for oil different from the world price. No National Energy Program, the much-hated Liberal legislation of 1980, could ever be set up again.

The FTA was about much more than trade. Ten of its twenty-one chapters dealt with such matters as technical standards, energy, movement of people for business purposes, investment, and financial services. The agreement also committed Canada and the U.S. to negotiate outside their borders in concert on issues such as agriculture, investment, and services. For the first time, one critic wrote, Canada "has accepted that its national negotiating stance in international affairs is a matter to be decided by provisions of an international treaty."

For the United States, the economic importance of the Free Trade Agreement was relatively small, though that country did manage to resolve some of its long-standing grievances with Canadian trade and investment policy. The deal would allow American investors to purchase Canadian industries, except in the areas of oil, gas, water, and uranium, valued at less than $150 million without any possibility of Canadian review; only larger acquisitions would face a governmental process. That was in effect the death knell for those Canadians who had supported the creation of federal bodies such as the Foreign Investment Review Agency and had worried about unchecked American investment. Nor would American industries be forced to relocate to take account of the Canadian market or Canadian competition. Instead, American industries might well be able to close down Canadian subsidiaries, set up to serve the small and protected market north of the forty-ninth parallel, and serve all of the North American market from plants in the United States. Greater size, in other words, could lead to rationalization and greater efficiency.

Economists and workers alike anticipated that some Canadian industries, the least cost-effective and efficient, would be driven out of business by the FTA. Workers were concerned about the loss of jobs, but many economists and the Conservative government were not. The survival of the fittest was a principle of economic life, and those Canadian firms that failed deserved to die; those that survived in the vigorous competition of the continental market would be "world-class" operations, industries on which the Canadian future could be built. The job losses in the dying industries, the rationale went, would eventually be more than made up by employment in the expansionist areas. In the meantime, there would be readjustment allowances for the dislocated.

The federal government flatly maintained that the FTA, just as the prime minister had promised, in no way affected Canada's social services. Critics expressed their concerns. As Duncan Cameron wrote, if Canada were to create a new national public sector day-care program, American day-care companies might have to be compensated for the loss of any potential benefits they might have earned in Canada. "These provisions of the accord," Cameron claimed, "make the costs of such a programme significantly higher than they would otherwise be. In fact, the cost of compensating American firms for their potential losses could be so high as to rule out the creation of new programmes in all areas where American firms already provide services.

THE GREAT DEBATE: THE 1988 ELECTION

The FTA, complicated as it was, was slow to take hold as a major issue. In the United States, it made almost no impact on the public and stirred only minimal response even among special interest groups. In Canada, the public's reaction was muted at first, although labour unions, women's groups, and nationalist organizations were quick to denounce the agreement's terms.

Over the vigorous, but necessarily ineffectual, opposition of the Liberal and NDP members of Parliament, the large Tory majority in the House of Commons passed the bill implementing the FTA on 1 September 1988. But that vote did nothing to persuade the Liberal-dominated Senate that the agreement was a good one. The Liberals in the upper chamber decided to block passage of the accord and to force the prime minister to go to the people. Mulroney duly obliged on 1 October, calling the election for 21 November. The people would have their chance to speak.

The Canadian electorate was feeling disillusioned in October 1988. The prime minister and the government were not popular, but the leader of the Liberal party stood low in public esteem, and only New Democratic Party leader Ed Broadbent consistently did well in public soundings. Nationally, by the time of the election call, the Conservatives had a small lead in the polls with a very substantial majority only in the West. The Liberals were strong in the Maritimes and almost even with the Tories in Ontario and Quebec. The NDP, which had led the parties in the polls several months before, had begun a steady decline. None of the three parties or leaders, in other words, started the campaign as certain winners, though inertia, to say nothing of the rumblings within the Liberal party over John Turner's lacklustre leadership, gave the government the edge.

Nothing in the campaign's opening days gave much reason for anyone to think that matters would change. The NDP leader, surprisingly and inexplicably, seemed to pay little attention to the FTA, despite its feared effects on the work force and its tighter linking of Canada to the United States. John Turner struggled to keep his campaign afloat in the face of continuing complaints about his leadership and difficulty in answering press queries about some confusing aspects of the Liberal platform. For his part, the prime minister blandly stayed above the fray to such an extent that the media began to complain about his being in a bubble, inaccessible and aloof. Certain groups, most notably the umbrella Pro-Canada Network, tried to rally opposition to the FTA, but their impact was small. The Network, however, did publish and distribute with newspapers across the country one stunningly effective pamphlet, brilliantly titled "What's the Big Deal?" Written by Rick Salutin and superbly illustrated by the Montreal cartoonist Aislin, the flyer posed hard questions and offered clear and simple answers.

It took Turner's performance in the leaders' debate to coalesce opposition to free trade. The media gave the decision to Turner, and the voters

Macdonald, Diefenbaker, Mulroney . . . what a difference a prime minister
makes. (Reprinted with permission—Toronto Star Syndicate.)

had already reached the same conclusion. Liberal canvassers going door-
to-door while the debate was on television found enthusiasm: "Your
leader is in the process of clobbering those guys," canvassers in Montreal
were told. One Conservative candidate in Saskatchewan thought the
campaign, until the debate, the dullest he had seen. Then the roof fell in
and he spent the remaining twenty-five days responding to accusations
that the FTA meant that Canada was selling its soul: "it was free trade at
every stop." The debate had been crucial, and for the rest of the election
campaign the country engaged in serious and sometimes heated discussion about its future.

What did Canadians want for themselves in the 1990s? Did they
want Canada to be linked economically with the United States? Or did
they prefer a more independent economic policy for their nation? Was
the FTA a political as well as economic turning point for Canada or, as
Mulroney claimed, just another agreement that could be cancelled on six

months' notice? And what were the implications of the trade agreement for Canada's social programs? Those questions and issues, some of them profoundly psychological, shaped the debate until 21 November.

The Tories tried to counter the sudden mood of doubt about the FTA. The prime minister, a good alley brawler who was more comfortable in a scrap than playing at being a statesman, began to attack for the first time, accusing the Liberals and NDP of using "scare tactics" by claiming that the FTA would jeopardize medicare. Nothing, Mulroney said, compromised Canada's social programs. At the same time, Tory strategists were whipping together new TV commercials to attack John Turner's credibility.

For a few days, as the NDP all but disappeared and the Conservatives scrambled to regroup, the Liberals had it their own way. Opinion polls showed that clear majorities believed Turner had won the debate, and substantial numbers now thought it more likely they would vote Liberal. As reporter Graham Fraser wrote in *Playing For Keeps*, the best study of the 1988 election, "it looked as if Turner might turn things around." The Liberals' TV advertisements were stunningly effective, particularly one that showed an American and a Canadian negotiator sitting in a room and discussing the FTA: "Since we're talking about the Free Trade Agreement, there is one line I'd like to change," the American said. "Which line is that?" came the reply. "This line here. It's just getting in the way." Then the American leaned over and erased the Canada–United States boundary on a map. The voice-over then asked, "Just how much are we giving away in the Mulroney free-trade deal? Our water? Our health care? Our culture? The line has been drawn—which side do you stand on? . . . This is more than an election, this is your future." The Liberals looked to be on the way to staging a remarkable victory.

But the well-financed Conservatives were soon hitting back harder than ever. Corporations, lobbied hard by "non-partisan" organizations such as the Business Council on National Issues, the Canadian Manufacturers' Association, and the Canadian Chamber of Commerce, canvassed their workers and urged support for the agreement and, by implication, for the Mulroney government. Ads placed by business groups and individual companies began to appear in the major newspapers to extol the virtues of the FTA. Workers were pressured by their bosses to understand the implications of a "no" vote: jobs would become scarcer in Canada if free trade were not enacted. Michael Wilson, the finance minister and a man whose integrity had survived largely intact through the scandals of the government's first term, hit John Turner with a straight-out attack that accused the Liberal leader of lying about the FTA's effects. The aged Emmett Hall, the father of Canada's medicare system and a retired justice of the Supreme Court, emerged to say that in his view medicare was safe under the FTA. Mulroney himself, the gloves now off for good, took on hecklers and engaged in a debate with a vociferous free trade critic. "I give you the assurance I gave my own mother," the prime minister said. "I would tell my mother, 'Ma, your medicare is O.K., your pension is O.K., everything is protected. What free trade is going to do is give Canada more money so we can do more for all of you.' And God bless you all." Tory commercials, openly acknowledging the impact of the Liberals' media campaign, featured a Canadian re-drawing the boundary line erased by the American on the map of North America.

The counterattack worked. The polls that had shown a swing to the Liberals demonstrated that the loose fish in the electorate had begun to swim back to Mulroney. In Quebec especially, where the fluently bilingual Mulroney was widely perceived as a francophone (despite his Irish parentage) and where his having pushed the Meech Lake Accord through was greatly appreciated, Tory support solidified massively. The Parti Québécois was in favour of the FTA, its leader saying that its implementation would lead to the breakup of Canada and the formation of an independent Quebec. How much weight that carried in 1988, a time when the PQ was going nowhere, is uncertain. Rather, most French-speaking voters appeared to view the FTA as a chance for Quebec's entrepeneurs to make it on the bigger North American stage. They seemed to care not a whit about the nationalist attacks on the agreement in English Canada. Still, if Turner looked as if he was going to win, Quebec voters probably wanted to be sure they had enough MPs on the Liberal side; if Mulroney looked safe, then Québécois would plump for him. Now that the prime minister seemed to have turned the tide, Quebec swung to the "*bleus.*" The support for the government in French Canada, in turn, probably reinforced the conviction, now beginning to spread in English Canada, that the Tories would be returned and the FTA would survive intact.

And so it was, despite the efforts of anti-FTA voters to cast their ballot "strategically" for the Liberal or NDP candidate with the best chance of beating the Tory. Early on election night, although the Tories had done poorly in Atlantic Canada, the CBC predicted a Conservative majority government on the basis of results from Quebec and Ontario ridings. Mulroney was exultant. But so too was an exhausted, vindicated John Turner, whose party doubled its support, and who noted that the Liberal and NDP popular votes together were a clear majority:

"Despite the fact that the Conservatives have a larger percentage of the popular vote, Canadians have certainly expressed their wish to keep this country strong, sovereign and independent."

When faced with a clear choice for a separate identity or a close link to the United States, Canadians had nevertheless returned the Progressive Conservative party and Brian Mulroney to power with a strong majority. The business community heavily supported the Conservatives, as did French-speaking Canadians. Yes, a majority of the voters had supported anti-FTA candidates, but elections in Canada are not decided by the popular vote, but by seats in Parliament. The FTA had won and it would be put into force.

Into an Uncertain Future

The trade agreement became law on 1 January 1989. The walls did not tumble down at once. Canadian visitors to the U.S. somehow seemed to believe that the FTA meant they could bring back their purchases without duty, and there were innumerable scenes at customs posts. Even without further reduced tariffs, American prices seemed and usually were lower. Shopping centres on the American side of the border experienced a boom in sales as Canadians, aggrieved by Mulroney's higher taxes, flooded their stores, ready to risk fines (and to brave long line-ups at border crossings) if caught smuggling clothes, stereos, and computers in their car trunks. Early in the 1990s, what became a Canadian mania for cross-border shopping was a major problem for harried politicans and concerned business folk along the frontier; it was also an indicator of a widespread Canadian irritation with their own country. Canadians still did not want to be Americans, but they clearly wanted their consumer goods at U.S. prices.

As critics of the FTA had feared, there seemed to be a flood of industries shutting down in Canada and re-locating to the U.S. Gillette closed a razor blade plant in Montreal and put 590 workers on the street; Pittsburgh Paint shut its Toronto factory; and even Northern Telecom, a Canadian high-tech giant, shut operations in Aylmer, Quebec, and Belleville, Ontario, costing 920 workers their jobs. The list of closures went on and on, and in the period from July 1989 to July 1990 more than 134 000 manufacturing jobs had evaporated, or one in every fifteen in the country. That total came from the Canadian Manufacturers' Association, an unabashed FTA supporter. Organized labour's estimates were usually higher—in December 1990, they claimed 226 000 lost jobs. How much of this could be directly attributed to the FTA was unclear. In the Canadian food processing industry, hampered by a short growing season, the losses were heavy indeed, and this was probably attributable to the FTA. But the industrial sector of North America had been contracting for years under the attack of more efficient Pacific Rim industries and, moreover, the Canadian economy was cooling down through 1989 and 1990 until even the federal government admitted that the country was experiencing a recession. The anti-inflationary policies of the Bank of Canada and the Department of Finance fixed Canada's interest rates much higher than those in the U.S. and helped to keep the Canadian dollar overvalued throughout 1989 and 1990. (The dollar went from a value of roughly 72 cents U.S. in 1984 to 86 cents in 1990.) Both factors combined to weaken Canadian manufacturing concerns' competitive advantages in the U.S. market. However it was examined, the FTA had been no panacea, and the "jobs, jobs, jobs" promised by the prime minister simply had not yet

Gone fishing. (AP/Wide World Photos)

materialized. Opinion polls at the end of 1990 showed that 52 percent of Canadians opposed the FTA, the highest level yet, while just 31 percent supported it.

The prospect of expanding free trade to include President Carlos Salinas de Gortari's Mexico with its population of 84 million also worried Canadians as the new decade began. Mulroney had taken Canada into the Organization of American States in 1989, overriding the fears of those who had long argued that this would be certain to subject the country to pressures from Washington to follow American policy directions in Latin and South America. Before the year was out, the U.S. had invaded Panama to depose Manuel Noriega, and the Canadian government had followed along, regretting, but supporting, the use of military force. In the 1990s, Washington's trade agenda seemed to be pulling Canada towards a giant commercial arrangement with Mexico and, if George Bush has his way, eventually with all the nations of the hemisphere: free trade from the North Pole to Terra del Fuego. Manufacturing wages in Mexico were as low as two dollars a day, and there were few of the social benefits such as medicare or unemployment insurance that run up production costs, almost certainly a magnetic attraction to Canadian (and American) industries seeking higher profits. Presidents Bush and Salinas were determined to get an agreement by 1992, and Canada felt obliged to protect its interests by joining in at the negotiating table. There were risks there, too, not least that Washington might seize the opportunity to re-open those areas of the FTA that it found not totally satisfactory.

Mulroney's alternative vision for Canada had been partially put in place midway through his second term. Privatization of government-owned enterprises was proceeding apace. The prime minister's efforts to bring Quebec into the Constitution, however, had foundered when the Meech Lake Accord failed to secure the required provincial consent and, as the 1990s began, the country faced an astonishing rebirth of Quebec nationalism, which seriously threatened national survival. Still, relations with the United States were closer economically and politically than ever before. Brian Mulroney had wanted to repair the relationship he inherited from Pierre Trudeau, and he had. He had hoped to link the Canadian and American economies inextricably, and with the FTA he had accomplished this. These were achievements of note, but they were not universally applauded.

CONCLUSION

At the beginning of August 1990, Saddam Hussein's Iraq invaded Kuwait, rapidly overrunning its neighbour's feeble defences and incorporating the country—and its vast reserves of oil—as a province of great Iraq. President George Bush quickly decided that the Iraqi takeover had to be resisted, and the United States began to move huge numbers of well-equipped troops to Saudi Arabia. In the capitals of the world and at the United Nations, the Americans pressed and pressured their friends and clients to assist in the effort and, before long, NATO nations, Arab states, and a variety of countries ranging from Australia to Afghanistan were sending or promising troops, ships, or aircraft to the American-led coalition.

At the UN, the Security Council, including the Soviet Union, agreed to slap tough economic sanctions on Iraq with the threat of even stronger action if the invader failed to disgorge its conquest. But Iraq continued to talk defiantly, and in January 1991, with the United Nation's sanction, air operations against Iraq began. Within a few days, the Iraqi air force had been eliminated as a threat and much of that nation's economic infrastructure was in ruins. Just over a month later, the ground forces of the coalition moved into Kuwait and southern Iraq, destroying the Iraqi army—and doing so virtually without casualties to its own forces. It was a unique modern example of the nations of the world uniting against an aggressor state and a devastating demonstration of the power of modern weaponry.

Prime Minister Brian Mulroney, when asked by President Bush if Canada could contribute to the American-led international force, duly and promptly replied that it could. On 10 August, just a week after the Iraqi invasion, Mulroney declared that Iraq had "flagrantly violated international law and offended against the most basic human values everywhere." Canada's expertise and reputation in the world was based on its peacekeeping role, he said, but that "does not remove from us the responsibility" to respond to attacks and threats against Canada's friends and allies. The country, Mulroney said stoutly, "must do everything it can" to restore Iraqi respect for international law. To that end, the prime minister ordered two destroyers, HMCS *Terra Nova* and *Athabaskan,* and a supply ship, HMCS *Protecteur,* to the Persian Gulf. This was soon followed by the dispatch of a squadron of CF-18 fighters and a field hospital. Once the fighting began, the Canadian pilots played a full part in the action.

In Canada, there was immediate criticism of the government's action. Much of the press and all the country's peace movements objected to the Canadian deployment and argued that Canada had become involved in an adventure that had nothing to do with respect for international law, but everything to do with U.S. interests and domestic politics. In other words, by supporting the U.S. in its "gunboat diplomacy" in the Gulf, Canada was acting yet again as a puppet of the United States, and moreover, in a way that could jeopardize its hard-won status as the pre-eminent supporter of United Nations peacekeeping.

There was an element of truth in those complaints. Canada, like other nations, had been pressed hard by the U.S. to support its effort against Iraq. There was a possibility that participation in the war could hurt the Canadian capacity to act as a peacekeeper, though that fear was exploded instantly when, within days of the end of the war, Canada was called on to supply troops for a UN force on the Iraq–Kuwait border.

As officials in Ottawa were quick to argue, however, there was much more to the story than Canada as compliant toady. Canada's role, they maintained, had been a traditional one as it attempted to constrain the United States from precipitate, independent action. How much better it would be, Ottawa insisted, if the Security Council could authorize economic sanctions as a first stage; surely it would be preferable to have the United Nations agree to the use of force if Iraq showed no willingness to budge from Kuwait; and if it came to the worst and war became inevitable, the Canadians (and others) suggested, then there had to be a joint command of the coalition's forces, albeit under American direction. These steps were followed, the U.S. accepting them with generally good grace. Canada's position, in other words, was very close to that it had taken during the Korean War: a staunch ally willing to carry its small share of the burden, but very interested in seeing the world community, and not solely the United States, involved in decision making.

None of this could satisfy the critics. Canada had sacrificed its independence to participate in an American war intended to protect oil supplies. It was all as the distinguished philosopher George Grant had predicted a quarter century before in his *Lament for a Nation*. Grant had argued that "Canada has ceased to be a nation," its fate certain to be a "social and economic blending into the [American] empire. . . . The dominant forces in the Republic do not need to incorporate us. A branch-plant satellite, which has shown in the past that it will not insist on any difficulties in foreign or defence policy, is a pleasant arrangement for one's northern frontier. The pin-pricks of disagreement are a small price to pay." George Grant argued that it was all over by 1965 and, for nationalists, the passage into law of the Canada–United States Free Trade Agreement and the subsequent Iraqi war seemed only to confirm his view.

The situation for Canadian nationalists was worsened immeasurably by the continuing constitutional crisis and economic recession that gripped Canada as the 1990s began. The failure of the Meech Lake Accord had renewed and redoubled Quebec separatism, and opinion polls in Quebec showed large and enthusiastic majorities for a much altered, decentralized Confederation and, if that was not forthcoming, for independence. In English-speaking Canada, on the other hand, the pollsters found strong resistance to further transfer of powers of the kind sought by the Quebec government and its people. And if Quebec left Confederation, the United States would be able to whipsaw Canada and Quebec, playing one against the other for economic and, possibly, defence concessions. So great might the pressure become, so difficult the task of communicating across a bifurcated Canada, that many might call for annexation. Better to live as Americans than as deprived Canadians in an economically depressed and highly taxed backwater. The future was nothing less than grim, and the United States watched closely and said little. Was the game up? Was Canada's life as an independent transcontinental nation nearing its end?

Historians are poor predictors of tomorrow and the next day. Our only utility is to be able to say something about how the past unfolded. Are Canadian–American relations as cut-and-dried as Grant and those who share his view believe? Or is the relationship a patchwork of inevitable conflict mixed with the co-operation that is every bit as inevitable? There can be no doubt that relations between the two countries (and, of course, between Quebec and Canada and Quebec and the U.S.) are now even more complicated, spanning virtually every area of modern life with a vast array of boards, commissions, treaties, agreements, corporate and trade union links, and personal and familial ties. There is also no doubt that the disparities in power are enormous, so much so that if the Americans exert themselves on any single issue they can virtually count on getting their way. But such big-stick diplomacy does not always suit the Americans' interest—and in any case the United States is composed of a plethora of competing interest groups.

Nor is the break-up of the stable and strategic country to their north devoutly to be wished by all or even most in Washington. Canadians, in other words, can work the margins, lobby and build coalitions, and get their way sometimes. It takes skill, persistence, and a shrewd understanding of the way Washington operates but, after all, who knows the Americans better than Canadians?

Nor is there any doubt that Canadian governments have stood up to the United States and slugged it out on innumerable occasions. From the Alaska boundary dispute to the trade disputes of the interwar years; from the insistence that Canada be given a place on some of the wartime combined boards to oil policy; and from fishing boundaries to softwood lumber imports, ministers and diplomats have fought and argued. Sometimes they have won, sometimes not; often there has been a compromise that everyone (or in a few cases no one) could live with. Whoever triumphs, the basic nature of the relationship continues to operate on a level of friendliness and interdependence that is unparalleled by any two other nations. As James Bartlet Brebner wrote in his classic *North Atlantic Triangle*, Canada and the United States are "the Siamese Twins of North America who cannot separate and live." Arthur R.M. Lower, another distinguished historian, looked at the relationship in much the same way in an article in 1939, using a phrase that especially commended itself to us: "Canadians and Americans, similar to each other in so many ways, and bound together by so many ties, resemble a married couple, who must take each other for better or for worse." Divorce is much more common today than it was a half-century ago, but the costs and consequences of ending a union are always severe. For better or for worse, Canada and the United States must share their continent and their fates.

BIBLIOGRAPHY

Introduction and General

A valuable general study, covering the eighteenth- and nineteenth-century background to modern Canadian–American relations (and a great deal more), is G.M. Craig, *The United States and Canada* (Cambridge, MA, 1968). There is also good material in C.P. Stacey, *The Undefended Border: The Myth and the Reality*, a Canadian Historical Association booklet (Ottawa, 1967); S.F. Wise and Robert Craig Brown, *Canada Views the United States: Nineteenth-Century Political Attitudes* (Toronto, 1967); Gaddis Smith, "The Legacy of Monroe's Doctrine," *New York Times Magazine*, 9 September 1984; and Kenneth Bourne, *Britain and the Balance of Power in North America 1815–1908* (Berkeley, 1967). More recently, two books have cast important new light on this early period: Jane Errington, *The Lion, the Eagle, and Upper Canada* (Kingston and Montreal, 1987), and R.C. Stuart, *United States Expansionism and British North America, 1775–1871* (Chapel Hill, NC, 1988). Both Errington and Stuart provide excellent bibliographies.

Overview histories of Canadian–American relations include, in addition to Craig, H.L. Keenleyside and G.S. Brown, *Canada and the United States* (New York, 1952); J.B. Brebner, *North Atlantic Triangle: The Interplay of Canada, the United States and Great Britain* (New Haven, 1945); E.W. McInnis, *The Unguarded Frontier* (New York, 1942); and E.E. Mahant and G.S. Mount, *An Introduction to Canadian–American Relations* (Scarborough, ON, 1989). Gordon Stewart of Michigan State University, working on a history of U.S. policies towards Canada, gives a preliminary view in "'A Special Contiguous Country Economic Regime': An Overview of America's Canada Policy," *Diplomatic History*, 6, 4 (Fall 1982). The Stewart article is reprinted in Norman Hillmer, *Partners Nevertheless: Canadian–American Relations in the Twentieth Century* (Toronto, 1989), which contains a wide variety of opinions on political, military, cultural, economic, and environmental relations, as well as an extensive bibliography.

For histories of the two countries' foreign policies, it would be hard to improve upon T.G. Paterson, J.G. Clifford, and K.J. Hagan, *American Foreign Policy*, 2 vols. (Lexington, MA, 1983) and C.P. Stacey, *Canada and the Age of Conflict*, 2 vols. (Toronto 1979–81).

Chapter One

There is an immense literature that bears on Canadian–American relations in the late nineteenth century. The most important book, and it is a very good one, is Robert Craig Brown's *Canada's National Policy, 1883–1900: A Study in Canadian–American Relations* (Princeton, 1964). Professor Brown is also the author of "The Nationalism of the National Policy," in Peter Russell, ed., *Nationalism in Canada* (Toronto, 1966), and, with S.F. Wise, *Canada Views the United States: Nineteenth-Century Political Attitudes* (Toronto, 1967). For a different view of the National Policy, see J.M. Bliss, "Canadianizing American Business: The Roots of the Branch Plant," in *Close the 49th Parallel etc.: The Americanization of Canada*, ed. Ian Lumsden (Toronto, 1970).

There is a great deal of valuable material in D.F. Warner, *The Idea of Continental Union: Agitation for the Annexation of Canada to the United States 1849–1893* (Lexington, 1960). Unfortunately, the volume is frequently unreliable. A better account of one slice of Warner's subject is to be found in Alvin Gluek, Jr., *Minnesota and the Manifest Destiny of the Canadian Northwest* (Toronto, 1965). The University of Toronto Press has a good edition, with an introduction by Carl Berger, of Goldwin Smith's *Canada and the Canadian Question* (Toronto, 1971). Professor Berger's *The Sense of Power: Studies in the Ideas of Canadian Imperialism 1869–1914* (Toronto, 1970) is the classic study of attitudes towards Canadian external relations at the turn of the century. An eloquent overview of Canada's formative years is P.B. Waite, *Canada 1874–1896: Arduous Destiny* (Toronto, 1971).

A number of distinguished historians have dealt with the Civil War and Confederation: to mention only some, D.G. Creighton, *The Road to Confederation* (Toronto, 1964); W.L. Morton, *The Critical Years: The Union of British North America 1857–1873* (Toronto, 1964); P.B. Waite, *The Life and Times of Confederation, 1864–1867* (Toronto, 1962); and Robin W. Winks, *Canada and the United States: The Civil War Years* (Baltimore, 1960). For the Fenians, see Hereward Senior, *The Fenians and Canada* (Toronto, 1978).

Although written some years ago, the best biographies of the leading Canadian politicians of the period are Donald Creighton, *John A. Macdonald*, 2 vols. (Toronto, 1955–56) and O.D. Skelton, *Life and Letters of Sir Wilfrid Laurier*, 2 vols. (New York, 1922). David Hall, *Clifford Sifton*, vol. 2, *1901–1929* (Vancouver, 1985) is strong on both Alaska and the 1911 election. We discovered the tale of Sitting Bull in John N. Jennings, "The North West Mounted Police and Indian Policy" (Ph.D. thesis, University of Toronto, 1979).

Norman Penlington, *The Alaska Boundary Dispute: A Critical Reappraisal* (Toronto, 1972) emphasizes the strength of Washington's position and the weakness of Ottawa's. J.A. Munro, ed., *The Alaska Boundary Dispute* (Toronto, 1970) is a collection of many points of view with a good bibliography. A recent account is Lewis Green, *The Boundary Hunters: Surveying the 141st Meridian and the Alaska Panhandle* (Vancouver, 1982).

Chapter Two

The first part of this chapter draws on four articles in the *Canadian Historical Review*: Roger Sarty, "Canadian Maritime Defence, 1892–1914," 71, 4 (December 1990); Peter Neary, "Grey, Bryce, and the Settlement of Canadian–American Differences, 1905–1911," 49, 4 (December 1968); Robert Bothwell, "Canadian Representation at Washington: A Study in Colonial Responsibility," 53, 2 (June 1972); and A.C. Gluek, "The Invisible Revision of the Rush-Bagot Agreement, 1898–1914," 60, 4 (December 1979). Dr. Gluek is also the author of a large number of other important pieces on this period, including "Pilgrimages to Ottawa: Canadian–American Diplomacy, 1903–13," Canadian Historical Association, *Historical Papers*, 1968.

L.E. Ellis, *Reciprocity 1911* (New Haven, 1939), is the standard monograph on the subject. Paul Stevens, *The 1911 General Election* (Toronto, 1970) collects documents and opinions. R.E. Hannigan, "Reciprocity 1911: Continentalism and American *Weltpolitik*," *Diplomatic History*, 4, 1 (Winter 1980) uses U.S. documents to argue a decidedly imperialistic cast of mind, while W.M. Baker, "A Case Study of Anti–Americanism in English–Speaking Canada: The Election Campaign of 1911," *Canadian Historical Review*, 51, 4 (December 1970), is a revealing canvass of Canadian views. Peter Morris, *Embattled Shadows: A History of Canadian Cinema 1895–1939* (Montreal, 1939), contributed interesting material on 1911, and on other subjects as well for this and the next chapter.

John E. Carroll has written instructively on the International Joint Commission in *Environmental Diplomacy: An Examination and a Prospective of Canadian–U.S. Transboundary Environmental Relations* (Ann Arbor, MI, 1983) and in other volumes. Also useful is Robert Spencer, John Kirton, and Kim Richard Nossal, eds., *The International Joint Commission Seventy Years On* (Toronto, 1981), which contains an article by N.F. Dreisziger, the authority on the origins of the IJC.

The First World War border defence section is derived from John Armstrong, "Canadian Home Defence, 1914–1917: and the Role of Major-General Willoughby Gwatkin" (M.A. thesis, Royal Military

College, 1982); Roger F. Sarty, "Silent Sentry: A Military and Political History of Canadian Coast Defence 1860–1945" (Ph.D. thesis, University of Toronto, 1982); Roger Sarty and John Armstrong, "Defending the Home Front," *Horizon Canada*, 8, 86; Martin Kitchen, "The German Invasion of Canada in the First World War," *International History Review*, 7 (May 1985); and Arthur S. Link, *Wilson: The Struggle for Neutrality 1914–1915* (Princeton, 1960) and *Wilson: Confusions and Crises 1915–1916* (Princeton, 1964). The material on the naval war in Canadian–American relations summarizes parts of Michael L. Hadley and Roger Sarty, *Tin–Pots and Pirate Ships: Canadian Naval Forces and German Sea Raiders 1880–1918* (Montreal and Kingston, 1991).

Chapter Three

There is no single detailed study of 1919–1935, the pivotal years in Canadian–American relations, but four works provide both the broad background to the period and a description of some of the events included in this chapter: James Eayrs, *In Defence of Canada*, vol. 1, *From the Great War to the Great Depression* (Toronto, [1964]); I.M. Drummond, *Imperial Economic Policy 1917–1939* (Toronto, 1975); Philip G. Wigley, *Canada and the Transition to Commonwealth: British–Canadian Relations 1917–1926* (Cambridge, 1977); Richard Veatch, *Canada and the League of Nations* (Toronto, 1975). Eayrs has strong and amusing words about Buster Brown's Defence Scheme No. 1, but Stephen J. Harris, *Canadian Brass: The Making of a Professional Army, 1860–1939* (Toronto, 1988) and Richard A. Preston, *The Defence of the Undefended Border: Planning for War in North America 1867–1939* (Montreal, 1977) give more convincing and comprehensive accounts.

Roger Graham is the sympathetic author of a full–scale biography, *Arthur Meighen*, 3 vols. (Toronto, 1960–65). R.M. Dawson and H. Blair Neatby counter with *William Lyon Mackenzie King*, 3 vols. (Toronto, 1958–76). There is as yet no adequate biography of R.B. Bennett. *The Memoirs of Herbert Hoover*, 3 vols. (New York, 1951–52) scarcely mention Canada. The autobiography of the first U.S. minister to Canada is William Phillips's *Ventures in Diplomacy* (Boston, 1952). On his Canadian counterpart, see Vincent Massey, *What's Past Is Prologue* (Toronto, 1963) and Claude Bissell, *The Young Vincent Massey* (Toronto, 1981). Captain J.T. Randell reminisced in *I'm Alone* (Indianapolis, 1930).

Richard N. Kottman, *Reciprocity and the North Atlantic Triangle 1932–1938* (Ithaca, NY, 1968), discusses the impact of high tariffs and the Depression on the Canadian–American economic relationship. Kottman has also written a number of relevant articles, the most important of which is "Herbert Hoover and the Smoot-Hawley Tariff: Canada, A Case Study," *Journal of American History*, 50, 3 (December 1975). Tom Traves, the author of *The State and Enterprise: Canadian Manufacturers and the Federal Government, 1917–1931* (Toronto, 1979), is the expert on the auto tariff. Cultural matters are covered from the Canadian point of view in Mary Vipond's sound survey, *The Mass Media in Canada* (Toronto, 1989). A recent book on Great Lakes liquor smuggling is C.W. Hunt, *Booze, Boats and Billions* (Toronto, 1988).

J.W. Dafoe, *Canada: An American Nation* (New York, 1935), is a collection of lectures that reveals the author's predilection for viewing Canada and international problems through a continental, North American lens.

A great deal of raw material can be found in various volumes of the Carnegie Endowment series on The Relations of Canada and the United States. Volumes helpful in preparing this chapter were: Herbert Marshall, F.A. Southard, and K.W. Taylor, *Canadian–American Industry* (New Haven, 1936); M.L. Hansen and J.B. Brebner, *The Mingling of the Canadian and American Peoples* (New Haven, 1940); and H.F. Angus, *Canada and Her Great Neighbor: Sociological Surveys of Opinions and Attitudes in Canada Concerning the United States* (Toronto, 1938).

Chapter Four

The relative lack of research on the years just before the Second World War, and on 1938 and 1939 in particular, is surprising and disappointing. The standard biography of Canada's dominant politician of the time is the third volume of the already noted *William Lyon Mackenzie King*: H. Blair Neatby's *1932–1939, The Prism of Unity* (Toronto, 1976). C.P. Stacey, *Mackenzie King and the Atlantic Triangle* (Toronto, 1976), is a brilliant essay on King's attitude towards the United States and Great Britain throughout his long career. Lawrence Martin's *The Presidents and the Prime Ministers* (Toronto, 1982) has a good chapter on the Roosevelt–King relationship. On FDR generally, Frank Freidel's *Franklin D. Roosevelt: A Rendezvous with Destiny* (Boston, 1990) and Robert Dallek's *Franklin D. Roosevelt and American Foreign Policy, 1932–1945* (New York, 1979) summarize much complicated scholarship in clear prose.

Richard Kottman, *Reciprocity and the North Atlantic Triangle 1932–1938* (Ithaca, NY, 1968), covers both the 1935 and the 1938 trade agreement. Kottman wrote before many sources became available. More up-to-date and wide-ranging in their research are Marc T. Boucher,

"The Politics of Economic Depression: Canadian–American Relations in the Mid-1930s," *International Journal,* 41 (Winter 1985–86) and Ian M. Drummond and Norman Hillmer, *Negotiating Freer Trade: The United Kingdom, the United States, Canada, and the Trade Agreements of 1938* (Waterloo, ON, 1989). The proceedings of the 1935–41 *Conferences on Canadian– American Affairs,* ed. A.B. Corey and R.G. Trotter, 4 vols. (Boston, 1936–41), are full of excellent contemporary assessments of economic and other relations.

Trade unions are the subject of Irving M. Abella, *Nationalism, Communism, and Canadian Labour: The CIO, the Communist Party, and the Canadian Congress of Labour 1935–1956* (Toronto, 1973). The Alaska Highway project is covered from many angles in Kenneth Coates, ed., *The Alaska Highway* (Vancouver, 1985).

James Eayrs, *In Defence of Canada,* vol. 2, *Appeasement and Rearmament* (Toronto, 1965), and Robert Bothwell and Norman Hillmer, eds., *The In-Between Time: Canadian External Policy in the 1930s* (Toronto, 1975) are also useful, although mainly for background.

Chapter Five

The official American history of the wartime relationship between Canada and the United States is Stanley Dziuban's *Military Relations Between the United States and Canada 1939–1945* (Washington, 1959). There is no directly comparable Canadian volume, though Charles Stacey's *Arms, Men and Governments: The War Policies of Canada 1939–1945* (Ottawa, 1970) comes closest. Mackenzie King's published diary, *The Mackenzie King Record,* vols. 1 and 2, *1939–44, 1944–45* (Toronto, 1960, 1968) is indispensable.

Other books include John English's biography of Pearson, *Shadow of Heaven: The Life of Lester Pearson,* vol. 1, *1897–1948* (Toronto, 1989); John Holmes, *The Shaping of Peace: Canada and the Search for World Order 1943–1957,* 2 vols. (Toronto, 1979, 1982); J.L. Granatstein, *Canada's War: The Politics of the Mackenzie King Government 1939–1945* (Toronto, 1990); and his *A Man of Influence: Norman A. Robertson and Canadian Statecraft, 1929–68* (Ottawa, 1981); Granatstein and Robert Cuff, *Ties That Bind: Canadian–American Relations from the Great War to the Cold War* (Toronto, 1977); Peter Neary, *Newfoundland in the North Atlantic World, 1929–49* (Kingston and Montreal, 1988); and Robert Bothwell and William Kilbourn, *C.D. Howe: A Biography* (Toronto, 1979). Robert Bothwell, Ian Drummond, and John English, *Canada 1900–1945* (Toronto, 1987) is a wonderful summary of many of the subjects and themes covered in this and earlier chapters.

Chapter Six

On the postwar years, the most useful guide to the course of Canadian–American relations are Holmes, *The Shaping of Peace* and J.W. Pickersgill, ed., *The Mackenzie King Record*, vols. 3 and 4, *1945–46, 1947–48* (Toronto, 1970). There is useful material on economic and defence relations in J.L. Granatstein, *Ties That Bind*, and in his *The Ottawa Men: The Civil Service Mandarins 1935–57* (Toronto, 1982), and in Robert Cuff and J.L. Granatstein, *American Dollars/Canadian Prosperity: Canadian–American Economic Relations 1945–1950* (Toronto, 1978). Denis Stairs, *The Diplomacy of Constraint: Canada, the Korean War, and the United States* (Toronto, 1974), illuminates Canada's difficulties in dealing with Washington during the Korean War, while Robert Bothwell and W. Kilbourn, *C.D. Howe* (Toronto, 1979) is a full and fair account of the "Minister of Everything" who so shaped Canadian policy. Lester Pearson's *Mike: The Memoirs of the Rt. Hon. Lester B. Pearson*, vol. 2, *1948–1957* (Toronto, 1973) provides a personal view, including diary quotations, by the prime maker of Canadian policy. Pearson's own view is supplemented and expanded gracefully by John English in the first volume of *Shadow of Heaven: The Life of Lester Pearson*, vol. 1, *1897–1948* (Toronto, 1990). On air defence, Joseph Jockel, *No Boundaries Upstairs: Canada, the United States, and the Origins of North American Air Defence, 1945–1958* (Vancouver, 1987), is careful and comprehensive.

Chapter Seven

There is a substantial Canadian literature on the Diefenbaker–Kennedy relationship and the nuclear arms question; unfortunately almost no American scholars or journalists have treated these themes in anything other than a glancing fashion. One of the earliest Canadian accounts was Peter Newman's *Renegade in Power* (Toronto, 1963), a book that may be truly said to have revolutionized political journalism in Canada. The Newman book holds up reasonably well on Canadian–American issues, but it has been largely superseded by several other works: journalist Knowlton Nash's *Kennedy and Diefenbaker: Fear and Loathing Across the Undefended Border* (Toronto, 1990); J.L. Granatstein's *A Man of Influence: Norman A. Robertson and Canadian Statecraft* (Ottawa, 1981) and *Canada 1957–67: The Years of Uncertainty and Innovation* (Toronto, 1986); and public servant Basil Robinson's *Diefenbaker's World* (Toronto, 1989). As one of Diefenbaker's external affairs' assistants, Robinson worked closely with the Chief for five years; his account is sympathetic but unsparing. Also useful is Peyton Lyon's careful and voluminous *Canada in World Affairs*, vol. 12, *1961–1963* (Toronto, 1968). Diefenbaker's own memoir, *One Canada: The Memoirs of the Rt. Hon. John G. Diefenbaker*, 3 vols. (Toronto, 1975–77) must be checked against the sources. Pearson's version in *Mike: The Memoirs of the Rt. Hon. Lester B. Pearson*, vol. 3, *1957–68* (Toronto, 1975) is more reliable.

Chapter Eight

For Canadian–American relations in the Pearson era, excellent sources include Pearson's own memoir, *Mike: The Memoirs of the Rt. Hon. Lester B. Pearson*, vol. 3, *1957–68* (Toronto, 1975) and Walter Gordon's *A Political Memoir* (Toronto, 1977). Peter Stursberg's *Lester Pearson and the American Dilemma* (Toronto, 1980) brings together interview transcripts with key participants, while Lawrence Martin, *The Presidents and the Prime Ministers* (Toronto, 1982), is a shrewd journalistic assessment of the LBP–LBJ relationship. Another fascinating view is provided in diplomat Charles Ritchie's diary, *Storm Signals* (Toronto, 1983).

On special issues, there are several useful sources: on Vietnam, see Douglas Ross, *In the Interests of Peace: Canada and Viet Nam 1954–1973* (Toronto, 1984) and Secretary of State for External Affairs Paul Martin's memoir, *A Very Public Life*, vol. 2, *So Many Worlds* (Toronto, 1985); on the Auto Pact, J.F. Kealey, "Cast in Concrete for All Time? The Negotiation of the Auto Pact," *Canadian Journal of Political Science*, 16 (June 1983), and Denis Smith, *Gentle Patriot: A Political Biography of Walter Gordon* (Edmonton, 1973). More generally, the account in J.L. Granatstein, *Canada 1957–1967: The Years of Uncertainty and Innovation* (Toronto, 1986), covers the whole decade.

Chapter Nine

Biographical studies of Pierre Trudeau include Richard Gwyn, *The Northern Magus* (Toronto, 1980) and Stephen Clarkson and Christina McCall, *Trudeau and Our Times*, vol. 1, *The Magnificent Obsession* (Toronto, 1990). Lawrence Martin studied the Trudeau–Nixon relationship in his *The Presidents and the Prime Ministers*, and there are snippets in Henry Kissinger's *The White House Years* (New York, 1979) and his *Years of Upheaval* (New York, 1982). Douglas Ross, *In the Interests of Peace* (Toronto, 1984) is the best book on Canadian involvement in Vietnam. On energy policy, see E. Erickson and L. Waverman, eds., *The Energy Question: An International Failure of Policy*, vol. 2, *North America* (Toronto,

1974); and on the Arctic, Franklyn Griffiths, ed., *Politics of the Northwest Passage* (Montreal, 1987).

More general treatments include Robert Bothwell, Ian Drummond, and John English, *Canada Since 1945* (Toronto, 1989); Peter Dobell, *Canada in World Affairs, 1971–1973* (Toronto, 1985); and J.L. Granatstein and Robert Bothwell, *Pirouette: Pierre Trudeau and Canadian Foreign Policy* (Toronto, 1990).

Chapter Ten

The most recent study of the later Trudeau government's relations with Washington is Granatstein and Bothwell, *Pirouette: Pierre Trudeau and Canadian Foreign Policy* (Toronto, 1990). Also very useful are Stephen Clarkson, *Canada and the Reagan Challenge: Crisis and Adjustment, 1981–85* (Toronto, 1985), and Charles Doran, *Forgotten Partnership: U.S.–Canada Relations Today* (Baltimore, 1984). Doran's is one of the few scholarly books on the relationship by an American.

There are a number of specialized accounts: on energy, G.B. Doern and G. Toner, *The Politics of Energy: The Development and Implementation of the NEP* (Toronto, 1985); on the law of the sea, Clyde Sanger, *Ordering the Oceans: The Making of the Law of the Sea* (Toronto, 1987); on the environment, Don Munton, "Reagan, Canada and the Common Environment," *International Perspectives* (May–June 1982); on the relations between Trudeau and the presidents, Lawrence Martin, *The Presidents and the Prime Ministers* (Toronto, 1982) and on the economy, D. Stairs and G. Winham, eds., *The Politics of Canada's Economic Relationship with the United States* (Toronto, 1985).

Biographical studies of Trudeau include the very helpful *Close to the Charisma: My Years Between the Press and Pierre Trudeau* (Toronto, 1986) by Patrick Gossage; Richard Gwyn's *The Northern Magus* (Toronto, 1980); and Stephen Clarkson and Christina McCall, *Trudeau and Our Times*, vol. 1, *The Magnificent Obsession* (Toronto, 1990).

Chapter Eleven

There are no serious studies thus far of Prime Minister Brian Mulroney or of the full range of the Mulroney government's policies towards the United States; there will be none until the documents of the government become available. Among the best available books are Richard Gwyn's *The 49th Paradox* (Toronto, 1985), David Bercuson, J.L. Granatstein, and

W.R. Young, *Sacred Trust? Brian Mulroney and the Conservative Party in Power* (Toronto, 1986), and Stephen Clarkson, *Canada and the Reagan Challenge*. The best examinations of the FTA's impact on the election are Graham Fraser, *Playing for Keeps: The Making of the Prime Minister, 1988* (Toronto, 1989), Robert Mason Lee, *One Hundred Monkeys* (Toronto, 1989), and Rick Salutin, *Waiting for Democracy: A Citizen's Journal* (Toronto, 1989). There was a large number of instant books on the FTA, too many to list here.

Popular assessments of Mulroney include the admiring book by L. Ian Macdonald, *Mulroney* (Toronto, 1987), the more restrained one by Michel Gratton, *"So What Are the Boys Saying?" An Inside Look at Brian Mulroney in Power* (Toronto, 1987), and the sharply critical Claire Hoy, *Friends in High Places* (Toronto, 1987). Mulroney collected some of his pre–prime ministerial speeches in *Where I Stand* (Toronto, 1983). John Turner is cruelly dissected in Greg Weston's *Reign of Error: The Inside Story of John Turner's Troubled Leadership* (Toronto, 1988). And Ronald Reagan tells his own story, which touches only briefly but very revealingly on Canada, in *An American Life* (New York, 1990).

Carleton University's Canada Among Nations series has thus far produced volumes on the 1984–1989 years; these valuable books contain studies of various aspects of foreign and defence policy. So too do the yearly volumes of *The Canadian Annual Review*, published by the University of Toronto Press.

INDEX